The Mathematics of Marriage

The Mathematics of Marriage
Dynamic Nonlinear Models

John M. Gottman, James D. Murray,
Catherine C. Swanson, Rebecca Tyson,
and Kristin R. Swanson

A Bradford Book
The MIT Press
Cambridge, Massachusetts
London, England

First MIT Press paperback edition, 2005

This book was typeset in LATEX by the authors and was printed and bound in the United
States of America.

Library of Congress Cataloging-in-Publication Data

The mathematics of marriage : dynamic nonlinear models / John M. Gottman ... [et al.].
    p. cm.
  "A Bradford book."
  Includes bibliographical references and index.
  ISBN 0-262-07226-2 (hard: alk. paper), 0-262-57230-3 (pb)
    1. Marriage—Mathematical models. 2. Marriage—Psychological aspects. 3.
  Marital psychotherapy. I. Gottman, John Mordechai.
  HQ728 .M328 2002
  306.81'01'51—dc21   2001044326

10 9 8 7 6 5 4 3 2

To the outsider, mathematics is a strange, abstract world of horrendous technicality, full of symbols and complicated procedures, an impenetrable language and a black art. To the scientist, mathematics is the guarantor of precision and objectivity. It is also, astonishingly, the language of nature itself. No one who is closed off from mathematics can ever grasp the full significance of the natural order that is woven so deeply into the fabric of physical reality.
– Paul Davies

Contents

Preface

The divorce rate in the United States has reached epidemic proportions. For first marriages, demographers Martin and Bumpass (1989) estimated that within a forty year span 67% would end in divorce. However, this is not a recent phenomenon; rather, it is a trend that has been in effect for at least a century (Cherlin, 1981). The rest of the world is not far behind the United States.

Furthermore, at this juncture the phenomenon is not well understood. Although sociologists have shown that the phenomenon of increasing divorce rates is related to the world-wide overdue economic and psychological emancipation and empowerment of women, it is not understood why some marriages end in divorce, but others do not. Of all the studies on divorce, only a handful have been prospective, longitudinal studies. These few studies have generally yielded little information about why some marriages end in divorce, but others do not.

Marital therapy is also at an impasse. The effects of marital therapy are owing primarily to the massive deterioration of distressed marriages in no-treatment control groups and not to the clinically significant gains of couples in treatment groups. Only approximately 35% of these treated couples make clinically meaningful gains in treatment, and within a year or two most of these couples relapse.

In our view, the field of marriage research is in desperate need of theory. Without theoretical understanding of key processes related to marital dissolution or stability, it will be difficult to design or evaluate adequately any new interventions. Personally we have the most respect for theories that are mathematical. We believe that scientific progress will be facilitated by mathematical models.

Using a multimethod approach to the study of marriages, our laboratory was fortunate in having been able to predict the longitudinal trajectories of marriages with a great deal of accuracy, more than 90% accuracy in three longitudinal studies. About five years ago, when we first discovered our ability to predict divorce and marital stability, Gottman began exploring alternative approaches to building mathematical models of this prediction, taught a seminar on the topic, and edited a book on the analysis of change. He was in a science book club that at one point featured James Murray's book, *Mathematical Biology*. After becoming enlightened that such modeling was proceeding at a rapid pace in many biological sciences, he invited James Murray to lecture in the seminar. A letter was sent to Oxford University, but it turned out that Murray had recently moved to the United States, and had actually begun to work at the University of Washington, where Gottman also was teaching. The two of them met at the faculty club with Gottman's graduate student Regina Rushe, and Gottman proposed a project of modeling the divorce prediction data. Murray was intrigued, and he agreed to discuss the idea with his students.

A work group was formed that included Julian Cook, Rebecca Tyson, Jane White, and Regina Rushe, James Murray, and John Gottman. This group met weekly for four years, watching tapes from Gottman's laboratory, talking about what was known about marital process, building a model, and eventually analyzing data. From this interaction, which Murray guided, the mathematical model of marriage emerged.

The model was remarkable. Immediately it gave us a new and parsimonious language for describing a marital interaction. It also gave us a set of parameters that we discovered were predictive of marital stability and marital quality. We have also applied the model to the study of preschool children interacting in six-person groups (Gottman et al., 1995). The model also worked well in that context, so we began thinking that perhaps the model was quite general in its representation of social processes.

As we modified our procedures and coding of the videotapes of couples in order to obtain more data points per interaction and to obtain them more rapidly, we modified the model. We then discovered new parameters that distinguish happily and unhappily married couples, such as the level of negativity required before a spouse reacts. We called this parameter the negative threshold effect. We began thinking about the relationship of this parameter to the fact that people delay getting marital therapy for an average of six years (Notarius and Buongiorno, 1992), and to the pervasive relapse effect in marital therapy. We began conceiving additional modifications to the model - for example, including a repair term that could explain why negativity does not always run unchecked but can take a positive turn. Similarly, there could be a term to assess damping, the opposite of repair.

Once we had the equations for a couple, the modeling allowed us to simulate marital interaction under different contexts, ones in which we had never observed the couple. This simulation was a first in the interaction field. For example, we could use the equations to ask what the interaction in this marriage might be like if the husband or wife started off very positively. This ability to simulate led naturally to experimentation to obtain proximal (not distal) changes in marital interaction. Most clinical trials are complex, multicomponent interventions designed to create large effects in the marriage. However, we were led to the idea of doing very clear and simple interventions designed to change parameters in the mathematical model for the second of two conversations a couple had in our laboratory. That is, rather than doing a clinical trial to change the whole marriage, we could try to change the couple's pattern of interaction only in the next conversation. We called these interventions our "marriage experiments." For example, we could see what effects just lowering a couple's heart rates or conversely, increasing their heart rates, would have onthe next conversation. Because these experiments were not clinical trials, but "exercises," we could manipulate an intervention variable by causing it to increase or decrease or even by leaving it unchanged. We were able to bring marriage into the social psychology laboratory for precise study.

Our pilot research on these marriage experiments was surprising because we found that we could change marital interaction quite dramatically for a brief time with very simple interventions. Previous clinical trials, when effective, often resulted in little gain in understanding (the interventions were so complex that it was difficult for investigators even to agree on what were the active ingredients of the change). On the other hand, armed with the mathematical model, we could do real experiments, very simple ones, and evaluate which processes our interventions were affecting. We are just at the threshold of this research.

It is time now for us to attempt to share our processes and methods with other researchers. We have had success in publishing our ideas and in explaining them clearly enough to a grant review panel clearly enough to be funded to do the marriage experiments. Hence, despite a pervasive math phobia among many of us, we wrote this book with a great deal of optimism. We are optimistic in part because for four years Gottman and Murray haved taught a very successful seminar jointly between the applied mathematics and psychology departments. The seminar brings graduate students in applied mathematics together with graduate students in psychology. The mathematicians have learned to become consultants, guided by James Murray, and the psychologists have learned to formulate their ideas more formally, guided by John Gottman.

We believe that our work represents the missing step necessary to complete the seminal thinking that the family general systems theorists started in the 1950s. We believe that this thinking is enriched by the mathematics we explain in this book- ideas such as catastrophe theory.

We revisit ideas such as homeostasis, developing them with concepts of phase space, null clines, influence functions, inertia, and uninfluenced and influenced stable steady states (attractors). We hope that these ideas will now be accessible to researchers who can weight their data with positive and negative weights, as we have done with Gottman's Specific Affect Coding System (SPAFF). Most coding systems in marriage are amenable to this weighting. These data already exist in most marriage research labs, so it is well within our readers' power to try these methods on their own. We also offer our computer programs for doing the computations.

Although the models are mathematical in the sense that they involve equations and mathematical concepts, the mathematical expertise required to employ these methods is minimal. Details of the mathematics are avoided in this book (or relegated to appendices) so that reader's can fully understand the models and the modeling process, the ideas and the results.

The process is seductive because we think what we will ultimately gain is understanding.

John M. Gottman
James D. Murray
Catherine C. Swanson
Rebecca Tyson
Kristin R. Swanson
Seattle, Washington

Personal Preface: John Gottman

I want to give the reader a sense of what an amazing gift of fortune it was for me to meet James Murray. I have a background in mathematics (an undergraduate major at Fairleigh Dickinson University, and a master's degree in mathematics from MIT.). When my wife was pregnant with our daughter in 1990 we took a trip to Yellowstone Park, and we had some of those rare great heart-to-heart talks that people can have only on a long car ride. I told her that I had come to the view that I could not respect my own work unless I could somehow make it theoretical and mathematical. I felt that I had to return to my childhood roots as a mathematician. I had a sense that this new route would lead me to explore various mathematical methods for the study of change, so I later taught a seminar on the analysis of change. As part of that seminar, I explored nonlinear differential equations and chaos theory, but the exploration left me very confused.

I had read probably fifty books on nonlinear dynamics and chaos before I read James Murray's book *Mathematical Biology*. The other books left the process of modeling mystical and somewhat romantic. I had no real idea how to apply these methods to my data. Fortunately I was in a book club that selected James' book, and once I started reading it, my eyes were opened. It contained example after example with real problems and real data. I began to see that it was possible to demystify these marvelous methods and bring them into my own laboratory. I wrote a letter to Oxford University (where the book said James lived) to invite James to come and talk in my seminar; a few weeks later my program coordinator, Sharon Fentiman, received a call from James. When she remarked that the connection was so clear for an international call, he said that he was at the University of Washington. She asked him how long he would be in town, and he told her that he had moved to Seattle. What an amazing coincidence! We arranged to meet at the Faculty Club with my graduate student Regina Rushe. We hit it off instantly James talked in my seminar, and at lunch one of the students suggested that James and I fit together so well that we ought to teach a course together. We looked at one another and decided to do just that. By the kindness of fate, neither of us had to teach very much at all, but we elected to take this on. What a joy it was, and a lifelong friendship began.

Aside from a sense of this friendship, which in my life has always been the seed of fruitful collaboration, I also want to give the reader a personal recollection of the modeling process. My goal here is to suggest that, in hindsight, it is easy to create models that enrich a scientific enterprise and give it shape and direction. When we first sat down with James and his students, they asked us questions about the "laws" of marital relationships that would guide us in writing down the equations. We shrugged and said that there were no laws, no real guides. But there were some phenomena I could suggest might be replicable findings. I pointed out the phenomenon of "the triumph of negative over positive affect," which was the reliable finding, at that point, that negative affect was a better discriminator of happy from unhappy couples than positive affect and a better predictor of marital outcomes. Eventually we were to discover the 5 to 1 ratio of positive to negative affect in stable couples and the 0.8 to 1 ratio in couples heading for divorce. We learned how to measure positive affect more accurately, and its role became much more important. Nonetheless, the phenomenon held. Negative affect was far more destructive than positive affect was constructive. Other phenomena also emerged (and were discovered) as we met and talked, including Fritz Heider's "fundamental attribution error," in which people in ailing marriages eventually blame their partners for their troubles and see small negative events and brief changes for the worse as owing to lasting defects in their partners' character, but are quite forgiving toward themselves. We decided that we needed to address the dimension of power if we were to develop an adequate model of the unfolding of mutual influence over time. The act of trying to write down equations and to build a model began to shape my thinking about my own work.

Very gradually Julian Cook (one of James' students), Jane White, Rebecca Tyson, and I started examining data to guide us in the choice of model. We all decided that we could dismantle a couple's behavior on our "point graphs" that divided marital outcome into self-influences, and other influences, and other influences. When way we tried dismantling the data, it did not work until we included a term for each person's starting point, the constant that each person brought to the interaction. Then the model fit the data. As soon as we were able to write down the model, we began teaching one another what the components of the model meant. We realized then that we had a new language for talking about interaction, one that was breathtaking in its simplicity and power. For the first time, systems theory concepts were not metaphors but something real and potentially disconfirmable. The model could grow and develop.

The model not only fit the data, but also led to a new discovery: the mismatch between spouses in influence functions predicted divorce. That discovery was entirely unexpected. For some couples, there were two attractors, a positive and a negative attractor, which meant that the concept of family "homeostasis" had to be modified to include more than one such attractor.

As we began using the model, questions arose, which is James' criterion for a good model. What should be the theoretical shape of the influence functions? If we used the bilinear model, perhaps all couples would theoretically have two homeostatic set points, a positive and a negative one. What would be the implications of that type of model? Could we measure the "strength" of an attractor, considering that it might be what changed after an intervention? Could we make the model less static and include a repair term? If there were a repair term, was there also an analogous damping term? If we were able to model interaction so well, what about our perception variable, the video recall rating dial that people turned when they watched their videotape and told us what they were feeling during the interaction? What about physiology? All three domains for two people were time synchronized, so could we build models for all three domains? What about models across domains and their predictive power? Could we describe anything fundamental about how interactive behavior, perception, and physiology were related for marriages with respect to predicting marital outcomes?

All this became possible once we wrote down our equations and sat back, and reflected on what they meant. In hindsight, it all seems easy, and we wrote this book to convince our readers to try the same process for their own data. It was a journey well worth taking.

John Gottman
Seattle, Washington

1

What Do We Mean by Theory?

In the history of science the word theory has been most successfully employed as *the explanation of a reliable set of phenomena.* That is the sense in which we use the term. For example, consider the development of the theory of gravitation. In Newton's theory of gravitation, the inverse square law of attraction between two bodies explained both the parabolic motion of a projectile fired on Earth as well as comets and Kepler's description of the motion of the planets. Among other things, it left unexplained how gravitational force could act at a distance and the very slow perihelion procession of the orbit of the planet Mercury around the sun.

Einstein's general theory of relativity presented a new theory of gravitation that linked inertial force and gravitation. In a famous Gedanken-experiment, or thought experiment, a scientist in outer space is imagined in an elevator that is being uniformly accelerated upward. She would be unable to distinguish this state of affairs from being in a uniform gravitational field, Einstein predicted that light would bend in a gravitational field. Einstein's prediction was confirmed by a dramatic observational study performed in Great Britain in 1919 that caused an international sensation. It was particularly dramatic that after World War I an English team of scientists had tested a theory put forward by a German scientist when the two countries had so recently been at war (although Einstein was a Swiss citizen, he taught in Berlin). Einstein's theory of gravitation postulated that the path light takes in space and time *is* the curvature of what he called space-time. He then showed that differential curvatures on the surface of space-time can explain gravitational attraction. The theory resolved the problem of action at a distance. The gravitational field equations also explained the perihelion procession of Mercury's orbit.

Both Newton and Einstein relied on mathematics to state their theories concisely, and they used the implications of the mathematics to explain the phenomena they were studying. Newton developed the differential calculus (as did Leibnitz [1]) to make his calculations using his second law of motion that force equals mass times acceleration. Acceleration was the rate of change of velocity. The second law, coupled with the inverse square law of gravitational attraction, made it possible to show that all orbits are sections of a cone, so that the parabolic motion of a projectile fired from Earth, the Kepler phenomena, the orbit of the moon around the Earth, and the motions of comets could all be derived from these ideas. In his book, *Principia,* Newton presented all his calculations using only geometry, probably because he thought that his new calculus of "fluxions" would not be accepted.

Einstein's general theory of relativity used field equations that stated that the gravitational field was equal to the curvature of space-time, a curvature based on the distribution of mass. To write these equations he used the tensor calculus of Riemann's differential geometry, which contained the idea of "geodesics," the shortest curve between any two points on a surface.

Both Newton and Einstein can be considered applied mathematicians because they developed or employed mathematical methods to model scientific phenomena. Both theories of gravitation explained existing phenomena, and the mathematics predicted new phenomena. In Einstein's case, these phenomena included the bending of light in a gravitational field, the gravitational red shift, the fact that clocks would run differently at different places in a gravitational field, the expanding universe, and the existence of black holes. These highly successful theories also fit together well, and in creating his theory of gravitation, Einstein correctly insisted that it must reduce to Newton's theory under everyday conditions that did not involve high velocities or high mass densities.

The simplicity underlying both theories of gravitation could only be described as beautiful. Einstein was so moved by the discovery of this underlying beauty that he referred to it as understanding the mind of God, whom he called "der Alter," the Old One. Newton was also led to write theology. So profound were the effects of these successful scientific theories and of others that we have come to *expect* this beauty and simplicity as characteristic's of true theories of natural law.

The theory we present here is no different from the theories of gravi-

---

[1] The controversy as to who discovered calculus first — Newton or Leibnitz — was bitter and acrimonious, primarily on Newton's part. It is now generally accepted among historians of mathematics that Leibnitz should be credited with its discovery.

tation in that it is a mathematical modeling of stable, natural phenomena. The phenomena in our case are social, human phenomena rather than physical. Ironically, biographers have noted that such phenomena were most problematic in the personal lives of these two scientists. The humor is not lost on us that it took a few hundred years since Newton before some scientific interest would shift from gravitational attraction between two inanimate bodies to social attraction between members of our own species. (Newton was not particularly agreeable, and, indeed, was vindictive in many of his interactions with his contemporaries.)

2

What Phenomena of Marriage Are We Modeling?

In some ways, we are at a disadvantage compared to Newton because we have no Kepler preceding us in selecting so precisely and neatly the phenomena of marriage. Marriage has now been studied scientifically for the past sixty years, and we can draw some general conclusions that guide our modeling of marital interaction. We run the risk of selecting the wrong phenomena on which to build theory, but in that event we hope that the methods and procedures we follow can be a guide for others who will, we hope correct our work. We have not selected all the phenomena of marriage to model, and for a more thorough discussion of how we view these phenomena we refer the reader to our other works (Gottman, 1994; Gottman, 1999).

We are motivated by trying to understand why some couples divorce, but others do not, and why, among those who remain married, some are happy and some are miserable with one another. There are high levels of divorce in today's world. In the United States the current estimate is that within a forty year span approximately 50% to 67% percent of first marriages will end in divorce; the figure is 10% higher for second marriage (Martin and Bumpass, 1989; Cherlin, 1981). Although the United States has the highest raw divorce rate in the world, the trends toward increasing rates of divorce over time exist worldwide. (The divorce rates in many European countries are skewed owing to the increasing tendency of couples not to get married.)

We began this modeling about seven years ago attempting to model only one phenomenon: the fact that in our laboratory we could predict from one variable which couples would eventually divorce and which would stay married. As first reported by Gottman and Levenson (1992), this variable indexed the balance between negativity and positivity. It described specific interaction patterns while the couple was discussing a major area of continuing disagreement in their marriage, and it was found to be predictive of marital dissolution or stability. We have now been able to replicate this phenomenon across three longitudinal studies. We set out to generate theory that might explain this phenomenon. In this chapter, we also selectively review the work of others on marriage and pick two other phenomena of marriage that will later prove useful in our mathematical modeling.

2.1 Brief Review of Research on Marriage

The Scientific Study of Marriage

As we noted, the divorce rate remains extremely high in the United States; current estimates of the chances of first marriages ending in divorce range between 50% and 67% (Martin and Bumpass, 1989). The rest of the world is not far behind. The data across studies suggest that failure rates for second marriages are either the same or about 10% higher than for first marriages. We also know that separation and divorce have strong negative consequences for the mental and physical health of both spouses – including increased risk for psychopathology; increased rates of automobile accidents with fatalities; and increased incidence of physical illness, suicide, violence, homicide, significant immunosuppression, and mortality from diseases (Bloom, Asher and White, 1978; Burman and Margolin, 1992). Marital disruption may not merely be related to the standard list of negative life events; it may actually be among the most powerful predictors of them. In the Holmes and Rahe (1967) scale of stressful life events, marital disruption weighs heavily among the major stresses in discriminating those who become ill from those who do not.

Also, there is now convincing evidence to suggest that marital distress, conflict, and disruption are associated with a wide range of deleterious effects on children, including depression, withdrawal, poor social competence, health problems, poor academic performance, and a variety of conduct-related difficulties (Cowan and Cowan, 1987, 1990,; Cowan et al., 1991; Cummings and Davies, 1994; Easterbrooks, 1987; Easterbrooks and Emde, 1988; Emery, 1982, 1988; Emery and O'Leary, 1982; Forehand et al., 1986). In a recent report from the Terman longitudinal study of gifted children (Friedman et al., 1995), survival curves showed that the combination of one's parents having divorced and one's own divorce reduced longevity by an average of approximately eight years. However, recently the active ingredient in divorce that hurts children has been uncovered. It is not divorce itself, but continued marital hostility between co-parents in which the children are used by one parent to hurt the other (Buchanan, Maccoby, and Dornbusch, 1991; Hetherington and Clingempeel, 1992). Many of the same effects of divorce on children have been observed in our laboratory in intact families as a result of continued marital hostility (see Gottman, Katz, and Hooven, 1996).

Given these grim statistics, our best scholars have concluded that, unfortunately, marital therapy is at a practical and theoretical impasse (Jacobson and Addis, 1993). Jacobson has shown that the outcome results in his studies (which are among the most effective) suggest that: *(a)* after therapy only 35% of couples are in the nondistressed range; *(b)* within a year after therapy approximately 30% to 50% of these couples relapse. In fact, the relapse data may be much grimmer than even these conclusions suggest. As far as we know, longer-term follow-up is likely to yield evidence of even greater relapse.

Psychology's Early Years in Studying Marriage

Psychology was a latecomer to the study of marriage. Sociologists had been studying marriages for thirty-five years before psychologists got wind of the idea. In the early 1970s, it was difficult to have papers on marriage even reviewed in a psychology journal. Editors would write back and politely explain that marriage was not psychology but sociology, and would recommend that the paper be submitted to a sociology journal. All that has changed. For example, the *Journal of Personality and Social Psychology* now has an interpersonal section. There is now an American Psychological Association journal called the *Journal of Family Psychology*. Family psychology doctoralprograms are springing up throughout the United States.

Marriage had indeed been the domain of sociologists until the early 1970s, although the first published study on marriage was by a psychologist, Louis Terman in 1938 (Terman *et al.*, 1938). What psychologists initially brought to the study of marriage was the use of observational methods, the design and evaluation of intervention programs, and an unbridled optimism that changing marriages was going to be easy, quick work. These contributions have had an enormous impact on the study of marriage.

Why Academic Psychology May Have Been Skeptical About Studying Marriage

The initial skepticism of psychology in the 1970s was probably largely owing to the difficulties personality theory was then having. Personality theory was facing a severe challenge from the work by Walter Mischel (1968). Mischel reviewed research on personality and suggested that personality theory had come far short of being able to predict and understand behavior. He concluded that correlations were quite low on the whole, that the field was plagued with common method variance (mostly self-reports predicting self-reports), and that the best predictors of future behavior were past behavior in similar situations. His book was a great stimulus to many researchers. It encouraged a new look at personality measurement, validity, and reliability (Wiggins, 1973), and stimulated new kinds of research in personality. However, it also contributed to a pessimistic view that research in interpersonal psychology would have very little payoff. These thoughts ran as follows: if it would take, say, 50 variables just to describe the individual personality, it would take at least 50 times 50, or 2,500 variables to describe two people who are interacting. The admonition was implicit: do not study relationships until we have understood the individual. At the time, this admonition seemed quite sensible.

But, in hindsight, this view was misguided. We are learning that, in fact, some of the order to be found in notions of consistency in individual personality exists at the interpersonal level. Patterson (1982), in his conclusion that there is a great deal of consistency across time and situations in male aggression, suggested that the aggressive trait ought to be rethought in interpersonal terms as the aggressive boy's recasting of people in his social world to play out dramatic coercive scenes shaped in his family. The same is true of gender differences: they appear to emerge primarily in the context of relationships (Maccoby, 1998).

It turns out that a great deal of order exists in people's behavior at an interpersonal level of analysis. Is this really so amazing? Let us consider von Frisch's studies of the behavior of bees. Von Frisch discovered the famous "dance of the bees," in which a bee who has found a nectar-rich field of flowers returns to the hive and does a complex dance that tells the other bees how to fly with respect to the sun and how far to fly (von Frisch, 1953). The strange dance of the bee can be understood only by realizing that the bee's dance is communication. Had von Frisch taken a solitary bee into the laboratory and placed it on a table, he would have concluded that bees are motivated only to bat their heads repeatedly against glass windows. The order he discovered in studying bees came from going directly to the hive and the fields of flowers that are the business of the hive. Are we Homo sapiens less social than bees? Maybe not. Hence, when modern social psychology brings an individual into a laboratory room, it must then become imaginative about how to "create" a social situation out of this isolated individual. This choice of paradigm is often made in the interests of experimental control of particular social processes, and then it may have great merit, but it has little to recommend it if the goal is to understand interpersonal relationships.

In fact, the use of self-report measures, including personality measures, initially dominated the field of marriage research. Unfortunately, even with the problem of common method variance, the self-report paper-and-pencil personality measures yielded relatively weak correlates of marital satisfaction (Burgess, Locke, and Thomes, 1971). As an example, psychoanalysis initially embraced Winch's complimentarity of need theory (Winch, 1958), which proposed that a happy marriage would be associated with spouses having complimentary needs (such as she needs to dominate and he needs to be dominated). No other theory in this field has ever been as soundly rejected as Winch's. Not until studies asked spouses to fill out questionnaires about their spouse's personality were substantial correlations discovered with marital satisfaction. Unhappily married couples were found to endorse nearly every negative trait as characteristic of their spouses (the negative halo effect), whereas happily married spouses were found to endorse nearly every positive trait as characteristic of their spouses (the positive halo effect) (Nye, 1988).

All this is not to say that personality theory will not ultimately make a substantial contribution to the study of marriage. However, the study of personality may have to move away from easily obtained but less-valid paper-and-pencil self-report measurement, and it may have to go back to such pioneering methods as those of the Berkeley Institute of Social and Personality Research when it worked with the Office of Secret Services during World War II in attempting to determine the ideal personality characteristics of spies. Subjects were studied using a variety of methods and observed in many different settings, each requiring some face-valid aspect of their behavior. We should recall that very early research reported that sociometric measures of other people rating an individual's popularity and leadership across repeated adhoc groups have revealed very high correlations (the correlation was .75 in Bell and French, 1950; see also the classic book by Gronlund, 1959). In many ways. the study of personality has become lazy methodologically, and it has paid the price.

The Glop Problem, and Refusing to Live with Glop

Bank, Dishion, Skinner, and Patterson (1990) wrote an important paper that was subtitled "Living with Glop." Glop refers to high correlations among variables obtained using a common method of measurement, usually with just one reporter. In the marital field, this method is usually to self-report data obtained from a single reporter. The point to be made about glop is an old one. Bank and his colleagues noted that reviews by Rutter(1979) and Emery (1982) showed consistent correlations between marital discord and child adjustment problems, but that Emery and O'Leary (1984) pointed out that in most of these studies both variables come from one person (usually the mother), who uses self-report measures. It was the experience of Emery and O'Leary and of other investigators that the correlations between parents' and teachers' reports of child behaviors were essentially zero. Structural Equations Modeling (SEM) was developed in part to deal with the problem of increasing reliability and validity in measurement of constructs. The SEM methods hark back to a classic paper in measurement by Campbell and Fiske (1959) in which they argued for the use of a multitrait-multimethod matrix. It is quite common to be able to create beautiful SEM models when all the data are collected by the same agent and self-report data are employed. However, once the issue of validity is introduced to the model (by adding the requirement that the data correlate with measurement of the same construct using a different reporter or different method), the models typically fall apart.

In the area of marriage, the glop problem is also of great theoretical concern. For example, it is commonly observed that measures of neuroticism are correlated with marital satisfaction (Kurdek, 1993). It is, however, difficult to demonstrate that one is really measuring neuroticism rather than distress associated with being unhappily married. It is well known that unhappily married people are more depressed, more anxious, more distressed, less optimistic, and so on. Is the personality measure assessing an enduring trait, or a state of wellness, or distress, or the current quality of life, which is essentially the same thing that the marital satisfaction measure taps? This is also a problem when one uses different reporters, as Kelly and Conley (1987) did when they had friends and acquaintances of the couple fill out the personality measures. Clearly, friends are likely to be familiar with the general dysphoria of their unhappily married friends, and they are likely to use the items of the personality tests they are given to report this fact. The conclusion we must reach from these studies is clear: we should refuse to accept constructs as explanatory if they have not dealt adequately with the glop problem. It is absolutely critical that any theory of marriage be very careful about how a construct was measured in drawing conclusions. This is a simple admonition that all studies of marriage employ multiple methods to operationalize central constructs.

The Reluctance to Observe Couples

Researchers have been reluctant to engage in the process of using systematic observation to study couples. The primary reason is that it is very costly and frustrating to do observational research. It takes lots of time and experience to develop a good coding system for marital interaction, and even then it takes lots of time to obtain actual numbers from tapes of the interaction. Reliability of measurement is a continual issue in an observational study, and the researcher must continually deal with problems of definition of categories, and inter-observer reliability drift and decay (Reid, 1970). It is so much easier to hand out a packet of questionnaires.

Also, observational measures are often atheoretical. They are usually designed to describe exhaustively all the behavior within a particular framework that can be observed in a particular situation. This type of measure is very different from a questionnaire, which is designed to measure a specific set of constructs, such as egalitarianism in the marriage, paranoid ideation in each partner, and so on. Once the researcher has collected observational data in a study, it is often quite unclear what he or she has measured. For this reason, a purely descriptive, hypothesis-generating phase of research is required to validate the observational measures. This added phase of research is often skipped by researchers who use observational methods. If it is not skipped, it adds a lot of time to any research program. Although observational data are often a richer source of hypotheses than questionnaire data and more satisfying to the truly voyeuristic researcher, they also require much more psychometric work to know what the researcher has actually measured. It is also the case that underlying the selection of categories for any observational system are a set of assumptions and some rudimentary theory about what behaviors are important to look for. For example, the Marital Interaction Coding System (MICS) emerged from behavioral marital therapy in which it was important to "pinpoint" the marital issue; as such, for example, vague statements of the problem were considered "negative," and specific statements were considered "positive." It is only relatively recently the case that Heyman, Eddy, Weiss, and Vivian (1995) have been able to conduct an important study of the structure of the MICS and to provide an empirically-based guide as to what it may measure. They used an archival data set of 995 couples' interactions coded with the MICS-IV. Their factor analysis yielded four factors: hostility, constructive problem discussion, humor, and responsibility discussion.

Furthermore, observational approaches to the study of families had been tried in the 1960s and had failed miserably. The story of this failure is very dramatic. First, a few maverick psychologists, psychiatrists, and anthropologists in the 1950s observed a strange pattern of interaction between adult schizophrenics and their mothers, when the mothers visited them in the hospital. The mothers would greet their children with warmth and then stiff coldness, all packaged in one embrace. The idea these researchers had was called the "double bind" theory of schizophrenia (Bateson *et al.*, 1956). It maintained that the mother sent a mixed message to her child and that this message put the child in a "double bind," meaning that he was damned if he responded to one part of the message and damned if he responded to the other (contradictory) part of the message. The way out of the double bind was to "metacommunicate"—that is, to raise the communication to a new level, commenting on the process of communication itself. They thought that the resulting double bind created the emotional withdrawal we have come to associate with schizophrenia. In 1964, a new journal called *Family Process*, was formed and dedicated to research on possible family origins of mental disorders. Much of this work was observatioal because the theories focused on communication. Unfortunately, the early quantitative observational research was very weak. Not a single hypothesis of these theorists, who called themselves "general systems theorists," received clear support from actual research, except for the finding that the communication of families with a schizophrenic member was more confusing than that of normal families (see Jacob, 1987). This state of affairs was hardly much of an encouragement to others to do observational research on families.

One of the more interesting hypotheses these theorists proposed was the hypothesis of the famous book *The Pragmatics of Communication* (Watzlawick, Beavin, and Jackson, 1968) that the basis of dysfunctional families was the absence of clear communciation, so that people used "mind-reading" instead of creating feedback loops to correct unclear communication. Messages could be decomposed into "channels" that included the verbal and nonverbal parts, and the "relational" part, which described the nature of the relationship between the two people at that moment. The therapists, role then became something like that of a cybernetic engineer, clarifying and dismantling complex messages, building in feedback mechanisms.

Unfortunately, this hypothesis never receieved much empirical support. Instead, the research results were considerably simpler than this fascinating hypothesis. It turned out that the affect (nonverbal and verbal) in dysfunctional marriages (and families) was simply more negative than the affect in functional marriages (and families). This discovery was facilitated by the fact that, in the early 1970s, several psychology laboratories began to use direct observation to study marital interaction. These laboratories were motivated by the idea that marriages could be helped with a behavioral approach that essentially taught couples new "social skills" for resolving conflict. Because all of these researchers came from a behavioral perspective, observational methods were part of the assumed assessment battery. The historical reason for this approach is worth noting. Early in the intervention research involving the families of children with problems, researchers at the Oregon Social Learning Center had noted that even if the children did not improve, the parents', in self-reports of satisfaction with treatment, claimed that their children were greatly improved. This claim bred a distrust of parental reports of child status and of a reliance on direct observation. The researchers found that the parents of these children were getting divorces at a high rate. They decided to do what they hoped would be a brief detour to design an intervention for marriages in distress. They confidently pushed forward and naturally employed observational methods to help distressed couples resolve their conflicts . In this way, in a classic book chapter published in 1973, by Weiss, Hops, and Patterson, observational research on marriage was born. This chapter was titled "A Framework for Conceptualizing Marital Conflict: A Technology for Altering It, Some Data for Evaluating It." It was an optimistic attempt to define an entire field in one paper. It did just that.

Early Work on the Terman Question

The first question that the psychology marital researchers tackled was the same question Terman raised: "What makes some marriages happy, but others miserable?" Although it continues to be criticized, marital satisfaction had shown itself to be a venerable criterion variable that researchers continued to use and the search was on for the observational correlates of marital satisfaction. There was a faith that an adequate theoretical background would be provided by coupling behavior therapy and social learning theory with principles of communication described by general systems theorists and by behavior exchange theorists (Thibaut and Kelley, 1959). For example, Weiss, Hops, and Patterson (1973) wrote:

> Relationships called marriage pose interesting, seductive, and troublesome challenges to those working within a behavioral framework. To understand continuing intimate adult relationships within a social learning framework requires first of all a translation of strongly held subjective truths into functional person-setting utility statements. It is alleged that marital behaviors, perhaps more than most other behaviors, are determined by cognitive factors, so that a suggestion

that spouses might track their daily exchanges of rewards and punishments is tantamount to introducing a foreign language. Yet this may be an accurate reflection of how the system functions, namely, that a considerable amount of mutual training in vagueness has indeed taken place and that for most adults living together in a marital relationship, assumptions and expectations about the spouse overshadow the data at hand. (p. 309)

The faith was that by bringing precision to the study of marriage, the truth would be revealed, and correct theory would emerge. These researchers simultaneously pursued two paths: the attempt to answer Terman's question with psychological constructs and the design and evaluation of marital therapies.

Laboratories Observing Couples Start Getting Consistent Results

New Methods, New Concepts. In the 1970s, another area of psychology converged methodologically with psychology's study of marriage, and a common approach to the study of social interaction began to emerge. The other area was developmental psychology. Perhaps the most important works that emerged were Lewis and Rosenblum's (1974) *The Effect of the Infant on Its Caregiver* and R. Q. Bell's (1968) paper on the bidirectionality of effects between parent and child. These works led researchers to view interaction as a process in which sequences of behavior unfold in time. Also in 1974, a landmark book was published by Raush, Barry, Hertel, and Swain called *Communication, Conflict, and Marriage*. In this book, the authors followed a cohort of newlyweds as they completed the transition to parenthood. Raush *et al.* introduced the use of Markov models of sequential interaction and an idea they called "adaptive probabilism." They said that marriages and families ought to be studied as systems. Although this idea was not new in the 1970s, what was new was that the book then proceeded to suggest how such studies could be done mathematically using information theory (Shannon and Weaver, 1949) for the study of sequential patterns of interaction. They noted that the mathematics of information theory change how interaction ought to be thought of, and they suggested that the mathematics implied a new approach. Hence, instead of this "systems" concept remaining a vague metaphor or a mathematical procedure for analyzing data, Raush *et al.* realized that it represented a whole new way of thinking. It was their intention to introduce the idea of "stochastic models" to researchers. Stochastic models are uniquely designed for thinking in terms of systems rather than individual behavior. They refer to the conceptualization of behavior sequences in terms of probabilities and the reduction of uncertainty in predicting patterns of interaction (for a systematic development of these concepts and their mathematics, see Bakeman and Gottman, 1986, Bakeman and Quera, 1995, Gottman and Roy, 1990.

New Findings. A complete review of findings is beyond our scope. However, a sampler, some general conclusions, and a flavor of the findings are in order. Restricting ourselves to studies that included some sequential analyses of the data, we would have the work of six laboratories: Raush's, Gottman's, Schaap's (Holland), Ting-Toomey's, the Max-Planck group (Revenstorf, Hahl weg, Schindler, Vogel) in Munich, and Fitzpatrick's. What were the results of various laboratories that investigated the Terman question, and in particular what were the results of sequential analyses?

Of the many studies involving observation of marital interaction, very few have employed sequential analyses. With the MICS, there are only two such studies (Margolin and Wampold, 1981, and Revenstorf *et al.*, 1980). They collapsed the many codes of the MICS into positive or negative, or into positive, negative, and neutral. Each study defined negativity in its own way. Margolin and Wampold (1981) reported the results of interaction with thirty-nine couples (combined from two studies conducted in Eugene, Oregon and Santa Barbara, California). Codes were collapsed into three global categories: positive (problem-solving, verbal and nonverbal positive), negative (verbal and nonverbal negative), and neutral. What were the results? Margolin and Wampold's (1981) results on negative reciprocity were that distressed couples showed negative reciprocity through Lag 2, whereas nondistressed couples did not demonstrate it to any significant extent. For positive reciprocity, they found that "whereas both groups evidenced positive reciprocity through Lag 2, this pattern appears to continue even into Lag 3 for distressed couples." (p. 559). Thus, reciprocating positive acts was more likely for distressed than for nondistressed couples. Gottman (1979) had reported similar results, suggesting that distressed couples showed greater rigidity (or inertia) and interactional structure than nondistressed couples.

Margolin and Wampold (1981) also defined a sequence called negative reactivity, which involves a positive response to a negative antecedent by one's spouse. They also proposed that there is a suppression of positivity following a negative antecedent in distressed couples. They found this supression for all four lags for distressed couples, but they found no evidence for this suppression of positivity by negativity for any lag for nondistressed couples! Revenstorf *et al.* (1980), studying twenty German couples, collapsed the MICS categories into six rather than three summary codes. These codes were positive reaction, negative reaction, problem solution, problem description, neutral reaction, and filler. Interrupts, Disagrees, Negative Solution, and Commands were considered Negative. The researchers employed both lag sequential analyses that allowed them to examine sequences as far out as four lags, as well as the multivariate information theory that Raush *et al.* (1974) had employed. From the multivariate information analysis, they concluded, "In problem discussions distressed couples respond differently from non-distressed couples .... In particular [distressed couples] are more negative and less positive following positive $(+)$ and negative $(-)$ reactions. At the same time they are more negative and more positive, that is more emotional, following problem descriptions (P) of the spouse. Above all distressed couples are more negative and less positive in general that non-distressed couples" (p. 103). They also found seventeen sequences that differentiated the two groups. There is some inconsistency in the group differences for sequences with similar names (e.g., "reconciliation"), so we will summarize only their clearest results. For what might be called "constructive" interaction sequences, they found that nondistressed couples engaged in more "validation" sequences (problem description followed by positivity) and positive reciprocity sequences (positive followed by positive). On the "destructive side," they found that distressed couples engaged in more devaluation sequences (negative follows positive), negative continuance sequences (which they called "fighting on" or "fighting back" in three-chain sequences), and negative start-up sequences (which they called "yes-butting," meaning that somewhere in the four-chain sequence negative follows positive). After an analysis of the sequences following a problem description, they concluded, "It appears as if the distressed couples would interact like non-distressed—had they only higher positive response rates following a problem description of the spouse. And vice versa. The non-distressed would react equally detrimentally as the distressed—were they to respond more negatively to problem description of their spouse. The way they handle problems [problem description statements] seems to be the critical issue—not the sheer number of problems stated" (p. 107). Revenstorf *et al.* also continued their sequential analyses for five lags and found that these reciprocity differences held across lags. They wrote: "In summary, different patterns of response tendencies emerge for distressed and non-distressed couples. After a positive statement the partner continues to reciprocate it positively in non-distressed, whereas no immediate response is likely in distressed couples. After a negative statement no immediate response is most likely in non-distressed, whereas in distressed couples both partners continue to reciprocate negatively. A problem description finally is repeatedly followed by a positive response in non-distressed. In distressed couples, negative statements follow repeatedly" (p. 109). Revenstorf *et al.* then described four types of sequences. The first type of sequence is continued negativity (they called it distancing). This sequence measures the extent to which negativity becomes an absorbing state. The second sequence type is positive reciprocity (which they called attraction). This sequence measures the extent to which positivity becomes an absorbing state. The third sequence consists of alternating problem descriptions and negativity (they called it "problem escalation). The fourth type of sequence consists of validation sequences, or sequences of alternating problem descriptions and positive responses to it (they called it problem acceptance). In most of the study graphs (e.g., for positive reciprocity), the differences between the groups are not very great. However, the evidence is very clear that negativity represents an absorbing state for distressed couples, but not for non-distressed couples. By Lag-2, non-distressed couples begin to escape from the negativity, but distressed couples cannot escape. These graphs provide dramatic information of group differences reflected in sequential patterning of MICS codes.

The consistent findings in these two studies and others that have employed sequential analysis (Raush *et al.*, 1974; Fitzpatrick, 1988; Schaap, 1982; Gottman, 1979; Ting-Toomey, 1982; for a review, see Gottman, 1994) is that: (1) unhappily married couples appear to engage in long chains of reciprocated negativity, and (2) there is a climate of agreement created in the interaction of happily married couples. More recently, Gottman and Notarius (2000) reviewed observational research on marital interaction and reported more widespread use of sequential analysis of observational data in the decade of the 1990s.

Negative Affect Reciprocity as the Failure of Repair Attempts

The basic sequential result is that greater reciprocated negative affective interaction is an absorbing state for dissatisfied couples. This result has profound implications for the interaction process. The result means that negativity becomes an absorbing state for dissatisfied couples; in other words, it is a state that is difficult to exit once entered. What are the potential implications of this fact? We need to know two additional facts about marital interaction. Vincent, Friedman, Nugent, and Messerly (1979) studied the interaction of distressed and nondistressed couples in a problem-solving task (the IMC). The two groups could be discriminated from one another on five out of six MICS summary codes, positive problem solving, and verbal and nonverbal positive and negative codes. They then asked distressed and nondistressed couples either to try to fake good or to fake bad during the next ten minutes. Both groups of couples were unable to fake their nonverbal behaviors. Hence, nonverbal behavior may be a better discriminator of distressed and nondistressed couples than verbal behavior alone. Second, most couples express the most negative affect during the middle arguing phase of the conflict resolution, and their major attempts at repair of the interaction are usually delivered in this phase as well. Attempts at interaction repair are often delivered with negative affect. For example, statements such as "Stop interrupting me!" or "We're getting off the subject" may be accompanied by irritation, tension, sadness, or some other form of distress. Thus, repair attempts usually have two components, a negative affective nonverbal component and a metacommunicative content component attempting to repair the interaction.

The implication of greater negativity being an absorbing state for dissatisfied couples is that they may attend primarily to the negative affect component of repair attempts, whereas satisfied couples attend primarily to the repair component. Thus, we come to the conclusion that repair processes will not work very well in dissatisfied marriages. Instead, what will predominate in dissatisfied couples' attempts to use these social processes is the negative affect. Hence, in various sequential analyses of the stream of behavior, if one spouse attempts a repair mechanism with negative affect, the other spouse is more likely to respond to the negative affect component with reciprocated negative affect in a dissatisfied marriage than in a satisfied one. The usual social processes present during conflict that repair the interaction (such as metacommunication) do not work in unhappy marriages. These processes are the mechanisms used by satisfied couples for exiting a negative state (Gottman, 1979). They include metacommunication, feeling probes that explore feelings, information exchange, social comparison, humor, distraction, gossip, areas of common ground, and appeals to basic philosophy and expectations in the marriage.

What goes hand in glove with this phenomenon is a constriction of social processes. The constriction of available social processes is the fascinating structural dynamic that maintains the absorbing state. How does this work? For example, assume that a message has two parts, one positive and one negative (for example, the message "Stop interrupting me," which is an attempt to repair the interaction, may have been said with some irritation). In a happy marriage, there is a greater probability that the listener will focus on the repair component of the message and respond by saying, "Sorry, what were you saying?" On the other hand, in an unhappy marriage, there is a greater probability that the listener will respond only to the irritation in the message and say something like, "I wouldn't have to interrupt if I could get a word in edgewise." In this case, the attempted repair mechanism does not work. The response to the negativity now continues for long chains of reciprocated negative affect in dissatisfied marriages. Negativity as an absorbing state implies that all these social processes have less of a chance of working because what people attend to and respond to is the negativity. Interestingly, a side effect of this analysis is that the interactions of dissatisfied couples show a higher degree of interaction structure, more predictability of one spouse's behaviors from those of the other, and less statistical independence than is found in the interactions of satisfied couples. The interaction of happily married couples is more random than that of unhappily married couples. This is precisely what Raush *et al.* (1974) predicted. One interesting finding that may be related to this phenomenon is that this greater structure may come to pervade positive as well as negative interaction. The latter result is not as consistently found across laboratories, but this problem may not be so much a failure to replicate as the lack of studies that do sequential analyses of data and the inconsistency across laboratories in conceptualizing, generating, and measuring positivity.

What is "Dysfunctional" in Ailing Marriages?

Research on the correlates of marital satisfaction represent only one way to address the Terman question. The second approach is to ask the longitudinal question about which marital interaction patterns and other variables predict marital stability and eventual happiness. There have been many suggestions about what is dysfunctional about ailing marriages. For example, Lederer and Jackson's (1968) book *Mirages of Marriage* spelled out what is dysfunctional about ailing marriages and how therapists ought to go about fixing them. They said that the sine qua non of marriage was the "quid pro quo": that in good marriages there was a reciprocal exchange of positive behaviors, and that in bad marriages we were witnessing, for various reasons (such as romanticism), the breakdown of these agreements, or contracts. This point of view was consistent with an economically based behavior exchange theory recommended ten years earlier in psychology by Thibaut and Kelly. The Lederer and Jackson book had an enormous impact. In marital behavior therapy alone, it led to the method of contingency contracting.

However, the book turned out to be totally wrong (Murstein, Cerreto, and MacDonald, 1977). Not only weren't happy marriages characterized by the quid pro quo, but it actually characterized unhappy marriages! Yet this erroneous and untested assumption not only spawned a new marital therapy, but also continued on as a major ingredient of marital therapy even when it was disproved. This would be like if a medical researcher, in battling AIDS, recommended as a treatment a biochemical process characteristic of patients losing the battle with AIDS instead of the process of those who might be winning it.

Marital therapy must be guided by a theory of both what is dysfunctional in ailing marriages and what is functional in successful marriage. This theory helps spell out the objectives of the treatment, the assessment of the marriage, although not necessarily the methods for producing change. In their book, Raush *et al.* (1974) raised two critical questions about what is dysfunctional in ailing marriages. The first question was why in some marriages minor conflicts "escalate far beyond their apparent triviality" (p.2). This question was also more broadly about what makes conflict constructive or destructive in marriages. Raush *et al.* gave the example of a couple arguing about which television show to watch. They were impressed by the fact that many couples got quite involved with their role-play improvisations. One wife became extremely upset and said, "Damn it, you always watch what you want to see. You're always drinking beer and watching football. Nothing else seems important to you, especially my wishes." The seemingly small discussion of which TV show to watch had led her to escalate and to express her complete exasperation with her partner and with the marriage. The second question was whether the avoidance of conflict in marriage was functional or dysfunctional. Raush *et al.* concluded that conflict avoidance is dysfunctional and that conflict or bickering about trivial issues is also dysfunctional (indicative of what they called symbolic conflict).

Many other hypotheses have been proposed, most of them stated as if they were truth, without much empirical backing. In addition to the two proposed by Raush, a baker's dozen follows: (1) a dominance structure is dysfunctional (Gottman, 1979); (2) the lack of a dominance structure is dysfunctional (Kolb and Straus, 1974); (3) a "demand-withdraw" pattern or a "pursuer-distancer" pattern is dysfunctional (e.g., Heavey, Christensen, and Malamuth, 1995); (4) not being able to change one another's behavior is dysfunctional (Jacobson and Margolin, 1979); (5) a good marriage is characterized by acceptance in which spouses accept one another as they are and do not try to get behavior change (Jacobson and Christensen, 1998); (6) poor problem solving is dysfunctional (Jacobson, 1989); (7) "mind-reading," or attributing motives or behaviors to one's spouse is dysfunctional (Watzlawick, Beavin, and Jackson, 1967); (8) not meta-communicating is dysfunctional (Bateson *et al.*, 1956); (9) need complimentarity is functional (Winch, 1958); (10) healthy marriage is not possible unless neuroses in one's primary family are resolved (Scharff and Scharff, 1991); (11) most marital conflict is projection (Meissner, 1978), but first the marriage needs to become "conscious" (Hendrix, 1988); (12) marriages start off happy, but over time "reinforcement erosion" occurs and that is the source of marital dysfunction (Jacobson and Margolin, 1979);(13) only equalitarian marriage is functional (Schwartz, 1994). The two questions we must ask are, first, are any of these contentions true, and, second, are these results fundamental or epiphenomenal? It will be important to consider this latter question when discussing the construction of theory. As to the first question, the two primary approaches taken to date toward answering it involve finding the correlates of marital satisfaction and the predictors of long-term stability and satisfaction.

The Criterion of Correlating with Marital Satisfaction. Gottman (1979) defined a dominance structure as asymmetry in predictability of one partner's behavior from the other's, and he used time-series analysis to assess its existence. Distressed couples had significantly greater asymmetry in predictability, with husbands being dominant. A study of 122 societies by Gray (1984) showed that female power is related to more positive sexual relations; however, a review by Gray and Burks (1983) concluded that wife-dominant marriages are the least happy. Because of the difficulty of operationalizing dominance and the lack of agreement among various measures of power and dominance (Rushe, 1996), we cannot conclude that the lack of a dominance structure is dysfunctional. The "demand-withdraw" pattern or a "pursuer-distancer" pattern as characteristic of unhappy marriage has been replicated a number of times (Gottman and Levenson, 1988; Heavey, Christensen, and Malamuth, 1995). In this pattern, it is the wife who raises and pursues the issues and the husband who attempts to avoid the discussion and tends to withdraw. A few results must qualify this conclusion. First, the pattern is also, to some degree, characteristic of happy marriages. Second, the pattern depends to some degree on whether the issue is the husband's or the wife's issue (Christensen and Heavey, 1990). To date there has been no research on the hypothesis that not being able to change one another's behavior is dysfunctional or that a good marriage is one in which spouses accept one another as they are and do not try to get behavior change. The hypothesis that poor problem solving is dysfunctional has yet to be tested independent of other processes of communication, such as negative affect; in therapeutic interventions the two aspects of interaction are also confounded. Mind-reading is a frequent way that couples begin discussing an event or probing feelings (Gottman, 1979). There is no evidence that mindreading, by itself, is dysfunctional. However, a potentially related process of negative trait attributions of one's spouse is indeed characteristic of unhappily married couples. The simple leap from mind-reading to negative trait attributions appears in statements phrased as "You always" or "You never." The genesis of the transformation from simple, specific complaints to these global complaints is unknown and unexplored, but Fincham and Bradbury (1992) offered a clue when they reported that attributions of

responsibility were correlated with the amount of anger displayed by
wives during a problem-solving interaction and the amount of whining
by both husbands and wives. There is no evidence that not metacommu-
nicating is dysfunctional; in fact, Gottman (1979) found that the amount
of metacommunication was the same for happily and unhappily married
couples. However, sequential analyses showed that happily married couples used short chains of metacommunication, often with agreement in
the chain, whereas unhappily married couples used reciprocated metacommunication with metacommunication. This latter sequence shows
that metacommunication in distressed couples is an ineffective repair
technique. There has been little support for the other hypotheses of
what is dysfunctional in ailing marriages.

The Longitudinal Criterion: Divorce Prediction Research. Gottman
(1994) reported that there were three types of stable couples. One
type of stable couple, called volatile, was very much like Raush's bickering couple', another type of stable couple was very much like Raush's
conflict-avoiding couples; and a third type of stable couple, called validators, were like Raush's harmonious couples. In other words, all three
types of couples Raush et al. identified turned out to be stable. The
three types of couples differed most dramatically in the amount and
timing of persuasion attempts: volatile couples had the most persuasion attempts and began them almost immediately; validators waited
to begin their persuasion attempts until the middle of the conversation;
and conflict avoiders avoided all persuasion attempts. The three types
of couples also differed in how emotionally expressive they were, with
volatile couples highest. validators intermediate, and avoiders lowest in
emotionality. The three stable types of couples differed in many ways
from couples on a trajectory toward divorce. First, using a balance theory of marriage, Gottman (1994) reported that the ratio of positive to
negative codes during the conflict discussion was about 5.0 for the three
types of stable marriages, whereas it was 0.8 for the unstable marriage.
Second, couples headed for divorce were high on four behaviors that
Gottman (1994) called the "Four Horsemen of the Apocalypse"; they
are criticism, defensiveness, contempt, and "stonewalling," or listener
withdrawal; consistent with the demand-withdraw pattern, women were
significantly more likely than men to criticize, while men were more
likely than women to stonewall.

What We Have Learned: The Psychology of Marriage

The View from Observing. Only a few phenomena are consistently characteristic of ailing marriages. The first we call "the triumph of negative
over positive affect." Once there is a neutral category, so that positive

and negative codes are not logically mirror images of one another (or very highly correlated), this phenomenon is that negative codes in a marital interaction coding system are consistently more likely to be negatively correlated with marital happiness and predictive of divorce than positive codes are to be positively correlated with marital happiness and predictive of stability

The second phenomenon is negative affect reciprocity, which is the greater than base rate likelihood that one partner will subsequently be negative if the spouse has just been negative. This reciprocation may be a result of the failure of repair processes. However, our recent research with newlyweds suggests that the major component of negative affect reciprocity that is dysfunctional is not the reciprocation of negative affect in kind (e.g., anger reciprocated by anger), which appears to be characteristic of all marriages during a conflict discussion. Instead, what is dysfunctional is the escalation of negative affect. Gottman *et al.* (1998) suggested that this escalation was an index of the rejection of influence—that is, that it tapped into a power struggle in the marriage.

The third phenomenon is the "demand-withdraw" pattern. This is a pattern in which one partner pursues solution of a problem and change, whereas the other partner is avoidant and tries to withdraw from the discussion. Usually this is a female-demand/male-avoid pattern. It seems to be characteristic of most marriages, but it is exacerbated when the marriage is ailing.

The fourth phenomenon is the presence of particular forms of negativity—namely, the Four Horsemen of the Apocalypse: criticism, contempt, defensiveness, and stonewalling—and their ability to predict divorce.

The View from Cognitive Psychology. A thorough review of this productive area in the study of marriage is not possible here (see Fincham, Bradbury, and Scott, 1990). There is a universal phenomenon in marriage that has to do with how spouses in happy and unhappy marriages think about positive and negative actions of their partner. In a happy marriage, if someone does something negative, the partner tends to think that the negativity is fleeting and situational. For example, the thought might be something such as "Oh, well, he's in a bad mood. He's been under a lot of stress lately and needs more sleep." So the negativity is viewed as unstable, and the cause is viewed as situational. Some external and fleeting situation has caused the negativity. On the other hand, in an unhappy marriage the same behavior is likely to be interpreted as stable and internal to the partner. The accompanying thought might be something such as, "He is inconsiderate and selfish. That's the way he is. That's why he did that." On the other hand, in a happy marriage, if someone does something positive, the behavior is likely to be interpreted as stable and internal to the partner. The accompanying thought might be something such as, "He is a considerate and loving person. That's the way he is. That's why he did that." On the other hand, in an unhappy marriage, the same positive behavior is likely to be seen as fleeting and situational. The accompanying thought might be something like "Oh, well, he's nice because he's been successful this week at work. It won't last, and it doesn't mean much." The positivity is viewed as unstable, and the cause is viewed as situational. Some external and fleeting situation has caused the positivity.

Holtzworth-Munroe and Jacobson (1985) used indirect probes to investigate when a couple might "naturally" search for causes of events and what they conclude when they do search for causes. The two researchers found evidence for the hypothesis that distressed couples engage in more attributional activity than nondistressed couples and that attributional thoughts primarily surround negative impact events. They also found that nondistressed couples engaged in relationship-enhancing attributions whereas distressed couples engaged in distress-maintaining attributions. Distress-maintaining attributions maximize the impact of negativity and minimize the impact of positivity of the partner's behavior. Moreover, there was an important gender difference. Distressed husbands generated more attributions than nondistressed, but the two groups of wives did not differ. These authors suggested that males normally may not engage in much attributional activity, but that they outstrip women once relationship conflict develops. Relationship-enhancing attributions were responses to positive partner behavior in both groups of couples. Relationship-enhancing attributions minimize the impact of negative and maximize the impact of positive behaviors of the partner.

In an experimental study by Jacobson et al. (1985), distressed and nondistressed couples were randomly assigned to instructions to "act positive" or to "act negative." They found that distressed couples were likely to attribute their partner's negative behavior to internal factors, whereas nondistressed couples were likely to attribute their partner's positive behavior to internal factors. Thus, these attributions, once established, make change less likely to occur. Behaviors that should disconfirm the attributional sets tend to get ignored, whereas behaviors that confirm the attributional set receive attention. Attributional processes may tap the way couples think in general about the marital interaction as it unfolds in time. For example, Berley and Jacobson (1984) noted that Watzlawick, Beavin and Jackson (1967) were talking about attributional processes when they discussed the punctuation fallacy. The punctuation fallacy is that each spouse views himself or herself as the victim of the partner's behavior, which is seen as the causal stimulus. Attributions and general thought patterns about negative behaviors may thus be theoretically useful in providing a link between the immediate patterns of activity seen in behavioral interaction and physiological response, on the one hand, and more long-lasting and more global patterns that span longer time periods on the other. It might be the case that these more stable aspects of the marriage are better at predicting long- term outcomes such as divorce than can be obtained from behavioral observation.

The content dimensions of negative attributions that have been studied include locus (partner, self, relationship, or outside events), stability (e.g., owing to partner's trait or to a state that is situationally determined), globality (how many areas of the marriage are affected), intentionality (negative intent, or selfish versus unselfish motivation), controllability, volition, and responsibility (e.g., blameworthiness). Bradbury, Fincham, and Scott (1990) reviewed experimental evidence for this phenomenon and concluded that, by and large, these patterns had been pretty well established by research. For attributions about negative events, all of the studies they reviewed supported differences between happily and unhappily married couples on the two dimensions of globality and selfish versus unselfish motivation. It is likely that it is these attributional phenomenona that make the self-report measurement of any aspects of the quality of the marriage so strongly related. It is also what becomes problematic in attaching any specificity to the measurement of marital satisfaction or marital quality (see Fincham and Bradury, 1987).

Weiss (1980) introduced another important cognitive dimension, called *sentiment override*. He suggested that reactions during marital interaction may be determined by a global dimension of affection or disaffection rather than by the immediately preceding valence of the stimulus. Notarius, Benson, and Sloane (1989) evaluated the validity of this hypothesis in a remarkably creative study in which they employed a sequential stream of behavior and cognitions to operationalize a number of hypotheses linking behavior and cognition. They found that distressed wives were more negative, were more likely to evaluate their partner's neutral and negative messages as negative (suggesting the operation of a negative sentiment override), and given a negative evaluation of their partner's antecedent message, were more likely to offer a negative reply than were all other spouses. Vanzetti, Notarius, and NeeSmith (1992) reported that distressed couples have more negative and less positive expectations; they measured relational efficacy, which is a shared belief that the couple can solve their problems, and found that couples high in relational efficacy chose relationship-enhancing attributions more often than did low-efficacy spouses. Low-efficacy marriages showed strong preferences for distress-maintaining attributions.

To assess a larger cognitive unit than attributions, Buehlman, Gottman, and Katz (1992) coded an interview with couples about the history of their marriage to assess the shared beliefs and narratives of couples about the history of their marriage and their philosophy of marriage. A few simple variables (such as the husband's fondness for his wife) were able to predict divorce or marital stability over a three-year period with a great degree of accuracy (100% for the divorcing couples and 94% overall). These results were recently replicated in an independent sample of newlyweds by Carrère *et al.* (2000).

Basic to these attributional patterns in marriage is the phenomenon that Fritz Heider (1958) called the fundamental attribution error, in which each spouse thinks that he or she is negative because of situational factors, but that the partner is negative because of negative personality defects. This is evident in one of our best predictors of divorce—criticism, in which a spouse presents a marital problem as a defect in the partner's personality. It is a suggestion that the marital issue is owing to a stable negative trait in the partner.

In this case, it seems to us that one is likely to see one's own negative behavior more compassionately as integrated over time with long-standing trends of positivity that offset this temporary negativity. On the other hand, one is more tuned into the immediate changes one's partner makes toward negativity, and then one establishes the attribution that this negativity is caused by a trait and not a state factor. It is as if one views one's own behavior with an integral and one's partner's behavior with a derivative, minimizing one's own negativity (balancing it out mentally in one's own mind with other positive acts), but somehow unable to do this with the partner's immediately negative behavior.

The View from Psychophysiology. A recent and productive approach to studying marriages has been a social psychophysiological procedure. Beginning with Kaplan, Burch, and Bloom (1964), simultaneous psychophysiological recording was taken from two conversing individuals. Their initial finding was that the galvanic skin responses of the two interacting people were correlated only when they disliked one another. Levenson and Gottman (1983) later extended this finding to the construct of "physiological linkage" —i.e., predictability of one person's physiology (across channels) from the other's (controlling for autocorrelation)— and reported greater physiological linkage for unhappily married couples compared to happily married couples. The linkage variable accounted for more than 60% of the variance in marital satisfaction. Levenson and Gottman (1985) later reported that measures of physiological arousal in cardiovascular channels and in skin conductance were able to predict drops in marital satisfaction over three years, controlling for the initial level of marital satisfaction. The pattern was later used by Gottman

(1990) to suggest that diffuse physiological arousal—that is, arousal in more than one physiological channel (but not necessarily more than one physiological system, e.g., increased heart rate as well as contractility, or blood velocity)—would be associated with decreased information-processing capability and a reliance on overlearned patterns of behavior and cognition, in particular those associated with fight or flight.

Brown and Smith (1992) studied forty-five married couples and found that husbands attempting to persuade their wives showed the greatest increase in systolic blood pressure before and during the discussion. In males, physiological effects were accompanied by increased anger and a hostile and coldly assertive interpersonal style. Although wives showed behavior patterns that were similar to husbands to some degree, they displayed neither elevated systolic blood pressure or anger. Also, Fankish (1992) found that both the size of the husbands' systolic blood pressure responses during marital conflict and their recovery times exceeded those of their wives. Malarkey, Kiecolt-Glaser, Pearl, and Glaser (1994) simultaneously studied the secretion of stress-related hormones in five samples of blood taken during the conflict interactions of ninety newlywed couples. Hostile behavior (coded with the MICS) correlated with decreased levels of prolactin and increases in epinephrine, norepinephrine, ACTH, and growth hormone, but not cortisol.

Physiological approaches have added something important theoretically. The general contribution they provide is in directing the organization and search for patterns of behavior and cognition within balance theories, in which positivity and negativity are in a state of dynamic balance around a steady state or set point (see Cook *et al.*, 1995). In the body, many systems are in a state of dynamic homeostatic balance around a steady state through the action of opponent processes (e.g., the regulation of the heart's rate through the parasympathetic and sympathetic branches of the autonomic nervous system).

Add to the discussion three additional concepts about how physiology may relate to interactive behavior. First, negative affect reciprocity may exist as a function of spouses' inability to soothe themselves and of the couple's inability to soothe one another. Evidence supporting this contention was reported by Gottman, Coan, Carrère, and Swanson (1998). Second, this variable of soothing may be the basis for the large relapse effect in marital therapy. The idea is that in therapy the therapist plays the role of soother instead of the couple; when therapy ends, the couple is unable to soothe one another, and old patterns of behavior and cognition reassert themselves. Third, Gottman and Levenson found that the husband's stonewalling (withdrawal as a listener) was related to his physiological arousal (reported in Gottman, 1994); also, Carstensen, Gottman, and Levenson (1995) in a study of older long-term marriages reported that the husband's but not the wife's physiological arousal was related to his self-report of feeling negative (in a video recall paradigm); they speculated that husband's withdrawal in the demand-withdraw pattern may be related to his physiological arousal, because it is known that males are more aware of their own physiology than women. Thus, physiological measures suggest a biological basis for the gender effect in the demand-withdraw pattern. This is not intended to mean that such a biological basis is unrelated to socialization.

2.2   The Problem of Power

In all of this research into the Terman question, the importance of negative and positive *affect* and of the reciprocity of negative affect emerged as most important. However, these findings were quite unsatisfying to sociologists and feminists, who were concerned with the concept of *power* and its distribution in marriages.

It's not that quantitative researchers were uninterested in the concept of power. On the contrary, there were scores of attempts to measure the distribution of power in a marriage. The problem is that these various strategies tended to be unrelated to one another. The concept of power proved elusive. Every attempt to define and measure the fabric of power led the fabric to come apart in the researchers' hands (Cromwell and Olson, 1975; Gray-Little and Burks, 1983; Olson and Rabunsky, 1972; Sprey, 1972; Turk and Bell, 1972). Strodtbeck's (1952) early investigation of three cultures was a first bold attempt at measuring power. Strodtbeck studied marital communication in a matrilineal culture (the Navajo), a patrilineal culture (the Mormon), and a supposedly more egalitarian culture (Anglo-Texan). He drove a van around the U. S. West and had couples make decisions in the back of the van. Women won most of the decisions in Navajo couples; men won most in the Mormon; and there was an equal distribution of winning in the Anglo-Texan couples. It seemed as if the study of power was off to a good start. Other definitions of power concerned the distribution of "resources" in the marriage, people's self ratings (Schwartz, 1994), the amount of housework done (doing little signifies power), who interrupts most, who cares about the marriage the most (the one who cares the least is supposedly the most powerful), asymmetry in speaking time (the one who talks more is more powerful), or visual gaze (the one who gazes at the partner the most is least powerful), judgments of power of each message in a conversation (Rogers and Farace, 1975), asymmetry in predictability in behavior (Gottman, 1979), And outcomes of various games (such as SIMFAM; Straus and Tallman, 1971). The problem was not a lack of measurement or definition, but the failure of these various definitions to relate to any important criterion variable or to one another.

In our modeling of marriage, we integrate the study of affect (emotions) and power. We broadly define power, or influence, as the ability of one person's emotions to affect the partner's emotions, but this definition has meaning throughout the emotion continuum. That is, we can assess the subsequent result on the wife of a husband's mild positive affect or mild negative affect, and so on. The same function can be defined for the wife. We thus complicate the study of power by making of "power" two functions. From this simple definition of power, we wind up defining two influence *functions* that specify the ability of each person's affect to influence the other person's affect which leads us to a discussion of the affect continuum (our "Dow-Jones Industrial Average" of a marital conversation), which we compute for modeling.

2.3   Review of Gottman and Levenson

Gottman and Levenson (1992) used a methodology for obtaining synchronized physiological, behavioral, and self-report data in a sample of seventy-three couples who were followed longitudinally between 1983 and 1987.

Creating a "Dow-Jones Industrial Average"–Type Graph of a Marital Conflict Conversation

Using observational coding of interactive behavior with the Rapid Couples Interaction Scoring System (RCISS) (Gottman, 1995), couples were divided into two groups, which we here call "high risk" and "low risk" for divorce. This classification was based on a graphical method originally proposed by Gottman (1979) for use with the Couples Interaction Scoring System, a predecessor of the RCISS. This observational system used as its unit the "interact," which is everything each of two people say in two conversational turns at speech during a fifteen-minute task in which they attempt to resolve a major area of continuing disagreement in their marriage. This unit provided an uneven number of interacts for each couple. The coding also took about six hours, and ten hours for a verbatim transcript.

We have now been able to derive the same data using a weighting of the codes of the Specific Affect Coding System (SPAFF; Gottman, 1995), which can be coded on-line in real time and, with a numerical weighting scheme for each coding category, provides 150 observations for each person in each couple. SPAFF also has the advantage that it can be

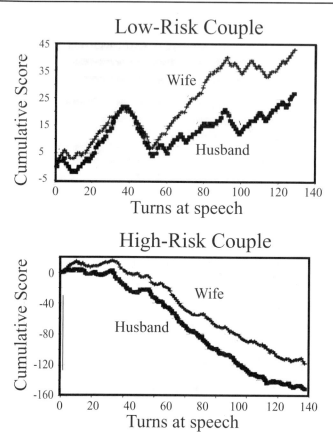

Figure 2.1: Cumulative RCISS speaker point graphs for a low-risk couple and a high-risk couple. The heavier line in each graph represents the husband's behavior, and the lighter line represents the wife's behavior.

coded for any conversation, not just for conflict resolution conversations. Later in this book, we discuss this new observational system.

On each conversational turn, the total number of positive RCISS speaker codes minus the total number of negative speaker codes was computed for each spouse. The classifications of "positive" or "negative" were based on previous studies that had sought to discriminate happy from unhappy couples from a scoring of the behavior they exhibited during conflictual marital interaction. Based on this review of the literature, the RCISS system was devised. Then the cumulative total of these points was plotted for each spouse (see figure 2.1). The slopes of these plots, which were thought to provide a stable estimate of the difference between positive and negative codes over time, were determined using linear regression analysis. If both husband and wife graphs had a positive slope, they were called low risk; if not, they were called high risk. This classification is referred to as the couple's affective balance. Using Cohen's Kappa, reliability for all RCISS subcodes taken together was 0.72. All couples, even happily married ones, have some amount of negative interaction; similarly, all couples, even unhappily married, have some degree of positive interaction. Computing the graph's slope was guided by a balance theory of marriage—namely, that those processes most important in predicting dissolution would involve a balance or a regulation of positive and negative interaction. Low-risk couples are defined as those for whom both husband and wife speaker slopes were significantly positive; for high-risk couples, at least one of the speaker slopes was not significantly positive. By definition, low-risk couples were those who showed, more or less consistently, that they displayed more positive than negative RCISS codes. Classifying couples in the current sample in this manner produced two groups consisting of forty-two low-risk couples and thirty-one high-risk couples. Figure 2.1 illustrates two cumulative graphs, one from the interaction of a low-risk couple and one from the interaction of a high-risk couple.

1987 Follow-up of the Couples

In 1987, four years after the initial assessment, the original subjects were Recontacted, and at least one spouse (70 husbands, 72 wives) from 73 of the original 79 couples (92.4%) agreed to participate in the follow-up. Marital status information was obtained.

Results from Gottman and Levenson (1992)

Figure 2.2 summarizes the Gottman and Levenson results for the dissolution variables of their dissolution cascade. The dissolution cascade is a *Guttman scale* (Guttman, 1944) in which precursors of separation and divorce were identified as continued marital unhappiness and serious thoughts of dissolution. Time-2 was 4 years later than Time-1. Low-risk couples were more happily married at Time-1, less likely to consider marital dissolution, and to separate and divorce by Time-2. Thus, the positive-minus-negative variable predicted an entire cascade of dissolution of the marriage.

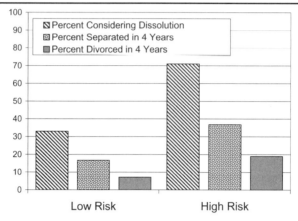

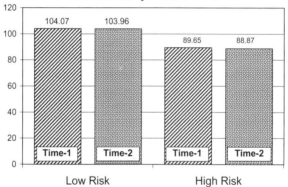

Figure 2.2: Outcome data from the marital dissolution cascade for high-risk and low-risk marriages (adapted from Gottman and Levenson, 1992).

Marital Typology

Gottman (1993) proposed and validated a typology of three types of longitudinally stable marriages with distinct Time-1 marital interaction patterns; these interaction patterns differed from the Time-1 interaction patterns of couples heading for dissolution. There were three groups of stable couples: validators, volatiles, and avoiders, who could be distinguished on problem-solving behavior, on specific affects, and, using log-linear analysis, on one variable designed to provide an index of the amount and timing of persuasion attempts. There were two groups of unstable couples: hostile and hostile-detached, who could be distinguished from one another on problem-solving behavior and on specific negative and positive affects; the hostile-detached group was significantly more negative (more defensive and contemptuous) than the hostile group.

Gottman reported one rough constant was invariant across each of the three types of stable couples. This constant, the ratio of positive to negative RCISS speaker codes during conflict resolution, was about 5.0, and it was not significantly different across the three types of stable marriage. The couples heading for divorce had a ratio of 0.8. Perhaps each adaptation to having a stable marriage, or each stable couple type, although the marriages were quite different, represents a similar kind of adaptation. The volatile couples reach the ratio of 5 by mixing a lot of positive affect with a lot of negative affect. The validators mix a moderate amount of positive affect with a moderate amount of negative affect. The avoiders mix a small amount of positive affect with a small amount of negative affect. Each partner does so in a way that achieves roughly the same balance between positive and negative.

We can speculate that each type of marriage has its risks, benefits, and costs. It is possible to speculate about these risks, costs, and benefits based on what we know about each type of marriage. The volatile marriage tends to be quite romantic and passionate, but has the risk of dissolving to endless bickering. The validating marriage (which is the current model of marital therapy) is calmer and intimate; these couples appear to place a high degree of value on companionate marriage and shared experiences, not on individuality. The risk may be that romance will disappear over time, and the couple will become merely close friends. The avoiding marriage avoids the pain of confrontation and conflict, but the risk may be emotional distance and loneliness. Gottman also found that the three types of stable marriages differed in the amount and timing of persuasion attempts. Volatile couples engaged in high levels of persuasion and did so at the very outset of the discussion. Validators engaged in less persuasion than volatile couples and waited to begin their persuasion attempts until after the first third of the interaction. Conflict-avoiding couples hardly ever attempted to persuade one another.

We wondered whether these five types of marriage could be discriminated using the parameters and functions derived from the mathematical modeling. For an extended analysis and review of the typology, see Gottman (1994).

2.4   What Phenomenon Are We Modeling?

There is clearly a large set of results to model in the marital area. We have selected only one, the ability of a sum of positivity and negativity (or a ratio) to predict whether or not couples will divorce. We call this sum (or ratio) the *Gottman-Levenson variable*. We will have occasion to determine whether or not the model derived from this phenomenon can "explain" other consistent results reviewed in this chapter.

2.5   Two Additional Mysteries in the Marital Research Area

We think that there are two major mysteries in the marital research area. The first is the *relapse effect*, which refers to a pervasive finding that initial gains in marital therapy relapse after one to two years (e.g., see Jacobson and Addis, 1993). What is the basis of relapse? How can it be controlled and minimized? The second mystery is the *delay effect*. In the public health field, one wishes to reduce the delay time from when a person discovers a symptom (e.g., angina, a lump in a breast) to the time when that person seeks professional help. These delay times, thanks to public education, are now a matter of weeks. However, Notarius and Buongiorno (1992) reported that the average amount of time a couple waits to get professional help from the time one of them detects serious problems in the marriage is a whopping six years! How can we explain these two effects? Later we propose that one parameter of our mathematical model of marriage, the negative threshold , can be used to explain both of these effects.

3

The Mathematics We Employ Is Nonlinear Dynamic Modeling

3.1 The General Systems Theory of von Bertalanffy

The application of a branch of applied mathematics to the study of marriage was presaged by von Bertalanffy (1968), who wrote a classic and highly influential book called *General System Theory*. This book was an attempt to view biological and other complex organizational units across a wide variety of sciences in terms of the interaction of these units. The work was an attempt to provide a holistic approach to complex systems. Von Bertalanffy worked with Boulding, Rapoport, and Gerard at the Palo Alto Center for Advanced Study in the Behavioral Sciences. The work fit a general Zeitgeist. As von Bertalanffy noted, his work fit with Wiener's (1948) *Cybernetics*, Shannon & Weaver's *Information Theory*, and VonNeumann and Morgenstern's (1947) *Game Theory*. The concepts of homeostasis (derived from the physiologist Cannon), feedback, and information provided the basis for a new approach to the study of complex interacting systems.

The mathematics of General System Theory was lost to most of the people in the social sciences who were inspired by von Bertalanffy's work. Von Bertalanffy believed that the interaction of complex systems with many units could be characterized by a set of values that change over time, denoted Q_1, Q_2, $Q_3, \ldots$. The Q's were variables each of which indexed a particular unit in the "system," such as mother, father, and child. He thought that the system could be best described by a set of ordinary differential equations of the form:

$$\frac{dQ_1}{dt} = f_1(Q_1, Q_2, Q_3, \ldots)$$

$$\frac{dQ_2}{dt} = f_2(Q_1, Q_2, Q_3, \ldots)$$

$$(3.1)$$

and so on.

The terms on the left of the equal sign are time derivatives —that is, rates of change of the quantitative sets of values Q_1, Q_2, Q_3,.... The terms on the right of the equal signs, $f_1, f_2, \ldots$, are functions of the Q's. Von Bertalanffy thought that these functions, the f's, would generally be nonlinear. The equations he selected have a particular form, called "autonomous," meaning that the f's have no explicit function of time in them, except through the Q's, which are functions of time. These are, in fact, among the type of equations we will work with. However, von Bertalanffy presented a table in which these nonlinear equations were classified as "Impossible" (von Bertalanffy, 1968, p.20). He was referring to a very popular mathematical method of approximating nonlinear functions with a linear approximation which is rather limited. He also had no idea what the Q variables should be.

In the applied mathematics world, such nonlinear equations have long been studied and several techniques are available to deal with them which give, at the very least, qualitative solutions. In fact, the modeling of complex deterministic (and stochastic) systems with a set of nonlinear difference or differential equations has become a very productive enterprise across a wide set of phenomena, across a wide range of sciences, particularly in the biomedical sciences. It is a significant part of a new field called "mathematical biology."

3.2   Modeling with More Than One Equation

In this section we will give the reader an overview of how our own modeling has differed from the one proposed by von Bertalanffy. We used a new approach to modeling social interaction using the mathematics of difference and differential equations. These equations express, in mathematical form, a proposed mechanism of change over time. They do *not* represent a statistical approach to modeling but rather they are designed to suggest a precise mechanism of change. This method has been employed with great success in the biological sciences (see, for example, the book by Murray, 1989). It is usually a quantitative approach that requires the modeler to be able to write down, in mathematical form, on the basis of some known or observed facts, the causes of change in the dependent variables, thus giving rise to a theory. For example, in the classic predator-prey problem, one writes down that the rate of change in the population densities is some function of the current densities (e.g., Murray, 1989). While this is a simple representation of the predator-prey phenomenon, it has served well as an initial exploratory model and in highlighting key questions. The equations are designed to write down the precise form of rates of change over time.

The ideal mathematical technique for describing change is the area of differential equations. In some fields, these equations usually use linear terms or linear approximations of nonlinear terms, and they often gave very good results. In fact, most of the statistics used in the field of psychology are based upon linear models. In the area of differential equations, linear equations simply assume that rates of change follow generalized straight line functions of the variables rather than curved line functions[1] and, for example, the sum of two solutions is another solution. Unfortunately, linear models are generally unstable, in that the solutions depend critically on the initial conditions. Linear models are seldom justified.

In recent years it has become increasingly clear that most systems are complex and must be described by nonlinear terms. Interestingly, by employing nonlinear terms in the equations of change some very complex processes can be represented with very few parameters. Unfortunately, unlike many linear equations, these nonlinear equations are generally not solvable in closed functional mathematical form. For this reason the methods are called "qualitative," and visual methods must be relied upon. For this purpose, numerical and graphical methods have been developed such as "phase space plots". These visual approaches to mathematical modeling can be very appealing in engaging the intuition of a scientist working in a field that has no mathematically stated theory. If the scientist has an intuitive familiarity with the data of the field, our approach may suggest a way of building theory using mathematics in an initially qualitative manner. The amount of mathematics needed is relatively minimal. The use of these graphical solutions to nonlinear differential equations makes it possible to talk about "qualitative" mathematical modeling. In qualitative mathematical modeling, one searches for solutions that have similarly shaped phase space plots.

We will soon describe these new methods of mathematical modeling in detail. But first we will also talk a bit about what is the conceptual gain inherent in the mathematics.

---

[1]For example, the equation $dy/dt = 2y$ is linear, whereas the equation $dy/dt = 2\sin(y)$ is nonlinear. For regions of y close to zero, however, $\sin(y) = y$ is a good approximation, and so the linear equation is a good approximation of the nonlinear equation but *only* when y is close to zero.

3.3   Outline of the Subsequent Chapters

Following this chapter we will present the mathematics necessary for understanding our modeling. Our goal is to make this book readable for researchers who do not necessarily have a mathematical background. For this reason, our appendices to chapters provide the more detailed mathematics. Please skip these appendices rather than be put off by the mathematics. They can be referred to for more detailed understanding later, if necessary. We provide instructions for obtaining our computer programs, so that any researcher who can put his or her dyadic data into two column vectors that contain zeroes, and positive and negative numbers can derive the models we discuss in this book. Because of this fact a researcher can read this book to find out how to interpret the model and its parameters, and then use our programs on his or her own data.

In chapter 4 we present an elementary introduction to the calculus. Readers familiar with the calculus can skip this chapter, or peruse it for a brief review. In chapter 5 we introduce nonlinear dynamic modeling with one equation. In chapter 6 we review catastrophe theory models of change, which, although not very popular today in biological modeling, appear to us to be potentially quite valuable in understanding the seemingly sudden changes observed in the breakdown of marital systems. In chapter 8 we extend the modeling to two equations instead of one. We also review the modeling of such examples as a linear model for marriage, Romeo and Juliet, and two-equation nonlinear models in the predator-prey, competition, and cooperation systems. In chapter 7 we present an intuitive discussion of phase space plots. We are building up an understanding of the necessary mathematics for understanding our modeling.

In chapter 9 we finally write down the equations of the marriage model. In chapter 11, titled "Who needs all this math?," we discuss the philosophical implications of this modeling. For example, we discuss how the old concept of homeostasis created an adversarial position between dysfunctional families and the therapist. The therapist is seen as battling valiantly against the family system, which keeps trying to maintain its dysfunctional homeostatic regulation. However, our modeling suggests that each family can have two or more homeostatic "set points," and one can be positive and one negative. Our model also integrates the study of affect with the study of power, by creating and estimating two "influence functions."

In chapter 10 we present the initial results of our modeling. In chapter 12 we extend our results with a specific form of the influence functions and apply the model to a new sample of newlyweds. We extend these results in chapter 13 in our modification of the model to include repair and damping. In chapter 14 we apply the model with repair and damping to a study of heterosexual and Gay and Lesbian couples, and to the study of mother-father-infant triads. In chapter 15, titled "The Core Triad of Balance," we extend the model to include perception and physiology as well as interactive behavior. In chapter 16 we illustrate our preliminary results with intervention in our "marriage experiments." The final chapter offers guidelines for preparing observational data for use with our programs.

4

Calculus—the Mathematics of Change

In this book, we occasionally use a bit of calculus because it is an important tool we can use to determine what behavior our model will exhibit after a long period of time. This chapter is designed for the reader who has only limited familiarity with calculus. It is intended as a conceptual introduction.

In A. A. Milne's *The World of Christopher Robin,* Winnie the Pooh and his friends play a game (Pooh sticks) in which they toss small twigs off a bridge onto the swirling river below. Many of us have gazed at the swiftly moving, eddying waters below a bridge. We can use the motions of the river to explain certain aspects of calculus, which is the mathematics of change. Calculus was invented simultaneously by Wilhelm Gottfried Leibnitz in Germany and by Isaac Newton in England. It was a marvelous invention because it made possible the description of the dynamical motion (motion over time) of all things. The invention of calculus was a singular achievement in a process begun by Galileo when he began to generalize the theories of Aristotle's physics. Aristotle had stressed "being at rest" and the idea of an object's "natural place" in the order of things. An object would remain at rest in its natural place unless disturbed, Aristotle asserted. Galileo, however, took this idea a huge step further. He carried out an interesting experiment in which he rolled an object down an inclined plane. As Galileo made his surface increasingly free of friction, the object kept moving at a uniform speed. From this experiment, he was able to recognize that he had come across a fundamental principle. Motion at a uniform velocity, he therefore declared, was the natural order, not rest.

Newton added the idea that changes in uniform motion— that is, acceleration— were proportional to forces in nature. One of his major feats was to suggest a form for gravitational force. Using his new calculus, he was able to explain the motions of the moon around the Earth, the motion of projectiles shot from cannons, and the orbits of the known planets. He did all this with one equation relating acceleration to force and mass.

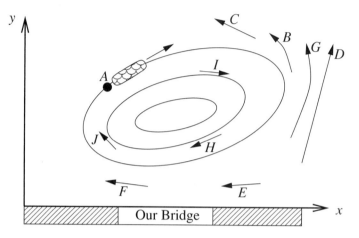

Figure 4.1: In the game of Pooh sticks, a twig or pinecone is dropped from a bridge onto the river below. This figure shows a twig on the river and arrows are drawn to indicate the flow lines of the water. The twig is currently circulating in an eddy that is turning clockwise, while to the right of the twig the main flow is in the direction of increasing y.

Newton was afraid his contemporaries would not accept the new calculus, so he used only geometric proofs in his book *Principia mathematica*. Some called this approach as great an accomplishment as inventing the calculus itself.

So calculus has a wonderful history. For our purposes, it is also useful. A small twig tossed off our bridge into the river is carried on a trajectory based on the velocities in each direction imparted to it by the flowing water. We can use calculus to help us describe this trajectory.

4.1 Dynamical Motion as Slope

If our little twig were to land in the water at point A, it would experience a force pushing it in the direction of the arrow shown as "A" in figure 4.1.

This arrow will move the twig in the direction of increasing y (away from our bridge) and also in the direction of increasing x (to our right).

At each point A through I on the water, in $x - y$ space, our twig would drift on a trajectory illustrated by the arrows at those points.

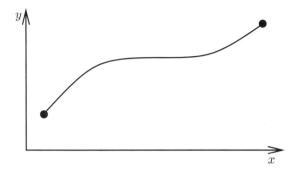

Figure 4.2: Possible movement of our Pooh stick twig in $x - y$ space on the surface of the river. The x–axis lies along the bridge in figure 4.1, and the y–axis points downriver. Notice that there is no indication of temporal information in the figure. The twig might have started from any point along the curve and then traced out and retraced the remainder of the curve over some unknown interval of time.

We can plot an overall relationship between y and x that contains only positional information with no reference to time (figure 4.2). We have no idea from this figure when the twig started. Also, unless we add some indication to the figure, we have no idea at which end the twig started, or even if it was at an end when it started. We only know the path along which it traveled.

But we are interested in motion over time. Thus, we also draw graphs of each component of the twig's movement over time, t. That is, we graph the twig's right/left position (x) against time, or its downriver/upriver position (y) against time (figure 4.3). These graphs do not give us a visual picture of the trajectory traveled, but they do tell us something about the twig's precise location at each moment in time.

In the middle section of time, the twig moved very quickly to our right. This is shown in figure 4.3 as a steep slope in the rightmost graph. However, during the same time interval, the twig moved very slowly in the upriver/downriver direction, which appears as a flatter slope in the leftmost graph of figure 4.3. So the slope of each of these curves contains information about the speed with which the twig is moving in

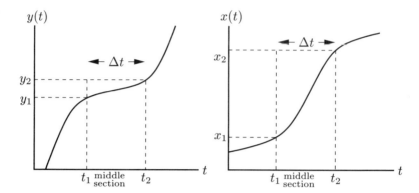

Figure 4.3: Graphs of the twig's movement over time (*t*). The graph on the left shows the downriver/upriver position of the twig as a function of time, and the graph on the right shows the right/left position of the twig as a function of time.

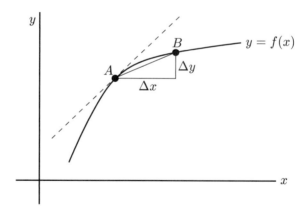

Figure 4.4: Graph showing how the slope of a line between two points A and B is calculated. The slope is calculated by taking the rise (Δy) and dividing it by the run (Δx). The slope of the line between A and B will differ from the actual slope of the curve at the point A. This slope is visualized as the dashed tangent line drawn through A.

each direction.

Recall that we calculate slope by selecting two points on the curve, and then by dividing the rise, or change in y (Δy), by the run, or change in x (Δx) (figure 4.4). In figure 4.3, the horizontal axis is labeled t instead of x, so the slope of the $y(t)$ curve over the time interval Δt is given by

$$\frac{\Delta y}{\Delta t} = \frac{y_2 - y_1}{t_2 - t_1}.$$

This slope is nearly flat, or close to zero. Over the same time interval Δt, the slope of the $x(t)$ curve is given by

$$\frac{\Delta x}{\Delta t} = \frac{x_2 - x_1}{t_2 - t_1}.$$

This slope is steep or fairly high.

By viewing the twig's motion in terms of its speed, or slope, at each point in time, we have isolated a quantity that we can measure easily and discuss. At the moment, however, our use of slope is still a little crude. Notice that the slope is found by determining the incline of the straight line drawn between two selected points on the curve, as shown in figure 4.4. Although this line can be said to approximate the actual curve, it is also clear from figure 4.4 there that the curve's slope is different from that of the straight line. Our description would be more accurate if we could talk about slope at an instant. In order to do this, we need to introduce the concepts of *function, limit,* and *derivative.*

4.2   The Concept of a Function

A *function* is usually a single-valued association between two variables. It is written

$$y = f(x),$$

where x is called the *independent variable,* y is the *dependent variable,* and f is the function. In other words, x is the input value, y is the output value, and f is the rule or machine whereby the output is calculated or produced from the input. A post office scale is a simple example of a function machine. In this case, the input is the weight of the letter, and the output is the postage required.

Functions may also be expressed graphically. In fact, graphical sketching can often replace algebraic expression in the initial stages of modeling. An example of a graph illustrating a function is shown in figure 4.5. For the post office scale, the function would look like a series of steps increasing to the right, with each price (output, or y value) corresponding to several weights (input, or x values).

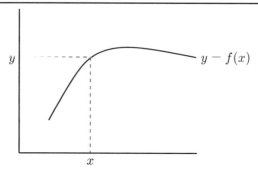

Figure 4.5: A graphical representation of a function. The horizontal axis is the axis along which input values are read, and the vertical axis is the one along which output values are read.

Inverse Functions

The inverse relationship to $y = f(x)$ is another relationship, $x = g(y)$. Graphically, it can be obtained by reflecting the curve around the line $y = x$ (figure 4.6). For $y = f(x)$, the input axis is called x, and the output axis is called y. The labels are reversed for $x = g(y)$. Notice that at any point where the curve f crosses the identity line, the input and output are equal, so the inverse relationship g also goes through that point. We sometimes have the choice of writing x as a function of y, or

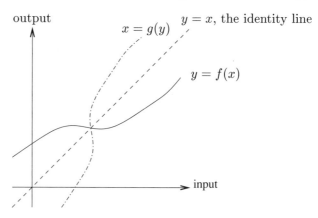

Figure 4.6: Inverse relationship $y = f(x)$ and $x = g(y)$.

y as a function of x, as in:

$$y = ax + b, \text{ or } x = \frac{y - b}{a}.$$

Commonly Occurring Functions

A few functions are so basic to a modeler's repertoire that they are to modeling as the alphabet is to spelling. Most models, at least at first, contain combinations of these basic functions. We list a few of them in this section.

1. *Polynomials* are a very important class of functions. What makes these functions so useful is that they can be used to approximate, with a high degree of accuracy, almost any existing function. Because polynomials are easy to handle, *vis-à-vis* calculus, we can avoid the headache of trying to deal with a very complicated function by using its polynomial approximation instead.

   Polynomials are simply functions that are expressed as sums of integer powers of the input variable. A general polynomial is written

   $$y = f(x) = a + bx + cx^2 + \cdots + Kx^P,$$

   where a, b, c, and K are numerical constants, and P is an integer. The value of P, which is the highest power in the sum, gives the degree of the polynomial. Polynomials of up to degree three have special names.

   Linear polynomials are polynomials of degree one and graphically appear as a straight line. Quadratic polynomials are polynomials of degree two and graphically yield a curve called a *parabola*. These curves are very important in daily usage. We find them in the cross-section of, for example, satellite dishes, flashlights, and the headlights on cars. The curve traced by water spouting out of a drinking fountain is also a parabola. Cubic polynomials are polynomials of degree three, which yield an N-shaped curve with long tails when graphed. Examples of all three polynomials are sketched in figure 4.7. Note that the cubic illustrated is a special one where the humps of the N-shape have been smoothed out to the point where essentially only the long tails (heading up and down) are left.

2. *Trigonometric functions* are found everywhere there exists a periodic process. The rise and fall of the tide, the general rise and

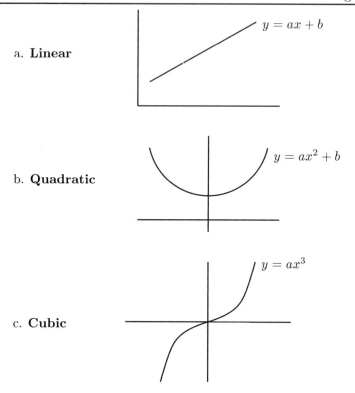

a. **Linear**

b. **Quadratic**

c. **Cubic**

Figure 4.7: A linear function (**a**), a quadratic function
(**b**), and a cubic function (**c**).

fall of temperature in one location over the seasons, or the periodic rise and fall of animal populations can all be approximated
by trigonometric functions.

There are six trigonometric functions, but the last three are simply
inverses of the first three, so there are simply three main trigonometric functions. They are called *sine, cosine,* and *tangent,* and
are written

(a) $y = \sin x$

(b) $y = \cos x$

(c) $y = \tan x = \dfrac{\sin x}{\cos x}$.

When graphed against the input variable, one can see that the sine and cosine functions are essentially the same function, differing only by a horizontal shift (figure 4.8).

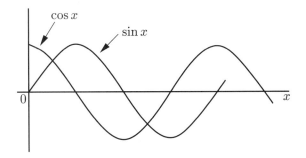

Figure 4.8: Graphical representation of the functions $y = \sin x$ and $y = \cos x$.

3. *Exponential functions* are both man's best friend and worst enemy. It has also been said that the fact that most people do not understand exponential growth is one of the biggest problems we face today.

   Additive processes appear to be straightforward for people to grasp. If I earn \$10 each day, then after 7 days I will have $7 \times 10 = \$70$. If I have a recipe for 2 servings, but I need 10, then I need $2 + 2 + 2 + 2 + 2 = 10$ servings, or 5 batches of the recipe. This is the kind of process that is modeled by a linear function.

   Exponential growth is based on a multiplicative process. The most common example is that of bacteria growing in an environment where there is plenty of nutrient. After a certain interval called the doubling time, each bacterium will split into two. After another doubling interval has passed, the bacteria will again split. So the number of bacteria after each doubling interval is twice the number there at the beginning. This means that the population is multiplied by two at each doubling time. After n doubling times, the number of bacteria will be $N_0 2^n$, where N_0 is the initial number of bacteria. What's so surprising about exponential growth is the rate at which a very small number can all of a sudden become enormous. If we pursue our bacteria example, then given an initial population of just 1 bacterium, and a doubling time of thirty minutes, then after five hours there will be 1,024 bacteria!

   This rapid growth rate is a boon in investments, where money earns interest at a given rate. The interest is calculated as a multiple of the original funds, so even if that multiple is fairly small (generally a good deal smaller than 2!), over time the money invested can grow substantially. This is the power of compounding. In populations, exponential growth tends to be a real problem. With humans, the difficulty is that the population can seem quite manageable, making precautions preventing excessive growth seem unnecessary. But the insidious thing about exponential growth is that a manageable population can grow so large so quickly that it swamps the available resources. In nature, this situation is typified by cycles between outbreak and refuge populations. When the organism has reached outbreak numbers, members rapidly die off until the population has been reduced drastically. Then exponential growth can begin again.

The multiplier rate at each interval can be any number (we had 2 for bacteria and a decimal numeral between 1 and 2 for interest rates). It is possible however, to express any multiplier as a power of another multiplier. Thus, mathematicians tend to express all exponential functions as powers of the special multiplier e. The standard exponential function $y = e^x$ is illustrated in figure 4.9.

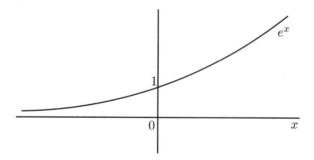

Figure 4.9: Exponential function, $y = e^x$.

4. *Logarithmic functions* are inverses of exponential functions. They are useful when trying to calculate the number of intervals (i.e., x) over which the multiplier has been applied. Mathematically we write this relationship as

$$y = e^x \Leftrightarrow x = \log y \ .$$

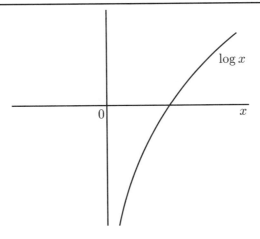

Figure 4.10: Logarithmic function, $y = \log x$.

4.3 Limits

A *limit* is the value to which a function or sequence tends as time gets very large. Consider a travel plan, where each day you cover half the distance between your current location and your ultimate destination. So the first day you cover $\frac{1}{2}$ of the total distance. The second day you cover half of the remainder or $\frac{1}{4}$ of the total distance, so your distance traveled is $\frac{1}{2} + \frac{1}{4} = \frac{3}{4}$ of the total distance. The third, fourth, and fifth days your distance traveled is $\frac{1}{2} + \frac{1}{4} + \frac{1}{8} = \frac{7}{8}$, $\frac{1}{2} + \frac{1}{4} + \frac{1}{8} + \frac{1}{16} = \frac{15}{16}$, and $\frac{1}{2} + \frac{1}{4} + \frac{1}{8} + \frac{1}{16} + \frac{1}{32} = \frac{31}{32}$ of the total distance. Each day you get closer to your destination, but never quite reach it. As the number of days of travel extends to infinity however, the fraction of the total distance traveled becomes indistinguishable from 1. We say that the limit of the sum is 1.

Thus, a limit is a value that is approximated ever more closely as time extends to infinity. We have seen an example in which the sum of a sequence of numbers (called a series) extends to a definable limit. The sequence itself may also have a definable limit. For example, the sequence

$$1, \frac{1}{4}, \frac{1}{9}, \frac{1}{16}, \cdots, \frac{1}{n^2}, \cdots$$

tends to the limit zero as n increases. In other words, the ratio $\frac{1}{n^2}$ comes closer and closer to 0. Other sequences and series do not have a definable

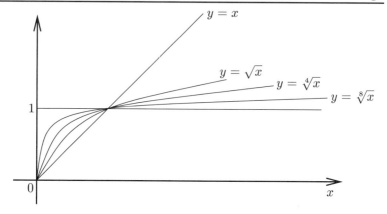

Figure 4.11: A series of functions that tend to the straight line $x = 1$.

limit. The series

$$\frac{1}{2} + \frac{1}{3} + \frac{1}{4} + \frac{1}{5} + \cdots, \frac{1}{n}, \cdots$$

keeps growing as n increases, and as n goes to infinity, the series goes to infinity as well. Thus, this series does not have a definable limit.

In a similar way, a series of functions can tend toward a limit. The functions $y_n = f_n(x) = \sqrt[n]{x}$ tend to the straight line $x = 1$ for n large, as shown in figure 4.11.

4.4   The Derivative Is a Limit

We can use this concept of limit to extend our definition of slope. Currently, our definition requires that there be two points so that

$$\text{slope} = \frac{\text{rise}}{\text{run}} , \tag{4.1}$$

where *rise* is the vertical distance between two points on the curve, and *run* is the horizontal distance between the same two points. Consider again figure 4.4. Imagine sliding point B toward point A along the curve. The straight line joining A and B will be a better and better approximation of the curve between A and B as the distance between the two points decreases. When B finally becomes A, what we end up with is the dashed line in the figure, also called the tangent line to the curve at A. The slope of the tangent line is the desired value of the derivative.

Mathematically, notice that this process of B sliding toward A means that Δx is approaching zero. Once B becomes A, and we are truly seeking the slope at the single point A, our definition (4.1) becomes a division by zero! To get around this difficulty, we say that the slope at a given point is the value that would be obtained in the limit as the run tends to zero. Thus, the derivative is a limit. This process of calculating the slope as point B approaches point A is written

$$\frac{dy}{dx} = \lim_{\Delta x \to 0} \left(\frac{\Delta y}{\Delta x} \right) . \tag{4.2}$$

If the point A has coordinates $(x, f(x))$, then the point B has coordinates $(x + \Delta x, f(x + \Delta x))$. Thus, the change in y can be written

$$\Delta y = f(x + \Delta x) - f(x)$$

and substituted into (4.2). If we also write $\Delta x = h$, as is commonly done, the equation for the derivative finally becomes

$$\frac{dy}{dx} = \lim_{h \to 0} \left[\frac{f(x + h) - f(x)}{h} \right] ,$$

which is the standard form.

4.5 Common Derivatives in Functional Form

Mathematicians have worked out the derivatives of commonly occurring functions. Below are derivatives of some of the polynomial and trigonometric functions discussed in section 4.2:

1. $\dfrac{d(\sin x)}{dx} = \cos x$

2. $\dfrac{d(ax)}{dx} = a$, where a is a constant

3. $\dfrac{d(a)}{dx} = 0$, where a is a constant

4. $\dfrac{d(ax^2)}{dx} = 2ax$, where a is a constant

5. $\dfrac{d(ax^3)}{dx} = 3ax^2$

6. $\dfrac{d(ax^n)}{dx} = nax^{n-1}$

4.6 Rules for Differentiation

When functions are combined, we take the derivative by applying some special rules. Here are five useful rules for taking derivatives of functions.

1. Derivative of a function multiplied by a constant a:

$$\frac{d}{dx}\left(af\left(x\right)\right) = a\frac{d}{dx}\left(f\left(x\right)\right)$$

2. Derivative of two functions added together:

$$\frac{d}{dx}\left(f\left(x\right) + g\left(x\right)\right) = \frac{d}{dx}f\left(x\right) + \frac{d}{dx}g\left(x\right)$$

3. Derivative of two functions multiplied together:

$$\frac{d}{dx}\left(f\left(x\right)g\left(x\right)\right) = \left[\frac{d}{dx}f\left(x\right)\right]g\left(x\right) + f\left(x\right)\left[\frac{d}{dx}g\left(x\right)\right]$$

4. Derivative of a function made by dividing one function by another:

$$\frac{d}{dx}\left[\frac{f\left(x\right)}{g\left(x\right)}\right] = \frac{g\left(x\right)\left[\frac{d}{dx}f\left(x\right)\right] - \left[\frac{d}{dx}g\left(x\right)\right]f\left(x\right)}{\left[g\left(x\right)\right]^{2}}$$

5. The *chain rule* is used for composed functions—that is, a function of a function. For example, if

$$f\left(g\right) = g^{p} \quad \text{and} \quad g\left(x\right) = x^{1/q}$$

where p and q are integers, then

$$y = f\left(g\left(x\right)\right) = x^{p/q}$$

and the chain rule is

$$\frac{dy}{dx} = \frac{df}{dg}\frac{dg}{dx}$$

$$= \left(pg^{p-1}\right)\left(\frac{1}{q}x^{\left(\frac{1}{q}-1\right)}\right)$$

$$= \frac{p}{q}x^{\left(\frac{p}{q}-1\right)}$$

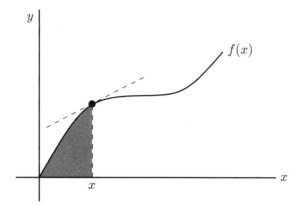

Figure 4.12: Graphical representation of an integral, the shaded area under the curve. The dashed line above the curve indicates the derivative of $f(x)$ at the indicated point.

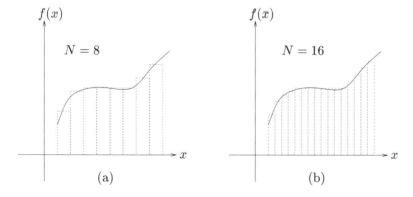

Figure 4.13: Two small rectangle approximations to the area under the curve $f(x)$. These constructions are called Riemann sums. In graph (a), eight boxes ($N = 8$) have been used, whereas in graph (b), 16 boxes ($N = 16$) have been used. It can be seen by inspection that the rectangles drawn in graph (b) cover an area that is a better approximation to the area under the curve $f(x)$ than is the area covered by the rectangles drawn in graph (a).

4.7   Integration—the Reverse of Differentiation

If the derivative is the slope of a curve at a point, the *integral* is the area under the curve up to that point (figure 4.12). The integral is written

$$\int_0^x f(x)dx .$$

It is the limit of a sum of small rectangles that approximate the area under the curve (figure 4.13). This sum is called a Riemann sum. If there are N of the little rectangles, then we write the integral as

$$\int_0^x f(x)dx = \lim_{\Delta x_i \to 0} \sum_0^{x_N} f(x_i)\Delta x_i .$$

The approximation obtained for the integral improves as N, or the number of rectangles, increases, as shown in figure 4.13.

The integral and derivative are inverse functions of one another. For example, the derivative of the log of x is

$$\frac{d}{dx}(\log x) = \frac{1}{x} ,$$

and the integral of $\dfrac{1}{x}$ is

$$\int \frac{1}{x}dx = \int \frac{dx}{x} = \log x + C .$$

The constant C appears because the derivative of a constant is zero. That is to say, the rate of change of something unchanging is null. Thus, there is always some ambiguity present when taking the integral, or *anti-derivative*, of a function, which means that we must add an unknown constant C to our answer.

4.8   Maxima and Minima

As function curves go up and down, they often have places where they reach peaks or troughs, just as a trail through a mountain range will have high and low points. Mathematically, we refer to these locations as maxima and minima (figure 4.14). Notice that the tangent to the curve at each maximum and minimum is a flat line with zero slope. Consequently, maxima and minima can be rigorously defined as those positions x where the derivative of the function is zero —that is, where

$$\frac{df(x)}{dx} = 0 .$$

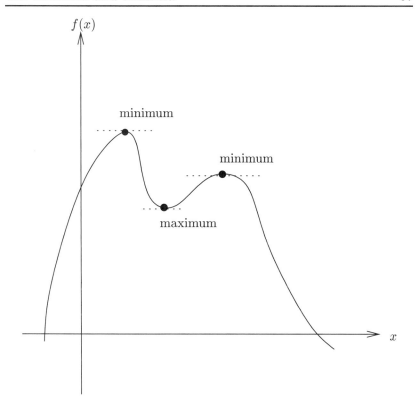

Figure 4.14: Graphical representation of minima and maxima on a function curve. The horizontal tangent lines (dotted) show that the derivative at these special points is zero—that is, $\frac{df(x)}{dx} = 0$.

Visually, it is straightforward to distinguish maxima and minima. It is important to be able to tell them apart mathematically, however, in the absence of a figure. We can do so by noticing how the derivative changes in each case. Following the curve from left to right through a minimum, we can see that the slope is negative at first, becomes zero at the minimum, and then becomes positive. For a maximum, we have the opposite sequence. The slope initially is positive, goes to zero at the maximum, and then becomes negative. Thus, for a minimum, the slope increases from negative to positive values, which means that the change in the slope is positive. Mathematically, this means that the *second* derivative is positive. Conversely, for a maximum, the slope decreases from positive to negative values, and so the *second* derivative is negative. This is called the *second derivative test.*

There also exist interesting points termed *points of inflection,* which often occur between maxima and minima. Visually, these points appear as locations where the tangent line is below the curve on one side of the inflection and above the curve on the other side of the inflection (figure 4.15). At points of inflection, the second derivative is zero.

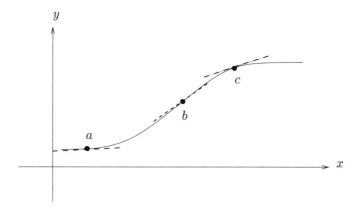

Figure 4.15: Graphical representation of the slope of the tangent line to a curve through a point of inflection. The points *a* and *c* are not points of inflection because the tangent emerges on the same side of the curve on either side of each point. The point *b* is a point of inflection because the tangent emerges on opposite sides of the curve as it passes through the point *b*.

4.9 Problem

We have learned enough calculus thus far to work through a simple problem. Suppose a farmer has only 140 feet of fence available. He wishes to create a rectangular space that provides the maximum area for his goat. What should the dimensions of this rectangle be?

Worked Solution
As shown in figure 4.16, the rectangle has dimensions *a* and *b*, and

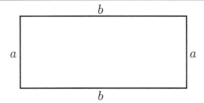

Figure 4.16: The farmer's fence

the sum of $2a$ and $2b$ is 140 feet. The area is given by

$$y = ab = a(70 - a)$$

$$= 70a - a^2 \tag{4.3}$$

So now we have a function $y = f(a)$, where $f(a)$ is given by (4.3). The derivative of this function is zero at the maximum, so

$$\frac{dy}{da} = 70 - 2a = 0 . \tag{4.4}$$

Equation (4.4) is satisfied when $a = 35$ feet and $b = 35$ feet. So the maximum rectangular area enclosed by a 140 foot fence is provided by a square of side length 35 feet.

We can also see this visually by plotting the area function $y = f(a)$ against the side length a (figure 4.17). Notice that the maximum of this curve occurs at $a = 35$.

It is also fun to ask whether a circular shape would afford a larger area than a square. The circumference of a circle is $2\pi r$, where r is the radius, so

$$r = \frac{140}{2\pi} = 22.28 \text{ feet.}$$

The area of this circle is $\pi r^2 = 1559.48$ square feet, instead of 1225 square feet for the square. The circle has approximately 1.27 times the area of the square.

4.10 Writing Differential Equations

We are now ready to discuss how the calculus tools we have described can be used in modeling. What becomes extremely powerful about these ideas is that we can extend them to situations where x and y represent more than spatial dimensions. For example, x might be plaque buildup

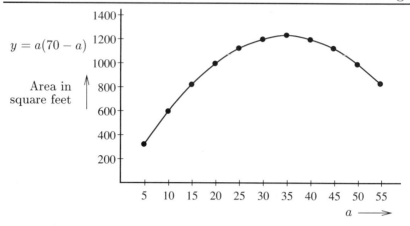

Figure 4.17: Plotting y against a, as given by equation 4.3, to obtain the maximum size of a rectangular area.

in a coronary artery over time, and y may be the amount of hostility an individual experiences over time. Then dy/dt is the *rate of change* of hostility over time. Thus, if we have a temporal process we wish to study, we can write equations that express how that process evolves over time.

We usually write equations with the derivatives —that is, the rates of change of our variables—on the left-hand side of the equal sign:

$$\dot{x} = ?$$

$$\dot{y} = ?$$

On the right-hand side of the equal sign is our best theory of what contributes to these rates of change. For example, suppose we were to write

$$\dot{x} = Ax + By \quad ; \quad A, B > 0 \tag{4.5}$$

$$\dot{y} = Cy \quad ; \quad C > 0\%, \tag{4.6}$$

where A, B, and C are positive constants. In the case of arterial plaque, for example, we are saying that the amount of arterial plaque (x) at any time increases with the amount of plaque already there, plus a fraction of the amount of this person's hostility. In equation (4.6), we are saying that a person's rate of change in hostility (y) increases as a function of his hostility at that time. This is a grim model indeed. It predicts an increasingly hostile individual on his way to a coronary.

The key first steps in modeling, then, are to identify the essential elements of the process one wishes to model and to then decide how they interact to effect change. Solving these differential equations is challenging. Over the centuries, mathematicians have worked out ways to solve these equations and have developed rules for doing so. In chapter 5 through chapter 9 we discuss various modeling and solution techniques, as well as what may be learned from them.

4.11   Taylor's series

We finish this chapter with a brief discussion of Taylor's series, because they are extremely important in all aspects of mathematics that deal with understanding the behavior of functions. We have already seen that the derivative of a function describes the rate at which it is changing. Thus far, with one small exception in section 4.8, the derivatives discussed in this chapter have all been first derivatives. We can extend this idea further. Once we have taken the derivative of some function $f(t)$ and have obtained $\dot{f}(t)$, we can repeat the process and take the derivative of $\dot{f}(t)$. This is called the *second derivative* of $f(t)$ and is written $\ddot{f}(t)$. The second derivative tells us how the first derivative is changing. We are most commonly used to these quantities as speed (the first derivative, or how position is changing) and acceleration (the second derivative, or how speed is changing). Two cars may have the same speed, but if one is accelerating and the other is not, then at some future time the cars will no longer have the same speed. Clearly, if we know only the speed of each car, we have only part of the picture. Knowing the acceleration enhances our knowledge of the situation.

This process can be continued ad infinitum. We can keep taking derivatives of derivatives, obtaining the fourth, fifth, tenth, and so on, derivatives. Writing all of those dots above the function name becomes confusing, so after the second or third derivative we start denoting nth derivatives as $f^{(n)}(t)$.

What can we do with all of these derivatives? Taylor made the incredibly useful observation that any well-behaved function (which includes just about any function you run into normally when using mathematics to describe everyday occurrences) can be approximated, with as much precision as is desired, by a sum of its derivatives. This sum is called a *Taylor's series*.

Instead of *sum*, we should really use the word *power series*, because the word *sum* implies that we write out the values of all of the derivatives and then add them up as we would add up a grocery bill. This isn't quite right. Instead, the value of each derivative is part of the coefficient of each term in a long sum that involves powers of t (where t represents time). Let us see how this works.

Consider, if you will, the situation of a train pulling out of a train station. Suppose that the train accelerates until it reaches a cruising speed of 80 miles per hour, at which point the train's speed remains constant. If we graphed the distance between the train and the station as a function of time, we would obtain the curve shown by the solid line in figure 4.18. This curve shows that the distance between the station and the train increases more and more quickly. Eventually the slope of the curve (which represents the speed of the train) would become constant, at the time when the distance between the train and the station increases at a constant rate (which is exactly 80 miles every hour).

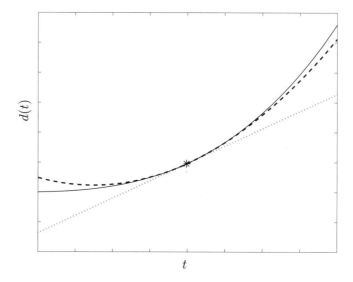

Figure 4.18: An illustration of Taylor's series approximations to a curve. The solid line is the curve we are trying to approximate. The point (given by the asterisk) is the zero-order Taylor's series approximation, the dotted line is the first-order approximation, and the dashed line is the second-order approximation. For most applications, we do not go beyond second order and so study the curve (solid line) in the region where the dotted or dashed line is a good approximation.

Now, suppose we didn't have the graph in figure 4.18. Instead, suppose we only knew that at 2 seconds the train was 48 feet from the station. Then, all we would know is the point shown by an asterisk on the graph. Suppose then we found out that the train, at 2 seconds, had reached a speed of 58 feet per second. Because distance equals speed times time (for example, if you are traveling at 60 miles per hour, then in half an hour you have traveled $60 \times \frac{1}{2} = 30$ miles), we then have $d(t) = 58t + c$, where c is some constant that makes the line go through the point (2,48). A little algebra tells us that $c = -68$. On our graph, this result becomes the dotted line in figure 4.18. The new line is a better approximation of the graph than is the single dot we had first.

Let us continue this process one step further. Suppose that we also find out that the train, at 2 seconds, is accelerating at 46 feet per second squared. We then have $d(t) = \frac{1}{2}(46)t^2 + c_1 t + c_2$, where the acceleration is part of the coefficient of the second order term (the one involving t^2). The $\frac{1}{2}$ part of the coefficient comes from Taylor's theorem and is part of why the function isn't simply a straight "sum" of the derivatives. Also, notice the pattern: the first term is constant, the second term is a function of t, and the third term is a function of t^2. This is what makes the Taylor's series a "power series": the power of t keeps increasing with each new derivative. The constants c_1 and c_2 must be chosen so that the first derivative of the function is still 58 feet per second, and so that at 2 seconds the train is at 48 feet. A little algebra gives us $c_1 = -34$ and $c_2 = 24$. The acceleration, or second derivative, addition to our function $d(t)$ gives us the dashed line shown in figure 4.18. Notice that our approximation is now even better.

We could continue this process, obtaining better and better approximations to the actual function until we had achieved the accuracy desired for our problem. Here we have approximated the distance function as a Taylor's series around the point $t = 2$ seconds. The process could be repeated for any time of interest.

What do we gain by approximating a function using a Taylor's series? Often, functions describing natural phenomena can be quite complicated, and difficult to work with. Rewriting such functions as Taylor's series around a point of interest considerably reduces the complexity involved in the mathematical analysis. Commonly, Taylor's series are only taken as far as the first order terms, in which case we are said to have *linearized* the function (the origin of this term is immediately obvious when we observe the dotted line in figure 4.18). This approximation is very crude and only true in a small neighborhood of the point of interest, but from behavior near a special point, such as a steady state, we can learn much about the behavior of the entire system. In fact, just from the linear approximation, we can tell if a steady state is an attracting or repelling state, and thus determine the ultimate behavior of the system.

5

Introduction to Nonlinear Dynamic Modeling

5.1 Philosophy of Modeling

In this chapter, we discuss the general philosophy of nonlinear dynamic modeling and present a few worked examples. Much of this work on nonlinear dynamics has been popularized with the presentation of chaos theory by James Gleick' (1987) best-selling book *Chaos! Making a New Science* and by many books on fractal geometry. There have been many positive consequences of this popularization. The most important consequence is the recognition that nonlinear equations can represent very complex systems with great parsimony and elegance. In the biological sciences, for example, phenomena as diverse as ecological systems, biological clocks, and disease processes such as tumor growth have been successfully modeled. The list of successful modeling examples is becoming astonishingly long.

In the social sciences, interest in nonlinear dynamic modeling has also been keen. Vallacher and Nowak (1994) edited a book titled *Dynamical Systems in Social Psychology*, which brought together social psychologists' thinking about dynamical systems modeling and the various functions of self-organization, catastrophe, and chaotic processes in understanding social processes. Nowak and Vallacher's (1998) book titled *Dynamical Social Psychology* is a brilliant and ambitious monograph that applies dynamical concepts to a wide array of social phenomena— including social judgment, interpersonal dynamics, and social influence— and to the study of the individual in society. In developmental psychology, researchers such as Vogel, Lewis, Newell, Molenaar, and Thelen have promulgated the intellectual power of dynamic mathematical concepts in understanding complex systems, from the development of walking to mother-infant interaction.

Noteworthy in the Vallacher and Nowak (1994) volume is the chapter by Tesser and Achee. These researchers modeled dating and mating by applying the cusp catastrophe, which we talk about below, with two variables, love for a partner and social pressure against the partner. In another chapter, Lantané and Nowak also applied the cusp catastrophe to the study of attitude change. Baron, Amazeen, and Beek studied two people's coordination of their limbs when they walk together. It turns out that two people both high in dominance have the greatest problem falling into the optimal phase relationship for walking together. The researchers then discussed extending their ideas to long-term dyadic relationships using Levinger's (1980) model. Newtson discussed dynamical concepts such as types of attractors, self-organizing systems, information flow, and chaos. He suggested viewing behavior as a wave and applied these ideas to generate time series from the way people segmented a videotape of people doing such things as setting a table or unloading a truck full of large boxes. Eiser applied dynamical concepts to the study of attitude consistency and change over time.

We applaud this interest. These writings increase the interest of scientists in dynamical concepts and in the study of the "unfolding" of processes over time. A dynamical view of social processes focuses attention on the temporal patterning of interaction instead of on a static view of social events. This point of view can only enhance interest in what actually occurs in social interaction and how this interaction is perceived.

However, we add a strong caution about using mathematical concepts without real hands-on experience with the mathematics. We think that the danger is that there is a tendency to romanticize the mathematics without full understanding of its power, flexibility, and *limitations*. This romanticizing could do some harm because it could lead to settling for only the metaphoric use of mathematical ideas, ideas that could be far more useful if they were applied to the precise formulation of these very real scientific problems. The practical solution of very complex problems with a very parsimonious equation or set of equations demonstrates how the concepts of nonlinear dynamic modeling can aid the construction of theory in fields previously thought to be impenetrable. Also, we can now see both the usefulness and limitations of the model, as well as ways to improve the model subsequently.

Modeling ought to be an interplay between science and mathematics. There should be a back and forth process, starting with the science, going to the mathematics, and then back to the science. In our view, a good model gets people to ask questions, especially ones that help generate ideas for new experiments within the science, thus keeping the interplay going. The goal in formulating the equation or equations for the study of a scientific problem is to write the *dynamics*—that is, the *mechanism* through which the system moves and changes over time. This means that the model itself is a *theory* the investigator develops about the phenomenon under study. The mathematics forces the development of precise theory about the mechanisms operating to create movement in the system. In the seminar that Gottman and Murray taught together, applied mathematics graduate students helped psychology graduate students in this process. First they defined a phenomenon and then formulated ideas that might explain the phenomenon, eventually arriving at an equation or set of equations. It isn't easy to do this, but it is feasible.

We hope to get creative investigators to move away from metaphors of dynamics toward real dynamical equations. There is one wonderful thing about nonlinear equations models: unlike linear models, they are usually impossible to solve in closed functional form, which means that what applied mathematicians call "qualitative" solutions and the digital computer's numerical capabilities are both extremely helpful. The qualitative and graphical methods that applied mathematicians developed (starting with Poincaré, 1893) are marvelous for engaging the intuition of scientists familiar with the phenomena under study. Hence, one of our goals in this book is to keep the interest of researchers and to teach them some of these graphical techniques. We want to avoid turning researchers off by presenting too much mathematics but we also want this book to teach enough mathematics so that the models can be understood. Our promise is that if researchers can stick with the book long enough to learn the qualitative graphical methods, their intuition will become engaged. We've always told students that if you can model marriage, you can model anything.

Once the model is written down in mathematical form, it automatically accomplishes a wonderful thing. In an area as apparently devoid of theory as the study of marriage, suddenly there is a *language* promulgated for describing what we picked as the basic phenomena of marriage. There is now a theory where before none existed. The theory may be dead wrong, but it is precise.

How important is it that the model provide a good fit to the data? In Murray's view (Murray, 1993), fitting the data does not tell you that you have the right mechanism. It is quite possible that a worse fit might be the right mechanism or on the right track toward the right mechanism, whereas a better fit might be the completely wrong mechanism. In Murray's book *Mathematical Biology*, there are many examples where adding a cubic term to a quadratic model might provide a better local fit to the data but imply a mechanism that is completely incorrect.

Ideally a good model allows us to ask questions that would never have occurred to us had we not written down the model. A good model also has surprises; it may organize a wider set of data than we had anticipated or even suggest some discoveries that are entirely new. This was the case with our initial model. It led us to a *mismatch hypothesis* about influence patterns predicting divorce, which was entirely unpredicted before the modeling.

It is our view, then, that we have to free ourselves from the idea that goodness of fit is the sine qua non of science. We would argue that it isn't. Of course, if we did produce the right model (assuming there is one right model) for the mechanism, a good fit would be obtained. Discovering the exact mechanism for any biological or psychological phenomenon is highly unlikely at this stage, but will certainly be the aim for the foreseeable future.

A good example of this model in the history of science is Ptolemy's model of planetary motion, in which the Earth was placed at the center of the planets, in contrast to the Copernican model, which placed the Sun at the center. Unfortunately, until Kepler's addition of elliptic orbits (a change he was quite reluctant to make because the circle was the Greek ideal of perfection), the Copernican model used circles. The Ptolemaic model, in contrast, used epicycles, or "wheels within wheels," to correct errors to the real data, and it gave a much better fit than the Copernican view, even though it was based on a totally false assumption.

5.2   A Bit of Dynamical Modeling History

In Peterson's (1993) book *Newton's Clock! Chaos in the Solar System*, he described the fascinating history of the "three-body problem." Newton had worked out with great precision the mathematics of gravitational attraction between two bodies, such as the earth and a projectile. He then invented a method called *perturbation theory* for describing a relatively small influence of another (third-body) gravitational force. However, perturbation theory never really worked very well for describing the motions of our moon, where the Earth, the Sun, and the Moon all interact. Newton tried to solve this very problem, but he remained dissatisfied with the accuracy of his own work on the problem.

The three-body problem continued to plague applied mathematicians for centuries, and they were not even sure they could prove that the solar system was stable for all time (or unstable), using Newton's laws. In the nineteenth century, a mathematician named Karl Weierstrass offered a prize to anyone who could resolve this problem of the solar system's stability or instability. The prize was a gold medal and a huge sum of 2500 crowns. Among the entrants was the twenty-seven-year-old Henri Poincaré, who won the prize by proving that there are many solutions to Newton's equations for the three-body problem that are not stable and that, in all likelihood, the solar system was not stable. Poincaré accomplished this analysis with qualitative geometrical methods he perfected or invented, such as phase-space maps. Peterson (1993) wrote that "To do this, he advanced the study of differential equations from numbers, formulas, and the manipulation of algebraic expressions to geometry, curves, and the visualization of flows. Instead of looking at the contents of his mathematical package, Poincaré looked at the package itself to obtain the clues he needed to determine whether a series converged and what the implications of the result were for the stability of a dynamical system" (p. 156). Subsequent work has confirmed the amazing long-term complexity of our solar system, with both stable and unstable, chaotic elements. The remarkable nature of chaos within a completely deterministic but nonlinear system was revealed by Poincaré's work. Its subsequent development is now bearing fruit today in physics and in other sciences as well.

5.3 One Equation: Malthus Revisited

In the year 1798, Malthus (an English country person, by all accounts a happy family man who enjoyed life and whose book had a major influence on Darwin and many others) suggested that the growth of the human population would be geometric, but the growth of food sources would be arithmetic, so unless population was controlled, there would be the catastrophe of mass starvation on the planet. He also suggested that population growth would also be controlled by disease and war. Indeed, the human population of the planet is estimated to have been 0.5 billion in the seventeenth century, 1 billion in the nineteenth century, 3 billion from 1918 to 1927, 4 billion in 1974, 5 billion in 1987, and 6 billion in 1999; it is projected to be 10 billion in the year 2050. In spite of the fact that world population has grown exponentially since about 1900, the Malthusian prediction is fairly unrealistic, and it has since been modified.

Here is how the Malthusian prediction would be modeled mathematically. If $N(t)$ represents the human population on the planet at time t, then the equation of Malthus for the rate of change of the human population, dN/dt, is given by the linear equation:

$$\frac{dN}{dt} = bN - dN. \tag{5.1}$$

The constants b and d are the birth rate and death rate respectively. This is a linear model because there are no powers or other nonlinear functions of $N(t)$ in the equation. In words, the model states that the rate of change in the human population, $N(t)$, equals the birth rate minus the death rate times the size of the population. The solution to (5.1) is

$$N(t) = N_0 e^{(b-d)t}, \tag{5.2}$$

where e represents the exponential function and N_0 represents the starting value of the population at time $t = 0$. If the birth rate exceeds the death rate, we obtain the exponential growth shown in figure 5.1. The terms b and d in the model are called the *parameters* of the model. If the birth rate is less than the death rate, the population tends to zero.

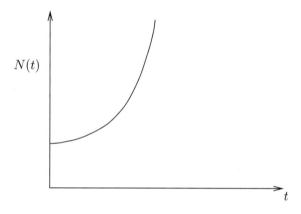

Figure 5.1: Exponential growth of the population, $N(t)$, as a function of time, t.

Unfortunately (or perhaps fortunately for us), the model does not fit the data very well. To make Malthus's model more realistic, we have to add a nonlinear regulatory term that subtracts an amount proportional to the square of the population as follows:

$$\frac{dN}{dt} = bN - dN - cN^2, \tag{5.3}$$

which can be rewritten as

$$\frac{dN}{dt} = rN(k - N). \tag{5.4}$$

In equation (5.4), r represents the linear growth rate, and k represents what is called the *carrying capacity* of the environment. Note that with

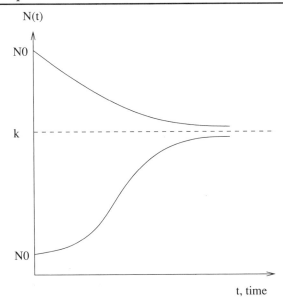

Figure 5.2: Logistic growth of a population with time, with k as the carrying capacity. If the initial population, N_0 is greater than k, then the population decreases toward the carrying capacity. Conversely, if N_0 is less than k, then the population increases until it reaches the carrying capacity.

the addition of the N^2 term, (5.4) models the *self-regulation* of the population if it gets too big. If N is larger than the carrying capacity, then dN/dt becomes negative, resulting in a decrease in population.

Equation (5.4) is called the *logistic* growth model. It has solutions (exact in this case) of the form shown in figure 5.2. The population asymptotically (that is, in the limit) approaches the straight line $N = k$, either increasing or decreasing toward it depending on the initial population N_0.

This model is a better representation of actual population data (Verhulst, 1838) than equation (5.1). However, we note in passing that the new model is not a universal law of growth. Agreement is good for bacteria, yeast, and other relatively simple organisms in constant conditions and without predators. It does not fit as well for fruit flies, flour beetles, and other organisms that have more complex life cycles. For more information, see Strogatz (1994), p. 24. We are reviewing these two forms of the Malthus problem because we wish the reader to see *how to write* the differential equations and to gain an appreciation of the different solutions that can be obtained.

The First Question: What Are the Steady States of the System?

One of the marvelous things about dynamical theory is that we can assess the stability or instability of particular steady states of the system, even without being able to solve the equation exactly. The question is, "Toward what values is the system drawn?" To answer the question we define a *steady state* as one for which the derivative dN/dt is zero. If the derivative is zero, this says in words that the rate of change of the population is zero, or that it is unchanging or constant. In general, if the differential equation is $dN/dt = f(N)$, we solve for the steady states by setting $f(N)$ equal to zero. In our case,

$$\frac{dN}{dt} = 0 = rN(k - N), \quad \text{when } N = 0 \text{ or } N = k. \quad (5.5)$$

Regulated Systems and the Second Question: Which Steady States Are Stable?

What does *stability* mean? It means precisely what we wish it to mean if the system we are studying is to be *regulated*. A regulated system (like a thermostat) has a *set point,* a *threshold,* an *error signal,* and some mechanism for bringing the system back to its set point if it deviates beyond the threshold of the set point. If the system is regulated, it also means that if you perturb the system slightly at a steady state (set point), it will return to that steady state. It is as if the steady state is an *attractor* that pulls the system back to the steady state, like a rubber band snapping back once pulled and released. On the other hand, if you perturb the system slightly at an unstable steady state, it will move away from that steady state.

Suppose we have the more general equation $N' = dN/dt = f(N)$. The steady states are just the solution of $f(N) = 0$. So if we plot $f(N)$ against N the steady states are simply the values of N where the curve crosses the axis. Figure 5.3 is an example with several intersections— that is, several steady states. It is easy to show (see section 4.10 and Appendix 5.1) that N^* is a stable steady state if the derivative of $f(N)$ with respect to N, or $f' = df/dN$, is less than zero at N^* and unstable if $f' = df/dN$ is positive at N^*.

This means that graphically all we have to do is to plot $f(N)$ and then look at the slope of $f(N)$ where it crosses the N-axis. If figure 5.3

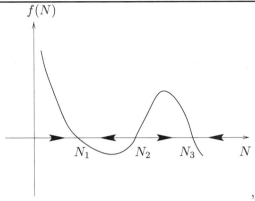

Figure 5.3: Hypothetical growth function. The steady states of $df/dt = f(N)$ are given by the Ns where $f(N)$ crosses the N-axis.

is a plot of a hypothetical $f(N)$, then N_1 and N_3 would be stable, and N_2 would be unstable.

Referring to figure 5.3, we can see intuitively why N_1 and N_3 are stable and N_2 is unstable. Suppose we choose an N greater than N_3, for example, on the N-axis. For this value, $N' = f(N) < 0$, which means that N decreases with time toward N_3. On the other hand, suppose we choose an N between N_2 and N_3. In this case, $N' = f(N) > 0$, which means that N increases with time toward N_3. N' is just the "velocity" we talked about in chapter 4. Basically, the velocity N' is positive above the curve $f(N)$, and negative below it. We can thus see why N_1 and N_3 are stable and N_2 is unstable. It is almost a universal rule that if you have continuous curves as in figure 5.3, and there are three (or more) steady states, then the steady states will alternate between stable and unstable.

If the function in figure 5.3 kept recrossing the N-axis, then each point of negative slope would imply a stable steady state and each point of positive slope would imply an unstable steady state. The arrows show how $N(t)$ changes if N_0 is in the regions shown in figure 5.3. The figure shows also that if we make a large enough perturbation about N_1 so that the new perturbed state is to the right of N_2, then $N(t)$ will move toward the steady state N_3. With nonlinear equations, stability of a steady state often requires a perturbation less than some maximum.

In our work with steady states, we sometimes refer to the stable steady states as *set points*, a term borrowed from research on the management of body weight. In this area, it has been noted that the body

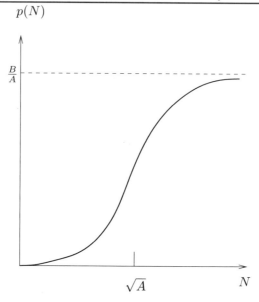

Figure 5.4: Graph of the predator function given by equation (5.7), which acts as a *switch*. For population levels to the left of the switch value $\sqrt{A}$, the predation term has a value near zero. Conversely, for population levels to the right of the switch value, the predation term has a much larger value near B/A. The transition from small to large values occurs in a small neighborhood around the switch value, so the change from little to much predation is abrupt and "switch-like."

defends a particular weight as a set point, adjusting metabolism to maintain the body's weight in homeostatic fashion. It is interesting that, as the general systems theorists noted, the existence of homeostasis (a regulated system) does not, by itself, imply that the system is regulated in a *functional* manner. Recently, a man who weighed one thousand pounds died in his early thirties; he had to be lifted out of his apartment with a crane. Yet his body defended that weight. Clearly this set point was dysfunctional for this man's health.

The Concept of Switch: Adding a Predation Term

To illustrate how the equations are written let us try a little exercise. We can easily modify the Verhulst equation (5.4) to add a term that represents the effects of a predator in the system, one that would be significant enough to affect the population. For example, if *Jurassic Park* were true, several tyrannosaurs would do the job nicely. The effect of the disease AIDS in sub-Saharan Africa is the equivalent of such a predator. In this case, the effects of the predation could be represented as a separate function, $p(N)$, and the differential equation would become:

$$\frac{dN}{dt} = rN(k - N) - p(N). \tag{5.6}$$

If we were to select as a predation function the expression

$$p(N) = \frac{BN^2}{(A + N^2)}, \tag{5.7}$$

then the predation term would have the form of a *switch* (figure 5.4.) Here, A and B are parameters. At $N = 0$, the value of the predation term is zero at zero population, but then increases to the value B as N increases. As A increases, the predator requires a larger population to start having an effect, which gives us some idea of how we can begin writing our equations to represent terms we think ought to be in our model. The reasoning behind such a predation term is that the predation is worth it only if enough prey are around, so it is low (lower than linear in N) for small N, and "switches" on around some critical population, which is approximately $\sqrt{A}$. It saturates because there is a limit to the predation however large N is.

Creating a Marriage Model with Two Steady States: Control Parameters

Suppose that our variable, instead of representing the size of a population, were to represent some aspect of a marital interaction that is changing over time. This variable could be the total time that husband and wife look at each other within some period of time. Or, for an example closer to what we actually do in our experiments, suppose that we use an observational coding of the positive and negative emotions in a husband and wife talking for fifteen minutes about an area of marital conflict. Suppose further that we compute a variable x that is the sum of positivity and negativity for both spouses over successive six-second blocks of time. We could even weight some behaviors more heavily if they were more highly correlated with some validity criterion (such as marital satisfaction), or the ability of the variable to predict divorce or stability of the marriage over time. In this section, we return to the main topic of this book, marriage, and attempt (in hindsight) to presage our subsequent chapters on the marriage model, but with only one equation. What sort of marriage model would yield two possible steady states?

In figure 5.3, we saw that if the hypothetical growth function $f(N)$ crossed the N-axis several times, stable and unstable steady states could alternate. Suppose that

$$\frac{dx}{dt} = f(x) = rx - B\tanh Cx. \tag{5.8}$$

The right-hand side of equation (5.8) is the difference between two functions, a straight line through the origin, which is rx, and a constant B times the hyperbolic tangent of Cx. The parameters r, B, and C are called the *control parameters* of the system. We selected the hyperbolic tangent because it has some very interesting properties (figure 5.5).

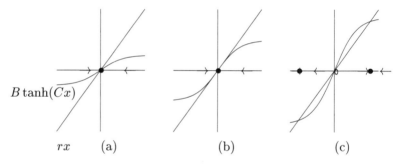

Figure 5.5: Solutions to a one-equation model (5.8) for marriage for different parameter values. Locations where the line and hyperbolic tangent intersect are points where the right-hand side of (5.8) is zero and thus where the population does not change. Depending on the relative steepness of the line with respect to the hyperbolic tangent, there may be one (a) or three (c) intersections. The transition between one and three intersections is shown in (b). The dots on the x-axis of each graph indicate the x value at the intersection points.

The hyperbolic tangent crosses the origin with a slope determined by the control parameter C. It then straightens out to asymptote toward the level of control parameter B on the right-hand side of the origin and toward $-B$ on the left-hand side of the origin. This means that we think that the rate of change of the couple's affect will be determined by two factors: (1) an autocorrelation control parameter r and its term

rx, which reflects the amount of inertia or sluggishness in the couple's overall affect, or the couple's tendency to remain in a negative or positive affective state (for example, if r is very small, rx does not affect dx/dt very much over short periods of time) ; and, (2) the influence function of the system, the B term. The choice of the hyperbolic tangent means that we propose that if the couple is in a positive affective state, the influence will be positive, asymptoting to B, whereas if the couple is in a negative affective state, the influence will be negative, asymptoting to $-B$. The rate of approach to these asymptotes is proportional to C (if C is large the approach is very quick.) Notice how the control parameters decide for us the qualitative behavior of this marriage. In practice, we would also need to design some algorithms for estimating these parameters from the observed behavior of a particular couple.

To determine the steady states of $f(x)$ we need to find where $f(x)$ is zero. A graphical trick for finding these steady states is to graph the straight line $y_1 = rx$ and also graph the hyperbolic tangent $y_2 = B \tanh Cx$. At the points where the two curves intersect, we know that $y_1 = y_2$, which means that $f(x)$ is zero (figure 5.5). As an example, suppose that $r = 1$. Then for $B < 1.0$, there is only one steady state for this marital system at the origin, and it is stable. For $B = 1$ or larger, there are two steady states for the system, one positive and one negative, in addition to the origin. These two steady states are stable, but the origin has now become unstable. For a general r, if $B > r$ we have three steady states, two of which are stable, with the origin unstable.

This marital model is very interesting because it posits that any marriage has two possible homeostatic set points. Basically it suggests that any marriage may be attracted to one of two states, one positive and one negative. We can make this model even more interesting by adding a constant control parameter x_0, which can reflect the starting value of the couple's interaction. Then the straight line need not go through the origin, and the two steady states need not be symmetric about the origin. The model thereby gains much more flexibility at the low cost of only one additional parameter.

Describing the Behavior of a Model

The next step in modeling is to describe the behavior of the model near each steady state and as the parameters of the model vary. We want to know what the model tells us *qualitatively* about how the system is supposed to act. Then, if the model isn't acting the way we think it ought to (given the phenomena we are trying to model), we alter the model to reflect a behavioral aspect we ignored in the first modeling attempt. This process can be represented with a flow chart for dynamic

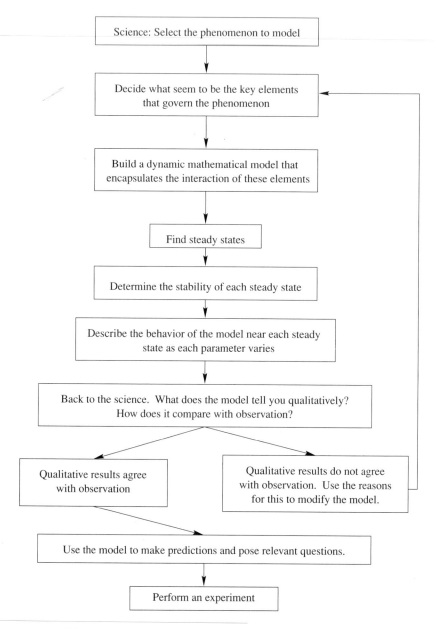

Figure 5.6: Flow chart for dynamic modeling of any process.

modeling of any process over time.

In the flow chart depicted in figure 5.6 we can see the process of modeling laid out in step-by-step fashion. We begin with identifying the phenomenon or phenomena we wish to model, which our insights and intuitions about the science give to us. Then we write the dynamic equations for building the model—a difficult task that requires some knowledge of mathematics and a good understanding of the key elements governing the phenomenon. Then we find the steady states of the model, those points where the derivatives are zero. Then we determine if these steady states are stable or unstable. Then we study the qualitative behavior of the model near the steady states. Then we study how the model behaves as we vary the parameters of the model. Finally, returning to the science, we ask whether this model is behaving in a manner that makes sense. If not, we modify the model by reevaluating our understanding of the processes that form the building blocks of the model.

Appendix 5.1: Stability Results

If $dN/dt = f(N)$ has steady-state solutions N^*, of $f(N) = 0$, we denote a perturbation about N^* by $n(t)$, where $n(t) = N(t) - N^*$ and where the magnitude of $n(t)$ is small—then, by the Taylor expansion,

$$f(N^* + n(t)) = f(N^*) + n(t)f'(N^*) + O(n^2), \qquad (A5.1)$$

where f' is the derivative of f, and $O(n^2)$ are terms of the order of n^2, which are small. By definition, $f(N^*) = 0$, and then we have the result that

$$\frac{dn(t)}{dt} = f(N^* + n(t)) \cong n(t)f'(N^*), \qquad (A5.2)$$

which has the solution

$$n(t) = n_0 e^{f'(N^*)t} . \qquad (A5.3)$$

This solution increases without bound if $f'(N^*) > 0$ (instability) and tends to zero if $f'(N^*) < 0$ (stability).

6

Modeling Catastrophic Change

In this chapter, we illustrate an extremely interesting characteristic of some models called *catastrophic change*. Catastrophe, in the mathematical sense, occurs when a parameter of the model changes continuously without changing the qualitative behavior of the model until a threshold value is crossed. Then the system's behavior changes dramatically and becomes qualitatively different; a catastrophe has occurred. A classic example is "the straw that broke the camel's back." The camel was fine as long as the weight it had to bear stayed below a critical threshold value. Once the weight crossed the threshold, even one straw's weight broke the camel's back. The field of psychology has historically been very interested in critical thresholds. There are critical thresholds in the fields of perception, in the imprinting of baby geese, and in the strength of stimuli required to release innate, instinctive fixed-action patterns. In our view, catastrophic behavior will turn out to be very important in understanding our models of marriage.

Catastrophe theory began with the publication of French mathematician René Thom's (1972) *Stabilité Structurelle et Morphogénése*. Thom had suggested applying topology to the dynamical systems work of Poincaré to model these sudden changes. The early excitement and extravagent claims about the universality of catastrophe theory gave way to a great deal of criticism, so that the theory has largely fallen out of favor. Introductory books are Saunders (1990), Arnold (1986), and Castrigiano and Hayes (1993). Our favorite introduction is the older book by Poston and Stewart (1978), as well as the selected papers of Zeeman (1987), which we review in this chapter. Zeeman's papers are interesting because they span such a wide range of applications, including war, the stock market, and anorexia nervosa and bulimia.

6.1 The Spruce Budworm Problem

The problem of managing balsam fir trees in a forest involves controlling
the population of spruce budworms that eat the foliage of these trees.
This turns out to be a beautiful example of catastrophe. The model
was first proposed by Ludwig *et al.* (1978). The equation we arrive
at for the budworm population is actually very similar to the Verhulst
equation (logistic growth) with a predator term, because birds eat the
budworms. The model we consider is, in fact, given by equations (5.6)
and (5.7). It can be shown easily that non-dimensionalizing the equation (see Appendix 6.5) for the budworm population $u(t)$ results in an
equation with only two positive parameters, r and q:

$$\frac{du}{dt} = f(u) = \left[ru\left(1 - \frac{u}{q}\right)\right] - \left[\frac{u^2}{(1+u^2)}\right]. \tag{6.1}$$

On the right-hand side of equation (6.1), the first term in the first square
brackets is the standard logistic growth function, and the second term
in the second square brackets is the predation term. The goal of the
modeling process is to understand how the population dynamics depend
on the parameters. One of the several questions we can ask is, "How
can we prevent an explosion of the budworm population?"

   First we find the steady states of the model—that is, those states
where the derivative is zero; these states are given by $f(u) = 0$. We are
looking for the values of u such that

$$\left[ru\left(1 - \frac{u}{q}\right)\right] - \left[\frac{u^2}{(1+u^2)}\right] = 0. \tag{6.2}$$

Obviously $u = 0$ is one such value. This steady state is unstable, however, because near $u = 0$, $du/dt \approx ru$, which is positive, so u increases
(exponentially) with time. If we concentrate on the other positive steady
states, we can divide our equation by u, and we then have the equation:

$$\left[r\left(1 - \frac{u}{q}\right)\right] - \left[\frac{u}{(1+u^2)}\right] = 0. \tag{6.3}$$

Note that this equation is a cubic equation. We must have at least a
cubic equation for catastrophes. Although one can solve a cubic equation
exactly, the solutions are quite complicated and in fact of little use in
understanding the dynamics of $u(t)$, the solution of (6.1). We next show
how a qualitative approach can provide a much fuller understanding of
the dynamics.

The solutions to (6.3) are those values of u for which the two bracketed terms are equal. We can find the solutions to this equation by graphically plotting the two bracketed terms as functions of u and seeing visually where they intersect. That is, we plot:

$$g(u) = r\left(1 - \frac{u}{q}\right),\tag{6.4}$$

which is a straight line, and we also plot

$$h(u) = \frac{u}{(1+u^2)}\tag{6.5}$$

and see where they intersect. To see what is going on, let us take q to be fixed and look at what happens for different values of r. If r is small enough or large enough, the straight line cuts the curve only once, so there is only one solution of (6.3). For a range of r, however, figure 6.1 shows as many as three points of intersection of the heavy dashed straight line with the solid curve $h(u)$.

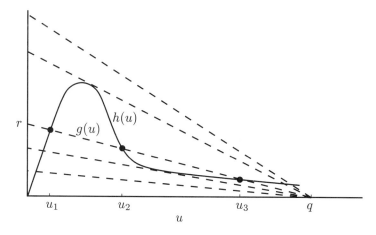

Figure 6.1: Budworm problem: the three potential points of intersection of the two bracketed functions in (6.3).

Notice that if we increase r (or decrease q), we can vary the angle of the straight line so that it has either zero, one, two, or three points of intersection with the curve in figure 6.1. This variation is represented by the five dashed lines in the figure. Hence, depending on the values of the two parameters, r and q, it is possible to have either 1, 2, or 3 steady states. Let's denote them by u_1, u_2, and u_3, where $u_3 > u_2 > u_1 > 0$.

We can see, using figure 6.1, with r and q in the range where we have three intersections (that is, three positive steady states), that the form of $f(u)$ from (6.1) must qualitatively look like the solid line in figure 6.2, which is similar to the curve in figure 5.3.

From figure 6.2 (and referring to figure 5.3), we can see that whenever three solutions exist, u_1 and u_3 are stable, but u_2 is unstable because at these points the gradient of $f(u)$ is respectively negative and positive. The steady state $u = 0$ is always unstable because $df/du = r > 0$.

The high value u_3 is a serious outbreak of the budworm, one value we would like to avoid. The smaller value of u_1 is really a "refuge." It is a nonzero population of the budworm, to be sure, but it is much better than the outbreak value. This result suggests that the goal of forest management should not be to eliminate the budworms entirely (an impossibility), but to manage their population to that of refuge size.

From a budworm-management point of view, the parameters we have at our disposal are q and r. The model tells us that $u = 0$ is not a stable solution, so there is no point in trying to eliminate the population altogether. Our options are to have the budworm population at u_1 or u_3. The former option is preferable, so we can alter the parameters r and q such that there is only one stable steady state at u_1. For example, we can reduce q by reducing the carrying capacity of the environment (see appendix 6.5 for details), perhaps by some systematic pattern of spraying trees. The model thus sends us back to the forest for more experimentation.

If we were to plot the steady states u_s versus the parameters r and q, we would obtain the three-dimensional figure depicted as figure 6.3. In the region where there are three steady states, there is a fold in the surface. The fold doesn't go back all the way on the surface because when r and q are small enough, there is only one steady state.

Let us now perform a thought experiment in which we keep q fixed at a sufficiently large value so that we are not on the $u_s = u_1$ only portion of the surface, and vary r from small to large values. We can track the steady-state solutions of (6.1) as r varies. With small values of r, we are on the A portion of the surface (figure 6.3), and we have only one solution. This situation corresponds to the lower dotted curve in figure 6.2. As we increase r, we eventually move past the B threshold on the surface into a regime where three solutions—u_1, u_2, and u_3— exist. Because we started with u_1, which is stable to small perturbations, we initially stay at this low steady state even though another stable steady state, u_3, is possible. As r increases further, it passes the critical threshold at the C portion of the surface, and u_1 disappears. At this point, the solution jumps "catastrophically" from a low-value (u_1) to a high-value (u_3) solution. This jump corresponds to the situation given by the upper dotted curve in figure 6.2. As we continue to increase r, we are on the D portion of the surface, where only one stable steady state, u_3, is possible

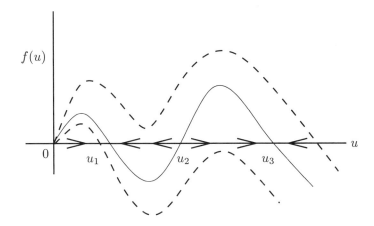

Figure 6.2: Qualitative form of $f(u)$ in equation (6.1) with r and q in the ranges where there are one or three nonzero solutions. The dotted lines are given by a large enough or small enough r such that there is only one stable steady state solution. For the highest dotted line, the only stable steady-state solution is u_3, and for the lowest dotted line we are left with u_1.

Suppose now that we perform our thought experiment in reverse, tracking the steady states as r decreases from large to small values. A particularly interesting aspect of such models is that we do not go from u_3 back to u_1 by the same route. As we reduce r, we move out of the D portion of the surface across the threshold C. This time however, because we started at u_3, which remains stable to small perturbations, we remain at u_3 even though the stable steady state u_1 has appeared. Eventually, however, u_3 disappears when r crosses the threshold value B. At this point, only the steady state u_1 is available, and there is a catastrophic change as the solution drops from u_3 to u_1.

In summary, if r increases from small to large values, the solution to equation (6.1) moves along the lower path $ABCD$, whereas in the reverse direction (r decreasing from large to small values) the solution moves along the upper path $DCBA$. The catastrophic jumps in the population occur at C on the way up and at B on the way down. This phenomenon, where a catastrophic jump occurs in a different location depending on the direction of parameter change, is called *hysteresis*.

We can now deduce some ecological implications of this analysis. If the tree foliage is sufficient to sustain an outbreak (a u_3 steady state) and the outbreak occurs, a much lower r is required to make it come back to a refuge (a u_1 steady state) than if the population was kept in check in the first place to keep the population on the lower branch ABC in figure 6.3.

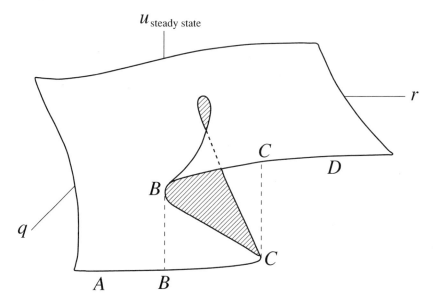

Figure 6.3: Fold plot of the cusp catastrophe. The surface shown is a plot of the stable and unstable steady states as a function of the parameters q and r.

We can view the information in figure 6.3 from another angle by projecting the three-dimensional figure onto the $r - q$ plane. In doing this, we obtain figure 6.4, which has a cusp at the point of the fold in figure 6.3. The parameter space in figure 6.4 is divided into three (strictly, only two) regions, one where there are three steady-state solutions, and two where there is just one steady-state solution.

Some catastrophe models do not exhibit hysteresis; they are instead irreversible. Once a state is entered, it is impossible to exit. Models displaying disease processes are likely to find this property desirable—that is, consistent with nature. Some perceptual phenomena are like that as well: once you see the illusion, you can never go back and see it any other way. For example, a number of illusions look like a random array of dots until someone points out a hidden figure, maybe a

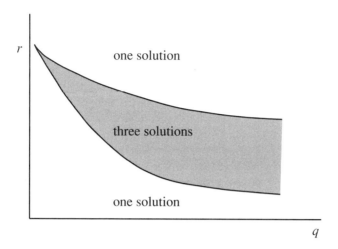

Figure 6.4: A cusp is formed when the surface in figure 6.3 is projected onto the $r - q$ plane.

cow. Subsequently, all you can ever see is the cow. There may be some processes in marriage that are similar. Once a particular event occurs, the marriage is forever changed. Examples might be a betrayal of the marriage contract, such as physical violence or an extramarital affair. In marriages, a catastrophic change for the worse could possibly be repaired, but with much more effort than if repair had been put in effect before the catastrophe. Hysteresis seems possible in such interactions. In our marital models, catastrophe configurations are possible in which the marital system loses its only positive stable steady state.

It is necessary to have at least a cubic equation for the steady states ($f(x) = 0$) in order for a catastrophe situation to be possible. Larger-order polynomials can lead to extremely complex catastrophe situations, which Murray has called "rococo." A more detailed analysis of catastrophe models can be found in Gilmore (1981). The concept and demonstration of rapid change as some parameter passes a critical value has been known to applied mathematicians and physicists for more than one hundred years. A simple fluid mechanics example is the breaking of a wave or the appearance of a shock wave (manifested by a sonic boom) when an object is moving through the speed of sound.

6.2   Courtship, Marriage, Divorce, and the Spruce Budworm Catastrophe

One of the major problems in marriage may be described as the *regulating* negative affect. The balance between negative and positive affect is absolutely critical in predicting the longitudinal fate of marriages (Gottman, 1993, 1994a). In a prospective study of newlywed couples, Gottman, Coan, Carrère, and Swanson (1998) found that, during a conflict discussion a few months after the wedding, only 30 seconds of positive affect (out of 15 minutes of interaction) differentiated couples who would eventually wind up either divorced, stable but unhappy, or stable and happy in the next six years. The happy stable couples had 30 seconds more positive affect (affection, humor, interest, or engaged listening) out of 900 seconds than the unhappy stable couples. The unhappy stable couples, in turn, had 30 seconds more positive affect than the couples who eventually divorced. Subsequent analysis of this positive affect showed that it was in the service of deescalation and physiological soothing only in the group of newlyweds who eventually wound up stable and happily married.

The idea of *balance* between positive and negative affect being important suggests that the goal of marital therapy is not the elimination of negative affect. Negative affect in marriage may have many positive functions. First, a marriage with no negative affect (e.g., irritability, anger, sadness, hurt, disappointment, tension, worries) is not real, so there is a constriction of the natural flow of emotions of everyday life. These negative affects are a natural part of close relationships. Familiarity and comfort make their expression natural. A marriage that was constricted to be totally cheerful and affectionate would be a nightmare. We have evidence that the suppression of affect predicts divorce, but in midlife (about sixteen years after the wedding) rather than within the first ten years after the wedding (in which divorce is predicted by high negative affect; Gottman and Levenson, 2000). Second, negative affect, like a predator population, culls those interactive patterns most likely to be counterproductive to the tasks of marriage, such as decision making. Newlywed disputes are, in part, designed to eliminate or minimize the most objectionable old bachelor and bachelorette habits that stand in the way of moving from *me-ness* to *we-ness,* in our laboratory's terminology. Third, negative affect may serve to regulate cycles of distance and closeness in a marriage and act to renew courtship continually. Fourth, being able to cope with the inevitable negative affect of living closely together may help give the couple a sense that they can handle conflict, and it may help redefine the relationship as needed for major life transitions. For example, in the transition to parenthood, sleeplessness and irritability often lead to depression, and it is well known that marital conflict increases by a factor of nine after the arrival of the first baby (Belsky and Kelly, 1994).

In this picture, the marital problem is quite like the spruce budworm problem. The amount of negative affect in a conflict discussion is the analogue of the budworm population. It is the variable u. Recast in terms of marriage, equation (6.1) states that the amount of negative affect generally reaches an asymptote, increasing over time to the couple's "carrying capacity". This description fits our experience with the conflict discussion, in which we find negative affect gradually increasing and then leveling off. The second term in equation (6.1) is a switch for turning off negative affect. It is the term that makes the regulation of negativity such an important balance.

The three steady-state solutions of the equation are: (1) an unstable steady state with no negative affect; (2) a stable steady state with intermediate levels of negative affect—that is, a managed state in which the spruce trees (positive affect) flourish, but are also culled by a nonzero budworm population (negative affect); and (3) a state of outbreak (runaway negative affect). These three solutions correspond very well to: (1) courtship, in which negative affect is minimized and positive affect reigns unabated; (2) real everyday marriage, in which positive affect generally thrives, but in which negative affect exists in regulated form; and, (3) a situation of outbreak, in which negative affect reigns supreme. This third situation is well documented as one precursor of divorce (e.g., Gottman, 1994a). Associated with it are the reliable cascades of increased distance and isolation as well as the other predictors of divorce.

This analogy suggests that it may be profitable to explore regulatory mechanisms for controlling an outbreak of runaway negative affect. Our recent results suggest that *repair attempts* may be that regulatory mechanism. Repair attempts are natural during conflict, even for very distressed couples, and occur at the rate of about one every three minutes. We have been studying what makes these repair attempts successful at downregulating negative affect. So far we have discovered that the success of these repair attempts during negative affect are determined only by the quality of the marital friendship (see Gottman, 1999).

6.3   Examples of Catastrophic Change: Christopher Zeeman

In a series of articles, Christopher Zeeman (1976) suggested some interesting applications of catastrophe theory that are relevant to psychology. Zeeman has written one of the few readable accounts of catastrophe theory. We review some of his models here. All of them are qualitative graphical models, unlike the quantitative budworm one, which came from the differential equation model.

Fight or Flight

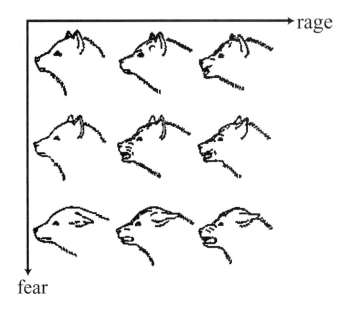

Figure 6.5: Rage and fear can be measured by facial expressions (after Lorenz, 1966).

The first model of catastrophe was an example from Konrad Lorenz's book *On Aggression* (1966), in which he says that fear and rage are conflicting factors that affect the outcome of aggression. He proposed that rage can be measured by how much a dog's mouth is open and the teeth are showing, and that fear can be measured by how much the ears lay back. Here, fear and rage are plotted along two axes labeled α and β (figure 6.5). Zeeman introduced a third axis, with its scale measuring the resulting behavior of the dog, from extreme behaviors such as fleeing or fighting, through intermediary or neutral behaviors such as growling and avoiding. The catastrophe theory view of this situation is reproduced in figure 6.6.

If there is only rage, then on the surface M of figure 6.6 there is the single point marked (1). This is the fighting dog. In case (2), we have

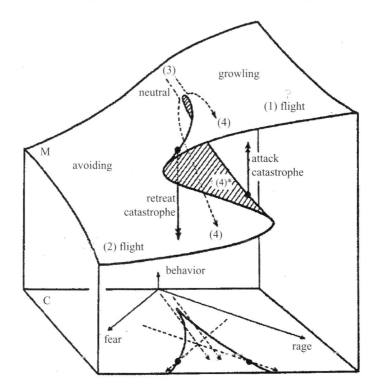

Figure 6.6: The cusp catastrophe illustrating fear and rage as conflicting factors influencing aggression.

the fleeing dog. Case (3) is in between, which is the neutral dog. But in the very interesting case (4), we have two possible points. There is a (4) above and a (4) below, on the lower surface. The distribution of the dog's behavior has gone bimodal. The shaded part of the drawing (marked 4*) shows the least likely neutral behavior of the dog. The least likely behavior of the dog is included in this graph because it makes the graph into a smooth surface. It also denotes the threshold between the two points: lower (4) for flight and upper (4) for fight. The curve on the surface where the upper and lower portions of the surface fold over is the *fold curve*. The projection of this curve on the horizontal plane is also called the *bifurcation set*. The cusp catastrophe looks much like the budworm problem we just studied, and we can see clearly what the projection of the catastrophe looks like in two-dimensional parameter space. Zeeman also suggested modeling fight or flight in fish guarding a nest from predators, in which the two parameters are the size of the predator and the closeness of the defender to the nest. This model was able to explain why in some fish the animal closest to the nest (either male or female) will defend it to the death, while the other animal flees. It should be possible to construct a differential equation model, incorporating the key observations, the solutions of which would generate such a behavioral surface and cusp catastrophe.

A Model for the Brain?

Zeeman was particularly interested in suggesting that the best models of the brain would be those that have catastrophe as a possibility. He argued that the model for the behavior of the dog might, in fact, be a model of the underlying neural mechanism for that behavior. He wrote:

> It is well known that non-linear oscillators can possess *attractors* (stable limit cycles), and that these attractors typically bifurcate according to the cusp catastrophe or higher dimensional catastrophes. Therefore we may expect elementary catastrophes to be typical models of brain activity, especially of activity in those parts of the brain such as the limbic system where the organs are more highly interconnected and consequently may tend to oscillate more as whole units (as opposed to the neocortex, whose parts can oscillate differently at the same time, and whose activity can therefore be much more complicated). According to Paul MacLean it is in the limbic system that emotions and moods are generated (while the neocortex determines the more complicated choice of behaviour within that mood). Therefore we might expect catastrophe theory to be the mathematical language with which to describe emotion and mood; and indeed it is striking that moods tend to persist, tend to delay before changing, and then tend to change suddenly, all of which qualities are typical of catastrophe theory. (Zeeman, 1976, pp. 12–13, emphasis in original).

Zeeman wrote that two-parameter cusp catastrophes have the five properties of bimodality (there are two main possible states), sudden jumps, hysteresis, inaccessibility, and divergence. In divergence, the difference between two paths on either side of the cusp point may be marginal but lead to a major change in behavior. Inaccessibility means that the system has equilibria that are unstable because even small perturbations can create dramatic changes in the system. Zeeman suggested that whenever we observe one of these qualities in nature, it would be sensible to look for the others and consider modeling the phenomenon with a cusp catastrophe model. Ideally, however, it would be much more informative if we could model the actual biological mechanism governing the phenomenon. With such a mechanistic model, catastrophes can then be found mathematically and be based on a knowledge of the underlying biology, as was the case with the budworm.

Anorexia Nervosa and Higher-Order Catastrophes

Anorexia nervosa is a psychologically based eating disorder in which mainly adolescent girls diet until they become so thin that their health is endangered. The disorder can also have bulimic cycles of binge eating and "purging" (usually vomiting). In some cases, the girls have a history of sexual abuse. Zeeman worked with a psychotherapist named J. Hevesi. The Anorexic Aid Society of Great Britain did a survey of more than 1,000 anorexics, and Hevesi's patients were the only ones who reported having completely recovered. The survey found that Hevesi had a success rate of 80% with the 60 out of 150 patients who were offered treatment with him. No other therapist had high success rates in this survey. Zeeman used what is known as the "butterfly catastrophe" to model the anorexic's behavior, as well as to model how the therapy might have its effects. In the butterfly catastrophe, the equation for determining the steady states is a fifth-order polynomial. There are four parameters in this case instead of two. The parameter of the quadratic term is called the *bias factor,* and its main effect is to swing the tip of the cusp to the right or left, which pulls the shape of the cusp right or left. There are two folds in the surface that represents the catastrophe. Zeeman used this idea to propose that anorexia has two phases. In the first phase, the patient is in a fasting modality, but in the second phase (which the patients calls "knock out") the pattern is a cycle of binge eating and purging. He also was able to model the therapy by proposing that its effects were to create a third alternative, which is the normal cycle of hunger, eating, and satiety.

Zeeman used the trimodal nature of the butterfly catastrophe (rather than the cusp catastrophe's bimodal character) to model conflicts (such as international war) in which compromise, in addition to fight or flight, is a third option.

6.4   Catastrophes in Perception

A series of now classic figures developed by Fisher (1967) demonstrate sudden changes in visual perception. Here, we describe one of these picture series and show that it is another example of a cusp catastrophe; it also exhibits perceptual hysteresis. We also present the results of an experiment carried out Murray that confirms the hypothesis. The specific example we describe has been studied in more depth by Zeeman (1987) and more generally by Stewart (1977).

Figure 6.7: Series of pictures exhibiting abrupt (catastrophic) visual change during the variation from a man's face to a sitting woman.

The mind can be triggered or moved in a major new thought or behavioral direction by a vast variety of cues in ways we cannot yet hope to describe in any biological detail. We can, however, describe the phenomenon and demonstrate its existence via example. [1] One example is given by the series of drawings shown in figure 6.7. For the purposes of

---

[1] An interesting example of a major change in a patient undergoing psychoanalysis is described by Zeeman (1987). The case involved a frigid woman whom Marie Claire Boons had been treating for two years without much success. "One day the patient reported dreaming of a frozen rabbit in her arms, which woke and said hello. The patient's words were 'un lapin congelé', meaning a frozen rabbit, to which the psychoanalyst slowly replied 'la pin con gelé?' We explain this somewhat elaborate pun: 'pin' is the french slang for penis, the female 'la' makes it into the clitoris, 'con' is the french slang for the female genitals, and 'gelé' means both frozen and rigid. The surprising result was that the patient did not respond for twenty minutes and the next day came back cured. Apparently that evening she had experienced her first orgasm ever with her husband."

Table 6.1: Results from a perception experiment

Figure number	1	2	3	4	5	6	7	8	Mean
number switching 1st run $\longrightarrow$	0	0	0	0	5	8	25	19	7.0
number switching 2d run $\longleftarrow$	0	1	1	17	29	6	3	-	4.8
number switching 3rd run $\longrightarrow$	-	0	3	19	19	12	3	1	4.9

Results obtained when fifty-seven Oxford undergraduates were asked to view the series of figures composing the visual transition from a man's face to a sitting woman (figure 6.7). The sequence of pictures shown to the students was 12345678765432123456789, and the students noted when they observed the illustration to change from the man's face to the seated woman or viceversa.

discussion, we number the pictures from left to right and top to bottom, so the upper-left-hand picture is number 1, and the lower-right-hand picture is number 8.

Picture 1 in the figure is clearly a man's face but picture 8 is clearly a sitting woman. Zeeman (1987) describes an experiment that demonstrates the sudden jump from seeing a man's face to seeing a seated woman. Following Zeeman (1987), one of the authors (Murray) carried out a similar experiment with a group of fifty-seven students in Oxford, none of whom had seen the series before or knew of such an example of sudden change in visual perception . The experiment consisted of showing the series three times starting with the man's face, picture 1, going up to the woman, picture 8, then reversing the sequence down to 1 and again in ascending order; that is, the figures were shown in the order 12345678765432123456789. The students were told to write down the picture number each time they noticed a major change in their perception. The results are presented in table 6.1.

The predictions were that during the first run through the series, that is from 1 to 8, the perception of most of the audience would be locked into the figure of the face until it became obvious that the picture was in fact a woman, at which stage there would be sudden jump in perception. As the pictures were shown in the reverse order, the audience was now aware of the two possibilities, so it could make a more balanced judgment as to what a specific picture represented. The perception change would therefore more likely occur nearer the middle, around 5 and 4. During the final run through the series, the change would again occur near the middle.

The results of table 6.1 are shown schematically in figure 6.8, where

Number of Students Perceiving

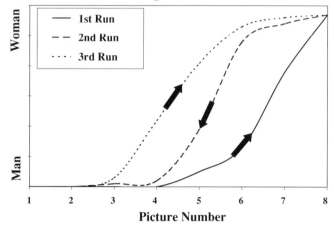

Figure 6.8: Schematic representation of the visual catastrophe based on the data in table 6.1 on three runs (12345678765432123455678) through the series of pictures in figure 6.7. On the vertical axis is plotted the number of students perceiving a change in their perception. At the level "man," all of the students perceive a man, and at the level "woman," all of the students perceive a woman. On the first run (solid line), all of the students see a man's face until the fifth picture, where a few students suddenly see a woman. The biggest jump occurs at the seventh picture. By the eighth picture, all of the students are seeing a seated woman. On the second run, most of the students continue to see a woman until the fifth and fourth pictures are presented, after which point most of the class is seeing a man's face. A similar pattern appears in the line for the third run, but the shifts in perception do not occur in the same place as they did for the second run. Thus these results are a good illustration of one-time hysteresis.

the vertical axis is perception, p, and the horizontal axis, the stimulus, is the picture number. The graph of perception versus stimulus is multivalued in a traditional cusp catastrophe way. For example, over part of the range there are two possible perceptions, a face or a woman. The relation with the example of the budworm population problem is clear. On the first run through, the switch was delayed until around picture 7, but on the run through the down sequence it occurred mainly at 5 and again around 5 on the final run through the pictures. There is, however, a fundamental difference between the phenomenon here and the budworm problem. In the latter there is a definite and reproducable hysteresis, whereas in the former this hysteresis effect occurs only once, after which the dynamics is single valued for each stimulus.

If we started instead with picture 8 and again ran the series three times, the results would be simply reversed. The jump would have first occurred around picture number 2, with the second and third switch again around picture number 5.

6.5 Chapter Summary

Although catastrophe theory can be profitably used to obtain some general insight into a wide spectrum of psychological and other phenomena, great care must be exercised not to overplay its use. In the field of biology, in particular, overenthusiastic proselytizing produced a major backlash in the scientific community. Even now, many bioscientists still view catastrophe theory with considerable skepticism, which has sadly been counterproductive. Used sensibly, however, catastrophe theory offers a modeling approach for situations in social science involving discrete states and sudden change brought on by very small changes in a model parameter.

In this chapter, we have presented some simple examples from biology, psychology, and visual perception, that exhibit catastrophic change as a single parameter is varied. The budworm problem is a very simple extension of the logistic growth problem, yet it demonstrates the phenomenon of catastrophe as a possibility, indeed a probability, if population is not controlled. This example shows how a complex situation can be represented with just a few parameters using a nonlinear dynamic model. More complex models are possible.

The phenomenon of catastrophic change both in behavior and in perception is widespread. An understanding of the underlying dynamics would clearly be of help in a great many modeling endeavors. Indeed, in our models for marital interaction, which we discuss in later chapters, sudden change occurring at a bifurcation value is evident, and true hysteresis is also possible.

Appendix 6.1: Nondimensionalization

Nondimensionalization is an important, if not absolutely essential, tool for preparing a model equation for mathematical analysis. Here we carry it out for a specific predator population model.

The model budworm population equation (Ludwig *et al.* 1978) is given by (5.6) with (5.7), namely,

$$\frac{dN}{dt} = rN(k - N) - \frac{BN^2}{A + N^2}. \qquad (A6.1)$$

The dimensions of the left-hand side are population/time, in whatever units you decide to use to measure time and the population. The right-hand side, of course, has to have the same dimensions. The carrying capacity, k, has dimension "population" so if $rN(k - N)$ has dimension population/time, r must have the dimension 1/(population $\times$ time). Analogously, A has the dimension (population)^2, and B must have, to be consistent, the dimension population/time. In (A6.1), there are four dimensional parameters A, B, r, and k. Let us introduce nondimensional quantities by setting

$$u = \frac{N}{\sqrt{A}}, \quad t^* = Bt, \quad r^* = \frac{kr}{B}, \quad q^* = \frac{k}{\sqrt{A}}. \qquad (A6.2)$$

If we divide both sides of (A6.1) by $B\sqrt{A}$, the equation becomes

$$\frac{du}{dt^*} = r^*u\left(1 - \frac{u}{q^*}\right) - \frac{u^2}{1 + u^2}. \qquad (A6.3)$$

All quantities here—namely, $u(t^*)$, t^*, r^* and q^*—are now pure numbers. Importantly, there are now only two parameters, r^* and q^*, that affect the dynamics. For example, u is now simply the fraction of the population relative to the switch population value $\sqrt{A}$. We can see, without doing any mathematics to get the solution, that a change in the linear birth r, say doubling it, could be compensated by a doubling of the maximum predation—that is, B, because this compensation leaves r^* unchanged. Equation (A6.3), with the asterisks omitted for notational simplicity, is equation (6.1).

7

An Intuitive Discussion of Phase Space Plots

In chapter 6, our discussion dealt entirely with single equation models. Often, however, it is useful to be able to simultaneously model two populations. Models of this sort are discussed in chapter 8. Before we can understand how these models behave, we must learn a little about how the results are presented. In this chapter, we try to familiarize the reader with Poincaré's phase space plots and how they actually emerge from real data. We do this with the data obtained for the marriage models we discuss.

7.1 Phase Space Portrait

For any set of data in which there is only one variable, it has become customary to create *phase space plots* by plotting the change in that variable against the variable itself. For example, if we are interested in the displacement of a real pendulum as it oscillates, and we call this displacement $x(t)$, then the phase space plot is a graph of dx/dt plotted against $x(t)$. Another example from this book is figure 6.2 from the budworm problem.

In the cases where we have two variables, we customarily plot these variables as functions of each other. We cannot also plot the changes in these variables on separate axes, because then we would have a four-dimensional plot. Once again, the plane defined by this plot is called the *phase space plot*. If the two variables are u and v, and the first data point at $t = 1$ is (u_1, v_1), and the second data point at $t = 2$ is (u_2, v_2), then figure 7.1 shows a phase space plot of these two points. Notice that time does not appear explicitly in this plot, but the sequence of points indicates movement through time. Another example of this type of plot already encountered in this book is figure 4.2, where u and v are x (horizontal position) and y (vertical position).

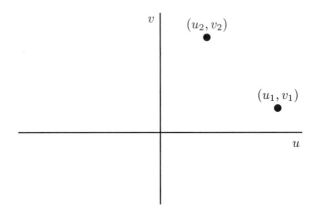

Figure 7.1: Phase space plot of two points, one at $t = 1$ and the second at $t = 2$, showing movement in time. Time is the hidden parametric variable in phase space.

7.2   Force Field Portrait

By simply mapping many data points on the phase plane and getting some idea of their motion over time, we can map the *flow field* that our equations create in phase space, just as we did in figure 4.1. We can also think of the field as a *force field*, where each arrow represents a force pushing our state (or twig) in the direction of that arrow.

Suppose again that the two equations under study in our modeling effort are written:

$$\frac{du}{dt} = f(u, v),$$
$$\frac{dv}{dt} = g(u, v).$$
(7.1)

We map the $u - v$ force field by tracking the signs of the functions g and f in different regions of the plane. Notice that if f is positive, then du/dt is also positive, which means that u is increasing. Thus, we have a force pointing in the direction of increasing u at that point. At the same point, g might be negative, which means that dv/dt is negative, and v is decreasing. Thus, at the same point, we also have a force pointing

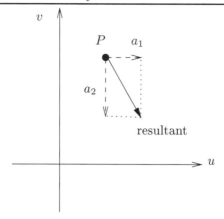

Figure 7.2: Creating a phase space plot. At the point P, we have $du/dt = f > 0$ and $dv/dt = g < 0$. Thus, the force field has a component a_1 in the direction of increasing u and a component a_2 in the direction of decreasing v. The sum of these two forces is found by drawing a box as shown (dotted line) and drawing the resultant arrow shown. This process can be repeated for any point in the phase space.

in the direction of decreasing v. What we end up with is the resultant arrow shown in figure 7.2.

7.3   Null Clines and Steady States

If we tested enough points in the phase space, we would end up with a full picture of the flow field. This is very time-consuming. A few observations can make this process of sketching a phase space plot much faster. Notice that if $f = 0$, then u doesn't change, and if $g = 0$, then v doesn't change. If we can find the curve along which $f = 0$, then on one side of the curve we will know that $f < 0$, and on the other side we will have $f > 0$. Thus, we can easily divide up phase space into regions where u is increasing or decreasing. Similarly, by plotting the curve along which $g = 0$, we can further subdivide the phase space into regions where v is increasing or decreasing. The curves $f = 0$ and $g = 0$ are called *null clines*.

At points where the null clines intersect, we have both $f = 0$ and $g = 0$. Thus, at these points neither u nor v are changing. We call these points *steady states* because the system will always stay there if not disturbed. Natural systems, however, are constantly being disturbed, so

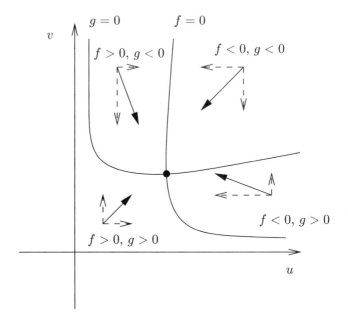

Figure 7.3: Qualitative portrait of vector force field in phase space. The curve labeled $f = 0$ is the null cline for the variable u, so along this curve u is not changing. Similarly, the curve labeled $g = 0$ is the null cline for the variable v, so along this curve v is not changing. At the point where the two curves cross, both f and g are zero, so neither u nor v is changing, and we have a steady state. The null clines divide the phase space into regions where f and g each have one sign. In the upper-right-hand region, f and g are both negative, so the resultant force field points in the direction of the solid arrow, or toward the steady state. In the upper-left-hand region, g is still negative, but f is now positive, so the resultant force field points in the direction of the solid arrow, or still toward the steady state. In the lower-left-hand region, both f and g are positive, so the resultant arrow points upward toward the steady state. Finally, in the lower-right-hand region, f is negative but g is positive, so the resultant arrow points back and up toward the steady state. Because the resultant arrow points toward the steady state in all four regions, we know that the steady state is a stable one.

the question then is to determine how the system will react to change. There are two possibilities. If the system is bumped away from the steady state, so that we are now in some nearby region in the phase plane, then the system can either relax back to the steady state or continue wandering off. In the first case we have a stable steady state, because the system tends to return to it, and in the second case we have an unstable steady state.

Consider figure 7.3, in which the two null clines $f = 0$ and $g = 0$ for a set of equations have been plotted. Note that the two curves cross in the middle of the graph. This intersection point is the steady state for our hypothetical system. Having located a steady state, we now plot the *force field* in the phase plane in order to determine if the steady state is stable or unstable.

In the upper-right-hand region of figure 7.3, both f and g are negative. Thus, u and v are both decreasing, as indicated by the dashed arrows, and the resultant force is toward the steady state. In the upper-left-hand region, g is still negative, but f has become positive. Thus, u is increasing, but v is decreasing, as shown by the dashed arrows. The resultant arrow (shown solid) still points toward the steady state. In the lower-left-hand region, both f and g are positive, and the resultant arrow points up and right toward the steady state. Finally, in the lower-right-hand region, f is negative and g is positive, again resulting in a net force toward the steady state. Because the net force in each region of phase space points toward the steady state, we can conclude that this steady state is a stable one.

Notice that we had to look at only one point in each region of phase space in order to know the general direction of the force field in the entire region. In this way, even a global glance at the signs of the two functions f and g gives us a *dynamic* idea of how points are impelled to move in each region of the phase plane.

It is perhaps helpful to think of phase space as a mountain range. There is a stable steady state at the bottom of each bowl-shaped valley and an unstable steady state at the top of each mountain. The *state of the system* can be represented by a stone tossed into the mountain range. If the stone is placed at the very top of a mountain, the first gust of wind that comes along will send it careening down the mountainside. Once the stone reaches a valley floor, however, it will stay there. If kicked up the mountainside by a hiker, the stone will fall back down to the valley bottom.

Clearly, stable steady states are very interesting, because we can predict that the system will ultimately end up there. We don't need to know exactly what path the stone took to get to the valley floor in order to know that it will end up there at some point. Thus, if we are interested in the long-term behavior of a system, which need not be very far away, we can obtain the answer simply by plotting the null clines and determining the stability of the steady states.

It is possible for the phase space of a mathematical model to have multiple steady states, just as a mountain range has multiple peaks and valleys. The greater the number of steady states, the more complicated the model. There is also the additional complication of determining at which steady state the system will end up. Most of the models we discuss in this book have one to five steady states, with only some of those being stable.

7.4   Chapter Summary

With these tools, we are ready to discuss dynamical systems with two equations, which are the subject of chapter 8. Just to summarize, the main steps in analyzing a two-equation model are

1. set up a phase space plot where each variable being modeled is plotted along its own axis;

2. graph the null clines;

3. locate the steady states;

4. determine the stability of the steady states by graphing the force field in phase space.

We go through this process for three different models in chapter 8.

Appendix 7.1: Phase Plane Analysis

We discuss here, only very briefly, general autonomous systems of first-order ordinary differential equations of the form

$$\frac{dx}{dt} = f(x, y), \quad \frac{dy}{dt} = g(x, y). \tag{A7.1}$$

We present the basic results that are required in the main text. Many books discuss phase plane analysis in varying depth, such as the excellent book by Strogatz (1994), which also discusses nonlinear dynamics and chaos in general. A particularly good, short, and practical exposition of the qualitative theory of ordinary differential equation systems, including phase plane techniques, is given by Odell (1980).

Phase curves or *phase trajectories* of (A7.1) are solutions of

$$\frac{dx}{dy} = \frac{f(x, y)}{g(x, y)}. \tag{A7.2}$$

Through any point (x_0, y_0) there is a unique curve except at *singular points* (x_s, y_s) where

$$f(x_s, y_s) = g(x_s, y_s) = 0.$$

Let $x \to x - x_s$, $y \to y - y_s$, then $(0,0)$ is a singular point of the transformed equation. Thus, without loss of generality we now consider (A7.2) to have a singular point at the origin; that is,

$$f(x,y) = g(x,y) = 0 \quad \Rightarrow \quad x = 0, \quad y = 0. \tag{A7.3}$$

We can expand f and g in Taylor's series about $(0,0)$, and, retaining only the linear terms, we get

$$\frac{dx}{dy} = \frac{ax + by}{cx + dy}, \quad A = \begin{pmatrix} a & b \\ c & d \end{pmatrix} = \begin{pmatrix} f_x & f_y \\ g_x & g_y \end{pmatrix}_{(0,0)}, \tag{A7.4}$$

which defines the matrix A and the constants a, b, c, and d. The linear form is equivalent to the system

$$\frac{dx}{dt} = ax + by, \quad \frac{dy}{dt} = cx + dy. \tag{A7.5}$$

Solutions of (A7.5) give the parametric forms of the phase curves; t is the parametric parameter.

Let λ_1 and λ_2 be the eigenvalues of A defined in (A7.4); that is,

$$\begin{pmatrix} a - \lambda & b \\ c & d - \lambda \end{pmatrix} = 0 \quad \Rightarrow \quad \lambda_1, \lambda_2 = \frac{(a+d) \pm [(a+d)^2 - 4 \det A]^{\frac{1}{2}}}{2}. \tag{A7.6}$$

Solutions of (A7.5) are then

$$\begin{pmatrix} x \\ y \end{pmatrix} = c_1 \mathbf{v}_1 e^{\lambda_1 t} + c_2 \mathbf{v}_2 e^{\lambda_2 t}, \tag{A7.7}$$

where c_1 and c_2 are arbitrary constants, and $\mathbf{v}_1, \mathbf{v}_2$ are the eigenvectors of A corresponding to λ_1 and λ_2 respectively: they are given by

$$\mathbf{v}_i = (1 + p_i^2)^{-1/2} \begin{pmatrix} 1 \\ p_i \end{pmatrix}, \quad p_i = \frac{\lambda_i - a}{b}, \quad b \neq 0, \quad i = 1, 2 \tag{A7.8}$$

Elimination of t in (A7.7) gives the phase curves in the (x, y) plane.

The form (A7.7) is for distinct eigenvalues. If the eigenvalues are equal, the solutions are proportional to $(c_1 + c_2 t)e^{\lambda t}$.

The above method is a very quick and succinct one. We arrive at the same solutions if we simply look for solutions of (A7.5) in terms of an exponential. In this case, it is probably simplest to differentiate the equations to eliminate y, say, to get a linear second-order equation for $x(t)$.

Catalog of (Linear) Singularities in the Phase Plane

1. λ_1, λ_2 real and distinct:

> **a.** λ_1 and λ_2 have the same sign. Typical eigenvectors $\mathbf{v}_1$ and $\mathbf{v}_2$ are illustrated in figure 7.4(a). Suppose $\lambda_2 < \lambda_1 < 0$. Then, from (A7.7), for example for $c_2 = 0, c_1 \neq 0$,
>
> $$\begin{pmatrix} x \\ y \end{pmatrix} = c_1 \mathbf{v}_1 e^{\lambda_1 t},$$
>
> so the solution in the phase plane simply moves along $\mathbf{v}_1$ toward the origin as $t \to \infty$ in the direction shown in figure 7.4(a), along PO if $c_1 > 0$ and along QO if $c_1 < 0$. From (A7.7), every solution tends to $(0,0)$ as $t \to \infty$ because, with $\lambda_2 < \lambda_1 < 0$, $e^{\lambda_2 t} = \omega(e^{\lambda_1 t})$ as $t \to \infty$, so
>
> $$\begin{pmatrix} x \\ y \end{pmatrix} \sim c_1 \mathbf{v}_1 e^{\lambda_1 t} \quad \text{as} \quad t \to \infty. \tag{A7.9}$$
>
> Thus, close enough to the origin all solutions tend to zero along $\mathbf{v}_1$ as shown in figure 7.4(a). This is called a *node* (Type I) singularity. With $\lambda_1 \leq \lambda_2 \leq 0$ it is a stable node, because all trajectories tend to $(0,0)$ as $t \to \infty$. If $\lambda_1 > \lambda_2 > 0$, it is an unstable node: here $(x,y) \to (0,0)$ as $t \to -\infty$.
>
> **b.** λ_1 and λ_2 have different signs. Suppose, for example, $\lambda_1 < 0 < \lambda_2$, then $\mathbf{v}_1 e^{\lambda_1 t} v_1 \to 0$ along $\mathbf{v}_1$ as $t \to \infty$, and $\mathbf{v}_2 e^{\lambda_2 t} \to 0$ along $\mathbf{v}_2$ as $t \to \infty$. There are thus different directions on $\mathbf{v}_1$ and $\mathbf{v}_2$: the solutions near $(0,0)$ are as shown in figure 7.4(b). This is a *saddle point* singularity. It is always *unstable*: except strictly along $\mathbf{v}_1$, any small perturbation from $(0,0)$ grows exponentially.

2. λ_1, λ_2 complex: $\lambda_1, \lambda_2 = \alpha \pm i\beta, \beta \neq 0$. Solutions (A7.7) here involve $e^{\alpha t} e^{\pm i\beta t}$, which implies an oscillatory approach to $(0,0)$.

> **a.** $\alpha \neq 0$. Here we have a *spiral,* which is stable if $\alpha < 0$ and unstable if $\alpha > 0$: figure 7.4(c) illustrates a spiral singularity.
>
> **b.** $\alpha = 0$. In this case, the phase curves are ellipses. This singularity is called a *center* and is illustrated in figure 7.4(d). Centers are not stable in the usual sense; a small perturbation from one phase curve does not die out in the sense of returning to the original unperturbed curve. The perturbation simply gives another solution. In the case of center singularities, determined by the linear approximation to $f(x,y)$ and $g(x,y)$,

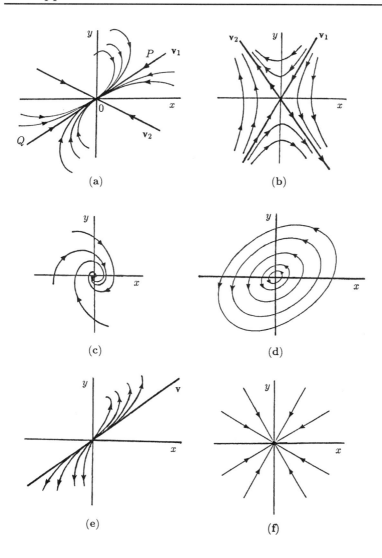

Figure 7.4: Typical examples of the basic linear singularities of the phase plane solutions of (A7.4). (**a**) Node (Type I): these can be stable (as shown) or unstable. (**b**) Saddle point: these are always unstable. (**c**) Spiral: these can be stable or unstable. (**d**) Center: this is neutrally stable. (**e**) Node (Type II): these can be stable or unstable. (**f**) Star: these can be stable or unstable. The arrows denote the stability, which is determined by the sign of $\mathrm{Re}\,\lambda$ if λ is complex.

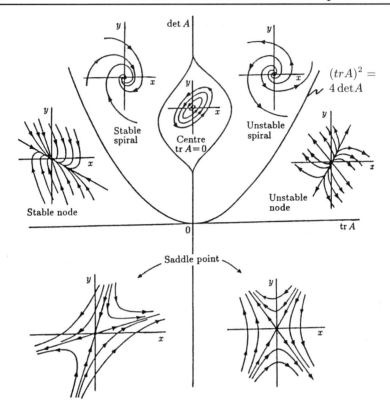

Figure 7.5: Summary diagram showing how $\operatorname{tr} A$ and $\det A$, where A is the linearization matrix given by equation (A7.4), determine the type of phase plane singularity for (A7.1). Here, $\det A = f_x g_y - f_y g_x$, $\operatorname{tr} A = f_x + g_y$, where the partial derivatives are evaluated at the singularities, the solutions of $f(x,y) = g(x,y) = 0$. (From Murray, 1993. Reproduced with permission.)

we must look at the higher-order (than linear) terms to determine whether or not it is really a spiral and hence whether it is stable or unstable.

3. $\lambda_1 = \lambda_2 = \lambda$. Here the eigenvalues are *not* distinct.

    a. In general, solutions now involve terms such as $te^{\lambda t}$ and there is only one eigenvector $\mathbf{v}$ along which the solutions tend to $(0,0)$. The t in $te^{\lambda t}$ modifies the solution away from $(0,0)$. It is called a *node* (Type II) singularity, an illustration of which is given in figure 7.4(e).

b. If the solutions do not contain the $te^{\lambda t}$ term, we have a *star* singularity, which may be stable or unstable, depending on the sign of λ. Trajectories in the vicinity of a star singularity are shown in figure 7.4(f).

The singularity depends on a, b, c, and d in the matrix A in (A7.4). figure 7.5 summarizes the results in terms of the trace and determinant of A.

If the system (A7.1) possesses a confined set (that is, a domain on the boundary of which the vector $[dx/dt, dy/dt]$ points into the domain) enclosing a single singular point that is an unstable spiral or node, then any phase trajectory cannot tend to the singularity with time, nor can it leave the confined set. The Poincaré-Bendixson theorem says that as $t \to \infty$, the trajectory will tend to a limit-cycle solution. This is the simplest application of the theorem. If the sole singularity is a saddle point, a limit cycle cannot exist. See, for example, Strogatz (1994) for a discussion of the theorem, its general application, and some practical illustrations.

8

Interacting Dyadic Systems: Two Equations Instead of One

In this chapter, we show how two differential equations can describe systems with two interacting elements. Dyadic systems have a long and venerable history in the population-ecology studies of two interacting species. We draw examples from that work in order to explain how dyadic models are developed and how they work. The model system can include linear or nonlinear equations, with the former resulting in much simpler models. In section 8.1, we discuss a model composed exclusively of linear equations, and then in the following sections we turn our attention to some nonlinear examples.

8.1 A Linear Marriage Model: Romeo and Juliet's Love Affair

We begin with a linear example that was designed to increase our understanding of love (and other) relationships. The example initially derives from the work of Anatol Rapoport (1960) in his classic book *Fights, Games, and Debates*. Strogatz (1994) independently described the same equations as the Romeo and Juliet model.

Suppose that at any time t, we could measure Romeo's love or hate for Juliet, $R(t)$, and Juliet's love or hate for Romeo, $J(t)$. Positive values of these functions indicate love, and negative values indicate hate. A very simple assumption would be that the change in Romeo's love for Juliet is a fraction of his current love plus a fraction of her current love. Similarly, Juliet's love for Romeo will change by a fraction of her current love for Romeo and a fraction of Romeo's love for her. This assumption leads us to the model equations

$$\frac{dR}{dt} = aR + bJ, \quad \text{(Romeo)}$$

$$\frac{dJ}{dt} = cR + dJ, \quad \text{(Juliet)}$$

$$(8.1)$$

where a, b, c, and d are parameters with numerical values.

The null clines of the Romeo and Juliet model (8.1) are

$$f(R, J) = aR + bJ = 0$$
$$g(R, J) = cR + eJ = 0,$$

$$(8.2)$$

where u and v from chapter 7 have been replaced with R and J. These equations are linear, so the graphs of f and g are straight lines in the $R - J$ plane.

If a and e are zero, then we are saying that Romeo's love changes as a fraction of Juliet's love for him and doesn't depend on the level of his own love at all. Similarly, changes in Juliet's love depend only on Romeo's love for her. In this case, the null clines are $f = 0 \Leftrightarrow R = 0$ and $g = 0 \Leftrightarrow J = 0$, which are the $J-$ and $R-$axes respectively. They intersect at the origin, $R = J = 0$, so this point is the steady state of the model. If we also assume that $b > 0$, but $c < 0$, then Romeo's love increases as does Juliet's, but Juliet's love only warms as Romeo's wanes. Then the force field in all four quadrants of the phase space gives us the trajectories shown in figure 8.1(a). These are closed trajectories along which Romeo and Juliet's love endlessly circles the steady state. Thus, the point $(R, J) = (0, 0)$ is termed a *neutrally stable* steady state because nearby states never get any farther away or any closer. The sad outcomes here are perpetual cycles of love and hate.

Many other scenarios are possible. Consider, for example, the case where Romeo is a cautious lover: that is, $a < 0$ and $b > 0$. These signs mean that Romeo's own love cools ($a < 0$) but that he is willing to increase his love if Juliet expresses hers ($b > 0$). Let us further simplify our example by supposing that the two lovers are identical: that is, $a = e$ and $b = c$. What sort of relationship can two such lovers have? The answer depends on the relative size of a and b.

The null clines (8.2) are the two straight lines $aR + bJ = 0$ and $bR + aJ = 0$. Their intersection is at the origin, $(R, J) = (0, 0)$, so this is the only possible steady state. It can be shown that when $a^2 > b^2$, the steady state is stable, and all trajectories lead to no feelings (neither love nor hate); the relationship fizzles out to zero, or mutual indifference (figure 8.1(b)). The lesson here is that too much caution leads to apathy.

When $a^2 < b^2$, the two of them are more daring and more sensitive to one another, but now the relationship is explosive, either a love fest or a war, asymptotically approaching the line $R = J$ (figure 8.1(c)).

Notice that this linear system is a poor representation of reality because it produces strange cycles or values that go to plus or minus infinity, or to zero (figure 8.1). This sort of behavior is characteristic of linear models, so for more realistic solution behaviors we need *nonlinear* models.

8.2   Predator and Prey Models (the Lotka-Volterra Equations)

Let us now look at a two-equation *nonlinear* example. When two species have strong interactions, their dynamics are best represented with two linked equations, one for the rate of change of the population of each species at time t. The interaction between the two species might be in the nature of competition, or cooperation, or as predator and prey. In the arena of marriage, we are interested in couples interacting at the level of behavior, where behavior over time can be a "species." For example, the running average over time of positive affect in one spouse could be "the prey" and of negative affect in the other person could be "the predator." The full repertoire of marital behaviors could, in fact, be viewed as an ecology of behavior, thought, and physiology of two people (see Gottman, 1993). Hence, the examples of the possible relationships between two species we discuss in this chapter will have general heuristic value.

In this section, we consider a model of a predator-prey relationship. In section 8.3, we study a competition model, and in section 8.4 we study a cooperation model.

In our predator-prey model, we use N to represent the prey population and P to represent the predator population. The well-known Lotka-Volterra[1] equations give the rate of change of N and P as

$$\frac{dN}{dt} = aN - bNP = N(a - bP), \quad \text{the prey equation}$$

$$(8.3)$$

$$\frac{dP}{dt} = -cP + eNP = P(eN - c), \quad \text{the predator equation.}$$

The constant parameters a, b, c, and e are positive. Notice that these equations are nonlinear because of the bNP and eNP terms.

---

[1]Lotka was a chemist who arrived at the same equations via a hypothetical chemical reaction which could exhibit periodic behavior. Volterra derived the equations as a model to explain the fluctuating fish catches in the Adriatic.

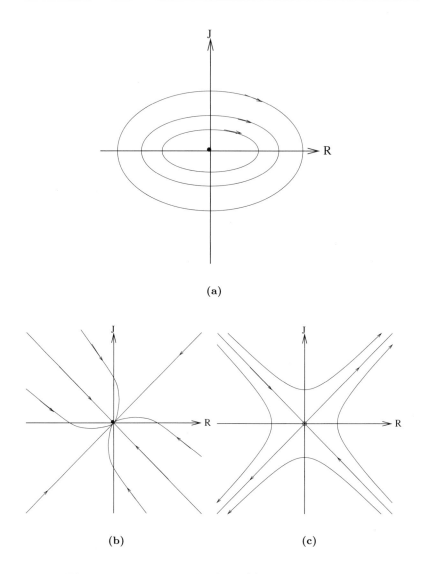

Figure 8.1: Romeo and Juliet. (a) Juliet's love warms as Romeo's wanes: perpetual cycles of love and hate; (b) Cautious lovers with $a^2 > b^2$: the relationship fizzles out to zero, or mutual indifference; (c) Cautious lovers with $a^2 < b^2$: the relationship is explosive, going to a love fest (positive infinity) or a war (negative infinity).

Consider the first of (8.3), the equation for the prey. The first term, aN, is analogous to the term aR, which we encountered in the Romeo and Juliet model. Here the model is stating that the prey's population at time t changes as a function of its current population. Often a is the birth rate of the population or the survival rate (births minus deaths). The second term in this equation, bNP, models the interaction between the prey and the predator. The minus sign indicates that the prey population is decreased by contact with the predator population. The choice of a simple product, NP, as the predator-prey interaction function is based on the assumption that contact between the two species happens at a rate proportional to the population of each species. The parameter b is, in some sense, the rate at which contact with a predator is fatal to the prey.

Notice that in the absence of the predator term, we have simply $dN/dt = aN$, where a is a positive number. Population numbers can never be negative, so the term aN is always positive, and the prey population increases without bound in the absence of the predator. This isn't entirely realistic, because eventually the carrying capacity of the environment must come into play. We can presume for the moment, however, that predator activity ensures that the carrying capacity of the environment is never reached.

The second equation of (8.3) is similar to the first one. The first term, again, depends only on the species' current population, whereas the second term models the interaction between the two species. The main difference between the first and second equations is in the signs. In the second equation, there is a minus sign in front of the first term, cP, and a plus sign in front of the interaction term, eNP. The assumption here is that interaction with the prey will increase the size of the predator population, while at the same time the predator population cannot sustain itself in the absence of interaction with the prey.

Before we begin analyzing this model, it is useful to try and reduce the number of parameters. We introduce here the technique of nondimensionalization, which reduces the number of parameters and highlights how different parameters can affect the solution in the same way. There are often several different ways to nondimensionalize. When this reduction has taken place (see appendix 8.5), the equations are left with just one significant parameter called α:

$$\frac{du}{dt} = u(1 - \alpha v), \quad \text{the prey equation}$$

$$(8.4)$$

$$\frac{dv}{dt} = v(u - \alpha), \quad \text{the predator equation.}$$

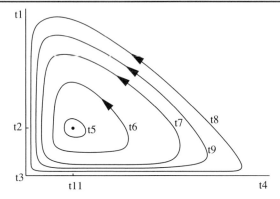

Figure 8.2: Schematic of closed phase space solutions
for the predator-prey Lotka-Volterra system. The point
at the center of the circular trajectories is the steady state
$(u, v) = (\alpha, 1/\alpha)$. Note the bunching of stable trajectories
near the axes. Initial conditions u_0 and v_0 determine the
trajectory, and because the solution trajectories are closed
curves, they imply periodic behavior.

The prey and predator populations N and P, have become the nondimensional populations u and v, respectively.

The null clines of this model are found by solving

$$
\begin{aligned}
f(u, v) &= u(1 - \alpha v) = 0 \\
g(u, v) &= v(u - \alpha) = 0
\end{aligned}
\tag{8.5}
$$

simultaneously. The solutions are four straight lines, $u = 0$ (the v-
axis), $v = 0$ (the u-axis), $u = \alpha$ (a vertical line), and $v = 1/\alpha$ (a
horizontal line). The steady-state intersections, where $f = g = 0$, occur
at $(u, v) = (0, 0)$ and at $(u, v) = (\alpha, 1/\alpha)$. If we graph the force field
in the $u - v$ phase plane, we obtain the solution trajectories shown
in figure 8.2. As with the Romeo and Juliet model, we find that the
$(u, v) = (\alpha, 1/\alpha)$ steady state is neutrally stable, and the model predicts
endless periodic oscillations about this steady state. The $(u, v) = (0, 0)$
steady state is unstable because none of the solution trajectories are
directed toward it.

Let us examine the cyclicity inherent in figure 8.2, beginning at a
point along the bottom edge (near the u-axis). When the prey population increases, the predator population also increases, until eventually
the predators wind up eating so many of the prey that their numbers

begin to decrease (upper right side of the triangular trjectories). Eventually, the predators eat too many of the prey, and then food becomes scarce, so the predator population drops (points near the v-axis), which allows the prey population to increase again, making more food available, so that the predator population may increase. Intuitively this process is why the two populations are cyclic over time. Depending on where we started the process (the "initial conditions"), we are on one or another of the curves shown in the $u - v$ phase space (figure 8.2). Figure 8.3 typical temporal behavior of each species. It can be noted in this figure that increases in the prey population (peaks in the prey curve) precede increases in the predator population (peaks in the predator curve), which is in line with our intuitive explanation above.

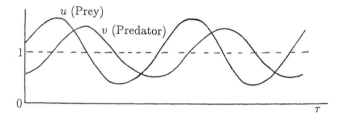

Figure 8.3: Schematic solutions of (8.4) for the predator, $v(t)$, and prey, $u(t)$, as functions of time. Note how the prey wave precedes the predator wave, in line with intuition.

Equations (8.4) can actually be rearranged to give a solvable relation between u and v. By dividing the two equations, we eliminate time and obtain the single differential equation:

$$\frac{dv}{du} = \frac{v(u - \alpha)}{u(1 - \alpha v)} \tag{8.6}$$

This equation is reasonably straightforward to integrate (that is, it has a first integral), yielding the solution equation

$$\alpha u + v - \ln(u^{\alpha} v) = H, \quad \text{a constant,} \tag{8.7}$$

where "ln" is the natural logarithm. This equation can be plotted in the $u - v$ plane and gives the periodic solution curves in figure 8.2, agreeing with our force field sketch.

If we examine figure 8.2 closely, we can see that to the left of the stable steady state (near the v-axis) the lines bunch closely together, whereas way out in the middle of the quadrant, where u and v are both large and positive, these same lines are quite spread out. Thus, if the system happens to be near the origin on one periodic cycle, a tiny perturbation can bump the system onto another periodic cycle many curves different. Close to the origin, the difference between the original and new periodic cycles is difficult to distinguish, but farther away from the origin, the difference becomes marked. These periodic solution trajectories are thus highly unstable, because a small change can have drastic effects. Murray (1993) explains: "This is a problem with any system which has a first integral, like [(8.7)], which is a closed trajectory in the phase plane. They are called *conservative systems;* here [(8.7)] is the associated "conservation law." They are usually of little use as models for real interacting populations" (p. 65, italics in original).

What we need is a model with a single stable periodic solution trajectory. Such a solution is termed a *limit cycle,* so called because any small perturbation dies out, and the solution returns to the limit cycle. Small disturbances cause only temporary changes in behavior. Although the limit cycle solution is periodic, it is a *stable* periodic solution.

Our predator-prey model can be improved along these lines by introducing a logistic term (logistic growth was introduced in chapter 5) for the growth or decline of each species and by putting a limit on predation, as follows:

$$\frac{dN}{dt} = N\left[r\left(1-\frac{N}{K}\right)\right] - N\left[\frac{cP}{(N+d)}\right],$$

$$\frac{dP}{dt} = P\left[e\left(1-f\frac{P}{N}\right)\right],\tag{8.8}$$

where r, K, c, d, e, and f are constants. Comparing (8.8) with (8.3), we see first that the aN term in (8.3) has been replaced with $N[r(1-N/K)]$. So now instead of having a constant survival rate a, we have a rate $r(1-N/K)$ which tends to zero as N approaches some limiting population density K. Thus, K is the carrying capacity of the environment for the prey. Similarly, the term bNP has been replaced with $N[cP/(N+d)]$. Now, instead of a constant damage rate b owing to contact with predators, we have a rate $c/(N+d)$, which goes to zero as the prey population increases and tends to some finite value as the prey population decreases. This process reflects the fact that predators can eat only so many prey, so their damage rate must go down as the prey population becomes overly plentiful.

The second equation of (8.8) is like a simple logistic equation for the predator, but with the carrying capacity directly proportional to the available prey; that is, the carrying capacity is N/f. Whatever the prey population is, if the predator population approaches N/f, then dP/dt approaches zero.

With these equations, we can get limit-cycle behavior, or the steady states will be stable to small perturbations, in the sense that perturbations soon die out. The behavior depends crucially on the parameters. This model is analyzed in detail in Murray (1993).

8.3 Competition Models

In competition models, two species compete for the same finite food source. Hence, each species inhibits the other's growth. Usually it is the case in nature that when two species compete for the same food source, one of the species eventually becomes extinct, the so-called *principle of competitive exclusion.* In species-competition equations, we write a symmetry that is very different from that in predator-prey models. We can start with realistic equations, which include logistic growth, and generalize the idea of *carrying capacity* to include two competing species. Our model is thus

$$\frac{dN_1}{dt} = r_1 N_1 \left[1 - \frac{N_1}{K_1} - b_{12} \frac{N_2}{K_1} \right],$$

$$\frac{dN_2}{dt} = r_2 N_2 \left[1 - \frac{N_2}{K_2} - b_{21} \frac{N_1}{K_2} \right],$$

(8.9)

where N_1 is the first species and N_2 is the second species.

Let's take a bit of time and examine equations (8.9). Notice first that they are symmetrical. Each species N_i has a carrying capacity K_i, and contact with the other species reduces the growth rate. The latter is a consequence of the minus sign in front of each interaction term ($-b_{12}\frac{N_2}{K_1}$ and $-b_{21}\frac{N_1}{K_2}$). Note that we generally have $b_{12} \neq b_{21}$, $r_1 \neq r_2$, and $K_1 \neq K_2$. This competition model is not a conservative system like the Lotka-Volterra predator-prey system.

If we nondimensionalize by writing $u_1 = N_1/K_1$, $u_2 = N_2/K_2$, $\tau = r_1 t$, $\rho = r_2/r_1$, $a_{12} = b_{12}K_2/K_1$, and $a_{21} = b_{21}K_1/K_2$, the resulting system of equations is:

$$\frac{du_1}{d\tau} = u_1(1 - u_1 - a_{12}u_2) = f_1(u_1, u_2),$$

$$\frac{du_2}{d\tau} = \rho u_2(1 - u_2 - a_{21}u_1) = f_2(u_1, u_2),$$

(8.10)

which have only three parameters instead of the original six. The null clines are given by

$$f_1(u_1, u_2) = 0, \quad f_2(u_1, u_2) = 0, \tag{8.11}$$

and they intersect at the steady states of the system. Solving (8.11), we find that the null clines are four straight lines in the $u_1 - u_2$ phase plane: $u_1 = 0$ (the u_2-axis), $u_2 = 0$ (the u_1-axis), $1 - u_1 - a_{12}u_2 = 0$, and $1 - u_2 - a_{21}u_1 = 0$. The number of intersection points in the realistic region $u_1 > 0$, $u_2 > 0$, depends on the parameter values a_{12} and a_{21}. In all cases, there are two intersection points, one on each axis, at $(0, 1)$ and $(1, 0)$. At $(0, 1)$, species 1 has become extinct, but species 2 survives. At $(1, 0)$, exactly the opposite situation exists. If a_{12} and a_{21} are appropriately valued, then there also exists a steady state at a point (u_1^*, u_2^*), where both species can coexist.

Figure 8.4 summarizes the possible outcomes of the competition system. In the first case, $a_{12} < 1$ and $a_{21} < 1$, and the positive steady state (u_1^*, u_2^*) exists. Analysis shows that the steady states on the axes are unstable, and the positive steady state is stable. Thus, in this case, both species can coexist.

All three steady states also exist in the second case, where now a_{12} and a_{21} are both larger than 1. This time, the two steady states on the axes are stable, but the positive steady state (u_1^*, u_2^*) is unstable. Thus, the system will end up either at the $(1, 0)$ or at the $(0, 1)$ steady state. The outcome depends on the initial starting point. It turns out that we can draw a curve called a *separatrix*, which divides the phase plane into starting points that will end up at $(1, 0)$ (region I in figure 8.4[b]), and starting points that will end up at $(0, 1)$ region II in figure 8.4[b]). Going back to our three-dimensional analogy, the separatrix is a flat ridge between the two neighboring valleys, which bottom out at $(1, 0)$ and $(0, 1)$. The point (u_1^*, u_2^*) is called a *saddle point* and it is unstable to small perturbations (see appendix 8.5 for a description and discussion). For these parameter values, then, the two species cannot coexist.

In the third and fourth cases, one of a_{12} and a_{21} is larger than 1, and the other is less than 1. The result is that the positive steady state (u_1^*, u_2^*) no longer exists, and coexistence of the two species is impossible. In the third case, no matter where we start, species 2 becomes extinct, and in the fourth case, no matter where we start, species 1 becomes extinct.

In summary, we can see from figure 8.4 that coexistence of two competing species is the exception rather than the rule.

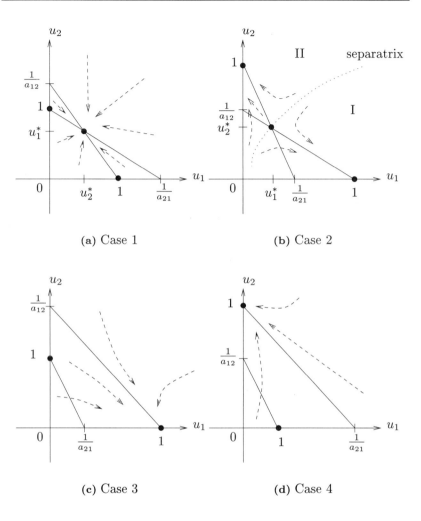

(a) Case 1   (b) Case 2

(c) Case 3   (d) Case 4

Figure 8.4: Phase space plots of the possible outcomes of competition. The axes and the two other straight lines drawn in each graph are the null clines. The heavy dots indicate the steady states. (a) Case 1: A stable steady state exists in which both species can survive. (b) Case 2: Depending on the location of the starting values with respect to the separatrix, either one or the other species will survive. (c) Case 3: No matter where u_1 and u_2 begin, only species 1 will survive. (d) Case 4: No matter where u_1 and u_2 begin, only species 2 will survive.

8.4   Cooperation Models

There are many examples in nature where the interaction of two species benefits the survival of both species. This beneficial interaction is the meaning of the term *cooperation*. Successful marriages ought to be more closely modeled by cooperation than by competition scenarios. Plants and the pollinators or dispersers of seeds are examples of mutually beneficial species.

Cooperation models look very much like the competition models except for the sign in front of the interaction terms. This time, because interaction is beneficial, we have a plus sign in front of each interaction term. Going straight to the nondimensionalized form, which is familiar from section 8.3, we have the cooperation model equations:

$$\frac{du_1}{d\tau} = u_1(1 - u_1 + a_{12}u_2) = f_1(u_1, u_2),$$

$$(8.12)$$

$$\frac{du_2}{d\tau} = \rho u_2(1 - u_2 + a_{21}u_1) = f_2(u_1, u_2).$$

The null clines are still straight lines in the $u_1 - u_2$ plane, with two of the null clines being coincident with the u_1-axis and u_2-axis. These lines intersect at the steady states $(1, 0)$, $(0, 1)$ and, for certain parameter values, at (u_1^*, u_2^*), where u_1^* and u_2^* are both positive.

It can be shown (Murray, 1993, p. 84) that in the event that $a_{12}a_{21} > 1$, unbounded growth occurs for both species (figure 8.5[a]). There is no positive steady state (u_1^*, u_2^*), and the other two steady states are unstable. If, on the other hand, $a_{12}a_{21} < 1$, all trajectories in phase space tend toward the positive steady state (u_1^*, u_2^*) (figure 8.5[b]). Note that at the positive steady state both species have assumed a population value greater than 1 (recall that the units have all be nondimensionalized at this point). The value of 1 is special, because that is the maximum possible population size (the carrying capacity) for each species in the absence of interaction with the other cooperating species. With the presence of cooperation, however, this model shows that the two species can coexist each at a higher population density than would be possible otherwise. Thus, an obvious benefit results from cooperation.

8.5   Chapter Summary

In this chapter, we introduced the idea of modeling the interaction of two elements using more than one equation, either linear or nonlinear. Fortunately, we had a long tradition on which to draw. We reviewed four different types of models. First, we looked at a linear example based on

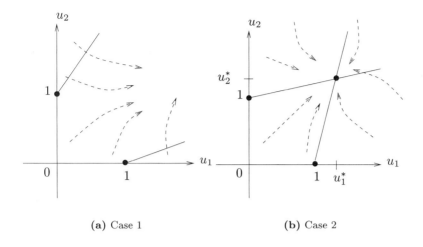

(a) Case 1   **(b)** Case 2

Figure 8.5: Phase trajectories for the cooperation model.
(a) Case 1: Unbounded growth in both species. (b) Case 2:
Positive steady state that exceeds the carrying capacities
of both species.

the interaction of two lovers, which gave unrealistic solutions. Then we
looked at three nonlinear models: the predator-prey model, which represents a situation where winners and losers are changing places; the
competition model, which generally represents a win-lose situation; and
the cooperation model, which has at least one outcome that improves
the lot for both species. These problems were a vehicle for us to explore many basic concepts in nonlinear dynamic modeling, including
phase space, null clines, and the basis for determining whether a steady
state is stable or unstable using a linearization of the equations near the
steady states (see appendix 8.5). We also introduced the idea of nondimensionalization. Murray (1993) discusses these concepts pedagogically
and presents many other examples.

Appendix 8.1: Nonlinear Modeling Concepts

Nondimensionalizing the Lotka-Volterra Equations

We carry out an analogous procedure to that for the budworm problem in appendix 6.5. Let:

$$u = \frac{eN}{a}, \quad v = \frac{bP}{c}, \quad t^* = at, \quad \alpha = \frac{c}{a}. \tag{A8.1}$$

Now the quantities u, v, t^*, and α are dimensionless. To see this, in the first equation of ((8.3), for example, dN/dt has dimensions population/time, as must each term on the right. So a has dimension 1/time, and b has dimension 1/[time $\times$ population]. Then, omitting the asterisks for notational simplicity, the equations become:

$$\frac{du}{dt} = u(1 - \alpha v), \quad \text{the prey equation}$$

$$\frac{dv}{dt} = v(u - \alpha), \quad \text{the predator equation.} \tag{A8.2}$$

Determining the Stability of Steady States

In many nonlinear equations, to determine the system's behavior around the steady state it is necessary to linearize the equations around this state. In our case, around the steady state of $(0,0)$, if x and y are small perturbations around zero, the linearized form of the equations from (A8.2) become:

$$\frac{dx}{dt} = x,$$

$$\frac{dy}{dt} = -\alpha y. \tag{A8.3}$$

Here we can solve the equations immediately because they are uncoupled. The solutions are

$$x(t) = x_0 e^t, \quad y(t) = y_0 e^{-\alpha t}, \tag{A8.4}$$

where x_0 and y_0 are initial values at $t = 0$. Because $x(t)$ grows exponentially, the steady state $(0,0)$ is unstable. A systematic way to examine such systems of equations is called *phase plane analysis* (see appendix ??). We now carry out this type of analysis.

In matrix form, equations (A8.3) become

$$
\begin{pmatrix} \dfrac{dx}{dt} \\[2mm] \dfrac{dy}{dt} \end{pmatrix} = \begin{pmatrix} 1 & 0 \\ 0 & -\alpha \end{pmatrix} \begin{pmatrix} x \\ y \end{pmatrix} = A \begin{pmatrix} x \\ y \end{pmatrix}. \tag{A8.5}
$$

This matrix has eigenvalues λ given by the characteristic equation: $\det\,(A - \lambda I) = 0$, where I is the identity matrix, and "det" is the determinant. This equation reduces to the following in the predator-prey model:

$$
|A - \lambda I| = \begin{vmatrix} 1 - \lambda & 0 \\ 0 & -\alpha - \lambda \end{vmatrix} = 0,
$$

which implies that $\lambda_1 = 1$, and $\lambda_2 = -\alpha$.

Because at least one eigenvalue, λ_1, is greater than zero, $x(\tau)$ and $y(\tau)$ grow exponentially. Therefore, $u = 0$ and $v = 0$ is a linearly unstable steady state. Because $\lambda_1 > 0$ and $\lambda_2 < 0$, this is a *saddle point* singularity.

Linearizing about the point $u = 1$, $v = 1$ results in a characteristic polynomial

$$
|A - \lambda I| = \begin{vmatrix} -\lambda & -1 \\ \alpha & -\lambda \end{vmatrix} = 0,
$$

which implies that $\lambda_1, \lambda_2 = \pm i\sqrt{\alpha}$.

In this case, the solutions in the neighborhood of the steady state $(1,1)$ are periodic with period $2\pi/\sqrt{\alpha}$, which in dimensional terms is $T = 2\pi\sqrt{(a/d)}$. The period depends strongly on natural growth and death rates. In general, if the real part of the eigenvalues is positive, the steady state is unstable, but if the real part of the eigenvalues is negative, the steady state is stable. If the real part is zero, the state is called neutral stability. If the imaginary part of λ is not zero, we have oscillatory behavior, because the solutions for the perturbations have terms $e^{(\mathrm{Re}\,\lambda \pm i\mathrm{Im}\,\lambda)t}$. Here it is $e^{i\sqrt{\alpha}t}$. This eigenvalue method is exactly equivalent to looking for solutions of (A8.3) in terms of exponential functions.

General Linearization around a Steady State

Suppose that our initial nondimensionalized equations are derivatives with respect to a transformed time, τ, and $du/d\tau$ and $dv/d\tau$ are denoted by u' and v' respectively:

$$u' = f(u, v),$$
$$v' = g(u, v).$$

(A8.6)

If we have a steady state (u^*, v^*), then the perturbations are defined as:

$$x(\tau) = u(\tau) - u^*,$$
$$y(\tau) = v(\tau) - v^*.$$

(A8.7)

Then, using a Taylor's series for x and y small, we obtain the linearization:

$$x' = f_u x + f_v y,$$
$$y' = g_u x + g_v y,$$

(A8.8)

where $f_u = df/du$ is evaluated at the steady state (u^*, v^*) and similarly for f_v, g_u and g_v.

In matrix form, this is:

$$\begin{pmatrix} x' \\ y' \end{pmatrix} = \begin{pmatrix} f_u & f_v \\ g_u & g_v \end{pmatrix} \begin{pmatrix} x \\ y \end{pmatrix} = A \begin{pmatrix} x \\ y \end{pmatrix}$$

(A8.9)

which implies that the characteristic polynomial is $\det(A - \lambda I) = 0$; that is,

$$\begin{vmatrix} f_u - \lambda & f_v \\ g_u & g_u - \lambda \end{vmatrix} = 0,$$

(A8.10)

which gives

$$\lambda^2 - \lambda(f_u + g_v) + (f_u g_v - f_v g_u) = 0,$$
$$\lambda^2 - \lambda(\operatorname{tr} A) + (\det A) = 0,$$

(A8.11)

where $\operatorname{tr} A$ is the trace of A (sum of its diagonal terms), and $\det A$ is the determinant of A evaluated at (u^*, v^*). We can solve for λ to get

$$\lambda = \left(\frac{1}{2}\right) \operatorname{tr} A \pm \sqrt{[(\operatorname{tr} A)^2 - 4 \det A]}$$

(A8.12)

The steady state (u^*, v^*) is stable if $\operatorname{Re} \lambda$ (the real part of λ) < 0, because the solutions of (A8.8) are given by solutions involving $e^{\lambda t}$. From (A8.10) we see that $\operatorname{Re} \lambda < 0$ if $\operatorname{tr} A < 0$ and if $\det A > 0$, because in this case λ has a negative real part. If $4 \det A > (\operatorname{tr} A)^2$, λ has an imaginary part $\operatorname{Im} \lambda \neq 0$, which implies oscillations in the perturbations about the steady state. Phase plane analysis is very powerful: see appendix 7.1.

9

Writing the Equations of Marriage

This chapter describes the process we went through in first developing the equations of marriage. Our initial dilemma was that we knew of no existing mathematical theory of marital interaction over time. This lack was in contrast to the existence of the models shown in the previous chapters. For these models, the quantities being modeled are quantitatively measurable: birth rates, immigration rates, death rates, etc. In psychology, it is more difficult to define an entity to measure, or perhaps we don't know how to measure it. For example, how do we quantitatively measure an individual's resistance to change?

We decided that we would focus on the situation created in our laboratory when a couple engages in discussion of an area of conflict in the marriage. Initially, the variable we used to drive the model consisted of the positive minus negative behaviors at each turn of speech during the conversation, using the Rapid Couples Interaction Scoring System (RCISS). As previously noted (section 2.4), we had found that the slopes of the cumulative point graphs of this variable predicted marital dissolution or stability. We referred to this variable as the Gottman-Levenson variable. Later in our work, this variable was replaced by an analogous variable constructed from our Specific Affect Coding System (SPAFF) by assigning positive and negative weights to the individual codes and by summing over a six-second period, which is the average length of a turn of speech. In this chapter, we discuss the modeling work based on the RCISS data.

Having decided on a measurable quantity to model, we began by creating qualitative, theoretical expressions for behavioral change over the course of a marital interaction. Based on years of marriage research,

Gottman used his intuitive understanding of the behavior of couples during conflict to create graphs of behavior and response to that behavior. Note that no numerical data was used at this point in the modeling process.

The next step was to move from our qualitative, graphical expressions to the formulation of equations, one for the husband and one for the wife. When writing down deterministic equations, one makes specific statements about behaviors and reactions to those behaviors, with no room for ambiguity. The equations we wrote expressed a theory describing how each person influenced his/her own and his/her spouse's subsequent behavior. At this point we had a model with parameters that had to be estimated.

We had at our disposal many files of behavioral observations of conflict discussions between couples in our marital interaction laboratory. This data we used to estimate the parameter values of the model. We then used statistical analyses to see if the parameter estimates significantly predicted outcome data for that couple e.g., if they stayed married or if they divorced, or what their marital satisfaction was at some point subsequent to the conflict discussion.

This approach is fundamentally different from another commonly used approach, which involves finding the curve that best fits the data and then considering that curve as "theory." We instead used the data to estimate parameter values of the *hypothesized* curve, which was developed *first* from our intuitive understanding of the system. Our approach yielded a model that had real meaning instead of a curve with no theory behind it. The test of how "good" the model was came from its ability to predict longitudinal outcomes in each marriage.

Why would one wish to pursue this kind of mathematical modeling at all? The answer is that it can provide two new things. First, we will see that the modeling provides a new language for thinking about marital interaction and change over time; and, second, once we have the equations for a couple, we can simulate the couple's behavior in circumstances other than those that generated the data. The second point is critical: no other approach allows us to do this. We can then do precise experiments to test whether these simulations are valid. In this manner, we build and test a theory using the modeling process. We show how this works when we discuss our modeling in the context of the *marriage experiments*.

The model presented in this chapter attempts to explain how the sequence of Gottman-Levenson scores is obtained. For the present, we have confined ourselves to a deterministic model, which means we regard any score as being fully determined by the recent history of the interaction and not by chance. That is, we seek to understand interactions as if individual behavior were based purely on predefined reactions to and interpretations of recent actions (one's own and one's partner's). This assumption may not be completely true, but it may be true enough that the results of the model suggest underlying patterns governing the way any particular couple interacts when trying to resolve conflict. We have also restricted cause and effect to the most recent two scores only. Because evolution of the behavior variable occurs in discrete chunks of time (turns at speech), we allow our time variable to have only integer values. Thus, we arrive at a discrete model to describe the individual's level of positivity in each turn at speech. The analysis of discrete models proceeds in much the same way as the analysis of continuous models outlined in chapters 7 and 8.

Our model building strategy follows the philosophy of Murray (1989). In this book, Murray has constructed fairly simple nonlinear models for complex biological problems. The strategy of model construction is first to propose equations that are good but simple representations of the underlying science. Subsequently, the models are extended and refined by other factors. Hence, we begin simply in modeling marital interaction. Later, we expect to extend our equations, for example, by suggesting that some of our parameters may not actually be fixed constants, but may vary with other variables in the experiment.

In section 9.1, we present the model formulas, and in section 9.2, we describe the methods for estimation of model parameters. In the subsequent sections, we discuss the mathematical behavior of the model. Detailed mathematical analyses can be found in the appendices at the end of this chapter.

9.1 The Model

The assumption that each person's score is determined solely by his/her own and his/her partner's immediately previous score suggests a particular class of mathematical models. If we denote W_t and H_t as the wife's and husband's behavior scores respectively at turn t, then the sequence of scores is given by an alternating pair of coupled difference equations:

$$W_{t+1} = f(W_t, H_t),$$
$$H_{t+1} = g(W_{t+1}, H_t).$$
(9.1)

Note that time is now discrete, taking values 1, 2, 3, etc. The functions f and g remain to be determined. The asymmetry in the indices is owing to the fact that we are assuming, without loss of generality, that the wife speaks first. We therefore label the turns of speech W_1, H_1, W_2, H_2, and so on.

To select a reasonable f and g, we make some simplifying assumptions. First, we assume that the past two scores contribute separately and that the effects can be added together. Hence, a person's score is regarded as the sum of two components: (1) interpersonal influence from spouse to spouse, termed influenced behavior, and (2) the individual's own dynamics, termed uninfluenced behavior. Influenced behavior depends on each individual's previous score only, and uninfluenced behavior depends on the score for the partner's last turn of speech.indexinfluenced behavior

The dismantling of the Gottman-Levenson variable into influenced and uninfluenced behavior represents our theory that the behavior variable consists of multiple components, each of which has an effect on the stability of the marriage. We are building a theory of the mechanisms that explain the power of this variable to predict the longitudinal course of marriage.

Uninfluenced Behavior

We first consider the uninfluenced component of behavior or the behavior one would exhibit if not influenced by one's partner. It seems reasonable to assume that some people would tend to be more negative when left to themselves, whereas others would naturally be more positive in the same situation. This "baseline temperament" we term the individual's uninfluenced set point or uninfluenced steady state. We suppose that each individual would eventually approach that set point after some time regardless of how happy or how sad the person was made by a previous interaction. The simplest way to model the sequence of uninfluenced scores is to assume that uninfluenced behavior can be modeled by the simple linear relationship

$$P_{t+1} = r_i P_t + a \ . \tag{9.2}$$

The variable P_t is the Gottman-Levenson variable score at turn t, r_i determines the rate at which the individual returns to the uninfluenced set point, and a is a constant specific to the individual. The constant r_i is analogous to the parameters a and c in the Romeo and Juliet model (equations (8.1)). Henceforth, we refer to the constant r_i as the emotional inertia or inertia parameter.

Based on the existing research on marital interaction, the *emotional inertia* positive or negative) of each spouse, which is each person's tendency to remain in the same emotional state for a period of time, is very important. The greater the emotional inertia, the more likely the person is to stay in the same state for a longer period of time. In marital interaction research, it has been consistently found that the reciprocation of negativity is more characteristic of unhappy couples than of happy couples. This finding has held cross-nationally as well as within the United States (for a review, see Gottman, 1994). Surprisingly, the tendency to reciprocate positive affect is also greater in unhappy than in happy couples (see Gottman, 1979). There is generally more time linkage or temporal structure in the interaction of distressed marriages and families. Another way of stating this finding is that there is more new information in every behavior in well-functioning family systems. The system is also more flexible because it is less time locked.

The *uninfluenced set point* is the steady state of the single equation (9.2). In chapter 7, we saw that the steady state of a differential equation is found by setting the derivative equal to zero which is equivalent to setting the change in the variable to zero. Here, time is discrete, so we do not have a derivative. But the change in our Gottman-Levenson variable is identifiable and is given by $P_{t+1} - P_t$. It is this quantity then that we wish to set to zero. Doing so, we set $P_{t+1} = P_t = P$ in (9.2) and solve for P. A little algebra gives us

$$P = a/(1 - r_i) . \tag{9.3}$$

We think of the uninfluenced set point as being the emotional state (and baggage) that each spouse brings into the interaction, before being influenced by his or her partner. Clearly this uninfluenced set point may be a function of the past history of the couple's interactions. It may also be a function of individual characteristics of each spouse, such as a tendency to dysphoria or optimism.

It turns out that we can also solve equation (9.2) exactly (see appendix 9.5) to get the solution

$$P_t = r_i^t P_0 + \frac{a(1 - r_i^t)}{1 - r_i}, \tag{9.4}$$

where P_0 is the starting P_t at $t = 0$. From equation (9.4), we can see that the behavior of the solutions P_t is governed by the value of r_i. If $|r_i| > 1$ then $|r_i|^t$ keeps growing which means that $|P_1| > |P_0|$, $|P_2| > |P_1|$, and so on, and P_t grows unboundedly. In this case, the system is not approaching a steady state, so the steady state is unstable. If instead $|r_i| < 1$, then $|r_i|^t$ tends to zero, and so does $|r_i|^t P_0$. Thus, P_t tends to $P = a/(1 - r_i)$, which is our steady state. In this case, the system tends toward the steady state regardless of the starting value P_0, so the steady state is stable.

Clearly we require the natural uninfluenced steady state to be stable, so we are interested only in the case in which the absolute value of r_i is less than 1.0. The magnitude of r_i determines how quickly the uninfluenced state is reached from some other state or how easily a person changes his or her frame of mind, hence the use of the word inertia.

Influenced Behavior

To determine the mathematical form of the *influence functions*, which describe the influenced component of behavior, we begin by sketching qualitative graphs. On the horizontal axis is the range of values of the behavior variable (positive minus negative at a turn of speech) for one spouse, and on the vertical axis is the average value of the influence of the one spouse on the other. It is crucial to note here that the influence functions represent averages across the whole interaction. We discuss later how influence is measured.

Because a "marital influence function" had never before been defined, we were free to choose any function that seemed reasonable. Using qualitative information about how a couple interacts, we settled on two basic functional forms, which we called the bilinear and ojive functions, both illustrated in figure 9.1.

There are only two assumptions built into the bilinear function, illustrated in figure 9.1(a). First, positive/negative behaviors have positive/negative influence. Second, the relationship is linear with a constant slope in each half of the graph. In other words, the more negative the behavior variable, the more negative the influence, and the more positive the behavior variable, the more positive the influence (reminiscent of Alexander's defensive/supportive cycle, e.g., Alexander, 1973). Thus, behavior and its influence can become arbitrarily large and positive or large and negative. Also, linearity implies that every behavior, no matter how small in positivity/negativity, has influence.

The assumptions that led to the ojive function figure 9.1(b) are a little different. First, behaviors are assumed to have thresholding properties. As before, positive behaviors have positive influence, and negative behaviors have negative influence, but there is a limit to the amount of positivity and negativity. Positive/negative behaviors by one spouse Below or above a certain threshold (T_+ and T_- in figure 9.1(b)) have a constant intermediate positive/negative influence on the other spouse. Behaviors by one spouse above the positive threshold and below the negative threshold have a constant large influence on the other spouse.

The parameters of these influence functions (e.g., the point at which the spouse's negativity starts having an effect) might vary as a function of the nature of the marriage, the cultures of the spouses, their marital satisfaction, the level of stress the spouses were under at the time, and so on. For example, a more reactive spouse has a lower positive threshold of response. These ideas can be specified at a later time to improve the model's generality, interest, and predictive ability.

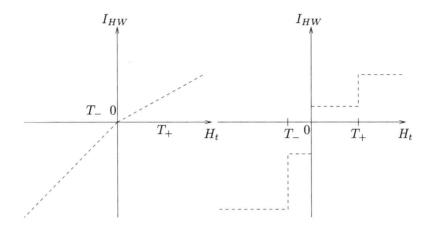

(a) The bilinear influence function

(b) The ojive influence function

Figure 9.1: Two forms of the influence function depicting the husband's influence on his wife: figure 9.1(b) the ojive influence function and figure 9.1(a) the bilinear influence function. On the horizontal axis, we have H_t, the husband's score at time t, and on the vertical axis we have I_{HW}, the husband's influence on his wife. Both influence functions have been drawn with asymmetry depicting the pervasive research finding that negativity has a greater impact than positivity. Thus, the left half of the ojive influence function is more negative than the right half is positive, and the left half of the bilinear function has a steeper slope than does the right half.

We can also be guided by the research literature in the selection of a theoretical shape for the influence functions. For example, one finding that has been fairly pervasive in the observational study of marital interaction is that negative affect by a marital partner has a greater impact on the spouse than positive affect. Thus, we would expect the influence functions to be somewhat asymmetric, as shown in figure 9.1.

We denote the influence functions by $I_{AB}(A_t)$, the influence of person A's state at turn t on person B's state at turn $t + 1$. This gives us

$$B_{t+1} = I_{AB}(A_t) \tag{9.5}$$

for the influenced component of behavior. In order to obtain values for
the influence function, averages are plotted across the entire interaction.
In this book we discuss both the bilinear and ojive functions we mentioned earlier. We find these functions are sufficient to make relevant
practical conclusions. The model can be made more complex later, once
that is shown to be necessary.

The Full Equations

With these assumptions, the complete model is:

$$W_{t+1} = I_{HW}(H_t) + r_1 W_t + a,$$

$$H_{t+1} = I_{WH}(W_{t+1}) + r_2 H_t + b. \tag{9.6}$$

Again, the asymmetry in the indices is owing to the fact that we are
using RCISS codes, where each increment in t represents a new turn of
speech, and we are arbitrarily assuming that the wife speaks first. For
most couples, this assumption is accurate.

9.2   Estimating of Parameters and Fitting the Influence Functions

The problem now facing us is estimation of our four parameters for the
uninfluenced component of the model, r_1, a, r_2, and b, and estimation of
the parameters for the two unknown influence functions, I_{HW} and I_{WH}.
We haven't listed any parameters for the functions I_{HW} and I_{WH}, but
as we sketch the influence functions, certain parameters emerge. Notice
in figure 9.1(a) that the *slopes* for the both the left half and the right half
of the influence function are important parameters for the bilinear form.
In the case of the ojive function (figure 9.1(b)), we have two parameters
indicating the heights of each part of the ojive. We have additional
parameters, the *thresholds of positivity and negativity*, denoted by T_+
and T_-. These thresholds represent how negative the husband has to
get before he starts having an impact on his wife (T_-) and how positive
he has to get before he starts having a positive impact on his wife (T_+).
In the process of modeling, two threshold parameters and four influence
parameters are obtained for each spouse.

Uninfluenced Behavior Parameters

To isolate and estimate the uninfluenced behavior we look only at pairs
of scores for one person for which the intervening score of his or her
partner was zero (about 15% of the data). By assumption, $I_{HW}(0) = 0$

and $I_{WH}(0) = 0$, so each equation (9.6) collapses to an equation of type (9.2), and we can use least squares on this subset of the data to estimate the two unknown constants for each person—that is, r_1, r_2, a, and b^1. Note that we can now compute the uninfluenced steady states from equation (9.3):

$$
\begin{aligned}
W_{\text{uninfluenced steady state}} &= \frac{a}{1 - r_1}, \\
H_{\text{uninfluenced steady state}} &= \frac{b}{1 - r_2}.
\end{aligned}
\tag{9.7}
$$

Influenced Behavior Parameters

Once we have estimated the uninfluenced component of each score, we can subtract it from the full score to find the observed influenced component. That is, following from equations (9.6), we obtain

$$
\begin{aligned}
I_{HW}(H_t) &= W_{t+1} - (r_1 W_t + a), \\
I_{WH}(W_{t+1}) &= H_{t+1} - (r_2 H_t + b).
\end{aligned}
\tag{9.8}
$$

For each value of the husband's score during the conversation, there is likely to be a range of observed values of the influence on his wife owing to noise in the data. Thus, if we plot his influence against his scores, we obtain a scatter plot of his influence function. If we have selected an analytical form for the influence function—e.g., bilinear or ojive as shown in figure 9.1— then we can use a fitting procedure to determine the influence function parameters of the plot that best fits his data.

9.3   Finding the Null Clines and the Influenced Set Points

In our model analysis, it is important to find the steady states of the phase plane, which we call the *influenced set points* for the marriage model. In terms of the experiment, we can think of the influenced set

---

[1]Note that if these zero points (where one of the spouses has a zero score) were rare for either spouse, it would be hard to obtain accurate estimates for the model parameters since the confidence intervals around these parameters would be large. While it seems like a strong assumption, the assumption that zero scores have zero influence is arbitrary. We could assume nonzero influences, make these additional parameters, and estimate these parameters as well. In fact, an asymmetry in these parameters would be theoretically interesting in characterizing a couple's interaction. In the interest of parsimony, we picked zero for these parameters.

point as a sequence of two scores (one for each partner) that is repeated
ad infinitum; if such a steady state is stable, then the sequences of scores
will approach that pair over time. It will also be interesting to examine
the difference between influenced and uninfluenced set points. We expect
that the influenced set point will be more positive than the uninfluenced
set point in marriages that are stable and happy.

Just as with the continuous functions in chapter 7 and chapter 8, we
find the steady states of our discrete model by plotting the null clines.
Again, just as with equation (9.2), our model equations (9.6) do not
contain any derivatives that we can set to zero. Instead, we set

$$
\begin{aligned}
W_{t+1} = W_t = W, \\
H_{t+1} = H_t = H,
\end{aligned}
\tag{9.9}
$$

forcing W_t and H_t to stay constant. Simple algebra in which we substitute W for all the wife terms and H for all the husband terms in the
first of equations (9.6) gives us:

$$
\begin{aligned}
W &= r_1 W + a + I_{HW}(H), \quad \text{or} \\
(1 - r_1)W &= I_{HW}(H) + a, \quad \text{or} \\
W &= \frac{(I_{HW}(H) + a)}{(1 - r_1)}.
\end{aligned}
\tag{9.10}
$$

Because we know the influence functions I and the parameter values,
this expression defines a curve in the (W, H) plane, along which W_t is
unvarying. The same procedure may be carried out with the second of
equations (9.6) to define a curve in the (W, H) plane, along which H_t is
unvarying. Together these curves give us

$$
\begin{aligned}
N_{HW}(H_t): \quad W(H_t) = \frac{[I_{HW}(H_t) + a]}{(1 - r_1)}, \\
N_{WH}(W_t): \quad H(W_t) = \frac{[I_{WH}(W_t) + b]}{(1 - r_2)},
\end{aligned}
\tag{9.11}
$$

where N_{HW} and N_{WH} are the null clines for the wife and husband
respectively (in chapter 8 we used the names f and g to denote the null
clines).

Note that each of the two right-hand sides in equations (9.11) contains an influence function that is shifted by a constant amount, (a or
b) and stretched by a constant amount, $((1 - r_1)$ or $(1 - r_2))$. In other
words, we have shown that *the null clines have the same shape as the
influence functions, they are moved up or down (translated) by a constant, and they are scaled (stretched) by another constant.* Null clines

play an important role in mathematical analysis because they give a visual indication of the dynamics of the system.

9.4 Steady States and Stability

We can now find the steady states by looking for points where the two null clines intersect, just as we did for the continuous functions in chapter 8. The pair of equations (9.11) define curves that can be graphed. If these two curves are plotted on the same graph, any point where they intersect gives a solution pair (H_t, W_t) that satisfies both equations and is a steady state. We call these steady states the *influenced set points* of the model.

The null clines for each couple are plotted in the $H_t - W_t$ phase plane—that is, the plane with the husband's and the wife's scores as coordinates. In figure 9.2(a) are plotted the null clines (9.11) for the bilinear influence function case, and in figure 9.2(b) we have the ojive influence function case. It can be seen that, as expected, the null clines in figure 9.2(a) look like the bilinear influence function stretched and shifted, and the null clines in figure 9.2(b) look like the ojive influence function also stretched and shifted.

Recall that the *null clines* are the curves in the phase plane for which the values of the Gottman-Levenson variable stay constant. Hence, a point in this plane is a pair representing the husband's and wife's scores for a particular interact (a two-turn unit). As time progresses, this point moves and charts a trajectory in phase space. These trajectories always move away from any unstable steady states and toward any stable steady states that exist in that phase space. Figure 9.3 illustrates consecutive points in time approaching a stable steady state. If the couple were later perturbed away from this steady state, they would be drawn back to it. A perturbation could be any random error or small change in behavior owing to factors that we can't measure. The "theoretical conversation" illustrated in figure 9.3 is constructed by simply applying equations (9.6) iteratively from some initial pair of scores. The potential existence of multiple stable steady states, each with its own basin of attraction, has practical implications. The model suggests that the final outcome (positive or negative trend) of a conversation depends critically on the opening scores of each partner.

Using the general formulation for the linearization of two nonlinear differential equations around a steady state, Cook *et al.* (1995) showed that, for the ojive influence function, the steady states alternate in being stable and unstable. A full description of how to determine the stability for the discrete marriage model equations is given in appendix 9.5. This

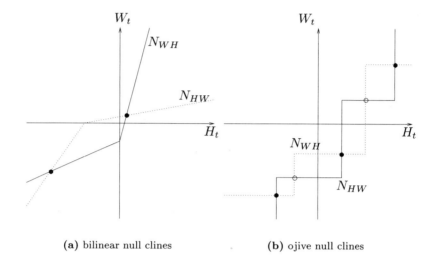

(a) bilinear null clines   (b) ojive null clines

Figure 9.2: Sketch of the possible configurations of the marriage model null clines using the figure 9.2(a) the bilinear form and figure 9.2(b) the form of the influence functions in equations 9.11. Notice that none of the null clines drawn pass through the origin, whereas the influence functions, by definition, do (figure 9.1). So the null cline for the husband (dotted line) is the husband's influence function on his wife moved to the left and stretched, and the null cline for the wife (solid line) is the wife's influence function on her husband moved down and stretched. The gray dots are the stable steady states, and the white dots denote unstable steady states. In the bilinear case (figure 9.2(a)), there are two steady states and both are stable. In the ojive case (figure 9.2(b)), there are five steady states, and three are stable. The stable steady states we call the influenced set points of the marriage model.

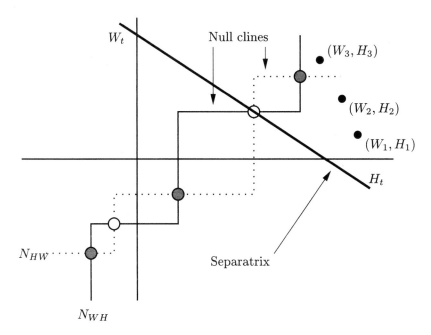

Figure 9.3: Null clines and a typical sequence of theoretical RCISS scores in the case of three steady states. The solid null cline is the husband's influence on the wife, and the dotted null cline is the wife's influence on the husband. Stable steady states and unstable steady states appear as gray and white circles respectively. A possible sequence of scores (small black dots) is shown approaching the positive steady state in the upper right on the graph. Each point corresponds to a consecutive pair of scores (W_t, H_t). Each stable steady states has a basin of attraction consisting of points starting from which a sequence of theoretical RCISS scores will approach that steady state. The separatrix, which is the curve separating the basins of attraction, is shown as a solid line. Pairs of scores above the separatrix will approach the upper-right-hand steady state, as shown. Pairs of scores below the separatrix (and above the separatrix which marks the boundary between the basins of attraction for the other two steady states - not shown) will approach the middle steady state. The long-term behavior of the sequence is therefore dependent upon the basin of attraction in which the initial pair of scores lies.

analysis shows that, in order for the steady state to be stable, there is a dialectic between the amount of influence each spouse should have on his or her partner and the level of emotional inertia in each spouse's uninfluenced behavior. Steady states tend to be stable when each person has a lower level of influence and a lower level of inertia. Another way of saying this is that if a marriage is going to have high levels of mutual influence, there needs to be lowered inertia in order for the steady states to be stable.

The situations drawn in figure 9.2 illustrate the maximum possible number of steady states for each type of influence function. For any given couple, the number of steady states can be the number shown or less. In our data, we have found that there usually is just one steady state for each couple, which means that the basin of attraction for this steady state is the entire phase plane. Consequently, no matter what the initial scores are, the sequence approaches this one steady state. If, on the other hand, there are two stable steady states, generally the plane will be divided into two regions (the basins of attraction). If the scores start in the basins of attraction of the first stable steady state, then, in time the sequence of scores will approach that steady state. The same goes for the second steady state and its basin of attraction.

For couples with just one steady state, the final pattern of behaviors will always be positive if their steady state is positive, or negative if their steady state is negative. Unhappy couples with a single negative steady state cannot hope to end up in a positive pattern of interaction unless something can be done to change their interactional dynamics enough so that their influence functions change and create a steady state in the positive region of behavior.

In contrast, high-inertia, high-influence couples, who are more likely to have multiple steady states, might potentially exhibit a positive conversation on one day and yet not be able to resolve conflict on another. The only difference might be the way the conversation began (their initial RCISS scores). The influence functions and uninfluenced parameters would be identical on each day. One of the interesting implications of the mathematical model is that even in the best of marriages *it is possible that there will be both a positive and a negative stable steady state.* In other words, depending entirely on starting values, there will be times that the couple will be drawn toward a very negative interaction. This may not happen very often in a satisfying and stable marriage, but the model predicts that *it might happen.* To some extent, these events are minimized if the strength of the negative steady state (or "attractor") is much smaller than the strength of the positive steady state. See appendix 9.5 for a detailed treatment of the strength of attraction.

This discussion makes concrete the general systems theory notion of first-order (or more superficial, surface structure) change and second-order (or more meaningful, deeper structure) change. In our model, first-order change means that the steady states may change but not the influence functions; second-order change would imply a change in the influence functions as well. The latter can come about only through fundamental change in the way a given couple interacts, possibly following counseling.

9.5   The Marriage Model and Catastrophes

Figure 9.4 illustrates what can happen to the influenced steady states when a parameter of the model is gradually changed. By way of example, we changed the parameter b, making it increasingly more negative, which moved the solid line to the left. This change corresponds to a negative shift in the husband's uninfluenced steady state. For a while, as the solid line was moved to the left, all three steady states, S_1, S_2, and S_3, continued to exist, though in slightly altered positions (figure 9.4(a)). Note what happened however, after a critical threshold was passed. Suddenly (figure 9.4(b)), when the husband's uninfluenced steady state became sufficiently negative, the marital system lost its only positive influenced steady state, S_1. Now, no matter where on the basin of attraction the spouses start their conversation, they will be inexorably drawn to one of the negative stable steady states, S_2 or S_3. That is all that is left to them in phase space!

Thus, all of the couple's conflict resolution discussions will degenerate into very adversive and highly negative experiences. Gottman (1994) found that when this degeneration happens, the couple enters a cascading series of behaviors that result in increased flooding, increased diffuse physiological arousal, increased arrangement of parallel lives (so that they interact less), and increased loneliness and vulnerability to other relationships. Here we see a model for a very gradual trend during which the couple often thinks that they are simply adapting to increasing stresses in their lives, getting used to seeing less of each other and fighting more often, but fully expecting that things will get better eventually. However, they are vulnerable to losing their positive stable influenced steady states, after which the model predicts marital catastrophe. After gradual drift, the marriage could change suddenly and become a qualitatively and entirely different relationship. Although the model predicts this sudden change, it also predicts hysteresis, so that this state of affairs ought to be reversible, at least within the short time span of the fifteen-minute conversation. Everyday experience suggests that once the marriage has been neglected for too long, reversibility is

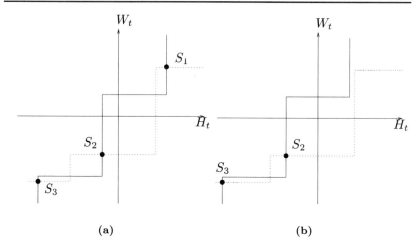

Figure 9.4: The curves in this figure illustrate how a steady state can be lost through a shift in one of the influence functions. The null clines of figure 9.4(a) illustrate a possible configuration for a couple. The couple has three stable steady states, S_1, S_2, and S_3, with one of them, S_1, being positive. The solid line is the husband's influence function, and the dotted line is the wife's influence function. In figure 9.4(b), the husband's influence function has been shifted to the left because his uninfluenced set point has become more negative. Now the couple has only two stable steady states, and both of them are negative. The positive steady state S_1 has disappeared altogether. Once this catastrophe occurs, no matter where the couple starts in phase space, their interaction will drift to the negative influenced steady state. A similar catastrophe could have occurred if instead the wife's uninfluenced steady state had become more negative. Positive catastrophes are also possible (a honeymoon phase).

probably no longer possible.

As we noted earlier, Notarius and Buongiorno (1992) reported that the average wait time for couples to obtain professional help for their marriage after they have noticed serious marital problems is approximately six years. This problem of "delay" in seeking help for an ailing marriage is one of the great mysteries in this field of inquiry. It may very well be related to another great mystery, which is the nearly universal "relapse phenomenon" in marital therapy. Some of our best scholars (e.g., Jacobson and Addis, 1993) have contended that marital therapy has relapse rates so high that the entire enterprise may be in a state of crisis. Consistent with these conclusions, the recent Consumer Reports study of psychotherapy (Seligman, 1995) also reported that marital therapy received the lowest marks from psychotherapy consumers. Marital therapy may be at an impasse because it is not based on a process model derived from longitudinal studies of what real couples do that predicts whether their marriages will be happy and stable, or unhappy and stable, or end in divorce.

Considering the long delay before a couple gets help, it makes some sense to propose that a positive hysteresis journey may be less likely than a negative one. Also, some key life transitions may make going back to a more positive state less likely. This is particularly true for the transition to parenthood. Half of all the divorces occur in the first seven years of marriage, and a great deal of stress is associated with the transition to parenthood. There are other vulnerable transition points for marriages in the life course. The low point cross-nationally for marital satisfaction is when the first child reaches the age of fourteen, although this phenomenon is not well understood. Retirement is also a delicate transition point. If these speculations are true, the model will have to be altered to accommodate these asymmetrical phenomena.

It does seem likely that there is something like a second law of thermodynamics for marital relationships, that things fall apart unless energy is supplied to keep the relationship alive and well. At this time in the history of Western civilization, marriages seem more likely to fall apart than to stay together. Hence, the hysteresis property of the model may turn out to be incorrect. However, our recent research with long-term first marriages (Carstensen, Gottman and Levenson, 1995) paints a far more optimistic picture, one that suggests that some marriages mellow with age and get better and better.

It should be pointed out that the model is designed to obtain parameters from a fifteen-minute interaction, and one useful way of extending the model is to attempt to model two sequential interactions, in which the parameters of the second interaction are affected by the first interaction. What is very interesting about the catastrophic aspects of the model is that it does tend to fit a great deal of our experience, in which we have observed that many marriages suddenly fall apart, often after having successfully endured a period of high stress.

Appendix 9.1: The Inertia Parameter

The single discrete equation for uninfluenced behavior is (9.2), namely

$$P_{t+1} = r_i P_t + a.$$

If P_0 is the starting state at $t = 0$, we have

$$P_1 = r_i P_0 + a,$$

$$P_2 = r_i P_1 + a = r_i[r_i P_0 + a] + a = r_i^2 P_0 + a(1 + r_i),$$

$$P_3 = r_i P_2 + a = \ldots = r_i^3 P_0 + a(1 + r_i + r_i^2),$$

$$\vdots \qquad\qquad\qquad\qquad\qquad\qquad\qquad\qquad (A9.1)$$

$$P_t = r_i^t P_0 + a(1 + r_i + \ldots + r_i^{t-1})$$

$$= r_i^t P_0 + \frac{a(1 - r_i^t)}{1 - r_i}.$$

We get the summation of the r_i series as follows. Let

$$S_t = 1 + r_i + r_i^2 + \ldots + r_i^{t-1},$$

so

$$r_i S_t = r_i + r_i^2 + \ldots + r_i^{t-1} + r_i^t,$$

which on subtracting gives

$$(1 - r_i)S_t = 1 - r_i^t.$$

We thus see that if $r_i > 1$, P_t will increase with each time step because of $r_i^t P_0$, whereas if $1 > r_i$ (and > -1), $r_i^t P_0$ tends to zero as t increases.

Appendix 9.2: Stability of the Steady States (Marriage Model)

We start with the marriage model equations (9.6). If the steady state is (W_S, H_S), then imagine a small perturbation (w_t, h_t) from it. That is,

$$W_t = W_S + w_t,$$
$$H_t = H_S + h_t,$$
$$(A9.2)$$

where w_t and h_t are small.

Substituting these equations into the equations (9.6), expanding in a Taylor series, and retaining only linear terms, we obtain:

$$W_{t+1} = W_S + w_{t+1} = I_{HW}(H_S + h_t) + r_1(W_S + w_t) + a$$
$$\approx I_{HW}(H_S) + h_t I'_{HW}(H_S) + r_1 W_S + r_1 w_t + a,$$
$$(A9.3)$$

where $I'_{HW}(H_S)$ is the $dI_{HW}(H_t)/dH_t$ evaluated at the steady state H_S and similarly for $I'_{HW}(H_S)$. But $I_{HW}(H_S) + r_1 W_S + a = W_S$ by definition of the steady W_S, H_S, so the last equation becomes

$$w_{t+1} = r_1 w_t + I'_{HW}(H_S) h_t. \qquad (A9.4)$$

With the husband's equation, we can show in a similar way that

$$h_{t+1} = I'_{WH}(W_S) w_{t+1} + r_2 h_t,$$

which, on using (A9.4) for w_{t+1}, gives

$$h_{t+1} = r_1 I'_{WH}(W_S) w_t + [r_2 + I'_{WH}(W_S) I'_{HW}(H_S)] h_t. \qquad (A9.5)$$

Equations (A9.4) and (A9.5) are two linear coupled difference equations for the perturbations w_t and h_t, which in matrix form are written as

$$\begin{bmatrix} w_{t+1} \\ h_{t+1} \end{bmatrix} = \begin{bmatrix} r_1 & I'_{HW}(H_S) \\ r_1 I'_{WH}(W_S) r_2 + I'_{WH}(W_S) I'_{HW}(H_S) \end{bmatrix} \begin{bmatrix} w_t \\ h_t \end{bmatrix} = M \begin{bmatrix} w_t \\ h_t \end{bmatrix},$$
$$(A9.6)$$

where M, defined by (A9.6), is called the stability matrix.

The standard way to find solutions of (A9.6) is to look for them in the form

$$\left. \begin{array}{c} w_t \\ h_t \end{array} \right\} \propto \lambda^t \qquad (A9.7)$$

and determine the λ. Because the system is second order (two equations), there will in general be two λs. Stability is then obtained if the magnitude of both λs (which can be positive or negative) is less than 1, because then the perturbation solutions of the form (A9.7) tend to zero at t increases.

Substituting (A9.7) into (A9.6) requires the λ to be solutions of the determinant

$$\begin{vmatrix} r_1 - \lambda & I'_{HW}(H_S) \\ r_1 I'_{WH}(W_S)r_2 + I'_{WH}(W_S)I'_{HW}(H_S) - \lambda \end{vmatrix} = 0. \qquad (A9.8)$$

This gives

$$\lambda^2 - (r_1 + r_2 + I'_{WH}I'_{HW})\lambda + r_1 r_2 = 0,$$

and so the λs are

$$\lambda_1, \lambda_2 = \frac{1}{2}\left[(r_1 + r_2 + I'_{WH}I'_{HW}) \pm \{(r_1 + r_2 + I'_{WH}I'_{HW})^2 - 4r_1 r_2\}^{\frac{1}{2}}\right].$$
$$(A9.9)$$

The solutions for the perturbations w_t and h_t are then given in matrix form by

$$\begin{bmatrix} w_t \\ h_t \end{bmatrix} = \mathbf{A}\lambda_1^t + \mathbf{B}\lambda_2^t,$$

where $\mathbf{A}$, $\mathbf{B}$ are constant column matrices. If the magnitude of λ_1 or λ_2, denoted by $|\lambda_1|$ and $|\lambda_2|$, is greater than 1, then w_t and h_t will grow with each increase in t. Stability then requires

$$-1 < \lambda_1 < 1 \quad \text{and} \quad -1 < \lambda_2 < 1 \qquad (A9.10)$$

because both w_t and h_t tend to zero as t increases. (See also appendix 9.5)

We now substitute the expressions for λ_1 and λ_2 from (A9.9) into (A9.10) to obtain the conditions on r_1, r_2, $I'_{HW}(H_S)$ and $I'_{WH}(W_S)$ for stability of the steady state W_S, H_S. Although we can do this for general r_1 and r_2, there is little point because we know that $0 \leq r_1 < 1$ and $0 \leq r_2 < 1$. If either were greater than 1, there would be no uninfluenced steady state because from (A9.1), it (the P_t) would get infinitely large for t large. So with these practical restrictions dictated by the model (and confirmed by the data), we can restrict the r_1 and r_2 as above.

The stability condition then is given by requiring the square bracket in (A9.9) to be less than 2. A little algebra shows that we must have at the steady state W_S, H_S

$$I'_{WH}(W_S)I'_{HW}(H_S) < (1 - r_1)(1 - r_2), \qquad (A9.11)$$

where $I'_{WH}(W_S) = dI_{WH}(W_t)/dW_t$ evaluated at the steady state W_S, H_S, and similarly for $I'_{HW}(H_S)$. Therefore, if we want to assess the stability of a steady state, we have to evaluate the derivatives of the influence functions and use (A9.11).

In general, we can say that steep influence functions and high inertia, the $r-$ parameters, are destabilizing for a steady state. For example, if each influence function has a slope greater than 1, then the steady state would be unstable irrespective of initial values. This conclusion agrees with our intuitive expectations if we interpret instability as the amplification of small perturbations. Influence is a measure of the effect that one partner has on the other being so large that changes in influence will result in amplification, or mutual instability. On the other hand, even couples with relatively flat (low-derivative) influence functions can have unstable steady states if the inertia of either of the partners is high (close to 1).

Condition (A9.11) can be interpreted graphically. The null clines either intersect as shown in figure 9.2(a) or figure 9.2(b). From equations (9.6), the equations for the null clines are (9.11), namely,

$$N_{HW}: \quad W = \left(\frac{I_{HW}(H) + a}{(1 - r_1)} \right),$$

$$N_{WH}: \quad H = \left(\frac{I_{WH}(W) + b}{(1 - r_2)} \right),$$

(A9.12)

where N_{HW} is the wife's null cline, and N_{WH} is the husband's.

If we now take the derivatives of these equations, respectively, with respect to H and W, we get

$$\left. \frac{dW}{dH} \right|_{\substack{\text{on wife's} \\ \text{null cline, } N_{HW}}} = \frac{I'_{HW}(H)}{1 - r_1}, \quad \left. \frac{dH}{dW} \right|_{\substack{\text{on husband's} \\ \text{null cline, } N_{WH}}} = \frac{I'_{WH}(W)}{1 - r_2}.$$

Thus, the stability condition (A9.11) becomes simply

$$\left[\frac{dH}{dW} \right]_{\substack{\text{on husband's} \\ \text{null cline, } N_{WH}, \\ \textbf{at } W_S, H_S}} \times \left[\frac{dW}{dH} \right]_{\substack{\text{on wife's} \\ \text{null cline, } N_{HW}, \\ \textbf{at } W_S, H_S}} < 1.$$

With the axes chosen, namely, W the vertical axis and H the horizontal one, the last expression guaranteeing stability can be written as

$$\left[\frac{dW}{dH} \right]_{\substack{\text{on wife's} \\ \text{null cline, } N_{HW}, \\ \textbf{at } W_S, H_S}} < \left[\frac{dW}{dH} \right]_{\substack{\text{on husband's} \\ \text{null cline, } N_{WH}, \\ \textbf{at } W_S, H_S}}$$

(A9.13)

That is, the product of the gradients at a steady state must be less than 1. So all we need to do is evaluate the gradients, and stability or instability is immediately obtained at each steady state. Let us now consider some examples using the null clines and steady states in figure 9.2 and figure 9.3.

Consider first figure 9.2 and the positive steady state. By inspection, the gradient on the wife's null cline is less than 1, as it is on the husband's null cline. On the husband's null cline remember the gradient in (A9.13) is dH/dW, which is also clearly less than 1. So the condition (A9.13) is satisfied, and the positive steady state is therefore stable. On the other hand, the negative steady state may or may not be stable; it clearly depends on whether or not (A9.13) is satisfied, which depends on the actual gradients of the null clines and the quantitative form of the influence functions.

If we now examine figure 9.3, at the open circle steady states the gradients are infinite, so the stability criterion (A9.13) is violated, and these steady states are unstable. The filled circles have zero gradients for (A9.13), so they are stable. Note how they alternate in stability and instability.

In conclusion, then, under these conditions on inertia $(0 < r_1 < 1, 0 < r_2 < 1)$ we can graphically determine not only the location of the steady states but also their stability. A simple corollary to this null cline intersection rule is that the stable and unstable steady states must alternate—i.e., any two stable steady states are separated by an unstable one and vice versa. If we assume that the influence functions are monotonic increasing functions, then the steady states can be ordered. By this we mean that both the steady-state values, W_S and H_S, will increase as we move from one steady state to the next. If we assume that influence functions saturate, then the highest and lowest steady state's are clearly stable (they must intersect as in figure 9.3): there must be an odd number of steady states that alternate between stable and unstable, and the first and last are stable.

Appendix 9.3: Measuring the Strength of Attraction of a Stable Steady States

In differential equations, the way to measure the strength of a stable steady state is by constructing an energy type of function (a Liapunov function) from the equations, which is not always easy. For difference equation systems, such as we have in the marriage interaction model, there is, as far as we know, no such equivalent. However, in the neighborhood of a stable steady state, we can derive a parameter that provides a comparative basis for the strength of the stable set point attractor.

The marital interaction equations are

$$W_{t+1} = I_{HW}(H_t) + r_1 W_t + a_1, \quad H_{t+1} = I_{WH}(W_{t+1}) + r_2 H_t + a_2.$$
$$(A9.14)$$

A steady state W^*, H^* is given by setting $W_t = W^*$ and $H_t = H^*$ in these equations, and solving for W^* and H^*. Doing that and rearranging the equations for the steady states gives

$$W^* = \frac{I_{HW}(H^*) + a_1}{1 - r_1}, \quad H^* = \frac{I_{WH}(W^*) + a_2}{1 - r_2}. \quad (A9.15)$$

These equations give two curves, called the null clines, in the W^*, H^* plane. The curves are just the influence functions translated by a_1 and a_2, and scaled by $1/(1-r_1)$ and $1/(1-r_2)$, so they look like figure 9.1 but just shifted and stretched as in figure 9.2. With the bilinear forms for the influence functions, there are two stable steady states, whereas for the ojive forms there can be one, three or five steady states. In the case of three steady states, for example, the most positive and the most negative are stable, but the one in between is unstable (see, for example, Cook *et al.* 1995). Where the interaction starts in the W_t, H_t plane determines which steady state the W_t and H_t end up at. There is a curve in the plane that delineates the areas of attraction of each stable steady state: these areas are called the basins of attraction of the steady states.

Each stable steady state is an attractor, and by linearizing about the steady state we can get a measure of the strength of the attractor. So we write

$$W_t = W^* + w_t, \quad H_t = H^* + h_t, \quad (A9.16)$$

where w_t and h_t are small perturbations from a stable steady state. Substituting these equations into the full equations (A9.14) and expanding the I_{HW} and I_{WH} by a Taylor series and keeping only the linear terms, we get the equations for w_t and h_t that we can solve. The linear equations are

$$w_{t+1} = r_1 w_t + h_t A, \quad h_{t+1} = r_2 h_t + w_{t+1} B, \quad (A9.17)$$

where

$$A = \frac{dI_{HW}(H)}{dH} \text{ evaluated at } H^*,$$

$$B = \frac{dI_{WH}(W)}{dW} \text{ evaluated at } W^*.$$

(A9.18)

To solve the linear equations (A9.17) we look for solutions in the form

$$w_t \propto \lambda^t, \quad h_t \propto \lambda^t$$

(A9.19)

and determine the λs. A little algebra shows that the λs satisfy the quadratic equation

$$\lambda^2 - (r_1 + r_2 + AB)\lambda + r_1 r_2 = 0,$$

and so the two λs, λ_1 and λ_2, are given by

$$\lambda_1, \lambda_2 = \frac{1}{2}(1 + r_1 + r_2 + AB) \pm \frac{1}{2}\left[(1 + r_1 + r_2 + AB)^2 - 4r_1 r_2\right]^{1/2}.$$

(A9.20)

The solutions for the perturbations about the steady state are then given by

$$w_t = L\lambda_1^t + M\lambda_2^t, \quad h_t = P\lambda_1^t + Q\lambda_2^t,$$

(A9.21)

where the L, M, P, and Q are constants (like constants of integration).

We can see from these solutions what we mean by stability. As long as the magnitude of λ_1 and λ_2 are less than 1, each successive time step makes w_t and h_t smaller, and after a long time they become negligible. So for stable steady states we know that $-1 < |\lambda_1| < 1$ and $-1 < |\lambda_2| < 1$. From the solution (A9.21), we see that if, for example, the magnitude $|\lambda_2| < |\lambda_1|$, then the $M-$ and $Q-$terms will die out more quickly and after a long time the perturbations will be dominated by the $L-$ and $M-$terms—in other words, the λ_1 contributions. The closer $|\lambda_1|$ is to 1, the more slowly the perturbations die out, and the *weaker* is the attraction of the steady state. So a measure of the strength, S, of the attracting stable steady state is given by

$$S = \frac{1}{\text{minimum of } |\lambda_1| \text{ and } |\lambda_2|}.$$

The larger S is, the stronger the attractor, or, alternatively, the closer S is to zero, the weaker the attractor.

10

Initial Computational Results of Our Modeling

10.1 Power and Affect: Influence Functions

In this section, we examine the results we obtained from analysis of the marriage model presented in chapter 9. The results presented here derive from experiments carried out on couples using the RCISS and MICS observational coding systems, and a turn of speech as the integer time unit. In our study, we ask the general question whether the shape of the influence functions varies qualitatively across types of couples. Here we refer to the marital typology presented in sections 2.3 and 2.4 of chapter 2.

As a way of presenting our results, and as a rough initial approximation to the shape of the influence functions (obtained from the data by least squares fitting), we concentrated on the bilinear two-slope influence function (recall figure 9.1) and computed the slope of the influence function separately for negative and positive values of the partner's behavior. The x-axis represents the range of positivity or negativity in each group.

Figure 10.1 is a summary of the empirically obtained functions for the three stable marriage types (volatile, validating, and conflict avoiding), and figure 10.2 is a summary of the empirically obtained functions for the two unstable marriage types (hostile and hostile-detached). Let us discuss these figures. In figure 10.1, the three right-hand graphs represent the theoretical (average) influence functions for the three low-risk marriages. The validators have an influence function that creates an influence toward negativity in a spouse if the partner's behavior is negative and an influence toward positivity if the partner's behavior

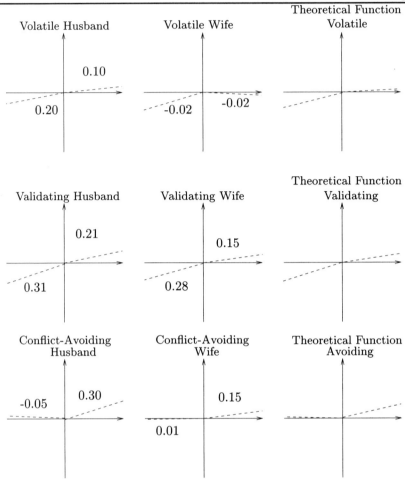

Figure 10.1: Empirically obtained influence functions using the bilinear functional form. These marriage types all fall into the category of low-risk marriages, and it is possible to determine a theoretical influence function for each type of marriage.

is positive. A surprising result was that volatile and conflict-avoider influence functions appear to be, respectively, one-half of the validators' influence functions, with volatiles having the right half of the curve with a slope close to zero, and the conflict avoiders having the left half with a slope near zero.

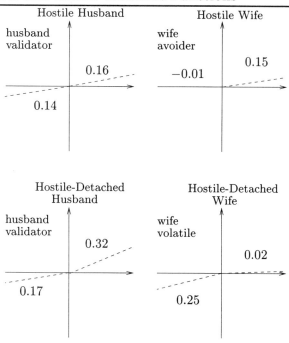

Figure 10.2: Empirically obtained influence functions using the bilinear functional form. These marriage types fall into the category of high-risk marriages. Note that there is a mismatch in slopes for these marriages. For example, in the hostile-detached graphs, the husband has an influence function characteristic of validator husbands, but the wife has an influence function characteristic of avoiding wives. Because of this mismatch, it is not possible to determine theoretical influence functions for these marriage types.

From an examination of the data, we can propose that validating couples were able to influence their spouses with both positive or negative behavior; positive behavior had a positive sloping influence, and negative behavior also had a positive sloping influence. This means that the negative x-axis values had a negative influence, whereas the positive x-axis values had a positive influence. For validators, across the whole range of RCISS point values, the slope of the influence function was a constant, upwardly sloping straight line. The data might have been generated by the process that in validating low-risk marriages there is a uniform slope of the influence function across both positive and negative values: in low-risk marriages, overall negative behavior has a negative influence, and positive behavior has a positive influence. Here we see that a full range of emotional balance is possible in the interaction. However, avoiders and volatile couples were nearly opposite in the shape of their influence functions. Avoiders influenced one another only with positivity (the slope was flat in the negative RCISS point ranges), whereas volatile couples influenced one another primarily with negativity (the slope was flat in the positive RCISS point ranges). The influence function of the avoiding couple is nearly the reverse of that of the volatile couple. This pattern of influence functions will be reflected in great differences in the stable steady states that are likely in each of these marriages.

A second surprise in these data comes from comparing husbands' and wives' influence functions. This observation of matching functions is summarized in the third column in figure 10.1, labeled "theoretical function." One observes that the functions have the same shape within stable couples.

Now examine the influence functions for the hostile and the hostile-detached couples (figure 10.2). It looks as if these data would support a mismatch hypothesis. Hostile couples appear to have mixed a validator husband influence function with an avoider wife influence function, and hostile-detached couples appear to have mixed a validator husband influence function with a volatile wife influence function.[1]

10.2   Mismatch Theory: The Possibility That Unstable Marriages Are the Results of Failed Attempts at Creating a Pure Type

Any theory attempts to subsume phenomena other than those that motivated its design. The very different shape of the influence curves thus led us to propose that the data on marital stability and instability can be organized by the rather simple hypothesis that hostile and hostile-detached couples are simply failures to create a stable adaptation to marriage that is either volatile, validating, or avoiding. In other words, the hypothesis is that the longitudinal marital stability results are an ar-

---

[1]Note that this match/mismatch idea is not the same as the Watzlawick, Beavin, and Jackson (1967, p.67) notion of symmetry versus complementarity, by which they meant interactional mirroring (as in assertive/assertive) versus one partner complimenting the other (as in assertive/submissive). We would expect, based on the typology reported in Gottman (1994), that couples in which the influence functions are mismatched would differ greatly in their desired levels of emotional distance and closeness, and have influence patterns that leave one person feeling overwhelmed and flooded while the other partner feels lonely. Gottman's typology is based extensively on the nature of influence patterns and their concomitants.

tifact of the prior inability of the couple to accommodate to one another and to have one of the three low-risk types of marriage. For example, in the unstable marriage, a person who is more suited to a volatile or a conflict-avoiding marriage may have married one who wishes a validating marriage. Their influence functions are simply mismatched.

These mismatch results are reminscent of a well-known empirical observation in the area of marital interaction, which is called the *demand-withdraw pattern*. In this pattern (e.g., Christensen, 1988; Christensen and Heavey, 1990), one person wishes to pursue the issue and engage in conflict, whereas the other attempts to withdraw and avoid the conflict. We propose the hypothesis that the demand-withdraw pattern is an epiphenomenon of a mismatch between influence functions and that the underlying dynamic is that the two partners prefer different styles of persuasion. The person who feels more comfortable with avoider influence patterns that use only positivity to influence will be uncomfortable with either validator or volatile patterns in which negativity is used to influence. Usually it is the wife who is the demander and the husband who is the withdrawer. These general results are consistent with our findings on criticism being higher in wives and stonewalling being higher in husbands.

Unfortunately, it is easier to propose our mismatch of influence hypothesis than it is to test it. The problem in testing this hypothesis is that the *marital* interaction is a means for classifying couples, as opposed to individual behavior. We also note that, although we have arbitrarily attributed the influence functions to the influencer, it may be that the influenced spouse also plays a part in determining the influence. The result is that the *marriage*—rather than each person's style or preferences—is described as volatile, validating, or avoiding. What is needed to test the mismatch hypothesis is an independent method for classifying each person's conflict resolution style. To begin to test this hypothesis, we computed the difference between husbands and wives on the RCISS positive and negative speaker codes. We argue that if the mismatch hypothesis were true, one would expect that the results of an *analysis of variance* between the groups would show greater discrepancies between husbands and wives for the hostile and hostile-detached group than for the three stable groups, which was indeed the case. The analysis of variance is a statistical procedure commonly used to test the hypothesis that several population means are equal. That is, it is used to test whether the observed differences between groups can be reasonably attributed to chance or whether there is reason to suspect there are true differences between the groups. If the reader is unfamiliar with the analysis of variance and the language associated with it (the F-ratio statistic, degrees of freedom, and the probability p which is the significance level of F), it is suggested they turn to an introductory statistics text in order to better understand the analyses presented in this and subsequent chapters.

We found that pooling the stable groups into one group and the unstable groups into another group, for the positive speaker code, $F(1, 70) = 4.12$, $p < 0.05$ (stable $= -.01$, unstable $= .08$); for the negative speaker code, $F(1, 70) = 10.42$, $p < .01$ (stable $= -.02$, unstable $= -.26$); and for the difference between positive and negative speaker codes, $F(1, 70) = 8.57$, $p < .01$ (stable $= .01$, unstable $= .34$). Thus, it could be that the unstable groups are examples of discrepancies in interactional style between husbands and wives that are reflective of the differences in their preferred types of marital adaptation.

10.3   Set Points and Inertia

Our analysis is incomplete without a discussion of the other parameters of our model for these five groups of couples—namely, inertia as well as influenced and uninfluenced set points. Note that we present no statistical tests here. Our purpose is the qualitative description of the data for generating theory. Recall that by theory we mean a suggested mechanism for the Gottman-Levenson prediction of marital instability.

Table 10.3 summarizes the mean set points (stable steady states) and inertias for the different types of couples. Let us begin by examining the inertia parameter. High-risk couples have higher mean emotional inertia than low-risk couples; the difference is four times greater for wives than for husbands (0.29 versus .07). Wives in high-risk marriages have greater emotional inertia than husbands, but this is not the case in low-risk marriages. Both the influenced and uninfluenced set points are more negative in high-risk compared to low-risk marriages, and this is especially true for wives (although we note again that the influenced set point is an attribute of the couple, not of the individual). The three stable types of couples also differed from each other. Volatile couples had the highest set points, followed by validators and then avoiders. Also, the effect of influence in high-risk marriages is to make the set point more negative, whereas, in general, the reverse is true in low-risk marriages. Perhaps it is the case that volatile couples need to have a very high set point to offset the fact that they influence one another primarily in the negative range of their interaction. The behavior of the wives was quite different from that of the husbands. Wives in low-risk marriages had a set point that was equal to or more positive than husbands. However, wives in hostile marriages had a set point that was more negative than their husbands, but the reverse was true in hostile-detached marriages.

The set points of wives in high-risk marriages was negative, and more negative than the set points of wives in low-risk marriages. Wives in hostile marriages had a more negative set point than wives in hostile-detached marriages.

Table 10.1: Parameter Estimates in the Mathematical Modeling of the RCISS Unaccumulated Point Graphs.

	Husband's Set Point			Wife's Set Point		
Group	Inertia	Uninfl.	Infl.	Inertia	Uninfl.	Infl.
Low-Risk Couples						
Volatile	.33	.68	.75	.20	.68	.61
Validating	.37	.38	.56	.14	.52	.59
Avoiding	.18	.26	.53	.25	.46	.60
AVERAGE	.29	.44	.61	.20	.55	.60
High-Risk Couples						
Hostile	.32	.10	.03	.51	−.64	−.45
Hostile-Detached	.40	−.42	−.50	.46	−.24	−.62
AVERAGE	.36	−.16	−.24	.49	−.44	−.54

Uninfl. = Uninfluenced; Infl. = Influenced

10.4   Validation of the Model Parameters

Table 10.4 summarizes the correlations of the parameters of our model with the low-risk/high-risk classification (shown as "marital type" in the table), the variables of the dissolution cascade, and physical health at Time-2. For example, the correlation between the wife's marital satisfaction at Time-1 and the husband's set point is .36, with a probability $p < 0.05$ that this correlation is actually zero in the population. Table 10.4 continues this summary with correlation of the parameters of our model with the summary behavior observation scales of the MICS and the RCISS, and with positive affect.

For predicting marital dissolution, these results suggest that: (1) the low-risk/high-risk classification (which was the Gottman-Levenson predictor of marital dissolution) was related to the wife's emotional inertia and to both the husband's and wife's uninfluenced set points; and, (2) the emotional inertia parameters are unrelated to the dissolution cascade variables, but both the husband's and the wife's uninfluenced set points are related to the dissolution cascade variables; both the husband's and

Table 10.2: Correlations of Model Parameters with Dissolution Cascade Variables.

	Parameters			
Variables	Husband Inertia	Wife Inertia	Husband Set Point	Wife Set Point
Marital Satisfaction at Time-1				
Husband	.05	−.08	.25	.26*
Wife	−.23	−.07	.36*	.28*
Marital Satisfaction at Time-2				
Husband	−.02	−.21	.31*	.27*
Wife	.00	−.21	.26*	.20
Thoughts of Dissolution				
Husb Considers Divorce	.02	.06	−.28*	−.22
Husb Considers Separation	.10	.06	−.34*	−.19
Husb Health Time-2	−.05	.01	−.31*	−.12
Thoughts of Dissolution				
Wife Considers Divorce	.00	.24	−.20	−.28*
Wife Considers Separation	.02	.24	−.22	−.28*
Wife Health Time-2	−.16	.21	.14	−.31
Dissolution				
Separation	−.07	.01	−.11	−.38**
Divorce	.05	.22	−.32*	−.42***
Marital Type	−.04	−.54***	.40***	.54***

* $p < 0.05$; ** $p < 0.01$; *** $p < 0.001$

wife's set points are significantly predictive of divorce.

We would like to know to what extent uninfluenced set points are independent of partner or independent of conversation; that is, to what extent are they intrinsic to the individual, and to what extent do they describe a cumulative quality of the relationship?

Emotional Inertia With regard to marital interaction, for the MICS codes, the husband's inertia was related to his criticism, whereas the wife's inertia was related to his withdrawal and to her own contempt; for the RCISS codes, the husband's inertia was related to his contempt, and her inertia was related to all the subscales.

Set Points For the MICS coding, the husband's set point variable was related to his criticism, his contempt, and his withdrawal, and to the wife's criticism and withdrawal; for the MICS coding, the wife's set point variable was related to all the variables for both spouses. For the RCISS coding, the husband's set point was related to all of his behavior and to all of the wife's behavior except for criticism; the wife's set point was related to all the husband's codes except for criticism and to all the wife's codes.

Table 10.3: Correlations of Model Parameters with Marital Interaction Behavioral Observation Variables.

	Parameters			
Variables	Husband Inertia	Wife Inertia	Husband Set Point	Wife Set Point
MICS Codes				
Husb Criticism	.37**	.21	−.30*	−.27*
Husb Defensive	.11	.07	−.22	−.28*
Husb Contempt	.01	.31*	−.38	−.31*
Husb Withdrawn	.14	.50**	−.46	−.61***
Wife Criticism	.11	.19	−.25	−.27*
Wife Defensive	.09	.21	−.05	−.38*
Wife Contempt	−.01	.36**	−.15	−.30*
Wife Withdrawn	.19	.19	−.30	−.30*
RCISS Codes				
Husb Criticism	.18	.25*	−.49***	−.24
Husb Defensive	.09	.52***	−.47***	−.46***
Husb Contempt	.26*	.33**	−.74***	−.50***
Husb Withdrawn	−.06	.38**	−.52***	−.55***
Wife Criticism	−.04	.45**	−.23	−.63***
Wife Defensive	.12	.55***	−.30*	−.41***
Wife Contempt	.18	.45***	−.64***	−.63***
Wife Withdrawn	−.08	.31**	−.42***	−.47***
Positive Affect				
Husb Laughter	−.15	−.15	.40***	.13
Wife Laughter	−.08	−.18	.32**	.28*
Husb Smiling	−.01	−.23	.22	.09
Wife Smiling	−.03	−.32*	.26*	.35**

* $p < 0.05$; ** $p < 0.01$; *** $p < 0.001$.

Positive affect Positive affect was coded entirely from facial expressions using the Ekman and Friesen Facial Action Coding System (EMFACS; Ekman and Friesen, 1978). We counted laughter and the occurrence of full smiles, which involve codes of both the mouth and the eyes, which are called "Duchenne" smiles. We observed the following relationships. Wives with more emotional inertia made fewer Duchenne smiles than wives with less emotional inertia. Husband and wife set points were related to fewer Duchenne smiles, but only for wives. On the RCISS, husbands with higher set points laughed more, but wives laughed more when either the husband's or their own set point was higher.

Summary Hence, there is evidence for the validity of the parameters of the mathematical model across different coding systems.

10.5   Discussion of Initial Modeling Results

The purpose of the dynamic mathematical modeling proposed in this book was to generate theory that might explain the ability of the RCISS point graphs to predict the longitudinal course of marriages. We found that the uninfluenced set point, when averaged by group, was enough to accomplish this task. This result alone is interesting, but what is this parameter? Is it what each person brings to the conflict discussion before being influenced? That's how we initially thought of it. However, subsequent attempts at theory construction may profit from making this parameter a function of other dynamic (time-varying) variables in the experiment such as indices of physiological activity. Perhaps the uninfluenced set point represents a cumulative summary of the marriage as well as what each individual brings to each marital conflict discussion. It might be useful to study what other variables (e.g., stress, ability to cope, power differences) are related to this index. How can these two ideas be separated out of the data? In chapter 11 we see that this test is possible, but it requires more data per couple than we have with the RCISS coding system, which is based on the rather large "turn at speech" unit.

On the basis of Time-1 interactive behavior on the RCISS (that is, at the first occasion of measurement), Gottman (1993) described three distinct types of couples who were more likely to have stable marriages and two groups of couples who were more likely to have unstable marriages. In this chapter, we have examined the influence functions for these five groups of couples and suggested that the influence functions might provide insight into the classification. Validating couples seemed to have a pattern of directly proportional influence over the whole range of their interaction; when they were more negative than positive, they had a negative impact on their partner's subsequent behavior, and, conversely, when they were more positive than negative they had a positive impact on their partner's behavior. Conflict-avoiding couples, on the other hand, resembled validating couples, but only in the positive ranges of their behavior. In the negative ranges they had nearly no influence on their spouses. Volatile couples resembled couples headed for marital dissolution in that they had no influence in the positive ranges of their behavior. They also differed from this group of couples only in having a more positive uninfluenced set point.

These results provide insight into the potential costs and benefits of each type of stable marriage. The volatile marriage is clearly a high-risk style. Without the high level of positivity, they may drift to the interactive style of a couple headed for dissolution. The ability to influence one another only in the negative ranges of their behavior may suggest a high level of emphasis on change, influence, and conflict in this marriage. On the other hand, the conflict-avoiding style seems particularly designed for stability without change and conflict. The validating style seems to combine elements of both styles, with an ability to influence one another across the entire range of their interactive behavior.

On the other hand, the marriages headed for dissolution had influence functions that were mismatched. In the hostile marriage, the husband, like a validating husband, influenced his wife in both the positive and the negative ranges, but she, like a conflict avoider, influenced him only by being positive. If we can generalize from validator and avoiding marriages, she is likely to seem quite aloof and detached to him, and he is likely to seem quite negative and excessively conflictual to her. In the hostile-detached marriage, we see another kind of mismatch. The husband again is like a validating husband, influencing his wife in both the positive and the negative ranges, but she, like a wife in a volatile marriage, influenced him only by being negative. If we can generalize from validator and volatile marriages, he is likely to seem quite aloof and detached to her, whereas she is likely to seem quite negative and excessively conflictual to him. These two kinds of mismatches are likely to represent the probable mismatches that might survive courtship; we do not find a volatile style matched to a conflict-avoiding style in our data. Perhaps they are just too different for the relationship to survive, even temporarily.

These results suggest that a mismatch of influence styles in the marriage can be predictive of marital instability. This result is interesting in light of the general failure or weakness of the concepts of "mismatched personality" or "areas of agreement" in predicting dissolution (Fowers and Olson, 1986; Bentler and Newcomb, 1978); it suggests that a study of process may be more profitable in understanding marriage than a study of individual characteristics.

Let us consider what one gains from our approach. As soon as we write down the deterministic model, we already gain a great deal. Instead of empirical curves that predict marital stability or dissolution, we now have a set of concepts that could potentially explain the prediction. We have the parameters of uninfluenced set point, influenced set point, emotional inertia, and the influence functions. We gain a language, one that is precise and mathematical, for talking about the point graphs. Marriages that last have more positive uninfluenced set points. Furthermore, interaction usually moves the uninfluenced set points in more positive directions, except in the case of the volatile marriage, in which the only way anyone influences anyone else is by being negative; in that case, a great deal of positivity is needed to offset this type of influence function. Marriages that last have less emotional inertia; they are more flexible and less predictable; and the people in them are more easily moved by their partners. Depending on the type of marriage the couple has, the nature of their influence on one another is given by the shape of the influence functions. We hypothesize that couples headed for divorce have not yet worked out a common influence pattern and that most of their arguments are about differences in how to argue, about differences in how to express emotion, and about differences in closeness and distance; all these differences are entailed by mismatches in influence functions (see Gottman, 1994a). Of course, we have no way of knowing from our data whether the mismatches in influence functions were there at the start of the marriage or emerged over time. We are currently studying these processes among newlyweds as they make the transition to parenthood.

We submit that the use of these equations as a new methodology for examining an experimental effect and for building theory can help a researcher get at the mechanism for an observed effect, as opposed to a statistical model. A statistical model tells us whether variables are related, but it does not propose a mechanism for understanding this relationship. For example, we may find that socioeconomic status is related to divorce prediction, but we will have no ideas from this fact how this effect may operate as a mechanism to *explain* marital dissolution. The differential/difference equation model approach can suggest a theoretical and mathematical language for such a theory of mechanism. The mathematical model differs fundamentally from the statistical approach in presenting an equation linking a particular husband and wife over time, instead of a representing husbands and wives, aggregated across couples as well as time.

10.6   Prospects for Extending the Model

The use of the ojive influence function may be the next step in developing the model, because the ojive model contains more parameters for describing the nature of the influence, such as threshold parameters. However, to accomplish this next step we need to use an observational system that provides much more data than the RCISS. After several years we have developed such a system. Gottman (1994a) found that his Specific Affect Coding System (SPAFF) was highly correlated with the RCISS speaker slopes, but the advantages of the SPAFF are that the couple's interaction can be coded on-line in real time, without a transcript, and the data can be summarized second by second instead of at each turn of speech; thus, the SPAFF makes it possible to obtain much more data for each couple.

With the ojive influence function, there is the possibility of five steady states (five intersection points for the null clines), three of which are stable.[2] The possible existence of more than one stable steady state for a given couple can be inferred from their data once we have written down the model with their influence functions and parameters. This means that we can describe the couple's behavior even in conditions in which they have not been observed in our study. Thus, the model can be used to *create simulations* of the couple's interaction that go beyond our data.

By varying parameters slightly, we can even make predictions of what might happen to this couple if we were able to change specific aspects of their interaction, which is a sort of quantitative thought experiment of what is possible for this particular couple. We are currently using this approach in a series of specific intervention experiments designed to change a couple's second interaction about a particular issue. The model parameters can be derived from the couple's first interaction in the laboratory, and an intervention designed to change a particular model parameter (whether it changes or not can be assessed). If the parameter is indeed changed when derived from the couple's second postintervention interaction, this change will give us feedback on the accuracy of our theory of the mechanism of change. In this way the model can be tested and expanded by an interplay of modeling and experimentation.

The qualitative assumptions forming the underpinnings of this effort are also laid bare by the process. For example, by postulating a different shape to the influence function, we are expressing a different theory about how the couple interacts. Then, subsequent correlational data can quantitatively test the new theory.

One simple way we might change the equations is to assume that the parameters are not fixed constants but instead functions of other fundamental theoretical variables. There are two central classes of variables we wish to consider. The first class of variables indexes the couple's physiology, and the second class of variables indexes the couple's perception of the interaction derived from our video recall procedure. We expect that physiological measures indicative of diffuse physiological arousal (Gottman, 1990) will relate to less ability to process information, less ability to listen, and greater reliance on behaviors that are more established in the repertoire in upsetting situations (e.g., fight or flight). Hence, it seems reasonable to predict that measures indicative of more diffuse physiological arousal may predict more emotional inertia. Similarly, we expect that a negative perception of the interaction

---

[2]Due to space limitations, we cut an appendix describing linear stability computations, that is, how to discern which steady states are stable or unstable. This appendix is in the original Cook *et al.* (1995) paper.

may go along with feeling flooded by one's partner's negative affect (see Gottman, 1993) and negative attributions (see Fincham, Bradbury, and Scott, 1991). Hence, it seems reasonable to predict that variables related to the video recall rating dial would predict the uninfluenced set point. If someone has an interaction with his spouse that he rates negatively, the next interaction may be characterized by a slightly less positive uninfluenced set point. The uninfluenced set point, to some extent, may index the cumulative effects of the marital balance of positivity over negativity, integrated over time. There is also the possibility that the uninfluenced set point might best be understood by an integration of personality traits with marital interaction patterns.

It is interesting to note that the model is, in some ways, rather grim. Depending on the parameters, the initial conditions determine the eventual slope of the cumulated RCISS curves. Unfortunately, this is essentially true of most of our data. However, another way the model can be developed further is to note that a number of couples began their interaction by starting negatively but then changed the nature of their interaction to a positively sloping cumulative RCISS point graph; their cumulative graph looked somewhat like a check mark. This result was quite rare (characterizing only 3.6% of the sample), but it did characterize approximately 14% of the couples for at least part of their interaction. This more optimistic type of curve suggests adding to the model the possibility of repair of the interaction once it has passed some threshold of negativity. This repair might be incorporated by changing the influence function so that its basic bilinear or ojive shape had the possibility of a repair jolt (or perhaps "repair nudge" would be closer to the data) in the negative parts of the x-axes of figures 10.1 and 10.2. Some strength in the marriage thus might be explored further. We discuss this extension in a subsequent chapter.

11

Who Needs All This Math?

When we analyze the metaphors of general systems theory as applied to the study of couples, we are at first struck by the advances in thought created by these ideas over and above a psychology that focused only on the individual. Previously unquestioned was the idea that some kind of order regarding human behavior, and marriage as well, would emerge from the study of personality traits. When initially approaching the study of marriage, psychologists such as Louis Terman (Terman *et al.*, 1938) began studying the personality of each spouse. They tried to apply ideas from the study of intelligence that led them to search for a general "marriage aptitude," one that would be reflected in an optimal profile of personality suited to marriage. The general systems theories of marriage focused instead on interaction and communication. This change in thinking was a major breakthrough in the study of marriage because it focused not on the individuals, but on the *temporal patterns* they create when they are together, much as one focuses on the harmonies of a jazz quartet.

Further thought, however, reveals some conceptual limitations of general systems theory. Let us consider four conceptual metaphors of general systems theory: homeostasis and feedback, the idea of "family dynamics," disconfirmability, and the idea that the "whole is greater than the sum of its parts."

11.1 Homeostasis and Feedback

Homeostasis was an idea that Von Bertalanffy attributed to the physiologist Walter Cannon. In homeostasis, some physiological quantity is regulated. A good example is body temperature, 98.6 degrees Fahrenheit. The body translates deviations from this fixed quantity into an *error signal*, and if the deviations exceed some fixed amount, a negative feedback loop is activated that restores the body to its target temperature value. The hypothalamus has been found to play a vital role in this process, which behaves very much like a thermostat regulating room temperature.

When applied to the study of interacting systems such as a couple, however, the concept of homeostasis is highly inadequate. It tells you only that the system is regulated, that it has one stable steady state or set point. What is wrong with this concept?

First, the system may have more than one stable steady state. In fact, one or more of these steady states may be entirely dysfunctional for the system, whereas another steady state may be functional. But how can we know how many stable steady states a system has unless we have a mathematical model for the system? In the case of the budworm problem, there were three steady states, and two of them were stable. One was the "refuge" situation, and the other was the "outbreak" situation, so one stable steady state of the system meant essentially death to the spruce trees and another meant survival. We learned from the mathematical model that a state of zero population for the budworm was a solution of the steady-state equations (derivative zero), but an unstable one. Thus, the budworm model gave us a goal for forest management— that is, to employ interventions that maintain the budworm population at refuge size. So, to find multiple or "hidden" steady states of a system we need the mathematics.

Second, there may be unstable steady states that the system will jump over in moving to a stable steady state. These unstable steady states may seem like refuges, but their long-term stability is illusory. In the predator-prey model, for example, there are even cycles of stability in an unstable system. In other systems, the instability can be of the *saddle point* variety, much like the seat of a saddle. Here a slight perturbation will drive a point easily off its apparently stable steady state. These states of affairs are similar to the relapse problem of marital therapy (Jacobson and Addis, 1993). Couples in most interventions make initial gains, but these gains largely erode after a few years. If we *expect* some steady states of the marital system to be unstable, we will not be surprised by the relapse of temporary gains. We can then direct the therapy toward having the couple experience these gains with the realization that they have changed their marriage *only* for a short time. They will then achieve a view of what is possible, with the expectation that it will not necessarily last. So again we need mathematics.

Third, knowing that a homeostatic point exists tells us nothing about the *nature of the regulation*. We have no idea what happens to the marital system once it is perturbed from its steady state. However, the mathematical model does suggest that we can draw a vector field in phase space that gives us the potential flow lines around a steady state. So again we need mathematics.

Fourth, the idea of homeostasis is actually quite static. It does not suggest a dynamic system that is capable of adapting to perturbations and incorporating these perturbations into its motion. For example, in physiology, the cardiovascular system resets such parameters as its cardiac output and fluid volume to new set points when it moves from rest to exercise or from rest to emergency. Different physiological mechanisms are responsible for these dynamic responses, but the cardiovascular system is not just maintaining a particular rate and contractility, independent of such factors as the needs of specific vascular beds in the body during muscular work or fight or flight. The nonlinear difference or differential equations of a realistic model can capture this dynamic adaptiveness. The case of the driven pendulum is one such mechanical example. It is a differential equation of a pendulum's motion, but one in which there is an independent input to the pendulum. Baker and Gollub's (1995) book on chaos theory is based entirely on the model of the driven pendulum and the extremely complex motions it can demonstrate, including chaos. So again we need mathematics.

Fifth, the concept of homeostasis doesn't easily describe the potential existence of sudden, catastrophic change or any other "bifurcations" in which the system has two possible paths it can take, depending on critical threshold values of the parameters. So again we need mathematics.

Finally, in the area of families, the metaphor of homeostasis doesn't provide anything quantitative, so it has remained in the realm of metaphor and literature, and has not ventured into the realm of science. Its use has been based primarily on clinical intuition, not on objective, quantitative assessment. Jackson (1957) discussed the term as follows:

> Family interaction [is] a closed information system in which the variations in output or behavior are fed back in order to correct the system's response (p. 79)

The concept has usually referred to some aspect of the family's or the therapist's perception of something stable in the family. For example, Rosenblatt (1994) wrote:

> Thus, the metaphor of system stability or change through negative or positive feedback obscures how much that is labeled stability or change and negative or positive feedback comes the standards and cognitive/perceptual/-interpretative processes of observers outside the family (pp. 137–138)

Without a solid empirical base, the concept of homeostasis and its allied concept of feedback cannot lead to the construction of an empirically testable theory, one that suggests experiments. Hence, its nonquantitative use has not led anywhere scientifically productive. The model's equations do all of these things. So again we need mathematics.

Modifying an Unfortunate Heritage

The idea of there being only one homeostatic set point for a family has an unfortunate consequence. Wile (1993) first pointed out that one homeostatic set point puts family therapists into an adversarial position against families:

> Practitioners from all major schools of systems theory start with the assumption that they must find some way of dealing with family homeostasis—that is, the tendency of families to maintain their pathological patterns and resist the therapist's constructive efforts. The major disadvantage of the concept of homeostasis is its assumption of an adversary relationship between therapist and family. Individual family members are viewed as active proponents of the family system, willing victims of this system, or both. Since the aim of systems oriented therapy is to challenge the family system, a task that requires disrupting the family's homeostatic balance, these therapists often see their goals as directly opposed to those of the family. ... [There is] the tendency of some to see family members as being duplicitous and manipulative, as using "ploys" (Jackson, 1959) or Eric Berne type games to get what they want. The systems approach thus appears to lead to a picture of the conjoint therapist struggling gallantly against great odds—against concerted family efforts to maintain homeostatic balance, against family forces sabotaging all attempts to change the family system, and against subtle maneuvers and deceits employed by family members. (pp. 28–29)

Wile went on to point out that this adversarial position has led to particular approaches to family therapy:

> Thus Ackerman (1966) deliberately charms, ridicules, and bullies family members; Haley (1963b) and Watzlawick, Weakland, and Fisch (1974) strategically manipulate them with paradoxical instructions; Jackson and Weakland (1961) tactically place them in therapeutic double binds; Haley (1977)

systematically browbeats certain partners who fail to do the tasks he assigns them; Minuchin and his colleagues (1967) "frontally silence" overbearing wives to "rock the system" and show their passive husbands how to stand up to them; Speck (1965) openly engages in "power struggles" with families; Satir (Haley and Hoffman, 1967) forcefully structures the therapeutic session and undercuts all attempts to challenge her control; and Zuk (1968) intentionally sides with one family member against another, challenges the whole family, and does so in inconsistent patterns in order to shake them up, keep them guessing, and "tip the balance in favor of more productive relating." It is perhaps surprising, considering the dramatic nature of these methods, that they have been incorporated into the couples and family therapy traditions with so little discussion and debate. An entrant into the field is often taught his general adversary orientation as if it were the only possible way of doing family and couples therapy. (p. 29)

We believe that these adversarial consequences are an unfortunate result of not actually doing the scientific work of writing real equations, which has led us to an incorrect view of what homeostasis is in family systems. Using the ojive or bilinear models of the influence functions, we see that more than one stable steady state is possible. Suppose it were the case that every family or couple potentially had two steady states, one positive and one negative. This means that every marriage is potentially a living hell or heaven. The goal of therapy could then be to reduce the strength of attraction of the negative steady stable state or to increase the strength of attraction of the negative stable steady state. In this case, the therapist is not in an adversarial position against the family, but aligned with the family in attempting to minimize negativity and maximize positivity.

11.2 Family Dynamics

Family dynamics usually refers to the interaction among the family members, which includes communication of all types—words, expressions, attitudes, expectations, emotions, thoughts—and forces outside the family, such as history, context, and so on. Rosenblatt (1994) wrote:

Family dynamics are most commonly....understood with properties derived from the previous experiences, preferences, and expectations of the individuals who have come together to

form the system. . . .The system can be understood to develop
as family members accommodate their pasts (if any), their
preferences, and their expectations to one another, to each
individual's development, and to myriad contextual forces.
The dynamics of a system must also accommodate major
changes in family context and membership. An important
aspect of family dynamics is understood to be the members'
accommodation to one another's differences, and accommodation that is ongoing as these differences develop and are
expressed. (p. 65)

In our analysis, we also talk about *dynamics*. What we mean by
dynamics, however, is how parts of the system affect the rate of change
in other parts of the system and how they specifically accommodate one
another. Whereas the use of the term *dynamics* in writings about family
from a general systems perspective is very general and vague, our use of
it is very specific. Once again, we need mathematics to make this so.

11.3 Disconfirmability

It is our goal to build a theory of how marriages succeed or fail that is
parsimonious and disconfirmable. It is our faith as scientists that when
we have accomplished this objective, the order inherent in the phenomena we have identified will be revealed. Even if we fail we have the hope
that the process of modeling and returning to the laboratory for new
experiments will reveal the order we believe is already there, waiting to
be discovered. Gregory Bateson was one of the original founders of the
general systems view of families. We contrast our point of view about
precision and disconfirmability with his. He responded to Mishler and
Waxler's (1966) critique of his "double bind" theory of schizophrenia,
in which they referred to an unnecessary "level of ambiguity and im-
precision" in the formulation of the theory. In response to this point,
Bateson (1966) wrote:

The authors have been generous and—so far as this was
possible—have been understanding in their critique of the
"double-bind" theory. They say with some justice that the
phrasings of the theory are sometimes ambiguous. They
might have gone further and said that (like much psychoanalytic theory) the double-bind theory of schizophrenia is
slippery—so slippery that perhaps no imaginable set of empirical facts could contradict it. . . . unfortunately, but necessarily, there is a basic formal truth about all abstract premises,

namely: the more abstract the premise, the more likely it is to be self-validating. (pp. 415–416)

To avoid this intolerable state of affairs, in which empirical findings are of no value and in which the ideas live on in spite of truth, we need mathematics.

11.4   The Whole Is Greater Than the Sum of Its Parts

Watzlawick, Beavin, and Jackson (1967) stated this axiom:

Nonsummativity, then, as a corollary to the notion of wholeness provides a negative guideline for the definition of a system. A system can not be taken for the sum of its parts; indeed, formal analysis or artificially isolated segments would destroy the very object of interest. It is necessary to neglect the parts for the gestalt and attend to the core of its complexity; its organization (p. 125)

This statement seems to describe an attempt to do two things. First, it is the authors' goal to find and describe something quite fundamental in the way the system is organized. Second, they want to show that the organization of parts of the system are inherently nonlinear—that is, nonadditive. We give voice to both goals. First, we have expressed the organization of the marital system in terms of how change comes about from within, through the interactions of it elements. That is, we say that the equations of the system are its organization. Second, our equations are nonlinear because linear equations are generally unstable. Thus, by using mathematics we can extend these goals from metaphors to precise scientific entities.

11.5   The Conceptual Power of the Mathematical Model: A New General Systems Language of Marriage

The model has accomplished a great deal just by dismantling the Gottman-Levenson variable into its components and parameters. Instead of just a variable that predicts the longitudinal course of marriages, we now can speak theoretically about the *mechanism* of this prediction. We can expect that compared to happy, stable marriages, what happens in marriages headed for divorce is that

- there is more emotional inertia;

- even before being influenced, *the uninfluenced set point is more negative*;

- when interaction begins, the couple influences one another to become even more negative rather than more positive;

- over time, as these negative interactions continue and become characteristic of the marriage, the couple may catastrophically lose its positive stable steady state.

We may also discover that the very shape of the influence functions are different for couples heading for divorce, compared to happy, stable couples.

The model has given birth to a *theoretical language about the mechanism of change*. We did not have such a language before the model was successfully constructed. The model provides the language of set point theory, in which a number of quantities, or parameters, may be regulated and protected by the marital interaction. It also provides a precise mechanism for change. The model itself suggests variables that can be targeted for change using interventions. In short, the model leads somewhere. It helps us raise questions, helps us wonder what the parameters may be related to and why. It raises questions of etiology. Why might a couple begin an interaction with a negative uninfluenced set point? Why and how would they then influence one another to be even more negative?

Thus, it is likely that the major contribution of the model will be the theoretical language and the mathematical tools it provides. It will give us a way of thinking about marital interaction that we never had before. Any model that accomplishes these things will be useful.

12

Applying and Modifying the Model to Understand Newlyweds

In this chapter, we describe the modification and application of our modeling to our longitudinal study of newlyweds. We present the results we have obtained with our new behavior data, developed using an on-line observational system, the Specific Affect Coding System (Gottman *et al.*, 1996), called SPAFF. The advantages of the SPAFF (over the older RCISS) are that it codes specific emotional behaviors of husband and wife, and that it can be coded in real time as the couple interact in the laboratory. The SPAFF coding system was designed to be usable for coding *any* marital conversation, whereas the RCISS was designed to code only conflict resolution discussions. The SPAFF also specifically discriminates among the *positive affects*, making fine distinctions between neutral, interest, affection, humor, and validation.

12.1 Developing the SPAFF Coding System

Positive affect models have received scant attention in describing marital interaction. An exception is Birchler, Weiss, and Vincent (1975), who used a self-report diary measure of "pleases" and "displeases," a precursor of the Spouse Observation Checklist, and a version of the Marital Interaction Coding System (MICS) to code both general conversation (when they were supposedly setting up the equipment) and the Inventory of Marital Conflict discussion (IMC, Olson and Ryder, 1970). In the summary MICS code, the positives were agreement, approval, humor, assent, laugh, positive physical contact, and smile. Distressed couples produced an average of 1.49 positives per minute, and nondistressed couples produced an average of 1.93 positives per minute, a significant difference. In the home environment, distressed partners recorded significantly fewer pleasing and significantly greater displeasing events than was the case for nondistressed partners.

Practical Advantages of the SPAFF

The previous RCISS system required a verbatim transcript of the couple's speech, usually taking about ten hours of a transcriber's time, after which it took six hours for an observer to code the conversation from tape and transcript. The unit of analysis for the RCISS was the *interact*, which is two "turns" at speech, one for the wife and one for the husband, and the number of interacts at speech varied a great deal from couple to couple, sometimes being as low as twenty-five turns in fifteen minutes, and at other times closer to eighty turns. The "turn" unit was everything one person said until the other began speaking, ignoring what are called "listener tracking backchannels" (Duncan and Fiske, 1977). These brief vocalizations (e.g., "Uh huh," "Yeah," "I see," and so on) are like eye contact, head nods, and facial movements that tell the speaker that the listener is tracking the conversation. These signals also regulate taking turns at speech.

The transformation from RCISS to SPAFF was a major technical breakthrough in our laboratory. First, it would make it possible to code on-line in real time, instead of waiting sixteen hours to obtain the coded data, and would thus streamline the lab's ability to conduct experiments. We would be able to see the effects of an experiment in the math model immediately after doing the experiment with a particular couple. Second, because of SPAFF's design, which applies universal codes suitable for any marital interaction, it would potentially make it possible to code *any* conversation the couple had, such as talking about the events of the day, talking about an enjoyable topic, or making everyday conversation as they spent twelve hours of videotaped time with no particular instructions at all in our new apartment laboratory. Third, we would be able to obtain a larger number of points per couple, which would move us toward more reliable data within each couple, as well as toward the differential equation form of the math model.

Converting SPAFF to Ordinal Data for the Model

We devised an arbitrary weighting scheme for the SPAFF, based on the differential ability of the specific codes to predict divorce. Thus, for example, the codes of criticism, contempt, belligerence, defensiveness, and stonewalling received more negative weights than codes such as anger and sadness because of their greater ability to predict divorce. Similarly, positive affects such as affection and humor received higher positive weights. The observational coding for the SPAFF was also computer assisted, so that the coding was synchronized with the video time code and the physiological data, as well as later with the couple's subjective recall of their own affects. The computer program that acquired the data sampled the observational coding station multiple times per second, and averaged these data to determine the dominant code for each second. This code received the appropriate weight, and then these weights were summed over 6−second time blocks. We chose 6 seconds because it has become a fairly universally used time block for averaging social interaction data in human interaction across many laboratories and many contexts. For the 900 seconds of the 15−minute conversation, this gave us 150 data points for the husband and for the wife.

12.2   Fitting an Ojive Model to Weighted SPAFF Data

We fit the mathematical model to the weighted time-series data described above, using the ojive form of the influence functions, with least squares fitting for all influence function parameters. An example of the time-series data for one couple is presented as figure 12.1.

Figure 12.2 illustrates the parameters of the ojive influence function. We were most interested in the negative threshold, which is marked F in figure 12.2 because it would tell us the critical level at which a spouse's negativity began having a real impact on the partner. Theoretically, negative threshold can be related to the couple's repair of the relationship on an ongoing basis. Finding differential predictability of a couple's eventual marital status and satisfaction by using their negative threshold parameters could model two problems in the marital therapy field: the twin problems of delay (in getting help through therapy) and relapse (from improvements in the marriage through therapy). Delay would be predicted if couples whose marriages ended in divorce were those who had a higher negative threshold for negative affect. In effect the higher negative threshold would suggest that each partner was better adapted to the spouse's negativity because the spouse had to be more negative to have an impact on the partner. We would then predict that couples with a lower negative threshold were repairing the marriage on an ongoing basis, rather than delaying getting help.

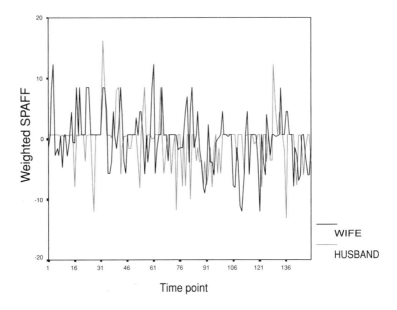

Figure 12.1: Weighted SPAFF time-series data for one couple.

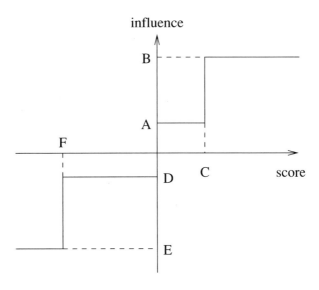

Figure 12.2: Sketch of the ojive influence function.

Negative Threshold and the "Marital Negativity Detector"

The threshold for negativity may be an important dimension of a couple's perception of the relationship. Consider figure 12.2. In this context, we say the threshold is "lower" when parameter F is less negative (i.e., closer to zero) That is, a lower threshold means you are more responsive to a stimulus. Setting the threshold for negativity lower for newlywed marriages that eventually wind up stable and happy could be called the *marital negativity detector effect*. For these spouses, it doesn't take much negativity from their partner to spark a response. In other marriages, people are adapting to and trying to accept negativity, raising their threshold for response to a much higher negative level. It is as if they are saying to themselves, "Just ignore this negativity. Don't respond to it until it gets much worse." It may be that this kind of adaptation to negativity is dysfunctional. It seems likely that having a lower threshold for negativity implies that people discuss issues before they escalate too much. They may follow the biblical principle in Ephesians 4:26, "Do not let the sun go down on your wrath," rather than the practice of the wife in Robert Burns' poem "Tam O' Shanter" who was "nursing her wrath to keep it warm."

A finding that the negative threshold is predictive of marital stability and quality could be important because it might explain the two mysteries we discussed in chapter 2. The first was the fact that people delay a very long time in getting help for an ailing marriage. A finding with the negative threshold parameter would suggest that people delay getting help for their marriage because they have inadvertently raised the negativity threshold. It would suggest that spouses in ailing marriages play a key role in the delay of seeking help by adapting to negativity. In marriages that work, spouses do not adapt to negativity.

The negative threshold effect could also explain the relapse effect in marital therapy. It suggests that relapse occurs because people adapt to increasingly higher levels of negativity, instead of repairing the relationship. Relapse and delay become parts of the same phenomenon—namely, adaptation to increasingly higher levels of negativity. So this finding would suggest that the key to avoiding decay in marriages is probably for the therapy to reset the *marital negativity detector* to a lower level of negativity and to build in some formal mechanisms for the couple to do repair on a continual basis.

12.3   Seattle Newlywed Study

This model application was completed for all the couples in a longitudinal study of newlyweds in Seattle. We now describe this study.

Participants

Between 1989 and 1992, a two-stage sampling procedure was utilized to draw a sample of newlywed couples from the Puget Sound area in Washington. Couples were initially recruited using newspaper advertisements. In order to be eligible to participate in the study, the couples had to meet requirements that it was a first marriage for both partners, that they were married within the six months prior to participating in the study, and that they were childless. Couples were contacted by phone, administered our telephone version of the Marital Adjustment Test (MAT) (Krokoff, 1987; Locke and Wallace, 1959), and surveyed to determine their eligibility on the other subject selection criteria. The MAT measures marital satisfaction. Higher scores on the MAT represent higher marital satisfaction. There were 179 newlywed couples that met the research criteria and participated in the initial survey phase of the study. In the survey phase of the study, both the husbands and wives were separately mailed a set of questionnaires to fill out that included measures of demographic characteristics and indices about their marriage, well-being, and health.

In the second phase of the study, 130 newlywed couples, who represented an even distribution of marital satisfaction, were invited to participate in a marital interaction laboratory session and complete additional questionnaires. These couples fit the demographic characteristics of the major ethnic and racial groups in the greater Seattle area, using the Seattle City Metropolitan Planning Commission Report. The demographic characteristics for these newly married couples were: (a) Wife age, mean or $m = 25.4$ (standard deviation or $sd = 3.5$); (b) Husband age, $m = 26.5$ ($sd = 4.2$); (c) Wife marital satisfaction, $m = 120.4$ ($sd = 19.7$); (d) Husband marital satisfaction, $m = 115.9$ ($sd = 18.4$). As regards the measure of marital satisfaction, newlyweds typically average 120 with a standard deviation of 15. Couples were seen in three yearly cohorts of approximately 40 couples per cohort, and followed through the sixth year of the study, so that the followup period varied from four to six years.

Procedures and Measures

Behavioral Observation Two remotely controlled, high-resolution cameras filmed frontal views of both spouses and their upper torsos during the interaction sessions. The images from the two cameras were combined in a split-screen image through the use of a video special effects generator. VHS video recorders were used to record the behavioral data. Two lavaliere microphones were used to record the couple's audio interactions. The computer synchronized the physiological data with the video data by utilizing the elapse time codes imposed on the video recordings. The SPAFF (Gottman, *et al.* 1996) was used to code the couples' conflict interactions and to index the specific affects expressed during the marital problem resolution session. SPAFF focuses solely on the affects expressed. It draws on facial expression (based on Ekman and Friesen's Facial Action Coding System; Ekman and Friesen, 1978), vocal tone, and speech content to characterize the emotions displayed. Coders categorized the affects displayed using five positive codes (interest, validation, affection, humor, joy), ten negative affect codes (disgust, contempt, belligerence, domineering, anger, fear/tension, defensiveness, whining, sadness, stonewalling), and a neutral affect code. Every videotape was coded in its entirety by two independent observers using a computer-assisted coding system that automated the collection of timing information; each coder noted only the onsets of each code. A time-locked confusion matrix for the entire video tape was then computed using a one-second window for determining agreement of each code in one observer's coding against all of the other observer's coding (see Bakeman and Gottman, 1986). The diagonal versus the diagonal-plus-off-diagonal entries in these matrices were then entered into a repeated measures analysis of variance using the method specified by Wiggins (1977). The Cronbach alpha generalizability coefficients were then computed for each code as the ratio of the mean square for observers minus the error mean square and the mean square for observers plus the error mean square (see also Bakeman and Gottman, 1986). The Cronbach alpha generalizability coefficients ranged between .651 and .992 and averaged .907 for the entire SPAFF coding of all 130 videotapes.

Physiological Measures During the first year of data collection, physiological measures were collected through the use of two Lafayette Instruments six-channel polygraphs and a standard PC-style computer with two Metrabyte DASH-16 boards to record and store the physiological data. Data acquisition and analysis software was developed by C. Swanson using the ASYST programming environment. During the remainder of the study, physiological measures were collected using Coulbourn Instruments bioamplifiers. Computer hardware and software used to collect data for the remainder of the study were the same as those used during the first year of the study. Techniques for applying the physiological sensors, recording the data using on-line computer input, and calculating the values of the physiological data were identical for all of the participants in this second phase of the study. The electrocardiogram (ECG) was collected using a bipolar configuration of miniature electrodes applied with redux paste. Interbeat intervals (IBI's) were calculated as the time in milliseconds (msec) between consecutive waves.

General somatic activity was indexed by an electromechanical transducer located under the platform supporting each spouse's chair.

Self-report of Affect Following the marital interaction, spouses viewed a videotape of their interaction and were asked to recall how they felt during the interaction, using a rating dial to provide a continuous self-report measure indexing their own emotional evaluation of the marital interaction. The instrument consists of a small box attached to each of the two chairs. On the box is a dial that can be turned in 180−degree radius from one side marked *extremely negative* to the other end of the radius marked *extremely positive*, with *neutral* indicated in the middle of the turning radius. The output of the rating dial is an analog voltage (−5 to +5 volts), which is directed to the data-collection computer.

Questionnaires The MAT (Locke and Wallace, 1959) was administered during the initial telephone interview. The MAT is used to assess marital satisfaction and is frequently used in marital research because of its strength in reliably and validly distinguishing between happily and unhappily married couples. The telephone version of the MAT has strong psychometric properties as well (Krokoff, 1987). Lower scores on the MAT represent lower marital satisfaction. The study participants filled out the Couple's Problem Inventory (CPI; Gottman, Markman, and Notarius, 1977), an index of marital problems, just prior to the marital discussion of disagreement areas during the marital interaction phase of the study. Couples used the CPI to rate the severity of various issues in their marriage. Items include standard marital problem areas such as in-laws, finances, and sex. Each item is rated on a scale of 0 to 100, with higher scores signifying that the problem is considered more severe.

Marital Interaction Laboratory Procedures

The marital interaction assessment consisted of the husband and wife discussing a problem area that was a source of ongoing disagreement in their marriage, plus two recall sessions in which the couple viewed their marital disagreement discussion. The couples were asked to complete the CPI. One of the experimenters then reviewed with the couple those issues they rated as most problematic and helped them to choose several issues to use as the bases for the problem area discussion. After choosing the topics for the discussion, couples were asked to sit quietly and not interact with each other during a two-minute baseline. The couples then discussed their chosen topics for fifteen minutes.

When the couple completed their discussion, they were asked to view the video recording of the interaction. In counterbalanced order, the husband and wife were asked first to view and rate their own affect during the discussion and then to view and rate their spouse's affect. Both the husband and wife used rating dials that provided continuous self-report data. Continuous physiological measures and video recordings were made during all of the interaction sessions, and data was averaged over 1−second intervals.

Four- to Six-Year Marital Status and the 3 Criterion Groups

In some sense, it is not adequate simply to predict divorce. We also want to know if those who remain married are happily or unhappily married. Once each year we assessed the marital status and satisfaction of the 130 couples in the study. At the end of the six-year period (called Time−2 in this book), there had been 17 divorces: 6, 6, and 5 in the first, second, and third cohorts, respectively. Of the couples who stayed married, we then identified the 20 couples who were the highest in marital satisfaction, and the 20 couples who were lowest in marital satisfaction, determined from the lowest of each couple's Time−2 Locke-Wallace marital satisfaction scores. The mean Time−2 marital satisfaction score of the stable and happily married group was 128.30 ($sd = 27.65$), and the mean Time−2 marital satisfaction of the stable but unhappily married group was 90.70 ($sd = 16.08$).

These three groups (the 17 divorced couples, the 20 happiest stable couples, and the 20 unhappiest stable couples) formed our criterion groups, setting the framework to allow us to determine whether the math model parameters of a Time-1 conflict discussion that took place within a few months after a couple married could predict their Time-2 marital status and marital satisfaction.

12.4 Initial Weighting for the SPAFF

Because previous research with the RCISS revealed the power of the negative codes in predicting divorce, the initial weighting scheme for the on-line SPAFF codes weighted more heavily those codes that were the best predictors of divorce in previous research: contempt, defensiveness, criticism, and belligerence. The positive affects were not heavily weighted in this scheme. The result was a scale that had a range from +12 to −24.

In the first application of the mathematical model discussed in Chapter 10, we explored the validity of the model parameters with correlations using data pooled across the types of couples. With this new application to the Seattle Newlywed Study, our goal was to determine if the parameters of the model were capable of predicting divorce or membership in

Table 12.1: Divorce Prediction with the Initial SPAFF Weights.

Variable	F-ratio	df	Means Stable	Unstable
Wife uninfluenced steady state	21.37***	1,123	.55	−2.58
Wife influence function				
Positive threshold	.42	1,123	4.04	3.65
Negative threshold	.20	1,123	−5.57	−6.00
Wife influenced steady state	.72	1,112	−1.37	−2.14
Husband inertia	4.18a	1,123	.44	.32
Husband uninfluenced steady state	15.96***	1,123	−.34	−2.16
Husband influence function				
Positive threshold	2.27	1,123	4.28	3.53
Negative threshold	3.69a	1,123	−5.13	−6.71
Husband influenced steady state	7.99**	1,112	−.59	−2.84

a $p < 0.10$; * $p < 0.05$; ** $p < 0.01$; *** $p < 0.001$.

one of the three criterion groups. For this reason, we used analysis of variance to predict group membership.

Divorce Prediction

Uninfluenced Steady States Table 12.4 shows the predictive validity of the parameters of the mathematical model using the initial weighting of the SPAFF. The F-ratio is a statistical test for comparing group averages. Its expected value is 1.0. If it differs markedly from 1.0 this indicates the sample averages probably came from different populations. As can be seen from the table, the wife's uninfluenced steady state, $a/(1 - r_1)$, was much more negative in the first few months of the newlywed phase for couples who eventually divorced. The same is true for the husband's uninfluenced steady state, although the effect size of the F-ratio was smaller, ($\omega^2 = .053$ versus .140 for the wife.)

Negative Threshold The husband's negative threshold was a marginally significant predictor of divorce, $F(1, 123) = 3.69$, $p = .057$, in the predicted direction, suggesting that there was a higher threshold for negativity for couples who eventually divorced, compared to those whose marriages turned out to be stable.

Inertia The husband's inertia parameter was not a significant predictor, with couples whose marriages remained stable having a higher inertia than those who divorced. This result is opposite to our initial finding with the RCISS data (Cook *et al.*, 1995).

Influenced Steady States In the early months of newlywed marriage, husbands who eventually divorced had an influenced steady state of −2.84, whereas those whose marriages turned out to be stable had an influenced steady state of −0.59. This parameter was thus a significant predictor of divorce. However, the wife's average influenced steady state was −2.14 for the group who eventually divorced and −1.37 for the group whose marriages turned out to be stable, and thus not significantly different for the two groups. Even after the influence process, the husbands are still very different across the two groups.

Three Criterion Groups

Table 12.4 summarizes these results. Using least significant difference subsequent tests to the analysis of variance, the husband and wife uninfluenced steady states were able to discriminate predictively all three groups from one another; for the wife's uninfluenced steady state, $F(2,48)$ = 11.82, p <0.001, with means .09, −.61, and −2.58 for happy stable, unhappy stable, and divorced groups, respectively; the husband's uninfluenced steady state, $F(2,48) = 5.85$, p <0.01, with means −.09, −.93, and −2.16 for happy stable, unhappy stable, and divorced groups, respectively. The husband's influenced steady state also predictively discriminated the three criterion groups from one another, with $F(2,46) =$ 6.02, p <0.01, with means −.71, .29, and −2.84 for happy stable, unhappy stable, and divorced groups, respectively. In these analyses, the inertia parameter and the negative threshold were no longer significant predictors.

12.5   Final Weighting Scheme for the SPAFF

For the newlywed data, we subsequently discovered that the SPAFF's positive affects were able to discriminate predictively the three criterion groups (see Gottman *et al.*, 1998). As a result of this finding, we reconsidered our weighting of the SPAFF codes and gave a higher positive weight to interest, affection, validation, and humor, which resulted in a scale that ranged from +24 to −24. The mathematical model with ojive influence function was re-run using the final weighting scheme for the SPAFF.

Table 12.2: Three Criterion Groups with the Initial SPAFF Weights.

			Means		
Variable	F-ratio	df	Happy, Stable	Unhappy, Stable	Divorced
Wife uninfluenced steady state	11.82***	2,48	.09	−.61	−2.58
Wife influence function					
Positive threshold	.83	2,48	4.71	4.11	3.65
Negative threshold	.23	2,48	−5.06	−5.47	−6.00
Wife influenced steady state	1.07	2,46	−.64	−1.48	−2.14
Husband uninfluenced steady state	5.85***	2,48	−.09	−.93	−2.16
Husb influence function					
Positive threshold	.85	2,48	4.12	4.29	3.53
Negative threshold	1.02	2,48	−5.00	−5.65	−6.71
Husband influenced steady state	6.02	2,46	−.71	.29	−2.84

*** $p < 0.001$.

Divorce Prediction

Table 12.5 shows the results with the final weighting scheme. The results are generally the same as those in table 12.4, with the exception that the husband's inertia parameter is no longer predictive and the husband's negative threshold is now significantly predictive. In the first few months of marriage, the negative threshold for husbands who stayed married was more positive than for husbands who eventually divorced. This means that for couples who stayed married, it took less negativity on the husband's part to have an impact on his wife's behavior than for couples who eventually divorced, suggesting that there is *less* adaptation to negativity on the part of those wives whose marriages wind up being stable.

Three Criterion Groups

Table 12.5 shows that, using the final weighting scheme, the husband and wife uninfluenced steady states were able to predictively discriminate the three groups from one another. Also, the husband's negative threshold was able to discriminate significantly the unhappy stable from the divorced group; the happy stable and the unhappy stable groups had the same husband negative threshold.

Table 12.3: Divorce Prediction with the Final SPAFF Weights.

			Means	
Variable	F-ratio	df	Stable	Unstable
Wife uninfluenced steady state	14.86***	1,123	.51	−2.26
Wife influence functions Positive threshold	.71	1,123	8.25	7.24
Negative threshold	.03	1,123	−6.23	−6.06
Wife influenced steady state	1.29	1,106	−.65	−1.95
Husband inertia	3.07a	1,123	.40	.30
Husband uninfluenced steady state	18.40***	1,123	.72	−1.89
Husband influence function Positive threshold	2.49	1,123	8.45	6.65
Negative threshold	8.25**	1,123	−5.36	−7.71
Husband influenced steady state	4.36*	1,106	.71	−1.49

a $p < 0.10$;   * $p < 0.05$;   ** $p < 0.01$;   *** $p < 0.001$.

Table 12.4: Three Criterion Groups with the Final SPAFF Weights.

			Means		
Variable	F-ratio	df	Happy, Stable	Unhappy, Stable	Divorced
Wife uninfluenced steady state	12.61***	2,48	1.07	−.03	−2.26
Wife influence function Positive threshold	.73	2,48	9.12	8.53	7.24
Negative threshold	.28	2,48	−5.76	−6.76	−6.06
Wife influenced steady state	1.60	2,41	−.05	−1.88	−1.95
Husband uninfluenced steady state	9.10***	2,48	1.06	−.41	−1.89
Husb influence function Positive threshold	.54	2,48	7.94	7.94	6.65
Negative threshold	2.22	2,48	−5.94	−5.29	−7.71
Husband influenced steady state	1.15	2,41	−.33	.31	−1.49

*** $p < 0.001$.

12.6   Understanding the Uninfluenced Steady States

We wished to assess whether the parameters we have been calling the *uninfluenced steady states* might actually contain some information about the relationship's prior history and information about enduring qualities of the individual, as well as how these influences might vary with the eventual fate of a marriage (happy versus unhappy stable or divorced). To understand the possible effect of immediate prior relationship history on the uninfluenced steady-state parameters, we divided the interaction into two equal halves and investigated the first half's predictors of the second half's uninfluenced steady-state parameters. We did this prediction separately for those couples who were eventually either divorced or stable but unhappy, compared to everyone else. There were two parts to answering this question. The first part was to assess whether or not there was a spillover of uninfluenced steady states from the first to the second half of the interaction (controlling the first half's influence parameters— that is, its influenced steady state and threshold parameters), and the second part was to assess whether the nature of the influence process itself in the first half affected the uninfluenced steady states of the second half (controlling the first half's uninfluenced steady state).

To test these hypotheses, we conducted a regression analysis with group as the main effects variable (group = 2 for the divorced and unhappy couples, and group = 1 for every other couple, so that increases in the grouping variable implied the declining health of the marriage) and with Group × Predictors as the interaction. The variables to be predicted were the second half's uninfluenced steady states. The regression had three steps. In the first step, we entered the relevant control variables. In the second step, the main effect variables were then stepped into the equation. In the third step, the interactions were stepped in (assessed by multiplying the group variable by the predictors, after first having stepped in the predictors themselves).

Assessing the Influence of Enduring Qualities of the Individual

When the wife's second-half uninfluenced steady state was predicted, controlling the interaction variables, the F-ratio-for-change was $F(7, 108)$ = 8.62, $p = .0041$. In the next step, the interaction with group was not significant: F-for-change $F(8, 107) = .79$. When the husband's second-half uninfluenced steady state was predicted, controlling the interaction variables, the F-ratio-for-change was $F(7, 107) = 17.72$, $p = .0001$. In the next step, the interaction with group was significant, F-for-change $F(8, 106) = 6.87$, $p < .05$. The interaction partial correlation was $-.25$ ($p < .05$), so that the degree of the stability of the husband's enduring quality was negatively related to marital health. Hence, the analysis showed that the uninfluenced steady state does contain a significant component that reflects the enduring qualities of the individual, and, for the husband, this component is related to negative marital outcomes.

The Effects of the Influence Process Itself

When the wife's second-half uninfluenced steady state was predicted, the F-ratio-for-change was $F(7, 108) = 3.76$, $p = .0019$. In the next step, the interaction with group was not significant, F-for-change $F(13, 102) = .93$. When the husband's second-half uninfluenced steady state was predicted, the F-ratio-for-change was $F(7, 107) = 5.95$, $p = .0000$. Hence, the influence process itself made significant contributions. In the next step, the interaction with group was not significant, F-for-change $F(13, 101) = 1.67$.

Summary

These analyses imply that the uninfluenced steady-state parameters contain significant information about both the enduring qualities of the individuals and their prior relationship influence history.

12.7 Chapter Summary

From a methodological standpoint, this chapter shows that it is possible to extend the early results of our modeling with the RCISS system to the SPAFF, a real-time coding system of specific affects that can be used for any marital conversation. This system also provides more observations for each couple (150 per couple in a fifteen-minute period), with the same number of observations for each spouse, so that the modeling is more likely to be reliable within each couple. Furthermore, the early results concerning the predictive validity of the model parameters might be extended to a new sample of newlyweds.

Finally, by extending the model to use the ojive form of the influence function, we were able to explore the importance of a parameter, the negative threshold, which could offer some explanation for the delay effect that Notarius amd Buongiorno (1995) had detected and potentially for the marital therapy relapse effect.

13

The Marriage Model with Repair and Damping

13.1 What Are Repair and Damping?

The model, as it stands, is very fatalistic. The outcome of any interaction between spouses is determined by their initial state. That is, the couple's conversation will inexorably be drawn toward the steady state in the basin of attraction in which they find themselves at the beginning of their conversation. If they arrive in a good mood, the conversation will go well. If they arrive in a bad mood, the conversation will go badly. Even worse, if there is only one steady state, and it is a negative one, then it doesn't matter how happy each spouse is at the beginning of the conversation: the couple will always end up at the only steady state they have. There is no possibility of any other outcome.

We would like to believe however, that couples do, at least theoretically, have the ability to reverse the trend of a conversation if it has become very negative. If the wife, say, is becoming despondent and upset, the husband might try to comfort her and point out the bright side of things. Or vice versa. These reversal attempts are called repair attempts and have, in fact, been specifically documented in our laboratory. In efforts to distinguish between happy and unhappy marriages, these repair attempts turn out to be extremely important.

The most consistent discriminator between distressed and nondistressed marriages that has been obtained across four nations is negative affect reciprocity. Negative affect reciprocity is the sequential pattern that negative affect by a spouse is more likely than his or her baseline after the partner has just been negative. In other words, for unhappy couples, negative behavior by the wife or husband generally produces a negative response by the spouse. This implies that it is very important that a couple be able to *repair* the interaction and exit a negative affect cycle, which may be the sine qua non of effective marital interaction during conflict. This view is further supported by the fact that happy couples do exhibit negativity—even a significant quantity. The predictors of divorce (criticism, defensiveness, contempt, and stonewalling) are not unknown in marriages that are stable and happy. The crucial difference appears to lie in the couple's ability to repair their negativity, not in their ability to avoid it entirely.

Once we began to study repair and its effectiveness, we realized that symmetric to the concept of repair is the idea of damping. If couples have the ability to turn a negative conversation into a positive one, we must also allow for the possibility that couples can turn a positive conversation into a negative one. Certainly, we can imagine a situation in which the relationship has deteriorated to the point where, for example, the husband finds even the wife's positivity intolerable and says something to hurt her. On a more subtle level, however, we can also imagine a situation in which, for example, the husband's tendency to worry makes him lend a negative light even to positive situations. Such behavior is analogous to the image of someone looking at a glass with water up to the halfway mark. A repairing person would see the glass as half full (or the interaction as half, or more, positive), whereas a damping person would see the glass as half empty (or the interaction as half, or more, negative).

We have been studying these repair processes and have discovered that in a conflict conversation (1) repair processes occur about once every three minutes, on the average; (2) they occur more often the more distressed the couple is; and (3) the success of the repair attempt cannot be predicted from any parameter of its delivery, context, or timing. Instead, M. Lorber, an honors student in our laboratory, discovered that the success of repair attempts is determined by a concept called positive sentiment override (PSO). He also observed negative sentiment override (NSO), which relates to damping.

The concept of sentiment override was first proposed in 1980 by R. Weiss, who suggested that reactions during marital interaction may be determined by a global dimension of affection or disaffection rather than by the immediately preceding valence of the stimulus. These overrides are determined experimentally by insider-outsider coding discrepancies, as follows: PSO, a spouse can say something with negative affect (as judged by observers), and the partner receives it as a neutral message, perhaps with italics, meaning that it is an important issue to the spouse; NSO, the partner receives even a neutral message (as judged by observers) as if it were negative. It is as if a person in NSO has a chip on the shoulder and is hypersensitive to sleights and insults. Notice that the two overrides aren't entirely symmetric. If they were, NSO would be observed when a positive message (as judged by observers) is received as if it were neutral. We employed Weiss's idea of PSO and NSO, and suggested that it has its basis in everyday, mundane, nonconflict interaction. Lorber found that what was critical was the *husband's* PSO. It determined the success of repair attempts during conflict resolution.

M. Hawkins in our laboratory recently discovered that the critical variable in PSO was the wife's perception of her husband's anger. In marriages that were destined to become happy and stable, the wife did not perceive her husband's anger negatively: she saw it as neutral. She noticed and responded to the anger, but did not evaluate it as negative using our video recall rating dial. In marriages headed for unhappiness or divorce, the wife's rating of her husband's anger was negative. It is important to note that this difference was a categorical difference and not a small quantitative difference. Wives in the marriages headed for stability and happiness were actually seeing their husband's anger as neutral, not just as less negative than did their counterparts in marriages destined for misery or divorce.

The theory we propose suggests that PSO mediates between positive affect in a couple's everyday interaction and their ability to regulate negative affect during the resolution of conflict. It is the basis of successful repair. Hence, we propose that what determines PSO is positive affect in *nonconflict* interaction which in our theory we call the "emotional bank account model" because it suggests that PSO is determined by how much "emotional money in the bank" the couple has. We now believe that this bank account is an index of the quality of the friendship between husband and wife. Our data to date supports this linkage in the theory. In addition, we have two new coding systems that we expect to provide data for testing the theory that everyday positive affect in nonconflict contexts mediates between PSO and the success of repair attempts during conflict. One of these observational coding systems (designed by J. Driver) is used to code bids for connection in our apartment laboratory, and either "turning toward" or "turning away" in response to those bids. The other observational coding system (designed by A. Tabares and J. Driver) is for coding repair during a conflict discussion. We are currently coding data using these two systems.

Similarly, we suggest that NSO is determined by the amount of negative affect in nonconflict interaction. This may be somewhat curious because negativity generally engenders or is accompanied by conflict. Negative affect and conflict, however, are not identical. In nonconflict interaction, a lack of interest or irritability or impatience can be negative without leading to conflict or a discussion of disagreement. Typically, in the nonconflict context, such negativity leads to emotional disengagement and distance. Both positivity and negativity can exist in daily, mundane interactions. To continue the analogy with the emotional bank account, where positive affect puts money into the account and negative affect removes it, we suggest that NSO and PSO are opposite ends of the same scale, PSO becoming NSO when the amount of negativity in the relationship outside conflict interaction exceeds the amount of positivity.

To summarize, the paired concepts of repair and damping are the cornerstones of the theory we are building. These terms added to the model appear to account for most of our prediction errors in predicting longitudinal outcomes in marriage. That is, the ability to repair negativity accounts for most of our prediction errors in which couples negative at Time-1 are seen as having stable, happy marriages upon longitudinal follow-up. We suggest that the basis of effective repair is PSO and that the basis of ineffective repair is NSO. Furthermore, we are exploring the hypothesis that the basis of PSO and NSO lies in the quality of the couple's friendship (not in conflict). That friendship can be assessed by examining the emotional bank account in nonconflict interaction in which we code bids for emotional connection and the partner's turning toward or away from the connection.

In the model, it would make sense to include switch terms that are turned on when the interaction becomes too negative (repair) or too positive (damping). The effectiveness of each switch and the frequency of its use can vary for each individual. Two terms would be necessary because PSO and NSO are not entirely symmetric, as observed above. The thresholds, frequency, and effectiveness will presumably be different for the two types of response.

13.2   The Repair and Damping Terms

Having thus introduced the general concepts of repair and damping, we need to define them very specifically so that we can include them in the marriage model. Because the two concepts are very similar, differing only in the ranges over which they operate (one in response to too much negativity, the other in response to too much positivity), we simplify this discussion by first talking only about the repair term.

The repair switch should satisfy a few simple characteristics. First, it should be asymmetrical, only kicking in when negativity has exceeded some critical threshold. Repair is not needed when the conversation is positive or when the negativity is slight and unthreatening. Second, it should appear abruptly once the threshold is crossed, being an on/off type of process. We assume a repair function of the form shown in

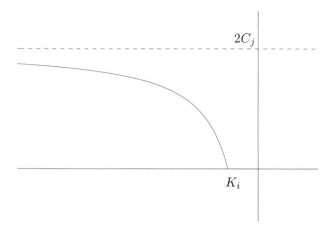

Figure 13.1: Graph of repair switch. After a specific negative threshold, the switch is turned on, serving as needed positivity to keep the reaction from becoming too miserable. Here $2C_j$ is the maximum repair possible.

figure 13.1.

In order to write down equations for this term, we need to decide what variables are being plotted on each axis of figure 13.1. There are several possible choices. Negativity in the conversation can come from four different places: negativity in one's own score, in one's partner's score, in the recent history of one's own scores during the conversation, and in the recent history of one's partner's scores during the conversation. The last two cases are described mathematically as the slope of each individual's conversation. The mathematical concept of slope is entirely analogous to the English one, used to refer to the inclining angle of a hillside, except that mathematically we can have both negative and positive slopes. A positive slope indicates that scores are increasing (becoming more positive/happy) over time, whereas a negative slope indicates that scores are decreasing (becoming more negative/unhappy) over time.

Both types of negativity, score and slope, are probably important in fully understanding the conversation. We can gain an enormous amount of information, however, by simply considering negativity in the score, and so for the moment we restrict our model and analysis to a repair term depending on negativity in score.

Because repair must be a reaction to the conversation as a whole and

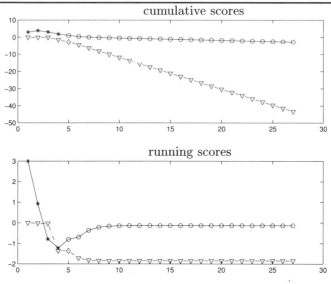

Figure 13.2: Marriage model run with repair attempts in response to self. Negativity thresholds were -1 for the running scores. The strength of repair was $+1$ for each partner. Influence functions for couple N006 with $K_w = -1$ and $K_h = -1$. The wife's score is denoted by a solid line (-) while the husband's score is represented by the dash-dot line (-.).

not simply an individual behavior operating in a vacuum, repair depending only on score must depend on the partner's score. This dependence creates a feedback loop and thus a connected conversation. We thus arrive at the conclusion that the horizontal axis in figure 13.1 represents one's partner's score, and the vertical axis represents the repair (positivity) added to one's own score. Simulations, shown in figures 13.2 and 13.3, confirm this point.

In figure 13.2, the simulation model was run with a disconnected conversation. That is, repair attempts by person A are in response to negativity by person A and affect person A's score. We see from the lower plot that the couple quickly evolves toward a steady state and stays there. The steady state scores are both negative, but significantly different in magnitude, which results in diverging cumulative scores as shown in the upper plot. Diverging cumulative score graphs are indicative of a lack of communication within the couple, so repair, when modeled this way, does not increase the connectivity of the couple's interaction.

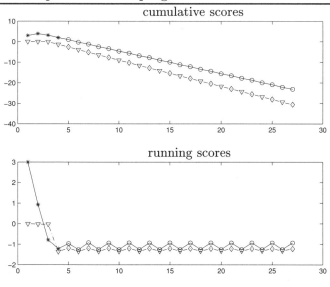

Figure 13.3: Marriage model run with repair attempts in response to spouse. Negativity thresholds were -1 for the running scores. The strength of repair was $+1$ for each partner. Influence functions for couple N006. The wife's score is denoted by a solid line (-) while the husband's score is represented by the dash-dot line (-.).

In figure 13.3, the picture is quite different. Here the simulation model was run with a connected conversation. That is, repair attempts by person A are in response to negativity by person B and affect person A's score. In this case, we see from the lower plot that the couple quickly evolves toward a cyclic steady state (recall the discussion of limit cycles in chapter 7). Again, the steady limit-cycle scores are negative for both the husband and wife, but they match quite closely. Thus, the cumulative scores, shown in the upper plot, parallel each other. Modeled this way, repair definitely increases the connectivity of the couple's interaction.

In a conflict discussion, the time sequence connected with repair would be something like this:

1. Individual notes that partner has become too negative.

2. In response, individual makes a repair attempt that affects his or her own score.

3. This repair attempt makes the individual's own score more posi-

tive, which then has the potential to make the partner's score more positive through the regular influence function for that couple.

The PSO present in the couple's interaction would show up in the strength of repair attempts. Generalizing the idea of PSO to repair, we propose that couples with plenty of PSO would be very responsive to negativity in their partner, seeing it as an indication of an important issue to the partner, and thus promoting a strong repair response in themselves. This allows them to elevate the positivity in the conversation. Graphically, this means that for some couples the curve in figure 13.1 would rise to a higher level than for others.

Mathematically, we write the repair term graphed in figure 13.1 as

$$\text{Repair}_j(x) = C_j \frac{|x - K_i| - (x - K_i)}{1 - (x - K_i)}, \tag{13.1}$$

where K_i is the negative threshold for individual i's running score, and C_j is the strength of the repair attempt by individual j. This multiplier is set to zero whenever repair is not being attempted.

Everything stated above with regard to repair applies to damping with a reversal of positivity and negativity. So damping occurs in response to too much positivity and is switched on once the partner's score reaches some positive threshold. The graph of damping looks like the graph of repair rotated through 180 degrees as shown in figure 13.4.

Mathematically, we write the damping term as

$$\text{Damping}_j(x) = -C_j \frac{|x - K_i| + (x - K_i)}{1 + (x - K_i)}, \tag{13.2}$$

where K_i is the positive threshold for individual i's running score, and C_j is the strength of the damping attempt by individual j. This multiplier is set to zero whenever damping is not being attempted. Note that the threshold (K_i) and strength (C_j) parameters for repair and damping are not the same.

The full model thus becomes

$$W_{t+1} = I_{HW}(H_t) + R_W(H_t) + D_W(H_t) + r_1 W_t + a,$$
$$H_{t+1} = I_{WH}(W_t) + R_H(W_t) + D_H(W_t) + r_2 H_t + b,$$

where

- W_t is the wife's score at time t.

- H_t is the husband's score at time t.

- $I_{HW}(H_t)$ is the influence of the husband on the wife (a function of the husband's most recent score obtained at time t).

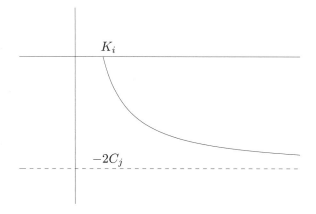

Figure 13.4: Graph of damping switch. After a specific positive threshold, the switch is turned on, serving as needed negativity to keep the interaction from becoming too euphoric. K_i is the positive threshold above which damping starts. $-2C_j$ is the maximum damping possible.

- $I_{WH}(W_t)$ is the influence of the wife on the husband (a function of the wife's most recent score obtained at time t).

- $R_W(H_t)$ and $D_W(H_t)$ are the repair and damping to the wife's score; both are functions of the husband's most recent score obtained at time t.

- $R_H(W_t)$ and $D_H(W_t)$ are the repair and damping to the husband's score; both are functions of the wife's most recent score obtained at time t.

The remaining terms of the equations are the terms describing uninfluenced behavior—that is, the natural behavior of each individual apart from the conflict discussion. The repair and damping functions are:

$$
\begin{aligned}
R_W(H_t) &= C_{rw}\frac{|H_t - K_{rh}| - (H_t - K_{rh})}{1 - (H_t - K_{rh})}, \\
D_W(H_t) &= C_{dw}\frac{|H_t - K_{dh}| - (H_t - K_{dh})}{1 - (H_t - K_{dh})}, \\
R_H(W_t) &= C_{rh}\frac{|W_t - K_{rw}| - (W_t - K_{rw})}{1 - (W_t - K_{rw})}, \\
D_H(W_t) &= C_{dh}\frac{|W_t - K_{dw}| - (W_t - K_{dw})}{1 - (W_t - K_{dw})},
\end{aligned}
\tag{13.3}
$$

bilinear influence function   ojive influence function

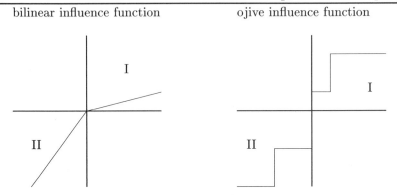

Figure 13.5: The bilinear and ojive influence function types. In region I, positive partner scores have a positive influence on spouse scores. In region II, negative partner scores have a negative influence on spouse scores.

where C_{rw} and C_{rh} are the strength of the repair attempts by the wife and husband, respectively. Similarly, C_{dw} and C_{dh} are the strength of the damping attempts by the wife and husband, respectively. The parameters K_{rw}, K_{dw}, K_{rh}, and K_{dh} represent the "switch" locations where repair and damping are turned on for the wife and husband. That is, when the husband's score H_t is less than K_{rh}, then the wife is repairing: $R_W(H_t) > 0$.

13.3   The Bilinear and Ojive Influence Functions

With the addition of repair and damping terms to the model, we are motivated to reexamine the influence functions of the model. We have, in previous chapters, introduced two types of influence functions: the ojive and bilinear forms. In our original work (Cook *et al.*, 1995), we used bilinear influence functions (figure 13.5). Under the bilinear influence function hypothesis, a partner's influence is divided into two halves as shown in figure 13.6. Whenever the husband, for example, exhibits positive affect (points *a* or *b*, for example), the wife is positively influenced (points *A* or *B*). The extent of this positive influence is directly proportional to the extent of positivity in the husband's score. So some positivity on the part of the husband (at *a*, say) generates a small positive influence on the wife's score (at *A*). If the husband's score is more positive (at *b*, say), then the husband's influence on his wife will be more positive (at *B*). If the husband's score is a great deal more positive, then the wife's score will also be a great deal more positive.

More importantly, even a tiny amount of positivity on the husband's part has some influence on the wife's behavior, and there is no limit to the amount of positivity the husband can impart to the wife. As his score increases, hers is more and more positively affected.

Recall that one of the most stable phenomena in marriage is that negative affect dominates (is more potent than) positive affect, so that we can expect the downward slope in the negative-negative quadrant to be steeper than the upward slope in the positive-positive quadrant.

In the region of negative affect, similar behavior is observed. If the husband is negative, then the wife is influenced to increase her negativity by an amount directly proportional to the increase in negativity in the husband's score. As above, even tiny amounts of husband negativity have an influencing effect on the wife, and there is no limit to the amount of negativity the husband can impart to the wife.

The arguments above also hold true if we reverse the roles of wife and husband in our description. The proportionality constants will be different, but the gross behaviors the same.

The model, then, is somewhat idealistic when we look at the influence owing to tiny and large amounts of positivity or negativity. It is much more likely that there is some limit to the amount of positivity one spouse can impart to another, and it is also plausible that there is some band of very slightly negative and very slightly positive behaviors that are so subtly different from neutral that the spouse receives them only as neutral. Thus, the ojive functions were introduced later to deal with these concerns. Under the ojive hypothesis, slightly positive or negative behaviors are the same as neutral ones in terms of their influence. At some threshold of positivity, however, the spouse is suddenly able to notice positivity on the part of the other spouse and to respond to it. As the amount of positivity exhibited by the influencing spouse increases, however, there is no increase in the amount of positivity received by the first spouse. That is, there is a range of positive and negative affects that have no influence, and then all positive affect influences to the same extent and all negative affect influences to the same extent outside of that range.

Both interpretations of the influence functions have proven very useful. Using the bilinear model, it was found (Cook *et al.*, 1995) that the slope of each half of the influence functions is useful in discriminating between the five types of couples (volatile, validating, conflict-avoiding, hostile, and hostile-detached). Using the ojive model, it was found (Gottman, Swanson, and Murray, 1998) that the location of the negativity threshold was critical in distinguishing distressed and nondistressed couples. It is clear that both approaches have some validity. It is also true, however, that although each one is a reasonable description

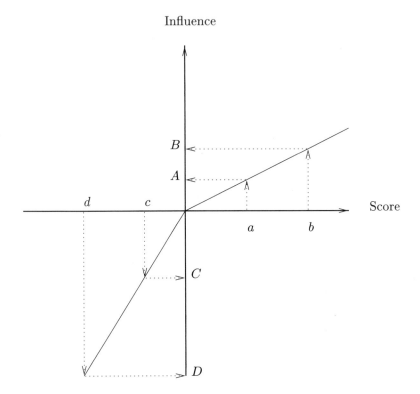

Figure 13.6: The bilinear influence function type. Partner's score is plotted along the horizontal axis, and partner's influence on spouse is plotted along the vertical axis. In this theoretical function, positive partner scores (examples are shown at a and b) generate positive influence on the spouse (A and B), and negative partner scores (examples are shown at c and d) generate negative influence on the spouse (C and D). More positivity in the partner score (points farther to the right on the horizontal axis) generates more positive influence on the spouse and more negativity in the partner score generates more negative influence on the spouse. There is no limit to the amount of positivity or negativity that can be imparted. Influence also occurs for very slightly positive and very slightly negative scores. The only neutral score (one that imparts no influence) is zero.

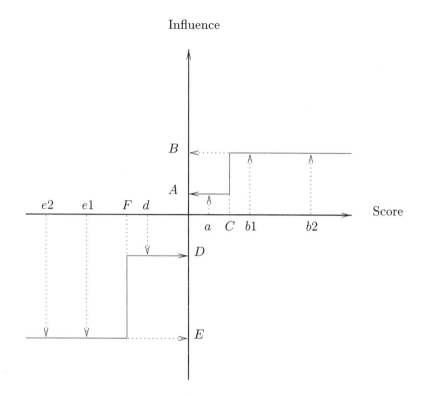

Figure 13.7: The ojive influence function type. Partner's score is plotted along the horizontal axis, and partner's influence on spouse is plotted along the vertical axis. Here, positive partner scores (*i.e.*, a, $b1$, and $b2$) generate positive influence on the spouse (A and B), and negative partner scores (*i.e.*, d, $e1$, and $e2$) generate negative influence on the spouse (C and D). Positive partner scores less (or greater) than the threshold C generate a constant moderate (or large) amount of positive influence. More positivity in the partner score (points even farther to the right on the horizontal axis) do not generate any increase in positive influence on the spouse. Negative partner scores less (or more) negative than the threshold F generate a moderate (or large) amount of negative influence. More negativity in the partner score (points even farther to the left on the horizontal axis) do not generate any increase in negative influence on the spouse. The only neutral score (one which imparts no influence) is zero.

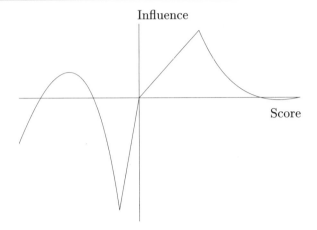

Figure 13.8: The bilinear influence function with repair
and damping. On the right, damping causes the influence
function to drop to a more negative value. On the left, repair causes the influence function to rise to a more positive
value.

of influence, each one has some less-reasonable assumptions built in. We
might do even better at modeling influence functions if we could come
up with some combination of the bilinear and ojive models.

It just so happens that the bilinear model, with damping and repair
terms (as described above) added, is just such a combination. The damping and repair terms provide the saturation behavior for the amount of
positivity or negativity that can be imparted, and the underlying bilinear model allows for a gradient in the amount of positivity or negativity
that is imparted.

In figure 13.8, we see that damping causes the influence function to
drop to a more negative value on the right, and repair causes the influence function to rise to a more positive value on the left. So repair and
damping contain the interaction within reasonable levels. Note, however, that there is one important difference between the ojive influence
function and the bilinear influence function with repair and damping. In
the former case, the containment values are absolute in the sense that
scores can never be more negative than F or more positive than C. In
our new scenario, scores will tend to be contained between the left-hand
maximum and the right-hand minimum, but if scores are ever allowed to
wander outside this region, the interaction can deteriorate to any level
of negativity or grow to any level of positivity. Thus, unbridled passion
or unrelenting misery are still possible with this model.

Table 13.1: Bilinear Model versus Ojive Model.

influence function type	average least squares error for repair type:			
	own slope/ own score	spouse slope/ spouse score	spouse slope/ own score	own slope/ spouse score
bilinear	84.12	92.79	95.09	91.09
ojive	324.53	469.63	469.60	465.77

With this combined model, we are able to obtain slope and threshold parameters that are as significant as they were for the previous models. We found that the "goodness of fit" provided by the combined bilinear/damping/repair model is much better than that provided by the ojive model alone. Even more significant, we found that the bilinear model with repair also fit the data more closely than the ojive model with repair.

Repair as we have chosen to model it depends only on the partner's most recent score. From previous discussion in section 13.2, however, we know that negativity can come from four places: (1) one's own score, (2) one's partner's score, (3) one's slope, and (4) one's partner's slope. In order to compare the ojive model with repair to the bilinear influence model with repair in terms of their ability to fit the experimental data, we did the following. We ran each of the models, ojive and bilinear, with the four different types of repair and for each of the couples, varying the parameters until we found those that best fit the experimental data. The fit was determined using a least squares comparison of the data points generated by the model and the data points obtained experimentally. The average difference across all couples between the model and experimental results was reported for each of the four repair types for each influence function type (ojive or bilinear). The results appear in table 13.1. For all four different types of repair, the errors reported for the ojive influence function model are an order of magnitude larger than those reported for the bilinear influence function model. That is, errors for the bilinear influence function model are in the tens, whereas the errors for the ojive influence function model are in the hundreds which strongly indicates that, as a model of marital interaction, the bilinear model with repair is superior to the ojive model with repair. For the remainder of this chapter, therefore, we restrict our study to the bilinear model with repair.

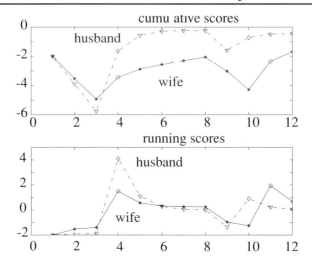

Figure 13.9: Graphs of cumulative and running scores generated by simulations of the marriage model with repair. In this example, two check mark patterns were observed in the graph of cumulative scores, and these patterns are marked by a diamond-point marker on the husband's trace and by a circle point marker on the wife's trace. The graph of running scores shows that the check mark patterns correspond to repair attempts (also shown as diamond- and circle-point markers) made by each partner. The wife's score is denoted by a solid line (-) while the husband's score is represented by the dash-dot line (-.). ($C_{rw} = C_{rh} = 5$

13.4   Simulations regarding Repair and Damping

Theoretically we are pleased with our repair function, and it captures the essential behavior we expect in a repair function. Now we must estimate the values for the eight model parameters, four for each partner: C_{rw}, C_{dw}, C_{rh}, C_{dh}, K_{rw}, K_{dw}, K_{rh}, and K_{dh}.

The search for a repair term was motivated first by the observation that a few couples had the ability to turn their negative conversation around and make it positive. Graphically, this ability showed most clearly in plots of the cumulative scores for each spouse over time. The remarkable incidence of a turning point in the conversation appears in the cumulative scores as a "check mark" pattern. Typically, the individual scores are first continually negative, so their sum (cumulative score) becomes increasingly negative, graphically giving the conversation a downward (negative) slope. Then a turning point occurs, and the couple manages somehow to start working more constructively, generating positive scores from then on. These positive scores then add to the cumulative score, tending to make it increase and graphically giving the conversation an upward (positive) slope (see figure 13.9).

Intuitively, we thought that these "check marks" must represent dramatic examples of successful repair attempts. Thus, we thought we could search the data for check-mark patterns and estimate the parameters from these segments of the data. The number of check marks would indicate the frequency of repair attempts, and the size of the check-mark would indicate the effectiveness. This approach, however, would give us no measure of the number of completely ineffective repair attempts made, which could be significant in distinguishing healthy and unhealthy relationships. That is, we would like to know if unhappy relationships are distinguished by many repair attempts with no effectiveness or by no repair attempts at all.

We nevertheless began studying this check mark idea by constructing simulations of potential data. We found that, further complicating the issue, check marks in the cumulative score graphs were not necessarily tied to repair attempts, and that even strong repair attempts did not necessarily produce check marks. The latter is possible because a marginally successful repair attempt may simply make the partner's score less negative, but not sufficiently less negative so that it becomes positive. Thus, the cumulative score would continue to decrease. Some examples obtained from simulations of the marriage model with repair are shown in figures 13.9, 13.10(a), and 13.10(b). Figure 13.9 is a graph of the model run with effective repair producing check marks in the cumulative score graph as anticipated.

Figure 13.10(a) shows a check mark pattern produced in the absence of repair, and figure 13.10(b) shows a cumulative score with no check mark in spite of the fact that repair with nonzero strength was present.

The simulations were surprising and led us to ask a number of questions. How can we distinguish the check marks caused by repair, and how can we determine the frequency and strength of repair when no check marks are present? Furthermore, when determining parameter values from the data, how can we tease apart the roles of the influence functions and repair? We eventually developed two approaches to this problem:

1. we can repeatedly fit the simulation model to the data using a range of parameter values, and take the parameters that give us the best fit;

2. we can try to distinguish repair attempts in the data (influence plots) and use that information to estimate the parameters.

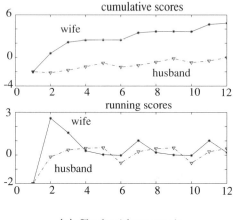

(a) Check without repair

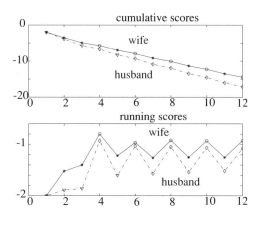

(b) Repair with no check

Figure 13.10: Graphs of cumulative and running scores generated by simulations of the marriage model with repair. In (a) a check mark pattern is observed in the cumulative scores, suggesting that a successful repair attempt was made. The repair switch, however, was never turned on. In (b) no check mark pattern is observed in the cumulative scores, suggesting that no repair attempts were made. The repair switch, however, was turned on frequently. The wife's score is denoted by a solid line (-) while the husband's score is represented by the dash-dot line (-.).($C_{rw} = C_{rh} = 1$)

Alternative 1: Repeated Simulations

We began by setting a reasonable range for each of the eight parameters: C_{rw}, C_{dw}, C_{rh}, C_{dh}, K_{rw}, K_{dw}, K_{rh}, and K_{dh}. Because the data has not been coded for repair, we had only our intuition and the SPAFF codes to guide us in our choice of parameter ranges.

For the negative score threshold appearing in the repair function, we set the range of K_r (for both husband and wife) to be -4 to 0. This range is reasonable because couples didn't often receive scores much less than -4. Thus, -4 is a fairly negative score, and we can assume that repair attempts will generally start happening before such strong negativity is reached. We might have examined a range of negative score thresholds that extends into the more negative scores, but a cursory set of simulations indicated that such an examination would not add any new information. For the upper limit, 0, we assumed that for some couples repair might be attempted the moment any negativity at all is detected.

Similarly, for the positive score threshold appearing in the damping function, we set the range of K_d (for both husband and wife) to be 0 to $+4$.

The remaining parameters in our list are the strength of repair and damping, C_r and C_d, for both husband and wife. These quantities have not been measured in experiment, so we have no experimental information giving us a plausible range for them. In the absence of any data, we simply chose C_r and C_d to be in the range 0 (no strength) to 8 (maximum strength). These numbers mean that repair/damping can increase/decrease one's score up to 16 points. Given that -4 and $+4$ are considered fairly extreme scores, an effect of 16 points is also quite extreme.

Having chosen a range of values for each parameter, we were ready to start comparing the simulation model to the data. We could choose between comparing the model and data scores at each timestep or comparing the cumulative model and data scores at each timestep. We selected the latter approach. A graph of the data showing, for one couple, the score obtained at each timestep indicates a large amount of variability in the moment to moment results. It is easy to become distracted by all of the wild-looking jumps in the data and to lose track of the progress of the conversation. In other words, it is difficult to "see the forest for the trees." In trying to understand the status of each couple's marriage, it is more instructive to look at graphs of the cumulative score for each spouse at each time point. In these graphs, the noisy-looking nature of the data is smoothed out, and we can see the general trend of the conversation. Were the scores generally negative? Generally positive? Generally neutral? We thus used the cumulative scores in our published papers (Gottman and Levenson, 1992) to predict the stability of each couple's marriage. Because the cumulative scores are the ones with predictive power, we want the model to capture the behavior of the cumulative scores and are not concerned with the fit with the moment to moment scores.

For each couple, we ran the simulation model with repair and damping using a large number of combinations of the possible parameter values. We did so by allowing each parameter to assume all of the integer values in the range between the minimum and maximum values chosen. The cumulative scores resulting from the simulation were then compared with the cumulative scores of the experimental data by finding the least squares difference between the two data sets. At each timestep, the difference between the two data points was calculated and squared. The values calculated at all of the timesteps were added up, and then the square root of that sum taken and divided by the number of timesteps which gave a measure of the difference between the two data sets. The errors computed for all combinations of parameter values were compared, and the smallest was deemed to be the best.

Alternative 2: Finding Repair Attempts in the Influence Plots

The second approach we took to viewing repair was to look at the plot of the influence of one spouse on the other at each data point. After calculating the uninfluenced parameters (r_1, r_2, a, and b), we subtracted the uninfluenced portion of each score to reveal just the influence of the spouse at each time point. Now these influence data points contain information regarding not only the influence function but also the repair and damping attempts. So we attempted to separate this influence into the three components: bilinear influence function, repair term, and damping term.

We expected to find these influence data points to lie mostly in the first and third quadrants of figure 13.11. That is, positive spouse scores should generally have a positive influence, and negative spouse scores should generally have a negative influence. A look at the data, however, showed that many couples had influence points in the second and fourth quadrants. Points in quadrant II are those where a negative spouse score produced a positive influence. These points, then, are repair points. The points in quadrant IV are points where a positive spouse score resulted in a negative influence. We identified these influences as damping points. Note here that there are also data points in quadrant III associated with repair attempts that were not sufficiently effective to induce a net positive influence. Similarly, there are points in quadrant I associated

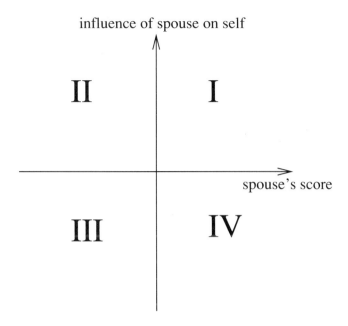

Figure 13.11: Normal influence function points lie in quadrants I and III. Repair points are positive influences occurring in response to negative spouse scores and lie in quadrant II. Damping points are negative influences occurring in response to positive spouse scores and lie in quadrant IV.

with damping attempts that were not sufficiently effective to induce a net negative influence. For our discussion, it is simple and intuitive to ignore this subtlety and to separate the four quadrants of the plane into one for repair, one for damping, and two for bilinear influence.

Because influence, isolated from repair and damping, is given only in quadrant's I and III, we used a linear least squares regression of these data points in each of these two quadrants to define the two straight-line portions of the bilinear influence function. Next, the bilinear influence contribution to each score was subtracted from the data points to reveal only that portion of the data associated with repair and damping. A nonlinear least squares algorithm was then used to fit the repair and damping coefficient to the remaining data.

Although the two alternative methods for estimating the model parameters are both accurate and useful, each has its own distinct advantages. "Repeated simulations" is probably capable of obtaining the

most accurate fit, but the computational cost of iterating over a large
set of parameter values can be quite large. Alternatively, "finding repair
attempts in the influence plots" allows us to gain intuition regarding the
couple's behavior without a significant amount of computational time.
The number of points (and their magnitude) in quadrants II and IV define the extent of repair and damping we expect from the couple before
the coefficients are even estimated.

13.5   Methods for Evaluating the Two Alternatives

To implement the method in Alternative 2, we used the data file containing weighted and summed SPAFF data that gave us 150 time points for
all 130 couples in the Seattle Newlywed Study. This is the same dataset
that is described in detail in Chapter 12. As described in previous chapters, a computer program was run on a Windows PC that calculated
the uninfluenced parameters (r_1, r_2, a, and b) and then subtracted the
uninfluenced portion from each score to yield an influence plot for each
spouse. The program then fit the influence data using the bilinear influence function with repair and damping, as described in section 13.4
above. The parameters of this model were stored in another data file for
subsequent statistical analyses. Note that the potential range of data for
each time point was $+24$ to -24, so it is also the potential range of the
positive and negative score threshold parameters under this alternative.
Note also that in addition to the threshold and strength parameters for
repair and damping, we also obtained the uninfluenced parameters and
the number and location of the influenced steady states in each quadrant.

To implement the method in Alternative 1, which is described in section 13.4, we used the data file that contained weighted SPAFF data for
each second of the fifteen-minute conflict discussion; the range of data
for each second was $+4$ to -4. This gave us 900 time points for all 130
couples in the Seattle Newlywed Study. A Matlab program [187] was
created and run to iterate over the range between the minimum and
maximum value for each parameter. The minimum and maximum for
strength of repair and damping was set to the range 0 to 8, with an
increment of 1. The negative score threshold for repair was set to the
range 0 to -4, with an increment of 1. The positive score threshold for
damping was set to the range 0 to 4, with an increment of 1. Note that
the potential range of data for each time point was $+4$ to -4, so it is also
the potential range of the positive and negative score threshold parameters under this alternative. The program computed simulated scores for
each couple at each possible combination of parameter values. It then
calculated the least squares difference with the actual observed scores

and kept track of which combination of parameter values most closely fit the observed scores. The final threshold and strength parameter values were stored in another data file for subsequent statistical analyses.

It is, of course, possible to use a finer resolution in the increment for the threshold and strength parameters. However, we found that the above simulation with an increment of 1 for all parameters took over 12 hours on a UNIX workstation to complete all 130 couples. Because this application is computationally intense, we did not think it was practical to use a finer resolution for the parameters.

13.6   Results

As in previous chapters, we were interested in the ability of each alternative to predict which couples would divorce, and also to discriminate predictively between the happy stable, unhappy stable, and divorced couples.

Divorce Prediction

Tables 13.2 and 13.3 summarize the results from an analysis of variance of the parameters of Alternative 2 (fitting the bilinear model with repair and damping to the influence plots for each spouse) and of Alternative 1 (simulation with best fit to observed cumulative scores). This analysis compared the 17 couples who were divorced at Time-2 to the 113 stable couples (results significant at $\alpha = .10$ or less). Recall that the Time-1 data were obtained within the first year after the wedding, and the Time-2 divorce/stability categorization was based on six-year follow-up data.

Table 13.2 shows the results of an analysis of variance of the parameters obtained under Alternative 2—i.e., fitting the bilinear model with repair and damping to the influence plots for each spouse. In addition to the threshold and strength parameters, this model also gave us the uninfluenced parameters and the number of influenced steady states in each quadrant. Compared to the stable couples at Time-1, the divorced couples had significantly more influenced steady states where both partners' behavior was negative and significantly fewer influenced steady states where both partners' behavior was positive. For both husbands and wives in divorced couples, the initial uninfluenced state was negative (where they started that conversation), as was the uninfluenced steady state (where they would tend to be behaviorally in the absence of any particular influence from spouses during the conversation). For the stable couples, the initial state and uninfluenced steady state were positive for both husbands and wives. In other words, looking at both partners'

Table 13.2: Divorce Prediction Using Parameters of Alternative 2: Fitting the Bilinear Model with Repair and Damping to the Influence Plots for Each Spouse.

Variable	F-ratio	df	Means Stable	Means Divorced
Number of Influenced Steady States				
where $(W+)$ and $(H-)$	0.00	1,129	0.12	0.12
where $(W-)$ and $(H-)$	7.55**	1,129	0.54	1.24
where $(W+)$ and $(H+)$	7.44**	1,129	0.95	0.24
where $(W-)$ and $(H+)$	1.37	1,129	0.16	0.00
Wife				
Inertia	0.18	1,129	0.39	0.42
Initial state	22.14***	1,129	0.28	−1.13
Uninfluenced steady state	15.01***	1,129	0.50	−2.26
Influence on husband				
Positive half slope	0.00	1,124	0.53	0.52
Negative half slope	1.13	1,127	0.52	0.62
Threshold, husb damping	0.53	1,124	5.64	5.02
Strength, husb damping	2.95^a	1,124	−4.63	−3.14
Threshold, husb repair	0.16	1,127	−4.74	−4.40
Strength, husb repair	0.01	1,127	3.90	3.83
Husband				
Inertia	3.09^a	1,129	0.40	0.30
Initial state	23.34***	1,129	0.45	−1.11
Uninfluenced steady state	18.70***	1,129	0.70	−1.89
Influence on wife				
Positive half slope	0.00	1,126	0.50	0.50
Negative half slope	0.65	1,124	0.58	0.46
Threshold, wife damping	0.04	1,126	5.75	5.58
Strength, wife damping	8.04**	1,126	−4.30	−2.07
Threshold, wife repair	0.11	1,120	−4.68	−4.95
Strength, wife repair	0.06	1,120	3.43	3.58

^{a} $p < .10$, * $p < .05$, ** $p < .01$, *** $p < .001$.
$(W+)$ Wife Positive, $(W-)$ Wife Negative.
$(H+)$ Husband Positive, $(H-)$ Husband Negative.

behavior over time and at the influence of each person's behavior on the other person's behavior, for the divorced couples conversation started out negative and tended to stay that way. In contrast, the stable couples started out positive and tended to stay that way. With respect to parameters of the influence function, both husbands and wives in stable couples were significantly more effective at damping their response to

Table 13.3: Divorce Prediction Using Parameters of Alternative 1: Estimated from the Best Fit to Observed Cumulative Scores.

Variable	F-ratio	df	Means Stable	Means Divorced
Wife				
Threshold, husb damping	0.03	1,129	0.40	0.35
Strength, husb damping	0.00	1,129	3.52	3.53
Threshold, husb repair	1.26	1,129	-1.88	-1.35
Strength, husb repair	0.14	1,129	3.84	3.53
Husband				
Threshold, wife damping	0.05	1,129	0.42	0.47
Strength, wife damping	0.27	1,129	3.22	3.65
Threshold, wife repair	0.43	1,129	-1.72	-1.41
Strength, wife repair	0.07	1,129	3.55	3.76

[a] $p < .10$, * $p < .05$, ** $p < .01$, *** $p < .001$.

their spouse's positivity when it exceeded the threshold level. Although this finding might at first seem counterintuitive, we show later in this chapter that damping has the ability to introduce a previously nonexistent positive steady state that is stable and attracting for the couple. So it may be that effective damping can be in service of long-term stability of the relationship.

Table 13.3 shows the results of an analysis of variance of the parameters obtained by finding the simulated scores that best fit the observed cumulative scores for each couple. With Alternative 1, none of the parameters (threshold and strength of repair and damping for both spouses) were able to discriminate between the divorced and stable couples with any significance.

Summary of Divorce Prediction Results

Alternative 2 was much better at discriminating between the divorced and stable couples. However, many of the significant results were from the uninfluenced parameters, and these results were the same as for the simple bilinear model without the repair and damping components added to the influence function. Therefore, we need to examine in particular what was gained by adding repair and damping to the model. In general, the findings for the repair and damping parameters themselves (threshold and strength) were not our most robust results. They were nonsignificant using Alternative 1, and only the strength of damping was significant using Alternative 2 (both husband and wife), although this result might have an interesting explanation. Alternative 2 did yield more robust results in the number of influenced steady states for each quadrant, which is one of the strengths of this alternative. It allowed us to compute the null clines for each spouse and therefore the number and location of influenced steady states. These results offered interesting insights into the marital processes that may distinguish divorced from stable couples.

Three Criterion Groups

Although divorce prediction is of great interest to us, we would also like to be able to predict marital misery or happiness of couples who stayed married. The first criterion group, seventeen couples who divorced, constituted a natural extreme group. The second criterion group—couples who were still married but had the lowest scores in marital satisfaction of all of the stable couples—in comparison to the divorced couples, allowed us to keep marital unhappiness constant while varying only marital stability. The third criterion group—couples who were still married but had the highest scores in marital satisfaction of all of the stable couples—in comparison to the second criterion group, held marital stability constant while varying only marital happiness. We selected samples for the second and third groups comparable in size to the number of divorced couples. This was the logic in constructing three criterion groups.

Tables 13.4 and 13.5 summarize the results from a second analysis of variance of the parameters of Alternative 2 (fitting the bilinear model with repair and damping to the influence plots for each spouse) and Alternative 1 (simulation with best fit to observed cumulative scores). This analysis determined which Time-1 parameters could significantly predict which group the couples wound up in: happy stable, unhappy stable, or divorced (results significant at $\alpha = .10$ or less). It compared the seventeen couples who divorced to the twenty most happily married and the twenty most unhappily married of the stable group. Recall that the data were obtained within the first year after the wedding, and the divorce/stability and marital satisfaction categorization was based on six-year follow-up data.

Table 13.4 shows the results of an analysis of variance of the parameters obtained under Alternative 2—i.e., fitting the bilinear model with repair and damping to the influence plots for each spouse. Recall that in addition to the threshold and strength parameters, this model also gave us the uninfluenced parameters and the number of influenced steady states in each quadrant. There was a significant difference between the three groups in the number of influenced steady states where both part-

Table 13.4: Three Criterion Groups and Parameters of Alternative 2: Fitting the Bilinear Model with Repair and Damping to the Influence Plots for Each Spouse.

			Means		
			Happy,	Unhappy,	
Variable	F-ratio	df	Stable	Stable	Div.
Number of Influenced Steady States					
where $(W+)$ and $(H-)$	0.05	2,55	0.15	0.15	0.12
where $(W-)$ and $(H-)$	4.78*	2,55	0.20	0.95	1.24
where $(W+)$ and $(H+)$	6.27**	2,55	1.20	0.55	0.24
where $(W-)$ and $(H+)$	0.42	2,55	0.01	0.01	0.00
Wife					
Inertia	0.32	2,55	0.37	0.41	0.42
Initial state	11.51***	2,55	0.64	−0.02	−1.13
Uninfluenced steady state	13.21***	2,55	1.17	−0.26	−2.26
Influence on husband					
Positive half slope	0.41	2,51	0.46	0.55	0.52
Negative half slope	0.39	2,54	0.51	0.65	0.62
Threshold, husb damping	1.30	2,51	5.15	6.82	5.02
Strength, husb damping	2.36	2,51	−3.41	−4.87	−3.14
Threshold, husb repair	2.79[a]	2,54	−6.27	−3.87	−4.40
Strength, husb repair	0.55	2,54	4.20	3.44	3.83
Husband					
Inertia	0.59	2,55	0.37	0.35	0.30
Initial state	9.77***	2,55	0.74	−0.04	−1.11
Uninfluenced steady state	10.34***	2,55	1.03	−0.47	−1.89
Influence on wife					
Positive half slope	1.00	2,54	0.51	0.39	0.50
Negative half slope	0.71	2,53	0.68	0.48	0.46
Threshold, wife damping	0.12	2,54	5.27	5.75	5.58
Strength, wife damping	3.05[a]	2,54	−3.98	−3.61	−2.07
Threshold, wife repair	0.02	2,50	−5.16	−5.03	−4.95
Strength, wife repair	0.51	2,50	3.34	2.94	3.58

[a] $p < .10$, * $p < .05$, ** $p < .01$, *** $p < .001$.
$(W+)$ Wife Positive, $(W-)$ Wife Negative.
$(H+)$ Husband Positive, $(H-)$ Husband Negative.

ners' behavior was negative and also in the number of influenced steady states where both partners' behavior was positive. The divorced couples were more than six times as likely to have a steady state where both partners' behavior was negative than were the happy stable couples.

Table 13.5: Three Criterion Groups and Parameters of
Alternative 1: Estimated from the Best Fit to Observed
Cumulative Scores.

				Means	
			Happy	Unhappy	
Variable	F-ratio	df	Stable	Stable	Divorced
Wife					
Threshold, husb damping	1.22	2,55	0.40	0.90	0.35
Strength, husb damping	1.88	2,55	2.50	4.40	3.53
Threshold, husb repair	0.70	2,55	−1.95	−1.45	−1.35
Strength, husb repair	0.60	2,55	3.15	4.20	3.53
Husband					
Threshold, wife damping	0.10	2,55	0.45	0.60	0.47
Strength, wife damping	2.01	2,55	2.10	4.00	3.65
Threshold, wife repair	2.83[a]	2,55	−2.20	−0.95	−1.41
Strength, wife repair	0.52	2,55	3.25	4.30	3.76

[a] $p < .10$, * $p < .05$, ** $p < .01$, *** $p < .001$.

Conversely, the happy stable couples were almost six times as likely as
the divorced couples to have a steady state where both partners' behavior was positive. In both cases, the unhappy stable couples had a mean
somewhere in between.

There was a strongly significant difference between the three groups
in the initial state (how they started out the conversation) and in the
uninfluenced steady state (where they would tend to be behaviorally in
the absence of any particular influence from their spouse during the conversation). For the divorced group, both the initial state and the uninfluenced steady state were negative (both husbands and wives). For the
unhappy stable group, both of these parameters were slightly negative
to near neutral (both husbands and wives). For the happy stable group,
both the initial state and the uninfluenced steady state were positive
(both husbands and wives). In other words, looking at both partners'
behavior over time and at the influence of each person's behavior on
the other person's behavior, for the divorced couples the conversation
started out negative and tended to stay that way. The case was the
opposite for the happy stable couples, and the unhappy stable couples
fell somewhere in between.

Looking at the threshold and strength parameters of the repair and
damping components of the influence function, there were two marginally
significant results. The wives in the happy stable group had to become

more negative than did the wives in the other two groups in order to trigger their husband's repair $(F(2, 54) = 2.786, p = .071)$. The other finding was that the wives in the stable couples (the 20 most happy and the 20 most unhappy) had higher strength of damping than did the wives in the couples who divorced $(F(2, 54) = 3.052, p = .056)$. This reinforces the finding in Table 13.2, where this parameter was seen to significantly discriminate between all 113 stable couples and the 17 divorced couples. Again we point out that although this finding might seem counterintuitive, we show later in this chapter that damping has the ability to introduce a previously nonexistent positive steady state that is stable and attracting for the couple.

Table 13.5 shows the results of an analysis of variance of the parameters obtained under Alternative 1—i.e., finding the simulated scores that best fit the observed cumulative scores for each couple. There was one marginally significant finding that the husbands in the happy stable group had to become more negative than did the husbands in the other two groups in order to trigger their wife's repair $(F(2, 55) = 2.827, p = .068)$. Although marginally significant, we found this finding to be somewhat puzzling because it counters the conclusions of Chapter 12, where we found for this same newlywed sample that there was less adaptation to husband negativity on the part of those wives whose marriages wound up being stable.

Summary of Results for the Three Criterion Groups

The results were strikingly similar to the divorce prediction results. Many of the same parameters that significantly predicted whether a couple would divorce or not were also able to discriminate predictively between the three groups. Again, it appeared that Alternative 2 was much better at discriminating between the three criterion groups. However, it was also again the case that many of the significant results were from the uninfluenced parameters, and we have pointed out that these results are the same as in the simple bilinear model without the repair and damping components added to the influence function. What was gained by adding repair and damping to the model? In general, the findings for the repair and damping parameters themselves (threshold and strength) were as follows. One marginally significant result was somewhat puzzling using Alternative 1, and two marginally significant results were puzzling using Alternative 2. Alternative 2 did yield more significant results in the number of influenced steady states for each quadrant, which again we note may be one of the strengths of this alternative.

Table 13.6: Divorce Prediction Using Couples with High
Husband Negativity at Time-1.

| | | | Means | |
Variable	F-ratio	df	Stable	Divorced
Alternative 2				
Threshold for husb repair	1.15	1,27	−5.81	−4.16
Strength of husb repair	4.39*	1,27	4.28	3.05
Threshold for wife repair	0.17	1,27	−5.56	−5.03
Strength of wife repair	0.54	1,27	3.16	3.61
Alternative 1				
Threshold for husb repair	0.04	1,27	−1.63	−1.50
Strength of husb repair	0.76	1,27	3.00	4.00
Threshold for wife repair	0.15	1,27	−1.94	−1.67
Strength of wife repair	2.13	1,27	2.44	4.08

^{a} $p < .10$, * $p < .05$, ** $p < .01$, *** $p < .001$

Couples with High Time-1 Negativity

We know from previous research that high levels of negativity during
the conflict discussion are predictive of divorce. Yet, in the Seattle
Newlywed Study, we also know that some couples who had high levels of
negativity in the Time-1 conflict discussion were still married at the six-
year follow-up. We were curious as to why some couples with high levels
of negativity at Time-1 remained married, but others were divorced at
Time-2. We hypothesized that the couples who stayed married might be
better at repairing negativity. They might repair at a lower threshold
or be more effective at repair or both.

To test this hypothesis, we found the median level of negativity for
the fifty-seven couples in the three criterion groups, for both husband
and wife. Total negativity was the number of seconds during the fifteen-
minute conflict discussion where they were SPAFF coded with contempt,
defensiveness, stonewalling, belligerence, or domineering. The sample
could then be split at the median, that is, the high-negativity couples
were the ones with total negativity above the median. We made this
split to select a subset with high husband negativity ($N = 28$), again
for high wife negativity ($N = 28$), and we also selected a subset where
either husbands or wives were above their respective median ($N = 36$).
For each of these subsets, we ran a univariate analysis of variance for
the four repair parameters (husband and wife thresholds and strength
of repair), for the two alternatives considered above.

All results were nonsignificant for the subset with high Time-1 wife negativity and for the subset in which either husbands or wives had high negativity at Time-1. The results of those analyses are therefore not given in a table here. However, as seen in table 13.6, there was a significant finding for the subset with high husband negativity at Time-1. Using the repair parameters from Alternative 2 (bilinear model with repair and damping terms in the influence function), the couples who stayed married had higher husband strength of repair than did the couples who divorced. Husband strength of repair was able to discriminate predictively between the couples who stayed married and the couples who divorced, when high husband negativity was coded during the Time-1 conflict discussion.

Even though the stable, high-negativity husbands did display a relatively large amount of negativity toward their wives, when they detected negativity in their wives above a certain threshold, they were better able to moderate their own subsequent behavior. They were better able to "tone down" their response to their wives' negativity. This is consistent with findings in Gottman *et al.* (1998) that de-escalation of negativity by the husband and concomitant physiological soothing of the male are predictive of positive outcomes in the marriage.

13.7   Model Behavior with Repair and Damping

Null Clines and Steady States

In chapter 7, we discussed the concept of null clines and their use in locating the steady states of the model system: the steady states are found at the inter-section of the null clines. Recall that the present model with repair and damping is given by equation (13.3). Along the wife's null cline, the wife's score W_t does not change in time: $W_{t+1} = W_t = W$. Similarly, $H_{t+1} = H_t = H$ along the husband's null cline. Substitution into (13.3) gives the following equations for the null clines:

$$N_{HW}(H): \ W = \frac{1}{1-r_1}\left(I_{HW}(H) + a + C_{rw}\frac{|H-K_{rh}| - (H-K_{rh})}{1-(H-K_{rh})}\right.$$
$$\left. + C_{dw}\frac{|H-K_{dh}| + (H-K_{dh})}{1+(H-K_{dh})}\right)$$

$$N_{WH}(W): \ H = \frac{1}{1-r_2}\left(I_{WH}(W) + b + C_{rh}\frac{|W-K_{rw}| - (W-K_{rw})}{1-(W-K_{rw})}\right.$$
$$\left. + C_{dh}\frac{|W-K_{dw}| + (W-K_{dw})}{1+(W-K_{dw})}\right),$$

$$(13.4)$$

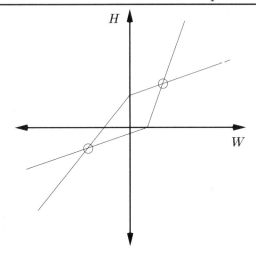

Figure 13.12: Null clines (solid line) and steady states
(circles) for the model without repair or damping.

where N_{HW} and N_{WH} are the null clines for the wife and husband,
respectively. These expressions are certainly complicated, yet with the
previous formulation of the model without repair and damping the geometry of the null clines is fairly simple.

Figure 13.12 shows a simple example of the null clines we might
expect from the model without repair and damping (equation (13.4)
with $C_{rw} = C_{rh} = C_{dw} = C_{dh} = 0$). In this simple case of bilinear null
clines, there could exist as many as two steady states.

With the introduction of repair and damping, the geometry of the
null clines becomes more complicated. Figure 13.13 shows three of the
many possible null cline geometries we might expect from the model with
repair and damping. The dotted line portion of the graphs represents
the null clines if repair and damping are not present. Note that although
there are only two steady states in figure 13.13a if we adjust the model
parameters to alter the null clines, the number of steady states can
change. Figure 13.13b shows four steady states, and figure 13.13c shows
five steady states. In later sections of this chapter, we discuss in detail
how changes in individual model parameters affect the location of steady
states. One conclusion surprised us. Damping is not necessarily a bad
thing. In figure 13.13(b), the couple would not have had a positive
steady state without damping.

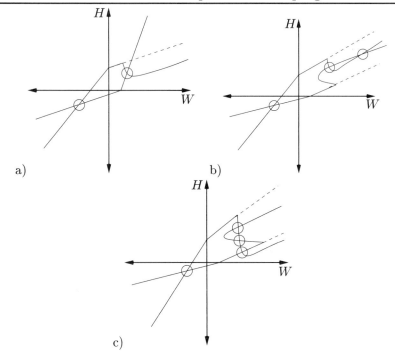

Figure 13.13: Null clines (solid lines) and steady states (circles) for the model with repair and/or damping.

Stability of Steady States

Now that we have located where the null clines intersect, we need to determine the stability of these steady states.

Following calculations similar to those presented in chapter 9 and detailed in appendix A, we found that for the model with repair and damping equation (13.3), a steady state is stable if

$$|r_1 + r_2| < 1 + r_1 r_2 - (\alpha_1 + \epsilon_1)(\alpha_2 + \epsilon_2) < 2, \qquad (13.5)$$

where r_1 and r_2 represent the inertia of the partners, α_1 and α_2 are the slopes of the bilinear portion of the influence at the steady state, and ϵ_1 and ϵ_2 are the slopes of the repair or damping portion of the influence at the steady state. Recall that the inertia parameters are positive and less than unity: $0 \leq r_1 \leq 1$, $0 \leq r_2$. The slopes of the bilinear influence function are constant and always positive: $\alpha_1 > 0, \alpha_2 > 0$. The slopes of the repair and damping portion of the influence are always

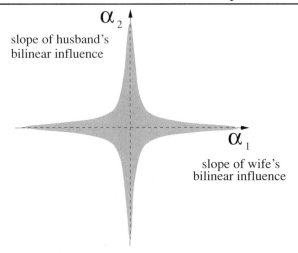

Figure 13.14: Region of the $\alpha_1 - \alpha_2$ plane where steady states of the model without repair or damping are stable as defined by equation (13.6).

negative, because if repair or damping is on and affect increases, then influence decreases (see figures 13.1 and 13.4). Equation (13.5) is fairly cumbersome, so we begin by first recalling the simpler case of the model without repair and damping.

Without Repair or Damping

Recall that without repair and damping, we have the condition

$$|r_1 + r_2| < 1 + r_1 r_2 - \alpha_1 \alpha_2 < 2 \qquad (13.6)$$

for stability of a steady state. This condition requires that, for given inertias r_1 and r_2, the slopes of the bilinear portion of the influence α_1 and α_2 have to be bounded. The shaded region of figure 13.14 defines the segment of the $\alpha_1 - \alpha_2$ plane defined by equation (13.6), for which the steady state is stable.

From figure 13.14, we see that if the slope of the influence function is small for both partners (i.e., α_1 and α_2 are small), then the steady state will be stable. In this case, a change in affect results in a small change in influence so that neither partner responds disproportionately. We can think of this case as "neutral", when changes in a partner's affect has little or no effect on the other partner's affect. These small reponses to changes in affect suggest that such a steady state would be a stable attractor for the couple. Although the couple can be perturbed away from this stable steady state, over a long time we would expect the couple to approach this neutral situation.

Alternatively, figure 13.14 also indicates that if one partner's influence function slope is large (say, α_1 large), the other partner's slope has to be small for the steady state to be stable. This case is represented by the long tails of the shaded region extending along the axes in figure 13.14. That is, one partner may respond disproportionately to small changes in the other's affect (α_1 large), as long as the other partner remains fairly controlled (α_2 small). In other words, one volatile partner can be counteracted by the other partner's neutrality to result in stability of the steady state.

Now that we understand the stability restrictions required for the model without repair and damping, we can explore the implications for our new model.

With Repair and Damping

Mathematically, by comparing equations (13.5) and (13.6), we see that repair and damping act to decrease the slope of the influence function α_1, α_2 in the stability condition. That is, the stability domain for a steady state from the model with repair and damping is defined by replacing α_i with $\alpha_i + \epsilon_i$ in equation (13.6), where ϵ_i is less than zero and represents the slope of the repair and damping term at the steady state. The portion of the $\alpha_1 - \alpha_2$ plane for which the steady state is stable is given in figure 13.15.

Recall that for the model without repair and damping we expect the neutral situation, when the slope of the influence function for each partner is small ($\alpha_1 \approx 0, \alpha_2 \approx 0$), to be stable. Because repair and damping act to decrease the slope of the influence function, this previously defined neutral situation of $\alpha_1 \approx 0$, $\alpha_2 \approx 0$ may be unstable for the model with repair or damping or both (see figure 13.15). In fact, the slope of the influence function can be high as long as the slope of the damping or repair portion of the influence is significant enough to counteract the steep bilinear influence at the steady state. This is manifested in the plot of the stability region defined by equation (13.5) in figure 13.15, for which the seemingly neutral case of $\alpha_1 \approx 0$ and $\alpha_2 \approx 0$ is unstable. Therefore, couples who repair or dampen extensively when it is not necessary (i.e., $\alpha_i \approx 0$, so a dramatic response is not necessary) can destabilize their neutral steady state. For stability in this case, the couple must respond more dramatically to small changes in affect (α_i large) to counteract their excessive repair or damping. This situation is

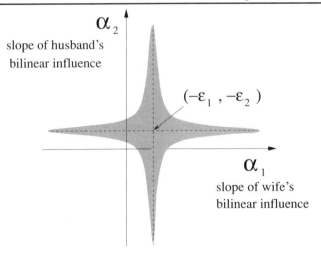

Figure 13.15: Region of the $\alpha_1 - \alpha_2$ plane where steady states of the model with repair or damping are stable. ϵ_1 and ϵ_2 are the slopes of the repair or damping terms at the steady state.

represented by a large number of couple data points in quadrant II and quadrant IV.

Assessing the Effectiveness of an Intervention

A key benefit of mathematical modeling is the ability to alter parameters theoretically in the system and predict the outcome. This type of information would be of considerable interest to marital therapists. By predicting the conditions necessary for a successful model marriage, the therapist can then make suggestions on how a couple may alter their behavior and perception for a stable and happy marriage. In this analysis, we are looking to identify criteria for the stability of the steady states as well as the location of the steady states. What good does the existence of a negative stable steady state provide for a couple seeking a long-term happy marriage?

In this section, we consider the effects of altering each of the model parameters on the resultant steady-state locations and stabilities.

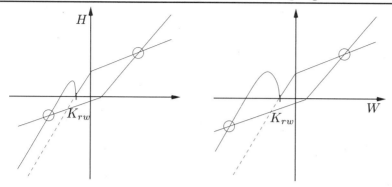

Figure 13.16: Increasing strength of repair coefficient C_{rh} for the case where repair begins early (K_{rw} is small and negative). As C_{rh} increases, the negative steady-state location moves more negatively. In this case, the stability of the steady state remains the same as C_{rh} increases.

Strength of Repair: C_{rw}, C_{rh}

A typical null cline geometry we may expect from the model without repair or damping is given in figure 13.12. To consider the effect of repair in determining the steady states of the model, we increase the strength of repair coefficient for only one of the partners, say C_{rh}. Figures 13.16 and 13.17 show the effect of increasing the strength of repair for two different cases. In the first case (figure 13.16), the husband begins to repair early (i.e., when negativity is small as defined by K_{rw} small and, of course, negative). In the latter case (figure 13.17), the husband begins to repair later (i.e., when negativity is large as defined by K_{rw} large).

"Early" Repair (K_{rw} Small)   Figure 13.16 demonstrates the effect of increasing the strength of repair coefficient C_{rh} on the resulting steady-state locations. As the husband's repair attempts become stronger, the negative steady state, originally located at the intersection of the solid and dotted lines, moves progressively more negatively. Because the slope of the intersection of the null clines at the negative steady state remains essentially the same with or without repair, we do not expect the stability of the negative steady state to change, although its location does change. Now as the negative steady state moves more and more negatively, if the positive steady state is stable, there is a better chance that the couple will be attracted to the positive steady state (i.e., the basin of attraction for the positive steady state increases in size).

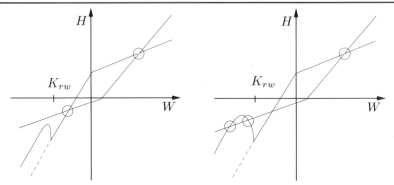

Figure 13.17: Increasing strength of repair coefficient C_{rh} for the case where repair begins late (K_{rh} is large and negative). As C_{rh} increases, the number of negative steady states increases.

"Late" Repair (K_{rw} Large)   Figure 13.17 shows the effect of increasing the strength of repair if the repair does not begin until the conversation is very negative (K_{rw} is large and negative). If the strength of repair C_{rh} is small, then the figure 13.17a shows that the steady-state location may not be affected. Alternatively, if the repair attempts are stronger, then two additional negative steady states can be introduced (see figure 13.17b). One of these steady states may be stable. So repair can act to introduce negative stable steady states. This result seems a bit counterintuitive because we expect repair to be helpful to the couple when in fact the increasing strength of repair introduces additional negative steady states, which may be stable attractors for the couple.

Threshold for Repair: K_{rw}, K_{rh}

For a fixed strength of repair, figure 13.18 shows how the negative steady-state locations change as the threshold for repair K_{rw} becomes more negative. When repair begins early and negativity is small, the negative steady state from the model without repair (defined as the intersection of the solid and dotted lines) is moved more negatively. When repair is switched on just after the location of the steady state for the model without repair, an additional steady state is introduced. If the repair switch is decreased further, then the additional negative steady states disappear, and we return to the case of only one negative steady state situated at the same location as that defined by the model without repair.

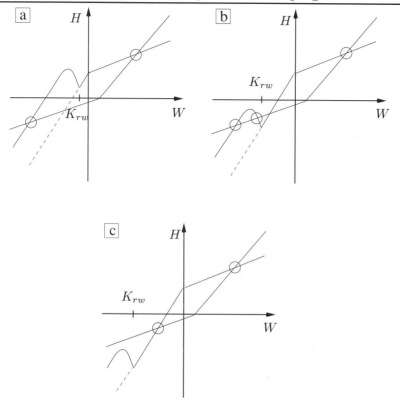

Figure 13.18: Increasing repair coefficient K_{rw}.

Strength of Damping: C_{dw}, C_{dh}

To consider the effect of damping in determining the steady states of the model, we increase the strength of the damping coefficient for only one of the partners, say C_{dh}. Figures 13.19 and 13.20 show the effect of increasing the strength of damping for two different cases. In the first case (figure 13.19), the husband begins damping early (i.e., when positivity is small as defined by K_{dw} small). In the latter case (figure 13.20), the husband begins damping later (i.e., when positivity is large as defined by K_{dw} large).

"Early" Damping (K_{dw} Small) As demonstrated by the decrease in positivity of the location of the positive steady state in figure 13.19, we expect the couple to be detrimentally affected by the excess negativity

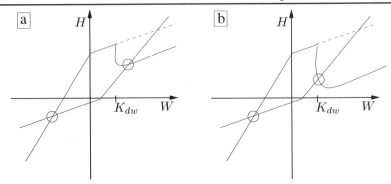

Figure 13.19: Increasing strength of damping coefficient C_{dh} for the case where damping begins early (K_{dw} small). The dashed line represents the null cline if damping is not active: (a) null clines for C_{dh} small, (b) null clines for C_{dh} large.

associated with early damping. Damping may be thought of as a means of controlling excessive positivity. If damping begins too soon, there is no exuberant positivity to mediate resulting in damping to the long-term happiness of the relationship. Figure 13.19 shows that in this case of an early damping switch (K_{dw} small), the steady state of the system decreases in positivity from the steady state we would expect if damping were not present (intersection of solid and dotted line).

Let us consider this example in a slightly different light by assuming that if the husband is not damping, then the steady state, defined by the intersection of the dotted line and the solid line in figure 13.19, is stable. The couple has a positive (quadrant I) stable steady state, suggesting that they may have a happy and stable relationship. Now once the husband begins damping, the steady-state location decreases in positivity for both the wife and the husband (the steady state moves from the intersecton of the dashed line and the solid line to the intersection indicated by the circle in quadrant I). Figure 13.19 shows the negative motion of the steady state as the strength of the damping C_{dh} increases.

Recall that the stability of the steady states depends critically on the slope of the null cline at the steady-state location. In figure 13.19a the slope of the null cline (the slope of the bilinear influence portion α_1 and the damping portion ϵ_1 in equation (13.5)) is similar to the slope at the nondamping steady-state location (circle), so we might expect this steady-state to be stable still. In this case, damping has altered the steady state location but has not affected the stability. Now, in

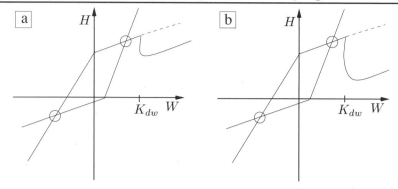

Figure 13.20: Increasing strength of damping coefficient C_{dh} for the case where damping begins late. The dashed line represents the null cline if damping is not active.

figure 13.19b the slope of the null cline is much steeper at the steady state than at the nondamping steady state, which indicates that the steady state is probably unstable. In this case, the increased damping by the husband has not only decreased the positivity of the steady state but also destabilized it. Upon closer consideration, we see also that as the strength of damping coefficient C_{dh} increases in magnitude, the wife's steady-state location approaches the damping switch value K_{dw}. If $W = K_{dw}$, then the slope of the null cline (the slope of the bilinear portion α_1 plus the slope of the damping portion ϵ_1) is infinite and the steady state must be unstable!

From this example, we might expect that if damping is small in magnitude, it may not significantly detriment the couple's ultimate happiness. Alternatively, as the magnitude of damping increases, the couple can lose the stability of their positive steady state and be attracted to another (perhaps negative) steady state.

"Late" Damping (K_{dw} Large)   Figure 13.20 shows that if damping does not initiate until the conversation has exceeded the steady-state location defined by the model without damping, then the location of the steady state will not be affected. Also, because the slopes of the null clines at steady states are unchanged, the stability of these states are unaffected by the damping.

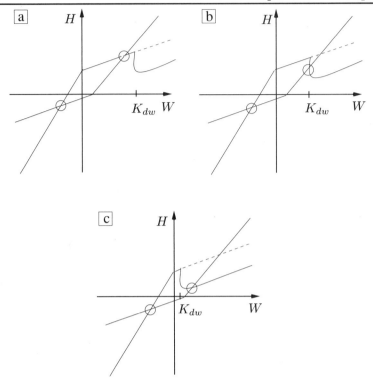

Figure 13.21: Increasing the damping coefficient K_{dw}

Threshold for Damping: K_{dw}, K_{dh}

We now consider what happens when it is only the threshold for damping K_{dw} that is adjusted. Figure 13.21 considers the effect of decreasing the damping switch K_{dw} such that the husband begins to dampen earlier and earlier. In figure 13.21a, we see that if damping does not initiate until the conversation is very positive, then it has no effect on the couple's steady state or stability. The location of the steady state is not adjusted by the introduction of damping.

As the damping switch decreases and the husband is damping earlier and earlier, figures 13.21b and c show the steady state decreasing in positivity. When damping initiates just before the location of the steady state without damping (intersection of the solid and dashed lines), then the slope of the null cline at the steady state (circle) can be very steep. Because stability depends critically on the slope of the null clines, the

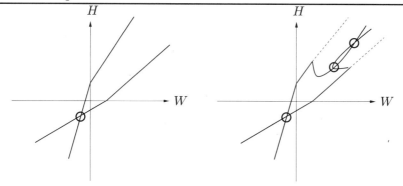

Figure 13.22: Beneficial damping for happy couples showing the null clines for the model (a) without damping and (b) with damping.

steady state in figure 13.21b may be unstable. But if the switch K_{dw} is decreased further, the steady state can become stable again. It seems clear that the location at which damping initiates is critical in the couple's long-term behavior.

13.8 Interpretations and Predictions

Damping Can Be Important Even for Happy Couples

Although it may not seem clear, damping can play an important role in controlling the positivity of a couple. If the husband and wife bilinear influence function slopes are sufficiently high, then it is possible for there to be no positive steady state (see figure 13.22), which means there can be one or more stable negative steady states. Therefore, no matter what the initial disposition of the couple's conversation, they are inevitably attracted to a negative steady state, although each partner responds with increasing positivity to the other's positivity. Figure 13.22a shows an example of such a case, where the rate of change of influence is high for positive affect values; therefore, the null clines do not intersect in the positive quadrant I. Damping has the ability to damp the positivity of the couple to introduce a previously nonexistent positive steady state, which could be stable and attracting for the couple. Figure 13.22b shows the same couple as in figure 13.22a but with effective damping by both the husband and the wife, inducing the introduction of two positive steady states. Mathematically, we know that at least one of these

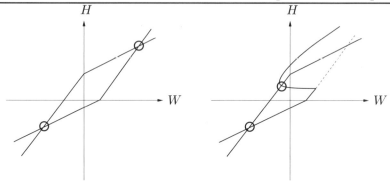

Figure 13.23: Detrimental damping for happy couples showing the null clines for the model (a) without damping and (b) with damping.

positive steady states will be stable. This problem is an interesting one for marital therapy; although it seems clear that it is critical that couples repair effectively, it may also be necessary for the couple to dampen effectively for long-term stability of the relationship. This model result agrees with the observation that happy stable marriages are not entirely without negativity.

One Happy Partner with One Unhappy Partner

Damping can also be detrimental to a happy couple. Figure 13.23a shows a couple with only one positive steady state. If the wife begins to dampen excessively, the steady state can move negatively so that it ends up in quadrant II (see figure 13.23b). If this steady state is stable, the wife will tend to be negative, and the husband will remain positive. Therefore, under our model, there can exist stable steady states for which one partner tends to be happy and content, but the other does not.

14

Extending the Marriage Model: Gay Male and Lesbian Relationships and Parent-Child Interaction

14.1   Gay Male and Lesbian Relationships

In 1983, *American Couples*, an important book published by Blumstein and Schwartz, reported the results of more than twelve thousand questionnaires and more than three hundred interviews with gay male, lesbian, married heterosexual, and cohabiting heterosexual couples on issues related to money, work, power, and sex. It was a landmark study, despite the fact that it preceded the AIDS epidemic, which was to have such a large impact on gay male and lesbian relationships (Andriote, 1999). However, even before 1983, in research done at the Kinsey Institute in the 1960s, Weinberg and Williams (1974) reported that 71% of their sample of gay men between the ages of thirty-six and forty-five were living with a partner, and in the 1970s Bell and Weinberg (1978) found that 82% of their sample of lesbians were currently living with someone. The AIDS epidemic increased this trend, and the preponderance of homosexual relationships are committed relationships. However, they may not be monogamous. Research on gay male and lesbian relationships by Kurdek (e.g., Kurdek, 1998) shows that they operate on the same principles (using a self-report model of cost-benefit analysis) as heterosexual relationships, except that there are fewer barriers to leaving, and gay male relationships emphasize autonomy more than do heterosexual relationships. Lesbian relationships report more intimacy, more autonomy, and more equality than heterosexual relationships. There are many myths about homosexual relationships, such as the "Butch/Femme hypothesis" and enmeshment in lesbian relationships, but Harry (1983) refuted many of these myths from a research standpoint.

This chapter reports the results of our mathematical modeling of gay male and lesbian relationships. To our knowledge, this is the *first longitudinal observational study* of gay male and lesbian relationships. This twelve-year longitudinal study was conducted in collaboration with Professor Robert W. Levenson of the University of California, Berkeley. We report only a few results here to illustrate the use of our mathematical modeling. Two samples of heterosexual couples were also part of the experimental design. One was a group of couples in which the woman presented a conflict issue to her husband. There was also a group of couples in which the man presented the issue to his wife. This presentation created a two-by-two factorial design in which one factor was who initiated the issue (man or woman), and the second factor was sexual orientation (heterosexual or homosexual). We could thus compare what it was like when a man presented an issue to a man he loved and was committed to with what it was like when a man presented an issue to a woman he loved and was committed to. Similarly, we could compare what it was like when a woman presented an issue to a woman she loved and was committed to with what it was like when a woman presented an issue to a man she loved and was committed to.

To our knowledge, there has been no direct observational research of gay male and lesbian committed relationships. Instead, studies have relied on self-report methods using questionnaires or interviews. By and large, these studies have concluded that the dynamics of gay male and lesbian relationships are not very different from those in committed heterosexual relationships (Blumstein and Schwartz, 1983).

Method

Samples of Gay Male and Lesbian Couples. Recruitment was done by advertising in the classified sections of the Berkeley and San Francisco gay newspapers, by posting flyers, by contacting various lesbian groups, and by using public service announcements with Bay Area radio stations stating "volunteer couples, including those with relationship problems, needed for a paid UC Berkeley research project on committed relationships." Couples had to be between the ages of twenty-one and forty and they had to have lived together in a committed relationship for at least two years. Couples who responded to the recruitment effort filled out a General Information Form and a Relationship-Adjustment Questionnaire for each partner. Couples were paid ten dollars for completing the questionnaires. Based on these data and on the selection of a wide range of relationship satisfaction scores, ten couples were invited to participate in the second phase of the study, which consisted of filling out a larger battery of questions and attending a total of three research sessions in the laboratory on the Berkeley campus. Our other selection criteria were: (1) no more than a ten year difference in ages between partners, (2) childless, (3) no previous committed heterosexual relationships (i.e. cohabitation), (4) discrepancy in Locke-Wallace relationship satisfaction scores no more than 25, and, (5) only English spoken at home. Both partners attended the first session together, and each partner attended one additional session separately. Each session lasted for two to three hours. Couples participating in this second phase were paid ten dollars for completing the battery of questionnaires and forty dollars for completing the laboratory sessions. During the first three-hour session, couples were asked to carry out three short, everyday conversations with each other while a video recording was made and we measured several physiological signals (such as heart rate, finger pulse, and skin conductance). Couples were asked to arrive in the laboratory after having been separated for at least eight hours so that they could begin by discussing the events of their day. Defining *happy* as having a Locke-Wallace mean for the partners greater or equal to 115, and *unhappy* as having a mean less than 115, we counted twelve happy gay male couples, and ten unhappy gay male couples, ten happy lesbian couples and eight unhappy lesbian couples.

Married Couple Sample The comparison married couple sample was selected from a larger longitudinal study that recruited couples from the environs of Bloomington, Indiana, beginning in 1983. Married couples were selected and matched to the gay male and lesbian samples in relationship satisfaction and length of their relationship; twenty married couples were selected for which the husband presented the conflict issue, and twenty married couples were selected for which the wife presented the issue. These married couples had undergone precisely the same experimental procedures as had the gay male and lesbian couples.

Demographics The lesbians were an average of 29.3 years old, and the gay men were an average of 32.5 years old. The married couples for which the women initiated the issue were an average of 28.7 years old, and the married couples for which the men initiated the issue were an average of 29.6 years old. The mean Locke-Wallace relationship satisfaction score of the lesbians was 113.2, and the mean Locke-Wallace relationship satisfaction score of the gay men was 116.0. The mean Locke-Wallace relationship satisfaction score of the married couples for which the women initiated was 121.8, and the mean Locke-Wallace relationship satisfaction score of the married couples for which the men initiated was 99.0.

Interaction Session The procedures employed in this experiment were modeled after those developed by Levenson and Gottman (1983). Couples came to the laboratory after having not spoken to each other for at least eight hours. After recording devices for obtaining physiological measures were attached, couples engaged in three conversations: (a) discussing the events of the day; (b) discussing a problem area of continuing disagreement in their relationship; and (c) discussing a mutually agreed upon pleasant topic. Each conversation lasted for fifteen minutes, preceded by a five-minute silent period. During the silent periods and discussions, a broad sample of physiological measures was obtained, and a video recording was made of the interaction. For the events of the day conversation, subjects were simply told to discuss what had happened during the day. Prior to initiating the problem area discussion, couples completed the Couples Problem Inventory (Gottman, Markman, and Notarius, 1977) , in which they rated the perceived severity of ten relationship issues on a 0 to 100 scale. Prior to initiating the pleasant topic discussion, couples completed a similar inventory, in which they rated the enjoyment they derived from sixteen topics on a 0 to 100 scale. The experimenter used these inventories to help couples select the topics they were to use in these two conversations.

Observational Coding SPAFF (Gottman *et al.*, 1996) was used to code the interaction of all subjects for the conflict discussion. The lesbian and gay male interactions during the events of the day conversation and the pleasant topic conversation were also coded with the SPAFF. The SPAFF was used to index specific affects expressed during the session of relationship problem resolution. SPAFF focuses solely on the affects expressed. The system draws on facial expression (based on Ekman and Friesen's system of facial action coding; Ekman and Friesen, 1978), vocal tone, and speech content to characterize the emotions displayed. Coders categorized the affects displayed using five positive codes (interest, validation, affection, humor, excitement/joy), ten negative affect codes (disgust, contempt, belligerence, domineering, anger, fear/tension, defensiveness, whining, sadness, stonewalling), and a neutral affect code. Every videotape was coded in its entirety by two independent observers using a computer-assisted coding system that automated the collection of timing information; each coder noted only the onset of each code. The result was a file for each observer containing 900 data points, which were the SPAFF codes observed at each second during the 15-minute conversation. A time-locked confusion matrix for the entire videotape was then computed using a one-second window for determining agreement of each code in one observer's coding against all of the other observer's coding (see Bakeman and Gottman, 1986). For the conflict segment for married couples, the Cronbach alpha generalizability coefficients summed over partners were: affection, .88; anger, .76; belligerence, .89; contempt, .92; defensiveness, .99; disgust, .62; domineering, .96; humor, .95; interest, .92; excitement/joy, .32; sadness, .82; stonewalling, .64; fear/tension, .98; validation, .97; and whining, .86. For the conflict segment for gays and lesbians, the Cronbach alpha generalizability coefficients summed over partners were: affection, .86; anger, .86; belligerence, .91; contempt, .67; defensiveness, .97; disgust, .37; domineering, .84; humor, .96; interest, .75; excitement/joy, .56; sadness, .72; stonewalling, .75; fear/tension, .95; validation, .96; and whining, .81. This coefficient has value between 0 and 1.0, and a higher value indicates better observer agreement.

Weighting of the SPAFF Codes For the mathematical modeling, we used the weighting scheme derived from previous prediction research (Gottman, 1994a) and described in chapter 12. Each SPAFF code received an appropriate positive or negative weight, and then these weights were summed over six-second time blocks. The weights are as follows: disgust, -3; contempt, -4; belligerence, -2; domineering, -1; anger, -1; fear, 0; defensiveness, -2; whining, -1; sadness, -1; stonewalling, -2; neutral, 0.1; interest, $+2$; validation, $+4$; affection, $+4$; humor, $+4$; and excitement/joy, $+4$. This weighting yields a potential range of -24 to $+24$. For each couple, this created two time series, each with 150 data points, one series for the initiator and one for the partner. For the conflict segment for married couples, combined across partners, the correlation for the two observers of total weighted SPAFF over the conflict interaction was .90 ($p < .001$). For the conflict segment for the gay men and lesbians, combined across partners, the correlation for the two observers of total weighted SPAFF over the conflict interaction was .52 ($p < .01$).

Results of the Conflict Conversations

The modeling was done using the influence function developed in chapter 13: bilinear with repair and damping.

Uninfluenced Steady States For the uninfluenced steady state of the initiator of the issue, there was a significant effect only for sexual orientation, $F(1,75) = 8.18$, $p = .005$. The homosexual mean was 0.61, and the heterosexual mean was $-.98$. There was no significant difference between gay male and lesbian relationships, $t(77) = 1.09$, ns, or between heterosexual couples in which the man or woman initiated, $t(77) = .45$. For the uninfluenced steady state of the partner, there was again only a significant effect for sexual orientation, $F(1,75) = 6.45$, $p = .013$. The homosexual mean was 0.37, and the heterosexual was

−1.09. There was again no significant difference between gay male and lesbian relationships, $t(77) = 1.37$, ns, or between heterosexual couples in which the man or woman initiated, $t(77) = .89$. Thus, the way the issue is presented and received in the conflict interaction is positive for homosexual couples and negative for heterosexual couples. These results suggest that homosexual relationships may be fundamentally different from heterosexual relationships.

Subsequent Analyses of Specific SPAFF Codes These analyses showed that homosexual initiators of the conflict issue compared to heterosexual initiators were characterized by less negative affect: less belligerence, $t(76) = 2.72$, $p < .01$ (homosexual mean $= 2.65$, heterosexual mean $= 10.57$); less domineering , $t(76) = 2.38$, $p < .05$ (homosexual mean $= 7.56$, heterosexual mean $= 33.18$); less fear/tension, $t(76) = 4.02$, $p < .001$ (homosexual mean $= 21.52$, heterosexual mean $= 121.76$); less sadness, $t(76) = 3.89$, $p < .05$ (homosexual mean $= 6.87$, heterosexual mean $= 30.21$); less whining , $t(76) = 1.97$, $p < .05$ (homosexual mean $= 2.30$, heterosexual mean $= 10.29$). The homosexual initiators of the conflict also demonstrated more positive emotions when compared with the heterosexual initiators: more affection, $t(76) = 1.75$, $p < .05$ (homosexual mean $= 1.82$, heterosexual mean $= .89$); more humor, $t(76) = 3.91$, $p < .001$ (homosexual mean $= 29.61$, heterosexual mean $= 9.45$); and more joy/excitement, $t(76) = 2.34$, $p < .05$ (homosexual mean $= .46$, heterosexual mean $= .007$). For the partner (i.e., the recipient of the conflict issue), homosexual compared to heterosexual partners showed less negative affect: less belligerence, $t(76) = 2.28$, $p < .05$ (homosexual mean $= 1.61$, heterosexual mean $= 5.96$); less domineering, $t(76) = 2.52$, $p < .05$ (homosexual mean $= 9.06$, heterosexual mean $= 38.88$); less fear/tension , $t(76) = 7.60$, $p < .001$ (homosexual mean $= 15.48$, heterosexual mean $= 94.71$). The homosexual partners also showed significantly more humor than the heterosexual partners, $t(76) = 3.86$, $p < .001$ (homosexual mean $= 29.71$, heterosexual mean $= 9.38$). These results suggest that homosexual relationships may be distinguished from heterosexual relationships in the expression of positive and negative affect during a conflict interaction.

Influenced Steady States For the influenced steady states, we computed the number of stable steady states in each of the four quadrants of phase space. The only significant difference between the types of couples was in the quadrant where both partners' behavior was positive, and again there was a sexual orientation effect, $F(1,75) = 5.25$, $p = .025$. The mean number of influenced stable steady states in this quadrant for the homosexual couples was .86 versus .32 for the heterosexual couples. There was also a marginally significant interaction between sexual orientation and the gender of the initiator, $F(1,75) = 3.89$, $p = .052$.

Subsequent tests showed that the lesbian mean of 1.14 stable steady states in the positive-positive quadrant was significantly higher than the mean for the other three types of couples (gay male mean = .57, man initiating to a woman mean = .50, woman initiating to a man mean = .19). Once again, these results suggest that influence processes in homosexual committed relationships may be dissimilar to the influence processes found in heterosexual couples. The findings imply that lesbian couples, when compared with the gay male and heterosexual couples, are more likely to remain stable in their behavioral interactions when both partners are positive in their communication content.

Repair Effectiveness There were no significant main effects owing to sexual orientation or to who initiates the issue for either the initiator's or the partner's repair effectiveness. However, subsequent t-tests revealed some interesting findings on partner's repair effectiveness. The mean was lower for gay male couples than the mean for any of the other three groups (gay male mean = 2.78, man initiating to a woman mean = 3.98, woman initiating to a man mean = 3.99, lesbian mean = 3.65). There was a significant difference between homosexual couples and heterosexual couples in which the man initiates, $t(69) = 1.70$, $p < .05$. There was also a significant difference between a woman initiating to a man (the most common occurrence in heterosexual couples) and a man initiating to a man in a gay couple, $t(69) = 1.80$, $p < .05$. These results suggest the following interpretation of the data: when a gay man presents the conflict issue to his partner and the initiator becomes too negative, his partner may not repair very effectively, suggesting that interventions for gay male couples in particular may do well focusing on the repair aspects of conflict regulation.

Repair Threshold There were no significant effects for the initiators' negative score threshold that triggered repair by their partner. However, there was a significant effect for the partners' threshold that triggered repair, and in this case the effect was due to who brought up the issue to be discussed, $F(1,69) = 5.14$, $p = .027$. The mean threshold when a man initiated the issue was -4.64, compared to a mean of -6.04 when a woman initiated the issue indicating that when a man initiates the issue, he detects negativity in his partner and attempts to repair sooner than a woman does when she is presenting the issue. In addition, there was a marginally significant interaction effect, $F(1,69) = 3.03$, $p = .086$. A subsequent t-test showed that this effect was owing to the fact that when a heterosexual man initiates the issue, he notices and responds to negativity in his partner at a much less negative threshold than in any other group, $t(69) = 2.48$, $p < .01$.

Damping Effectiveness There was a significant effect for the initiator's effectiveness of damping, and the effect was owing to sexual orientation, $F(1,73) = 4.98$, $p = .029$. The mean initiator's effectiveness of damping for homosexual couples was -4.85, as compared to -3.11 for heterosexual couples. It is the magnitude and not the sign of this measure that is important (it is expected to be a negative number precisely in order to have a damping effect on the underlying influence function). In addition, there was a marginally significant effect for the partner's effectiveness of damping, and the effect was also owing to sexual orientation, $F(1,70) = 3.91$, $p = .052$. The mean partner's effectiveness of damping for homosexual couples was -5.03, as compared to -3.37 for heterosexual couples. Thus, when either partner in the homosexual couples detected that the other person had become "too positive" (perhaps treating a serious issue with too much levity), they were more effective at damping down this tendency than were the heterosexual couples.

Affect and Influence Patterns In every study we have conducted with heterosexual couples using the mathematical modeling, the slope of the influence functions in the negative affect range is steeper than the slope in the positive affect range. Gottman (1994a) has referred to this as "the triumph of negative over positive affect," meaning that it is easier to hurt one's partner with negative affect than it is to have a positive influence with positive affect. In the present study, when we compared homosexual relationships with heterosexual relationships, we found some indication that for homosexuals there was a reversal of the pattern. The variable used in this analysis was the slope for positive affect minus the slope for negative affect, so a negative value indicates the negative affect slope is steeper (i.e., the usual finding). For the initiator's influence function there was a marginal interaction effect, $F(1,66) = 3.05$, $p = .085$ (man initiates to woman mean $= -.086$, woman initiates to man mean $= -.283$, gay male mean $= -.331$, lesbian mean $= -.122$). The means suggested a difference between the heterosexual men initiating to their wives and all other groups, but a subsequent t-test did not find this difference to be significant. However, for the partner's influence function, there was a marginally significant effect for sexual orientation, $F(1,68) = 2.83$, $p = .097$ (heterosexual mean $= -.19$, homosexual mean $= -.002$). Hence, with increased power, we may find a lessening of the effect of the triumph of negative over positive affect in homosexual couples.

Gender Effects In addition to the gender threshold effect for the repair trigger previously noted, several other significant main effects for gender were found. Regardless of sexual orientation, men were angrier than women when presenting an issue, $t(77) = 1.75$, $p < .05$ (female mean $= 1.55$, male mean $= 3.99$), and women were more excited/joyful than men, $t(77) = 2.86$, $p < .003$ (female mean $= .49$, male mean $= .004$). For the partner, regardless of sexual orientation, women were sadder when receiving a conflict issue than men, $F(1,76) = 6.03$, $p = .016$ (female partner mean = 16.64, male partner mean = 2.06).

Differences between Gay Males and Lesbians. There was inadequate power for the math modeling comparisons. However, there was enough power to find significant differences in affect. The SPAFF coding revealed that, for the initiator of the issue, lesbians were angrier than gay males, $t(76) = 1.66$, $p < .05$ (gay male mean = 4.97, lesbian mean = 15.10), used more humor, $t(76) = 2.15$, $p < .05$ (gay male mean = 21.88, lesbian mean = 37.33), and showed more excitement/joy, $t(76) = 3.55$, $p < .01$ (gay male mean = .007, lesbian mean = .86). For the partner, SPAFF coding revealed that lesbians showed more humor, $t(76) = 1.76$, $p < .05$ (gay male mean = 23.29, lesbian mean = 36.14) and that lesbians showed more interest, $t(76) = 1.95$, $p < .05$ (gay male mean = 1.24, lesbian mean = 6.00). These results suggest that lesbians are more emotionally expressive than gay men.

Summary and Discussion

We applied the mathematical model to this first observational study of gay male and lesbian relationships. What is most striking about the observational data is that they reveal a different pattern of social interaction for homosexual relationships when compared to heterosexual relationships. Homosexual relationships appear to operate on a different set of principles. Although these ideas were not greatly emphasized in their work, Kurdek (1998) and Blumstein and Schwartz (1983) also suggested that some different principles may operate in gay male and lesbian relationships compared to heterosexual relationships. They suggested that autonomy was more important for gays and intimacy more important for lesbians, and equality more important for both compared to heterosexuals. Based on the analyses of our observational data, gay male and lesbian couples operate very differently than heterosexual couples. They begin a conflict discussion much more positively and are then also more likely to accept influence to move them to even more positive set points. This pattern is opposite to what we previously discovered (Cook et al., 1995) were the destabilizing patterns in heterosexual couples! Hence, it may be the case that heterosexual couples might learn something vital from gay male and lesbian relationships.

14.2 Parent-Baby Interaction: Extending the Marriage Model to Triads

This analysis was part of a study of newlywed couples' transition to parenthood, conducted in collaboration with our graduate student Alyson

Fearnley Shapiro. In this procedure, parents came to our laboratory with their three-month-old infants and participated in the Lausanne Triadic Play (LTP; Fivaz-Depeursinge, 1991; Fivaz-Depeursinge and Corboz-Warnery, 1995). The LTP is a semistructured task in which the parents and the baby are seated at the vertices of an equilateral triangle, and parents are asked to play with their baby in four phases: (1) one parent plays with the baby, while the other parent is simply present; (2) the parents switch roles; (3) both parents play with the baby; and (4) the parents talk to one another, while the baby is simply present.

Method

Participants The participants were part of our study of 130 newlywed couples whom we have been following for many years. For the purposes of this analysis, 9 couples high in marital satisfaction and 8 couples low in marital satisfaction were selected from the 50 couples who had gone on to become parents.

Coding The mother, father, and baby were each coded individually over time for facial affect (positive, neutral, negative) and direction of gaze using a system developed by Shapiro. Parents were additionally coded for giving infants space versus overstimulating them and for including or excluding their partner. Codes were assigned weights and summed, for each second and for each person, resulting in one score that we termed *interactive state*. This gave us three time series, one for each parent and one for the baby. Only the first 17 families (out of 50) were coded for this analysis.

Modeling At the time this study was done, we had not yet developed the repair/damping form of the influence function. The ojive form of the influence function was used in the mathematical model for these analyses (see chapter 12). The median interactive state was determined for each father during his family's triadic play session (i.e., when the parents were instructed to play together with the baby). Then a special version of the marriage model was applied to the time series data coded for the mother and baby during the triadic play segment. This model made two passes through the data. On the first pass, all model parameters were estimated using only those data points when the father was below his median state. On the second pass, all model parameters were estimated using only those data points when the father was above his median state. Breaks in the time sequence were taken into account when estimating the parameters of the mother's and the baby's influence functions. Data points where the father's state was equal to his median were alternately assigned to the below-median and above-median subsets.

We ended up with two sets of math model parameters, which we

Figure 14.1: Mother's uninfluenced steady state when father is relatively negative and relatively positive in low and high marital satisfaction families.

examined with respect to the father's relative state (relatively positive or relatively negative) and to the couple's marital satisfaction category (low or high) by using repeated measures analysis of variance. All tests were two-tailed.

Results

The first seven results, shown in figures 14.1 through 14.7, found effects owing to marital satisfaction, to the father's relative state, or to the interaction of these two factors.

There was a significant interaction effect for the uninfluenced steady state of the mothers, $F(1,14) = 4.61$, $p = .05$ (low satisfaction means were 8.75 for father negative and 4.13 for father positive; high satisfaction means were 4.28 for father negative and 10.52 for father positive). As seen in figure 14.1, the uninfluenced steady state of happily married mothers when interacting with their babies reflected their synchrony with their husbands. In contrast, the uninfluenced steady state of mothers with low marital satisfaction indicates that they were "out of synch" with their husbands, which may have been a result of competition between the parents or enmeshment of one and withdrawal of the other.

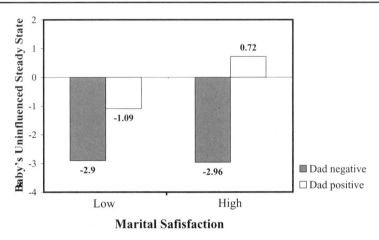

Figure 14.2: Baby's uninfluenced steady state when father is relatively negative and relatively positive in low
and high marital satisfaction families.

There was also a significant interaction effect for the baby's uninfluenced steady state, $F(1,14) = 4.83$, $p = .05$ (low satisfaction means were
-2.90 for father negative and -2.96 for father positive; high satisfaction
means were -1.09 for father negative and $.72$ for father positive), as
shown in figure 14.2.

As seen in figures 14.3 and 14.4, both mothers and babies had a
higher negative minimum score in their interactive state when marital
satisfaction was low, which for the babies was accentuated when the father was relatively more negative. There was a significant difference owing to marital satisfaction in the mother's most negative score, $F(1,15)$
$= 6.14$, $p = .03$ (low satisfaction means were -4.25 for father negative
and -4.75 for father positive; high satisfaction means were -1.11 for
father negative and -1.00 for father positive). For the babies, there was
also a significant difference in their highest negative score owing to marital satisfaction, $F(1,14) = 4.78$, $p = .05$ (low satisfaction means were
-8.00 for father negative and -7.38 for father positive; high satisfaction
means were -6.33 for father negative and -5.22 for father positive).
For the babies, there was also a marginally significant difference owing
to father's relative state, $F(1,15) = 3.15$, $p = .10$.

There was a significant interaction effect between father's relative

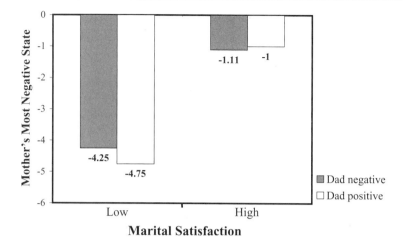

Figure 14.3: Mother's most negative state, marital satisfaction, and father influence.

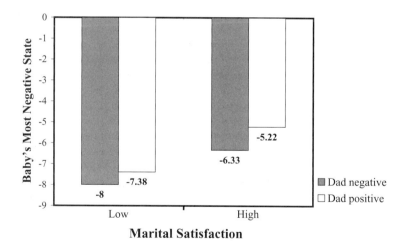

Figure 14.4: Baby's most negative state, marital satisfaction, and father influence.

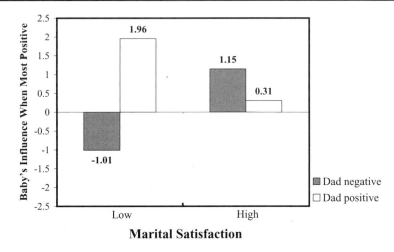

Figure 14.5: Baby's influence on mother when most positive, marital satisfaction, and father influence.

state and marital satisfaction on the influence the baby exerts on the mother when the baby is most positive, $F(1,7) = 8.86$, $p = .02$ (low satisfaction means were -1.01 for father negative and 1.96 for father positive; high satisfaction means were 1.15 for father negative and .31 for father positive). See figure 14.5. This finding was for the ojive influence function parameter marked B on figure 12.2. In happily married families, this level of the baby's influence on the mother was positive regardless of whether the father was relatively negative or positive (although the baby's influence was more strongly positive when the father was relatively negative). In contrast, in unhappily married families the baby's influence on the mother was *negative* when the father was relatively negative, whereas it was quite positive when the father was relatively positive. In other words, quite the opposite pattern occurred between the high- and low-satisfaction groups.

Figure 14.6 shows that marital satisfaction had a significant effect on the influence the baby exerts on the mother when the baby is most negative, $F(1,14) = 5.10$, $p = .04$ (low satisfaction means were -2.10 for father negative and -3.64 for father positive; high satisfaction means were $-.74$ for father negative and $-.05$ for father positive). This finding was for the ojive influence function parameter marked E on figure 12.2. The baby's influence was significantly more negative in the low-marital-

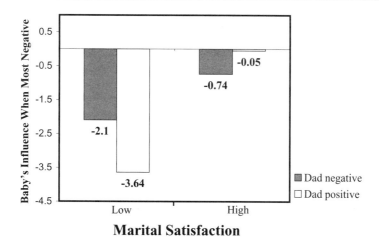

Figure 14.6: Baby's influence on mother when most negative, marital satisfaction, and father influence.

satisfaction families when the baby was in a more negative interactive state.

As shown in figure 14.7, marital satisfaction had a significant effect on the baby's negative threshold, $F(1,14) = 5.48$, $p = .035$ (low satisfaction means were -2.75 for father negative and -3.00 for father positive; high satisfaction means were -2.38 for father negative and -1.88 for father positive). This finding was for the parameter of the ojive influence function marked F on figure 12.2 in chapter 12, and it indicates the point at which there is a change in the baby's negative influence on the mother as the baby becomes more negative. The baby's threshold was significantly higher in the unhappily married families, which means the baby had to become more negative to change the influence on the unhappily married mother than was the case in the happily married families. In other words, in the happily married families the mothers were more responsive to increasing negativity in their baby.

For the next two analyses, we found significant effects only owing to the father's relative state, so the graphs show only the effect of this dimension. As seen in figure 14.8, the baby's most positive state was more positive when the father was relatively positive during the triadic play, $F(1,15) = 4.02$, $p = .06$ (means were 5.00 for father negative and 6.59 for father positive).

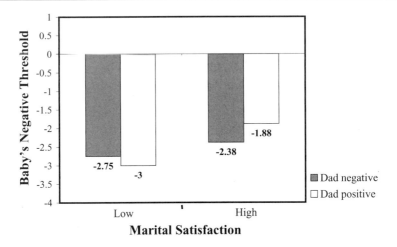

Figure 14.7: Baby's negative threshold, marital satisfaction, and father influence.

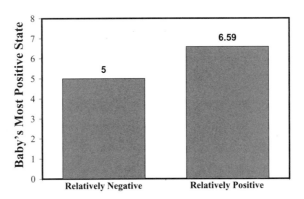

Figure 14.8: Baby's most positive state relative to father's state.

There was a nonsignificant trend suggesting that the mother's interactive state was more positive when the father was relatively positive, $F(1,15) = 2.63$, $p = .14$ (means were 16.88 for father negative and 17.41 for father positive), as shown in figure 14.9.

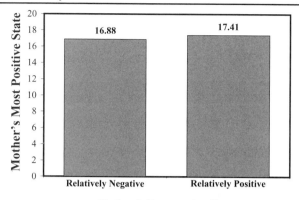

Figure 14.9: Mother's most positive state relative to father's state.

Discussion

Both marital satisfaction and the role of the father appear to have an impact on the mother and baby within the family triad in terms of how they begin an interaction, how negative they become during the interaction, and what influence the baby has on the mother. The situation appears to be particularly problematic when there is low marital satisfaction and the father is relatively negative, compared to other fathers from both high- and low-satisfaction families.

Overall, the role of the father appears to be important in the dynamics of the family triad. Fathers and their babies, in particular, appear to be "in synch" during triadic play. The baby's interactive state (affect and gaze) was positive when the father was relatively more positive during the play session. Findings relating the father and baby interactive state but not the mother and father interactive state may indicate that parents are more attuned to their baby than to each other during triadic play. In addition, parents may influence each other indirectly rather than directly during play when all three family members are present, as suggested by the negative influence the baby exerts on the mother when the baby is relatively positive but the father is relatively negative in low-marital-satisfaction families. It may be the case that the father is influencing the mother indirectly through his effect on the baby.

14.3   Chapter summary

In this chapter, we have shown other applications for the marriage model. In the first case, we used the model to show other types of dyadic relationships (for committed gay male and lesbian couples), and we showed that a meaningful comparison of homosexual versus heterosexual conflict interactions can be made if a psychologically meaningful subclassification of the partners in those two groups can be made. In this case, we chose to classify the partners based on who presented the issue in the conflict discussion. We know from previous research that in marriages it is usually the wives who present the issue, so it is interesting to see what differences there are in marriages where the husbands present the issue. In turn, it is interesting to see how this compares to same-sex relationships where by default it will always be either a man or a woman presenting the issue. Also, we know that the way the initiator starts up the conversation has great bearing on the trajectory of the conversation. Again, it is interesting to see if there are differences when it is a man or a woman presenting the issue, and if there is a difference within that presentation when it is a heterosexual or a homosexual partnership.

We also showed that the model can be applied to a triadic interaction. The solutions for a true three-equation model are extremely complex and may not be solvable. However, by modeling the interaction of two of the members of the triad while controlling for some level of affect of the third person, we can still make some interesting and meaningful comparisons that apply to the entire triadic system.

15

The Core Triad of Balance

In this chapter, we illustrate the power of the mathematical modeling approach by extending its application to variables other than behavior. In particular, we construct a model that explores the relationship between the trinity of measurement domains: behavior, perception, and physiology during a fifteen-minute conflict discussion between married couples. For this work, we continue using the influence function developed in chapter 13: bilinear with repair and damping.

This chapter also offers a good example of how to move from data gathered in the laboratory, which does not have a natural positive to negative range, to a variable that does have this property and is comparable across individuals. Because the model estimates the influence on the spouse of positive to negative values of whatever variable is being used, it is necessary to cast the data in those terms. It is also necessary for this variable to have a "neutral" value or range that makes sense in terms of what the variable is measuring, and that this value or range is obtained often enough to allow for estimation of the uninfluenced steady state.

15.1 What Is the Core Triad of Balance?

In *What Predicts Divorce? The Relationship between Marital Processes and Marital Outcomes* (1994a), Gottman proposed a theory that he called the *core triad of balance*. This theory suggests bidirectional linkages between Q-space (the perception of well-being and safety in the relationship, or the opposite perception), P-space (the flow over time of positive and negative behaviors), and Phy-space (physiological responses such as heart rate, vascular constriction, respiratory pattern, sweating, and the like). In our laboratory, we referred to this as "Q-P-Phy" theory, or just QPPhy.

Figure 15.1 illustrates the core triad of balance theory. Each element of the core triad of Q-space, P-space, and physiological responses has both positive and negative aspects. The Q-space component has the perception of well-being as a balancing force for perceptions of hurt/perceived threat or hurt/anger-contempt. In P-space, the behavioral flow is measured as the sum of positive minus negative behaviors over time. In Phy-space, physiological responses linked to negative affect can lead to increased reactivity and diffuse physiological arousal. Physiological responses linked to positive affect have the potential to buffer arousal through physiological soothing. Each component in the core triad can affect the other in a bidirectional fashion, and each component has the potential for balance.

At the core of the formulation shown in figure 15.1 is a balance theory, an ecology of marital behaviors in which a ratio of positivity to negativity, which is overall more positive than negative, needs to be maintained. If it is not, then in Q-space the perception of well-being is replaced by one of distress (hurt/anger or hurt/perceived attack). A long time spent in negative Q-space can lead to a state of being flooded by one's partner's negative affect, diffuse physiological arousal (DPA), negative sentiment override (NSO), and negative attributions of the partner. Flooding begins the distance and isolation cascade, which entails perceiving one's marital problems as severe and as better worked out alone than with the spouse, arranging one's life so that it is more parallel to the spouse's life than it used to be, and loneliness within the marriage. Eventually one's perception of the entire relationship is affected, and the entire history of the marriage may be recast in negative terms. Ultimately, this state of affairs may lead to divorce.

In contrast, couples whose marriages are stable may use positive affect and persuasion in ways that buffer them from the physiological stresses of DPA and from the perception of their partner's negative emotions as being disgusting, threatening, overwhelming, and impossible to predict. They are in a state of positive sentiment override (PSO). They may see negative emotion in their partner as an aberration or even as a call for help, so they may even have a *positive* response to negativity.

15.2   On What Data Do We Base the Model?

The source of data for the core triad modeling work was the Seattle Newlywed Study described in chapter 12. In that chapter, we detailed the procedures for obtaining behavioral data using the SPAFF coding system, physiological measures, and self-report of affect using the video

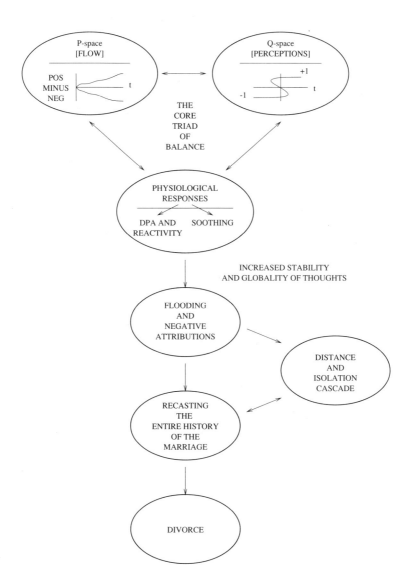

Figure 15.1: The core triad of balance suggests a unique role for physiology (and soothing) in mediating between P-space and Q-space and in predicting divorce. From Gottman (1994a), fig. 15.7 (p. 370).

recall procedure and the rating dial device. Data from all three sources were gathered continuously for a fifteen-minute conflict discussion in the marital interaction laboratory. The data were coordinated in time and were averaged over one-second intervals.

We wanted to explore whether and how these three types of data are linked in the interaction between husband and wife. In previous chapters, we showed that parameters of the behavior model discriminate between divorced, happy stable, and unhappy stable couples. We now asked the question, Would we find other significant patterns if the source of influence on one's behavior is the spouse's physiology or perception rather than his or her behavior? What if we change what is being influenced? Is a wife's physiology influenced by her husband's behavior? Can it be influenced by his perception of his own emotional state?

Behavior Data from Objective Observers

As presented in chapter 12, the data for husband and wife behavior was derived from the SPAFF coding, using the weighting scheme that gave equal weight to positive and negative codes. Each second was assigned a value of -4 to $+4$ depending on the SPAFF code for that second and the weight assigned to that code. These weights were then summed over six-second intervals throughout the fifteen-minute interaction, yielding 150 time points with data values in the range -24 to $+24$. We chose the six-second time block because it is a fairly universally used time block for averaging social interaction data. It is also the average time each person holds the floor in a dyadic marital conflict discussion (excluding vocal backchannels). The next immediate task was to construct scales for perception and physiology for the same time blocks.

Perception Data from Self-report of Affect

The rating dial has a pointer that moves from "very negative" through neutral to "very positive," so that subjects can continuously rate how they were feeling as they view a replay video of the marital interaction. The device emits a voltage range that is converted by our data collection program to values between 1 (very negative) through 5 (neutral) to 9 (very positive). These values were continuously sampled and then averaged over one-second intervals. It is therefore a simple transformation to convert the value for each second to a weight between -4 and $+4$ by subtracting 5 from the dial value. Then -4 is "very negative," 0 is "neutral," and $+4$ is "very positive." These weights are then in the exact same range that was derived for the weighted SPAFF codes. The weights are summed over the same six-second time intervals, yielding

150 time blocks for perception data in the range -24 to $+24$.

Physiology Data

The ECG waveform was continuously sampled, and these data were later analyzed to extract the interbeat interval (IBI), or time in milliseconds between R-spikes. An average IBI was computed for each of the 900 seconds in the 15-minute conflict discussion. Note that the inverse of IBI is heart rate in beats per minute (IBI $= 60,000/$HR). The problem we confronted was that the IBI does not have a natural positive to negative range, or a predefined value that means "neutral." Every person has a baseline rate and his or her own normal range of data that is a function of sex, body size, and physical fitness. We did think that slower heart rate (calmer or higher IBI) would be considered "positive" and that faster heart rate (aroused or lower IBI) would be considered "negative." In addition, there was one absolute notion of negativity in heart rate that we wanted to incorporate into our scale. In a healthy, normal adult heart, the pacemaker rate is about 100 beats per minute (600 IBI). At heart rates faster than 100 beats per minute (IBI less than 600), secretion of noradrenaline and adrenaline creates increased myocardial contractility as well as increased heart rate, which makes it more difficult to listen and respond to one's partner. The subject moves toward a state of severe and even toxic physiological arousal (Rowell, 1986). We needed to consider this physiology of arousal, which is discontinuous, in our modeling of arousal using the IBI data.

For each subject, we found the minimum and maximum IBI for the fifteen-minute interaction. We also calculated their mean IBI during the two-minute baseline preceding the conversation, when they are instructed to sit with their eyes open but without speaking to their spouse, and wait for the signal to begin talking. We used this as a base value for that person, instead of the mean from a separate, eyes-closed baseline, which was almost always a slower heart rate (higher IBI). We wanted a base value that was reflective of some arousal, in an anticipatory state in the presence of their spouse, and that would fall in the midrange for the next conversation. In other words, we wanted a value that would represent "neutral" for the conversation itself and around which the heartbeat data could be assessed as slower (calmer, more positive) or faster (aroused, more negative).

It was necessary to consider an area around the base value to be *neutral* to provide uninfluenced data so that the initial state and inertia parameters could be estimated in the mathematical model. We found that setting aside 30% of the positive side and 30% of the negative side around the base value provided adequate data for this purpose. In other

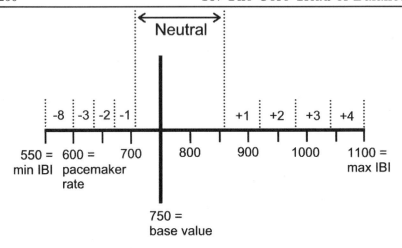

Figure 15.2: Assigning weights to IBI data.

words, the upper end of neutral fell 30% of the way from the base value
to the maximum IBI (slowest heart rate) for a subject. The lower end
of neutral fell 30% of the way from the base value to the minimum IBI,
or the pacemaker rate of 600 if the subject's minimum fell below that.
See figure 15.2. Note that the absolute range of IBI values in the neutral
band was not the same on the positive and negative sides of the base
value.

After we established the neutral band, we could assign weights to
IBIs on each side of that band. On the positive side, the range of IBI
values between the upper end of neutral and maximum IBI (slowest
heart rate) for a subject was divided into four equal parts and assigned
weights from +1 to +4. On the negative side, the range of IBI values
between the lower end of neutral and the pacemaker rate (IBI = 600),
or the minimum IBI if it was above pacemaker rate, was divided into
three equal parts and assigned weights from −1 to −3. Any IBI below
600 was assigned a weight of −8. The decision to weight more heavily
IBIs below the pacemaker rate was based on the physiology of the heart
mentioned earlier.

This weighting scheme was applied to the IBI for each of the 900
seconds, then the weights were summed over the same 6-second intervals
as were used above. This yielded 150 time points for physiology data in
the potential range of −48 to +24.

15.3   Brief Review of Behavior-Based Models

Up to this point, the mathematical modeling of marital interaction explored the influence of each partner's behavior (as coded by an independent observer) on the other partner, as well as the enduring effects of each partner's own behavior on his or her own subsequent behavior. That is, in the difference equations

$$W_{t+1} = I_{HW}(H_t) + r_1 W_t + a,$$

$$H_{t+1} = I_{WH}(W_{t+1}) + r_2 H_t + b$$
(15.1)

the Hs and Ws referred to a measure of positive or negative behavior at time t, $t + 1$, etc. The influence functions in these equations can take several forms, so they have been purposely expressed in a generic way above. However, in this chapter, we use the bilinear influence function with repair and damping (see figure 13.8).

To briefly recap chapter 9, the parameters a and b in equations 15.1 are the *initial behavioral state* for each spouse—that is, the initial uninfluenced behavior with which they enter the interaction. The parameters r_1 and r_2 reflect the influence of each persons immediate past behavior on their own self and are called *behavioral inertia* (at time $t + 1$, how likely are they to remain behaviorally the same as at time t?).

The Is are the influence functions. I_{HW} is the influence of the husband on the wife when his behavior is H_t. Conversely, I_{WH} is the influence of the wife on the husband when her behavior is W_t. The equations are saying that the behavior of the spouses at the next time point is modeled as a combination of forces: the initial state that each person brought to the interaction, that person's inertia or tendency to stay the same as his or her immediate past behavior, and the influence of his or her spouse's behavior.

We have hypothesized a number of shapes for these influence functions and fitted them to the actual behavioral data for each couple. In previous chapters, we considered the simple bilinear and ojive forms of the influence function and later showed that a bilinear influence function with repair and damping terms provides both a more interesting theoretical framework for describing the interaction, and a better fit to the data.

Using both the ojive shape of the influence function and the bilinear shape with repair and damping, we found that several parameters of the behavior math model significantly discriminated between newlywed couples who divorced and those who stayed married. Also, certain parameters of the model significantly discriminated among three groups: divorced, happy stable, and unhappy stable couples.

15.4   Core Triad Model Specification

We now expand on our previous work and write nine sets of equations to describe the interactions between behavior, perception, and physiology within the core triad of balance theory.

The variables being modeled are:

- WB, HB = Wife and Husband Behavior

- WP, HP = Wife and Husband Perception of Own Emotion (Self-rating)

- WI, HI = Wife and Husband Physiology (IBI)

We have chosen to name these variables using two same-font letters in order to make the equations themselves more readable. Thus the variable WP means "Wife Perception", and does not denote the multiplication of a variable named W times a variable named P. As a further example, in the equations below, WP_{t+1} means "Wife Perception at time $t + 1$."

Model 1: Both Partners' Behavior (original model)

$$WB_{t+1} = I_{HW}(HB_t) + r_{11}WB_t + a_1,$$
$$HB_{t+1} = I_{WH}(WB_t) + r_{12}HB_t + b_1 \tag{15.2}$$

Model 2: Wife Behavior and Husband Perception

$$WB_{t+1} = I_{HW}(HP_t) + r_{21}WB_t + a_2,$$
$$HP_{t+1} = I_{WH}(WB_t) + r_{22}HP_t + b_2 \tag{15.3}$$

Model 3: Wife Behavior and Husband Physiology

$$WB_{t+1} = I_{HW}(HI_t) + r_{31}WB_t + a_3,$$
$$HI_{t+1} = I_{WH}(WB_t) + r_{32}HI_t + b_3 \tag{15.4}$$

Model 4: Wife Perception and Husband Behavior

$$WP_{t+1} = I_{HW}(HB_t) + r_{41}WP_t + a_4,$$
$$HB_{t+1} = I_{WH}(WP_t) + r_{42}HB_t + b_4 \tag{15.5}$$

Model 5: Both Partners' Perception

$$WP_{t+1} = I_{HW}(HP_t) + r_{51}WP_t + a_5,$$
$$HP_{t+1} = I_{WH}(WP_t) + r_{52}HP_t + b_5 \tag{15.6}$$

Model 6: Wife Perception and Husband Physiology

$$WP_{t+1} = I_{HW}(HI_t) + r_{61}WP_t + a_6,$$

$$HI_{t+1} = I_{WH}(WP_t) + r_{62}HI_t + b_6 \tag{15.7}$$

Model 7: Wife Physiology and Husband Behavior

$$WI_{t+1} = I_{HW}(HB_t) + r_{71}WI_t + a_7,$$

$$HB_{t+1} = I_{WH}(WI_t) + r_{72}HB_t + b_7 \tag{15.8}$$

Model 8: Wife Physiology and Husband Perception

$$WI_{t+1} = I_{HW}(HP_t) + r_{81}WI_t + a_8,$$

$$HP_{t+1} = I_{WH}(WI_t) + r_{82}HP_t + b_8 \tag{15.9}$$

Model 9: Both Partners' Physiology

$$WI_{t+1} = I_{HW}(HI_t) + r_{91}WI_t + a_9,$$

$$HI_{t+1} = I_{WH}(WI_t) + r_{92}HI_t + b_9 \tag{15.10}$$

Example of What the Equations Mean

Each equation expresses the proposed link between one measure from the core triad in the wife with a different measure in the husband. For example, equations (15.5) express the following model:

Wife's *perception* at the next time point is a function of:

- her initial state of perception (a_4)

- her perception inertia (r_{41}), i.e., how much her previous perception is likely to stay the same

- the influence of her husband's current behavior on her perception

Husband's *behavior* at the next time point is a function of:

- his behavioral initial state (b_4)

- his behavioral inertia (r_{42}), i.e., how much his previous behavior is likely to stay the same

- the influence of his wife's current perception (feelings) on his behavior

Note that Models 1, 5, and 9 are the "pure models"; the measure from the core triad is the same for both husband and wife. Also, Model 1 is the original behavioral model with some changes to the parameter labels.

15.5   Core Triad Model Results

Using the methods described in section 15.2 above, we constructed a
data file that contained Time-1 behavior, perception, and physiology
data for 150 time blocks for all 130 couples in the Seattle Newlywed
Study. A specially modified version of the math model program was
run that fit the model using the bilinear influence function with repair
and damping, for each of the nine equations detailed in section 15.4
above. The parameters of each model were stored in another data file
for subsequent statistical analyses. As in previous chapters, we were
interested in which models had the ability to predict which couples would
be divorced at Time-2 and also which models were able to discriminate
predictively between the happy stable, unhappy stable, and divorced
couples.

Divorce Prediction

Tables 15.1 through 15.9 summarize the significant results from an analysis of variance of the parameters of the nine core triad models. This
analysis compared the 17 couples who were divorced at Time-2 to the
113 stable couples (results significant at $\alpha = .10$ or less). Recall that the
behavior, perception, and physiology data were obtained within the first
year after the wedding (Time-1), but the divorce/stability categorization
was based on six-year follow-up data (Time-2).

In table 15.1, we see that Model 1, our original model, tells the familiar story. The couples who eventually divorced had significantly more
influenced steady states where both partners' behavior was negative and
significantly fewer influenced steady states where both partners' behavior was positive. For both husbands and wives in divorced couples, the
initial uninfluenced state was negative (where they started that conversation), as was the uninfluenced steady state (where they would tend
to be behaviorally in the absence of any particular influence from their
spouse during the conversation). For the stable couples, the initial state
and uninfluenced steady state were positive for both husbands and wives.
In other words, looking at both partners' behavior over time and at the
influence of each person's behavior on the other person's behavior, the
divorced couples started out negative and tended to stay that way. In
contrast, the stable couples started out positive and tended to stay that
way. Looking at parameters of the influence function, both husbands
and wives in stable couples were significantly more effective at damping
their spouse's positivity when it exceeded the threshold level. Although
this finding might at first seem counterintuitive, recall that in chapter 13
we showed that damping has the ability to introduce a previously nonex-

Table 15.1: Divorce Prediction Using Parameters of Core Triad Model 1: Both Partners' Behavior.

			Means	
Variable	F-ratio	df	Stable	Divorced
Number of Influenced Steady States				
where $(W+)$ and $(H-)$	0.00	1,129	0.12	0.12
where $(W-)$ and $(H-)$	7.55**	1,129	0.54	1.24
where $(W+)$ and $(H+)$	7.44**	1,129	0.95	0.24
where $(W-)$ and $(H+)$	1.37	1,129	0.16	0.00
Wife				
Inertia	0.18	1,129	0.39	0.42
Initial state	22.14***	1,129	0.28	−1.13
Uninfluenced steady state	15.01***	1,129	0.50	−2.26
Influence on husband				
Positive half slope	0.00	1,124	0.53	0.52
Negative half slope	1.13	1,127	0.52	0.62
Threshold, husb damping	0.53	1,124	5.64	5.02
Strength, husb damping	2.95^a	1,124	−4.63	−3.14
Threshold, husb repair	0.16	1,127	−4.74	−4.40
Strength, husb repair	0.01	1,127	3.90	3.83
Husband				
Inertia	3.09^a	1,129	0.40	0.30
Initial state	23.34***	1,129	0.45	−1.11
Uninfluenced steady state	18.70***	1,129	0.70	−1.89
Influence on wife				
Positive half slope	0.00	1,126	0.50	0.50
Negative half slope	0.65	1,124	0.58	0.46
Threshold, wife damping	0.04	1,126	5.75	5.58
Strength, wife damping	8.04**	1,126	−4.30	−2.07
Threshold, wife repair	0.11	1,120	−4.68	−4.95
Strength, wife repair	0.06	1,120	3.43	3.58

^{a} $p < .10$, * $p < .05$, ** $p < .01$, *** $p < .001$
$(W+)$ Wife Positive, $(W-)$ Wife Negative
$(H+)$ Husband Positive, $(H-)$ Husband Negative

istent positive steady state that is stable and attracting for the couple, so it may be that effective damping can be in the service of long-term stability of the relationship.

In table 15.2, we see that Model 2 looks at the interplay between the wife's behavior and the husband's self-perception. One interesting result was that the stable couples had significantly more steady states in the quadrant where her behavior is positive and his self-rating is positive. In other words, these couples were more likely to wind up at a place where her affective behavior (as judged by observers) was positive and he had a sense of well-being, than were the couples who were divorced at Time-2. The finding for the uninfluenced steady state for the wife confirms one result from Model 1, which is that the divorced wives tended to be much more negative than the stable wives in the absence of influence from their husbands. However, in this case, it means that the divorced wives tended to be behaviorally negative even when their husbands were feeling neutral. The findings for the husbands from this model indicate that the stable husbands had significantly higher perception inertia (it took more influence from their wives to change how they felt) than the divorced husbands. Also, the divorced husbands started out the conversation feeling slightly negative, compared to the stable husbands, who started out feeling slightly positive.

In table 15.3, we see that Model 3 considered the relationship between the wife's behavior and the husband's physiology (heart rate). The divorced couples had significantly more steady states where the husband's physiology was negative (higher arousal) and the wife's behavior was also negative. In fact, the divorced couples had more than one such steady state on average (mean = 1.18). The next two findings were for the slopes of the wife's influence function— i.e., the strength of the influence of her behavior on his heart rate. We immediately saw that by using both positive and negative emotion, the wives in the divorced group drove their husbands' heart rates more than did the stable wives. However, the divorced husbands were better able to moderate this influence than were the stable husbands. Perhaps they found it more necessary to do so because they were so much more reactive to their wives' behavior. We saw this moderation through the effectiveness of repair and damping parameters, which were greater in magnitude for the divorced husbands. Two other interesting results from this model concerned the level of physiological arousal in the husbands. The husbands in the divorced group started the conversation in a much greater state of physiological arousal than did the stable husbands (initial state), and their physiological arousal also tended to be much greater even in the absence of emotional influence from their wives during that particular conversation (uninfluenced steady state). Thus, these husbands may

Table 15.2: Divorce Prediction Using Parameters of Core Triad Model 2: Wife's Behavior and Husband's Perception.

			Means	
Variable	F-ratio	df	Stable	Divorced
Number of Influenced Steady States				
where $(W+)$ and $(H-)$	0.31	1,115	0.18	0.27
where $(W-)$ and $(H-)$	0.83	1,115	0.66	0.93
where $(W+)$ and $(H+)$	5.49*	1,115	1.11	0.33
where $(W-)$ and $(H+)$	0.80	1,115	0.38	0.60
Wife				
Inertia	0.18	1,115	0.33	0.35
Initial state	3.55^a	1,115	0.35	−0.45
Uninfluenced steady state	4.82*	1,115	0.31	−1.21
Influence on husband				
Positive half slope	0.05	1,110	0.29	0.27
Negative half slope	0.53	1,114	0.38	0.48
Threshold, husb damping	1.75	1,110	6.76	5.18
Strength, husb damping	1.34	1,110	−2.33	−1.43
Threshold, husb repair	2.19	1,114	−4.18	−3.06
Strength, husb repair	0.86	1,114	1.86	2.41
Husband				
Inertia	7.28**	1,115	0.78	0.63
Initial state	5.18*	1,115	0.25	−0.29
Uninfluenced steady state	0.29	1,115	1.12	−0.60
Influence on wife				
Positive half slope	0.20	1,113	0.81	0.70
Negative half slope	1.42	1,106	0.60	0.40
Threshold, wife damping	0.72	1,113	4.66	3.66
Strength, wife damping	1.19	1,113	−4.29	−5.35
Threshold, wife repair	0.46	1,106	−5.40	−6.29
Strength, wife repair	1.36	1,106	3.45	4.96

^{a} $p < .10$, * $p < .05$, ** $p < .01$, *** $p < .001$
$(W+)$ Wife Positive, $(W-)$ Wife Negative
$(H+)$ Husband Positive, $(H-)$ Husband Negative

Table 15.3: Divorce Prediction Using Parameters of Core Triad Model 3: Wife's Behavior and Husband's Physiology.

			Means	
Variable	F-ratio	df	Stable	Divorced
Number of Influenced Steady States				
where $(W+)$ and $(H-)$	0.14	1,120	0.46	0.53
where $(W-)$ and $(H-)$	4.53*	1,120	0.67	1.18
where $(W+)$ and $(H+)$	0.25	1,120	0.27	0.18
where $(W-)$ and $(H+)$	1.60	1,120	0.14	0.29
Wife				
Inertia	2.15	1,120	0.41	0.53
Initial state	0.50	1,120	0.01	−0.26
Uninfluenced steady state	2.00	1,120	−0.13	−1.14
Influence on husband				
Positive half slope	8.24**	1,117	0.38	0.64
Negative half slope	8.64**	1,118	0.53	0.95
Threshold, husb damping	0.04	1,116	6.28	6.05
Strength, husb damping	3.30^a	1,116	−3.72	−5.65
Threshold, husb repair	0.68	1,118	−3.41	−2.89
Strength, husb repair	5.50*	1,118	3.27	4.90
Husband				
Inertia	0.62	1,120	0.24	0.20
Initial state	9.94**	1,120	−1.81	−5.17
Uninfluenced steady state	10.04**	1,120	−2.35	−5.52
Influence on wife				
Positive half slope	0.69	1,119	0.81	0.62
Negative half slope	0.02	1,120	0.45	0.46
Threshold, wife damping	1.40	1,119	3.20	4.06
Strength, wife damping	0.58	1,119	−4.90	−3.64
Threshold, wife repair	1.93	1,120	−4.19	−5.84
Strength, wife repair	0.94	1,120	3.11	2.61

^{a} $p < .10$, * $p < .05$, ** $p < .01$, *** $p < .001$
$(W+)$ Wife Positive, $(W-)$ Wife Negative
$(H+)$ Husband Positive, $(H-)$ Husband Negative

be experiencing diffuse physiological arousal, which we have theorized is one factor leading to the distance and isolation cascade.

We now consider table 15.4. The first three models concerned the interaction of the wife's behavior with one of the core triad measures in the husband. We have some interesting findings from each of these models that involve the wife's behavior, each of which tells the same story in a somewhat different way. In Model 4, we turn to the first pairing of the husband's behavior with a different core triad measure in the wife—namely, the interaction between his behavior and her self-perception. We immediately saw one result that mirrors that of Model 2, which is the same pairing of core triad measures, but with the spouses reversed. There was a marginally significant finding ($F(1, 111) = 3.55$, $p = .062$) that the stable couples were more likely than the divorced couples to wind up in a place where his affective behavior (as judged by observers) was positive and she had a sense of well-being. The findings for the husbands' behavior from this model are in line with those from Model 1. They indicate that the stable husbands had significantly higher behavioral inertia than the divorced husbands (it took more influence from their wives to change how they behaved, but in this case the influence was owing to her perception rather than to her behavior). There were significant differences in both the husband's initial state and his uninfluenced steady state, with the stable husbands behaviorally positive, but the divorced husbands quite negative.

In table 15.5, we consider Model 5—the second of the "pure" models, in which we considered the relationship between both partners' perception. The wives in the divorced group had significantly higher perception inertia, meaning it took more influence from their husband to change how they felt, in comparison to the wives in stable marriages. This is the reverse of the inertia pattern for the husbands' perception. Looking at the parameters for the wives' influence functions, we saw a significantly higher positive half slope for the divorced wives. That is, in terms of the underlying bilinear influence function, when their perception was positive, the divorced wives had a much stronger positive influence on their husbands' perception (before damping was triggered) than did the wives in stable marriages. However, in the same divorced group, the husband's effectiveness of damping was also significantly stronger, meaning that once these wives passed a certain threshold of positive perception, the husband was much more effective at moderating the positive influence on his own perception, bringing it back down to a lower level. Also, the husbands in the divorced group had a fairly negative initial state (they went into the discussion feeling pretty negative), compared to the stable group, where the initial state was slightly positive.

In table 15.6, we see that Model 6 paired wife perception with hus-

Table 15.4: Divorce Prediction Using Parameters of Core
Triad Model 4: Wife's Perception and Husband's Behavior.

Variable	F-ratio	df	Means Stable	Means Divorced
Number of Influenced Steady States				
where $(W+)$ and $(H-)$	2.29	1,111	0.36	0.69
where $(W-)$ and $(H-)$	2.30	1,111	0.55	1.08
where $(W+)$ and $(H+)$	3.55^a	1,111	1.13	0.38
where $(W-)$ and $(H+)$	0.89	1,111	0.22	0.08
Wife				
Inertia	0.84	1,111	0.81	0.86
Initial state	0.21	1,111	0.00	-0.14
Uninfluenced steady state	0.17	1,111	-0.66	-1.70
Influence on husband				
Positive half slope	0.46	1,110	0.92	1.13
Negative half slope	0.08	1,98	0.56	0.52
Threshold, husb damping	0.21	1,110	4.32	3.75
Strength, husb damping	0.55	1,110	-4.94	-4.01
Threshold, husb repair	1.50	1,98	-5.72	-7.58
Strength, husb repair	1.76	1,98	3.08	4.37
Husband				
Inertia	9.27**	1,111	0.35	0.09
Initial state	12.43**	1,111	0.55	-1.47
Uninfluenced steady state	4.06*	1,110	1.01	-1.43
Influence on wife				
Positive half slope	0.16	1,109	0.26	0.22
Negative half slope	0.09	1,108	0.26	0.28
Threshold, wife damping	2.07	1,108	6.44	4.90
Strength, wife damping	0.11	1,108	-2.43	-1.85
Threshold, wife repair	0.71	1,105	-4.47	-5.25
Strength, wife repair	0.04	1,105	1.83	1.97

^{a} $p < .10$, * $p < .05$, ** $p < .01$, *** $p < .001$
$(W+)$ Wife Positive, $(W-)$ Wife Negative
$(H+)$ Husband Positive, $(H-)$ Husband Negative

Table 15.5: Divorce Prediction Using Parameters of Core Triad Model 5: Both Partners' Perception.

			Means	
Variable	F-ratio	df	Stable	Divorced
Number of Influenced Steady States				
where $(W+)$ and $(H-)$	0.86	1,104	0.49	0.23
where $(W-)$ and $(H-)$	0.05	1,104	1.03	0.92
where $(W+)$ and $(H+)$	0.03	1,104	1.22	1.15
where $(W-)$ and $(H+)$	0.06	1,104	0.53	0.46
Wife				
Inertia	6.36*	1,104	0.78	0.95
Initial state	0.25	1,104	−0.07	−0.23
Uninfluenced steady state	2.15	1,104	0.90	8.89
Influence on husband				
Positive half slope	11.68**	1,103	0.42	1.79
Negative half slope	0.57	1,94	0.41	0.30
Threshold, husb damping	0.01	1,103	4.82	4.98
Strength, husb damping	7.78**	1,103	−2.59	−7.06
Threshold, husb repair	0.30	1,93	−5.63	−4.85
Strength, husb repair	0.01	1,93	2.72	2.63
Husband				
Inertia	0.00	1,104	0.74	0.74
Initial state	6.61*	1,104	0.17	−1.71
Uninfluenced steady state	0.06	1,104	0.66	1.17
Influence on wife				
Positive half slope	1.83	1,103	0.30	0.43
Negative half slope	0.01	1,97	0.32	0.34
Threshold, wife damping	1.58	1,103	5.73	3.91
Strength, wife damping	0.01	1,103	−2.20	−2.26
Threshold, wife repair	0.00	1,97	−5.28	−5.34
Strength, wife repair	0.41	1,97	2.36	2.93

[a] $p < .10$, * $p < .05$, ** $p < .01$, *** $p < .001$
$(W+)$ Wife Positive, $(W-)$ Wife Negative
$(H+)$ Husband Positive, $(H-)$ Husband Negative

Table 15.6: Divorce Prediction Using Parameters of Core Triad Model 6: Wife's Perception and Husband's Physiology.

Variable	F-ratio	df	Means Stable	Means Divorced
Number of Influenced Steady States				
where $(W+)$ and $(H-)$	0.13	1,109	0.74	0.64
where $(W-)$ and $(H-)$	0.11	1,109	0.82	0.93
where $(W+)$ and $(H+)$	0.14	1,109	0.38	0.29
where $(W-)$ and $(H+)$	0.26	1,109	0.21	0.29
Wife				
Inertia	0.77	1,109	0.83	0.89
Initial state	0.30	1,109	-0.09	0.11
Uninfluenced steady state	0.75	1,109	1.05	-6.73
Influence on husband				
Positive half slope	3.90^a	1,107	0.67	1.47
Negative half slope	1.34	1,96	0.50	0.71
Threshold, husb damping	0.20	1,107	4.88	5.46
Strength, husb damping	1.48	1,107	-3.46	-4.75
Threshold, husb repair	1.96	1,96	-5.22	-7.21
Strength, husb repair	1.45	1,96	3.69	4.79
Husband				
Inertia	9.74^{**}	1,109	0.25	0.01
Initial state	6.03^*	1,109	-2.02	-4.86
Uninfluenced steady state	2.40	1,109	-2.47	-4.46
Influence on wife				
Positive half slope	0.39	1,109	0.40	0.32
Negative half slope	0.04	1,109	0.33	0.35
Threshold, wife damping	0.16	1,109	3.90	3.54
Strength, wife damping	0.50	1,109	-2.66	-2.00
Threshold, wife repair	0.00	1,109	-5.52	-5.51
Strength, wife repair	0.03	1,109	2.57	2.37

[a] $p < .10$, * $p < .05$, ** $p < .01$, *** $p < .001$
$(W+)$ Wife Positive, $(W-)$ Wife Negative
$(H+)$ Husband Positive, $(H-)$ Husband Negative

band physiology. Significant differences between the stable and divorced couples were found for this model that concerned the level of physiological arousal in the husbands. The husbands who eventually divorced started the conversation in a much greater (initial) state of physiological arousal than did the stable husbands, and their physiological inertia was near zero (the contribution of their current physiological state to their state at the next time point was almost nil, and thus any change was driven almost entirely by the wife's influence). In addition, there was a result for the positive half slope of the wife's influence function—i.e., the strength of the influence of her positive perception on his heart rate. For the divorced wives, this influence was stronger ($F(1, 107) = 3.90$, $p = .051$, or very close to significance at the $\alpha = .05$ level). These results echo those from Model 3, where the wives in the divorced group drove their husbands' heart rates more than did the stable wives. In this case, however, the influence was owing to the wife's perception rather than to her behavior.

In table 15.7, we see that Model 7, which paired wife physiology with husband behavior, yielded little in the way of significant results in comparison with Model 3, which used the same two core triad measures but with the spouses reversed. That model showed significant differences between the two groups in which husbands in the divorced group were more physiologically aroused than the stable husbands, and the wives in the divorced group seemed to be driving their husbands' physiology more. We did not see the same sorts of patterns emerge from Model 7, where husband and wife are reversed. The only significant finding was for husbands' behavioral initial state, which was quite negative in the divorced group and slightly positive in the stable group.

In table 15.8, we turn to Model 8. This model paired wife physiology with husband perception and also yielded little in the way of significant results. Curiously, there was a significant difference between the stable and divorced groups with regard to wife's uninfluenced steady state, which was quite negative for wives in the stable group and near zero for the divorced wives, indicating that the stable wives had heart rates higher than their baseline in the absence of influence owing to their husband's perception, which is difficult to interpret. The other finding from this model was that the divorced wives began damping at a lower level; as their husbands' perception became increasingly positive, they began to moderate the positive influence on their own physiology sooner.

In table 15.9, we see that Model 9 is the third "pure" model: it explored the relationship between both partners' physiology (heart rate). This model did not yield many significant results in terms of distinguishing the divorced and stable couples. The stable wives had a significantly more negative initial state, meaning they began the conflict discussion in

Table 15.7: Divorce Prediction Using Parameters of Core Triad Model 7: Wife's Physiology and Husband's Behavior.

Variable	F-ratio	df	Means Stable	Means Divorced
Number of Influenced Steady States				
where $(W+)$ and $(H-)$	2.94^a	1,113	0.09	0.31
where $(W-)$ and $(H-)$	0.61	1,113	0.81	1.08
where $(W+)$ and $(H+)$	0.44	1,113	0.29	0.15
where $(W-)$ and $(H+)$	2.56	1,113	0.58	0.23
Wife				
Inertia	0.14	1,113	0.37	0.35
Initial state	0.07	1,113	-3.13	-2.83
Uninfluenced steady state	0.78	1,113	-5.29	-3.79
Influence on husband				
Positive half slope	0.14	1,113	0.37	0.35
Negative half slope	0.04	1,113	0.44	0.50
Threshold, husb damping	0.79	1,112	3.21	2.58
Strength, husb damping	0.18	1,112	-4.22	-3.79
Threshold, husb repair	0.42	1,113	-7.95	-6.35
Strength, husb repair	0.01	1,113	4.02	3.77
Husband				
Inertia	1.14	1,113	0.35	0.23
Initial state	10.97^{**}	1,113	0.26	-1.47
Uninfluenced steady state	0.27	1,113	8.71	-2.32
Influence on wife				
Positive half slope	1.60	1,112	0.56	0.39
Negative half slope	0.26	1,108	1.02	0.81
Threshold, wife damping	1.77	1,111	6.42	4.83
Strength, wife damping	2.07	1,111	-5.72	-3.60
Threshold, wife repair	0.58	1,106	-3.80	-4.34
Strength, wife repair	0.03	1,106	5.61	5.21

[a] $p < .10$, * $p < .05$, ** $p < .01$, *** $p < .001$
$(W+)$ Wife Positive, $(W-)$ Wife Negative
$(H+)$ Husband Positive, $(H-)$ Husband Negative

Table 15.8: Divorce Prediction Using Parameters of Core Triad Model 8: Wife's Physiology and Husband's Perception.

Variable	F-ratio	df	Means Stable	Means Divorced
Number of Influenced Steady States				
where $(W+)$ and $(H-)$	0.10	1,103	0.25	0.18
where $(W-)$ and $(H-)$	0.03	1,103	1.11	1.18
where $(W+)$ and $(H+)$	1.07	1,103	0.52	0.18
where $(W-)$ and $(H+)$	0.01	1,103	0.88	0.91
Wife				
Inertia	0.04	1,103	0.36	0.34
Initial state	1.03	1,103	-3.81	-1.89
Uninfluenced steady state	4.04*	1,103	-5.61	0.02
Influence on husband				
Positive half slope	1.02	1,102	0.78	0.32
Negative half slope	0.15	1,103	0.28	0.32
Threshold, husb damping	0.23	1,102	3.05	3.44
Strength, husb damping	0.13	1,102	-3.18	-2.60
Threshold, husb repair	0.66	1,103	-8.59	-6.46
Strength, husb repair	0.01	1,103	2.74	2.68
Husband				
Inertia	2.60	1,103	0.85	0.68
Initial state	0.25	1,103	-0.03	0.30
Uninfluenced steady state	0.13	1,103	-23.95	-1.49
Influence on wife				
Positive half slope	0.00	1,103	0.85	0.86
Negative half slope	0.25	1,96	0.85	0.69
Threshold, wife damping	5.36*	1,102	5.42	2.29
Strength, wife damping	0.90	1,102	-5.06	-3.52
Threshold, wife repair	0.17	1,96	-4.36	-4.92
Strength, wife repair	1.27	1,96	5.08	3.46

[a] $p < .10$, * $p < .05$, ** $p < .01$, *** $p < .001$
$(W+)$ Wife Positive, $(W-)$ Wife Negative
$(H+)$ Husband Positive, $(H-)$ Husband Negative

Table 15.9: Divorce Prediction Using Parameters of Core
Triad Model 9: Both Partners' Physiology.

Variable	F-ratio	df	Means Stable	Means Divorced
Number of Influenced Steady States				
where $(W+)$ and $(H-)$	0.33	1,110	0.25	0.36
where $(W-)$ and $(H-)$	0.28	1,110	0.93	1.07
where $(W+)$ and $(H+)$	1.13	1,110	0.26	0.00
where $(W-)$ and $(H+)$	0.20	1,110	0.39	0.29
Wife				
Inertia	1.30	1,110	0.35	0.48
Initial state	5.22*	1,110	−2.98	0.48
Uninfluenced steady state	0.02	1,110	−10.20	−8.10
Influence on husband				
Positive half slope	0.33	1,108	0.74	0.88
Negative half slope	0.15	1,110	0.42	0.38
Threshold, husb damping	1.49	1,108	3.11	2.26
Strength, husb damping	0.20	1,108	−4.86	−4.13
Threshold, husb repair	0.08	1,110	−8.58	−7.89
Strength, husb repair	0.50	1,110	4.13	3.29
Husband				
Inertia	1.76	1,110	0.27	0.11
Initial state	1.12	1,110	−1.37	−2.25
Uninfluenced steady state	1.05	1,110	−1.79	−2.78
Influence on wife				
Positive half slope	3.66^a	1,109	0.84	1.53
Negative half slope	1.01	1,110	0.84	0.67
Threshold, wife damping	0.18	1,109	3.53	3.20
Strength, wife damping	2.26	1,109	−5.16	−7.82
Threshold, wife repair	0.45	1,110	−4.94	−5.99
Strength, wife repair	0.23	1,110	6.64	5.18

^{a} $p < .10$, * $p < .05$, ** $p < .01$, *** $p < .001$
$(W+)$ Wife Positive, $(W-)$ Wife Negative
$(H+)$ Husband Positive, $(H-)$ Husband Negative

a more physiologically aroused state. There was a marginally significant finding for husbands' positive half slope ($F(1, 109) = 3.664$, $p = .058$) that indicated that the divorced husbands had a stronger influence on their wives' heart rates than did the stable husbands, when the husbands were physiologically soothed compared to baseline.

Summary of Divorce Prediction Results

Model 1, our original model pairing both partners' behavior, had the most strongly significant results; that is, it was the "best" at distinguishing the couples who eventually divorced from the stable couples.

In general, we found many more significant results from the models that involved at least one person's behavior (the exception being Model 7, husband behavior and wife physiology). Models 1, 2, and 3, taken together, indicated differences between stable and divorced couples when the wife's behavior affects any of the three of the core triad measures in the husband (behavior, perception, and physiology). Interestingly, though, the reverse is not quite true. Model 1, of course, did indicate that husband behavior affects wife behavior. There is some indication of a link between husband behavior and wife perception (Model 4) in the fact that stable couples had significantly more steady states where both spouses were positive in their respective domain. However, the results for Model 7 do not suggest much of a linkage between husband behavior and wife physiology. For some reason, in dysfunctional marriages wife behavior drives husband physiology, but not the converse.

For the models that did not include behavior, the significant results tended to confirm the findings for these parameters from the models that did include behavior. For example, Model 6 showed that the husbands in the divorced group started the conversation in a much greater state of physiological arousal than did the stable husbands (initial state), which was also seen in Model 3. This parameter is estimated from the moments when wife was neutral, i.e. noninfluencing; the finding held when that influence was owing to her behavior or to her own perception. Likewise, Model 5 showed that the husbands in the divorced group started the conversation with a negative perception, compared to the stable husbands, who started with a slightly positive perception; this result was also seen in Model 2.

Models 7, 8, and 9, taken together, showed few significant results and therefore the lack of a strong tie between wife's physiology and any of the three core triad measures in the husband (behavior, perception, or his own physiology), at least in terms of distinguishing the stable couples from those who eventually divorced. That is, the husband was not influencing the wife's heart rate no matter how we measured his influence in any of the three domains. Conversely, and probably not surprisingly, her physiology did not have an influence on his behavior, perception, or physiology.

Three Criterion Groups

Although divorce prediction is of great interest to us, we would also like to be able to predict the marital misery or happiness of couples who stay married. For these comparisons, we reasoned as follows. We wanted to compare the divorced couples to other couples who stayed married but were comparable in terms of having low marital satisfaction. This comparison controlled for marital satisfaction, varying only marital stability or instability. The next comparison controlled for stability (examining the stable groups) while varying marital satisfaction (happy or miserable). We selected samples for these analyses comparable in size to the number of divorced couples. This was the logic in constructing three criterion groups.

Tables 15.10 through 15.18 summarize the results from a second analysis of variance of the parameters of the nine core triad models. This analysis determined which Time-1 parameters could significantly predict which group the couples wound up in: happy stable, unhappy stable, or divorced (results significant at $\alpha = .10$ or less). It compared the seventeen couples who eventually divorced to the twenty most happily married and the twenty most unhappily married of the stable group. Recall that the data were obtained within the first year after the wedding, and the divorce/stability and marital satisfaction categorization was based on six-year follow-up data. This analysis also determined if a significant linear trend existed for the values of each parameter as it moved from the happy stable group to the unhappy stable group to the divorced group.

In table 15.10, we examine Model 1, which is our original model pairing both partners' behavior. There was a significant difference between the three groups in the number of influenced steady states where both partners' behavior was negative and also in the number of influenced steady states where both partners' behavior was positive. There was also a significant linear trend across the three groups for both of these steady-state locations ($F(1, 55) = 8.93$, $p = .004$ for linear trend in the steady state where both spouses were negative; $F(1, 55) = 12.04$, $p = .001$ for linear trend in the steady state where both spouses were positive). The divorced couples were more than six times as likely to have a steady state where both partners' behavior was negative than were the happy, stable couples. Conversely, the happy stable couples were almost six times as likely as the divorced couples to have a steady

Table 15.10: Three Criterion Groups and Parameters of Core Triad Model 1: Both Partners' Behavior.

Variable	F-ratio	df	Happy, Stable	Unhappy, Stable	Div.
			Means		
Number of Influenced Steady States					
where $(W+)$ and $(H-)$	0.05	2,55	0.15	0.15	0.12
where $(W-)$ and $(H-)$	4.78*	2,55	0.20	0.95	1.24
where $(W+)$ and $(H+)$	6.27**	2,55	1.20	0.55	0.24
where $(W-)$ and $(H+)$	0.42	2,55	0.01	0.01	0.00
Wife					
Inertia	0.32	2,55	0.37	0.41	0.42
Initial state	11.51***	2,55	0.64	−0.02	−1.13
Uninfluenced steady state	13.21***	2,55	1.17	−0.26	−2.26
Influence on husband					
Positive half slope	0.41	2,51	0.46	0.55	0.52
Negative half slope	0.39	2,54	0.51	0.65	0.62
Trigger, husb damping	1.30	2,51	5.15	6.82	5.02
Strength, husb damping	2.36	2,51	−3.41	−4.87	−3.14
Trigger, husb repair	2.79[a]	2,54	−6.27	−3.87	−4.40
Strength, husb repair	0.55	2,54	4.20	3.44	3.83
Husband					
Inertia	0.59	2,55	0.37	0.35	0.30
Initial state	9.77***	2,55	0.74	−0.04	−1.11
Uninfluenced steady state	10.34***	2,55	1.03	−0.47	−1.89
Influence on wife					
Positive half slope	1.00	2,54	0.51	0.39	0.50
Negative half slope	0.71	2,53	0.68	0.48	0.46
Trigger, wife damping	0.12	2,54	5.27	5.75	5.58
Strength, wife damping	3.05[a]	2,54	−3.98	−3.61	−2.07
Trigger, wife repair	0.02	2,50	−5.16	−5.03	−4.95
Strength, wife repair	0.51	2,50	3.34	2.94	3.58

[a] $p < .10$, * $p < .05$, ** $p < .01$, *** $p < .001$
$(W+)$ Wife Positive, $(W-)$ Wife Negative
$(H+)$ Husband Positive, $(H-)$ Husband Negative

state where both partners' behavior was positive. In both cases, the unhappy stable couples had a mean somewhere in between.

There was a strongly significant difference between the three groups in the initial state (how they started out the conversation) and in the uninfluenced steady state (where they would tend to be behaviorally in the absence of any particular influence from their spouse during the conversation). There was also a strongly significant linear trend in the initial state ($F(1,55) = 22.51$, $p = .000$ for linear trend in wife's initial state; $F(1,55) = 19.37$, $p = .000$ for linear trend in husband's initial state), as well as in the uninfluenced steady state ($F(1,55) = 26.15$, $p = .000$ for linear trend in wife's uninfluenced steady state; $F(1,55) = 20.67$, $p = .000$ for linear trend in husband's uninfluenced steady state). Looking at the means, we saw that for the divorced group, both the initial state and the uninfluenced steady state were negative (for both husbands and wives). For the unhappy stable group, both of these parameters were slightly negative to near neutral (for both husbands and wives). For the happy stable group, both the initial state and the uninfluenced steady state were positive (for both husbands and wives). In other words, looking at both partner's behavior over time and at the influence of each person's behavior on the other person's behavior, for the divorced couples the conversation started out negative and tended to stay that way. The case was the opposite for the happy stable couples, and the unhappy stable couples fell somewhere in between.

Table 15.11 shows the results from Model 2, which looks at the interplay between the wife's behavior and the husband's perception. There was a marginally significant difference ($F(2,49) = 2.61$, $p = .084$) between the three groups in the number of steady states where her behavior is positive and his self-rating is positive, and there was a significant linear trend across the three groups ($F(1,49) = 5.16$, $p = .028$ for linear trend). The happy stable couples had more than one such steady state on average and were approximately four times as likely as the divorced couples to have such a positive steady state; the unhappy stable couples fell about halfway in between. In other words, the happy couples were more likely than either the unhappy or the divorced couples to wind up at a place where her affective behavior (as judged by observers) was positive and he had a sense of well-being. The finding for the uninfluenced steady state for the wife confirms one result from Model 1, which is that the divorced wives tended to be much more negative than the wives in the other two groups in the absence of influence from their husbands. However, in this case it means that the divorced wives tended to be behaviorally negative even when their husbands were feeling neutral. Again, there was a significant linear trend across the groups ($F(1,49) = 7.33$, $p = .009$), with the happy stable wives having a positive uninfluenced

Table 15.11: Three Criterion Groups and Parameters of Core Triad Model 2: Wife's Behavior and Husband's Perception.

Variable	F-ratio	df	Means Happy, Stable	Unhappy, Stable	Div.
Number of Influenced Steady States					
where $(W+)$ and $(H-)$	0.03	2,49	0.21	0.24	0.27
where $(W-)$ and $(H-)$	0.86	2,49	0.47	0.59	0.93
where $(W+)$ and $(H+)$	2.61[a]	2,49	1.26	0.88	0.33
where $(W-)$ and $(H+)$	0.71	2,49	0.21	0.53	0.60
Wife					
Inertia	1.45	2,49	0.24	0.35	0.35
Initial state	2.41	2,49	0.79	0.01	−0.45
Uninfluencedsteady state	3.66*	2,49	0.94	−0.01	−1.21
Influence on husband					
Positive half slope	0.64	2,45	0.32	0.40	0.27
Negative half slope	1.99	2,48	0.25	0.43	0.48
Trigger, husb damping	4.62*	2,45	5.36	8.59	5.18
Strength, husb damping	3.74*	2,45	−2.02	−4.43	−1.43
Trigger, husb repair	1.29	2,48	−4.28	−4.46	−3.06
Strength, husb repair	1.65	2,48	1.40	2.48	2.41
Husband					
Inertia	3.39*	2,49	0.77	0.82	0.63
Initial state	3.04	2,49	0.01	0.37	−0.29
Uninfluencedsteady state	0.28	2,49	−0.44	3.15	−0.60
Influence on wife					
Positive half slope	0.53	2,47	0.54	0.78	0.70
Negative half slope	0.81	2,45	0.52	0.36	0.40
Trigger, wife damping	0.38	2,47	3.62	4.54	3.66
Strength, wife damping	1.32	2,47	−3.40	−4.10	−5.35
Trigger, wife repair	1.35	2,45	−4.37	−6.49	−6.29
Strength, wife repair	0.59	2,45	2.78	3.48	4.96

[a] $p < .10$, * $p < .05$, ** $p < .01$, *** $p < .001$
$(W+)$ Wife Positive, $(W-)$ Wife Negative
$(H+)$ Husband Positive, $(H-)$ Husband Negative

steady state and the unhappy stable wives near neutral. The findings for the husbands from this model indicate a significant difference in perception inertia, although for this parameter it wasn't quite linear across the groups. The happy and unhappy stable husbands were similar and had higher perception inertia (it took more influence from their wives to change how they felt) than the divorced husbands.

Table 15.12 shows the results from Model 3, which considers the relationship between the wife's behavior and the husband's physiology (heart rate). Although there was no significant difference between the three groups in the locations of the steady states, there was a marginally significant linear trend ($F(1, 50) = 3.09$, $p = .085$) in the number of steady states where the husband's physiology was negative and the wife's behavior was also negative, with the divorced couples having more than one such steady state on average (mean $= 1.18$) and the happy and unhappy stable couples about half that many. The next two findings were for the slopes of the wife's influence function—i.e., the strength of the influence of her behavior on his heart rate. We immediately saw that by using both positive and negative emotion, the wives in the divorced group drove their husbands' heart rates more than did the happy and unhappy stable wives. Moreover, there was again a significant linear trend across the three groups for these slopes, although the happy and unhappy stable means appear to be quite close ($F(1, 47) = 6.77$, $p = .012$ for linear trend in wife's positive slope; $F(1, 49) = 6.27$, $p = .016$ for linear trend in wife's negative slope). There was a marginally significant difference among the three groups in the husband's effectiveness of repair ($F(2, 49) = 2.88$, $p = .066$), but this was with significant linear trend ($F(1, 49) = 4.40$, $p = .041$).

Surprisingly, we found for Model 3 that the divorced husbands were almost twice as effective at moderating negative influence from their wives than were the happy or unhappy stable husbands. Perhaps they found it more necessary to do so because they were so much more reactive to their wives' behavior. There were two other significant results from this model that concerned the level of physiological arousal in the husbands. The husbands in the divorced group started the conversation in a much greater state of physiological arousal than did the husbands in the other two groups (initial state), and their physiological arousal also tended to be much greater even in the absence of emotional influence from their wives during that particular conversation (uninfluenced steady state). Again, there was a significant linear trend across the three groups for both initial state ($F(1, 50) = 5.82$, $p = .020$) and uninfluenced steady state ($F(1, 50) = 7.89$, $p = .007$), although the mean for the divorced group was much more negative in both cases, and the means of the happy and unhappy stable groups were more similar to each other.

Table 15.12: Three Criterion Groups and Parameters of Core Triad Model 3: Wife's Behavior and Husband's Physiology.

Variable	F-ratio	df	Means Happy, Stable	Unhappy, Stable	Div.
Number of Influenced Steady States					
where $(W+)$ and $(H-)$	1.33	2,50	0.65	0.22	0.53
where $(W-)$ and $(H-)$	1.84	2,50	0.59	0.67	1.18
where $(W+)$ and $(H+)$	0.58	2,50	0.41	0.50	0.18
where $(W-)$ and $(H+)$	0.46	2,50	0.12	0.22	0.29
Wife					
Inertia	1.08	2,50	0.37	0.47	0.53
Initial state	1.27	2,50	0.66	−0.12	−0.26
Uninfluencedsteady state	0.58	2,50	0.41	0.50	0.18
Influence on husband					
Positive half slope	4.22*	2,47	0.30	0.32	0.64
Negative half slope	4.32*	2,49	0.41	0.40	0.95
Trigger, husb damping	0.32	2,47	5.11	5.67	6.05
Strength, husb damping	2.28	2,47	−3.49	−2.86	−5.65
Trigger, husb repair	0.46	2,49	−3.62	−3.47	−2.89
Strength, husb repair	2.88[a]	2,49	2.79	2.84	4.90
Husband					
Inertia	0.67	2,50	0.27	0.27	0.20
Initial state	4.36*	2,50	−0.97	−0.56	−5.17
Uninfluencedsteady state	5.98**	2,50	−1.39	−0.94	−5.52
Influence on wife					
Positive half slope	0.50	2,49	0.79	0.62	0.62
Negative half slope	0.02	2,50	0.45	0.45	0.46
Trigger, wife damping	0.63	2,49	3.97	2.97	4.06
Strength, wife damping	2.00	2,49	−5.47	−3.10	−3.64
Trigger, wife repair	0.80	2,50	−4.51	−3.60	−5.84
Strength, wife repair	0.48	2,50	2.67	3.13	2.61

[a] $p < .10$, * $p < .05$, ** $p < .01$, *** $p < .001$
$(W+)$ Wife Positive, $(W-)$ Wife Negative
$(H+)$ Husband Positive, $(H-)$ Husband Negative

Thus, the husbands who eventually divorced might have experienced diffuse physiological arousal, which we have theorized is one factor leading to the distance and isolation cascade.

The first three models all concerned the interaction of the wife's behavior with one of the core triad measures in the husband. We have observed some interesting findings from each of these models that involve the wife's behavior, each model telling the same story in a somewhat different way. In Model 4 we turned to the first pairing of husband's behavior with a different core triad measure in the wife—namely, the interaction between his behavior and her self-perception. These results are shown in table 15.13. We immediately saw one result that mirrors that of Model 2, which is the same pairing of core triad measures but with the spouses reversed. There was a significant difference between the three groups in the number of positive steady states, where his affective behavior (as judged by observers) was positive and she had a sense of well-being. There was also a significant linear trend across the three groups for this measure $(F(1, 45) = 8.17, p = .006)$, with the happy stable couples almost five times as likely as the divorced couples to have a positive steady state and the unhappy stable couples about three times as likely. The findings for the husbands' behavior from this model are in line with those from Model 1. They indicate that the happy and unhappy stable husbands had significantly higher behavioral inertia, with significant linear trend $(F(1, 45) = 4.38, p = .042)$, than the divorced husbands (it took more influence from their wives to change how they behaved, but in this case the influence was owing to her perception rather than to her behavior). There was a significant difference in the husbands' initial state for the three groups, with significant linear trend $(F(1, 45) = 6.44, p = .015)$, such that the happy and unhappy stable husbands started out behaviorally positive, but the divorced husbands were quite negative. Although there was no statistical difference between the three groups in the husbands' uninfluenced steady state, there was a significant linear trend $(F(1, 45) = 4.13, p = .048)$, with the happy stable husbands fairly positive, the unhappy stable husbands just slightly positive, and the divorced husbands fairly negative.

Model 5 is the second of the "pure" models, in which we considered the relationship between both partners' perception. These results are shown in table 15.14. With regard to the parameters for the wives' influence functions, there were a few marginally significant findings. There was a marginal linear trend across the 3 groups $(F(1, 45) = 3.52, p = .067)$ for positive half slope, with a much higher slope for the divorced wives than for the wives in the other two groups. That is, in terms of the underlying bilinear influence function, when their perception was positive, the divorced wives had a much stronger positive influence on

Table 15.13: Three Criterion Groups and Parameters of Core Triad Model 4: Wife's Perception and Husband's Behavior.

Variable	F-ratio	df	Happy, Stable	Unhappy, Stable	Div.
				Means	
Number of Influenced Steady States					
where $(W+)$ and $(H-)$	1.29	2,45	0.68	0.20	0.69
where $(W-)$ and $(H-)$	1.11	2,45	0.89	0.40	1.08
where $(W+)$ and $(H+)$	4.11*	2,45	1.84	1.20	0.38
where $(W-)$ and $(H+)$	1.34	2,45	0.37	0.13	0.01
Wife					
Inertia	0.79	2,45	0.82	0.79	0.86
Initial state	0.06	2,45	−0.01	−0.20	−0.14
Uninfluencedsteady state	0.14	2,45	−0.59	−0.21	−1.70
Influence on husband					
Positive half slope	1.00	2,45	0.71	1.33	1.13
Negative half slope	0.05	2,43	0.47	0.53	0.52
Trigger, husb damping	0.72	2,45	5.07	3.46	3.75
Strength, husb damping	0.82	2,45	−4.30	−6.33	−4.01
Trigger, husb repair	2.15	2,43	−4.53	−4.45	−7.58
Strength, husb repair	2.19	2,43	2.25	2.67	4.37
Husband					
Inertia	3.29*	2,45	0.36	0.38	0.01
Initial state	4.27*	2,45	0.44	0.39	−1.47
Uninfluencedsteady state	2.08	2,45	2.31	0.19	−1.43
Influence on wife					
Positive half slope	0.60	2,44	0.35	0.37	0.22
Negative half slope	0.07	2,43	0.25	0.25	0.28
Trigger, wife damping	3.65*	2,44	5.54	8.15	4.90
Strength, wife damping	1.35	2,44	−2.34	−6.45	−1.85
Trigger, wife repair	1.77	2,43	−4.99	−3.09	−5.25
Strength, wife repair	0.65	2,43	3.01	1.80	1.97

[a] $p < .10$, * $p < .05$, ** $p < .01$, *** $p < .001$
$(W+)$ Wife Positive, $(W-)$ Wife Negative
$(H+)$ Husband Positive, $(H-)$ Husband Negative

Table 15.14: Three Criterion Groups and Parameters of
Core Triad Model 5: Both Partners' Perception.

			Means		
			Happy,	Unhappy,	
Variable	F-ratio	df	Stable	Stable	Div.
Number of Influenced Steady States					
where $(W+)$ and $(H-)$	1.04	2,45	0.74	0.40	0.23
where $(W-)$ and $(H-)$	0.57	2,45	1.21	1.60	0.92
where $(W+)$ and $(H+)$	0.24	2,45	1.37	1.53	1.15
where $(W-)$ and $(H+)$	1.11	2,45	1.00	0.60	0.46
Wife					
Inertia	1.92	2,45	0.79	0.77	0.95
Initial state	0.01	2,45	-0.27	-0.27	-0.23
Uninfluencedsteady state	0.66	2,45	1.30	0.15	8.89
Influence on husband					
Positive half slope	2.22	2,45	0.38	0.48	1.79
Negative half slope	2.74^a	2,43	0.21	0.54	0.30
Trigger, husb damping	0.40	2,45	6.06	4.66	4.98
Strength, husb damping	2.01	2,45	-2.49	-2.22	-7.06
Trigger, husb repair	0.41	2,43	-5.32	-6.33	-4.85
Strength, husb repair	1.30	2,43	1.82	4.06	2.63
Husband					
Inertia	0.34	2,45	0.80	0.71	0.74
Initial state	1.25	2,45	-0.14	0.25	-1.71
Uninfluencedsteady state	1.13	2,45	-1.30	3.17	1.17
Influence on wife					
Positive half slope	1.59	2,44	0.37	0.22	0.43
Negative half slope	0.06	2,41	0.34	0.31	0.34
Trigger, wife damping	7.03**	2,44	4.46	9.20	3.91
Strength, wife damping	0.23	2,44	-2.87	-2.90	-2.26
Trigger, wife repair	0.01	2,41	-5.13	-5.12	-5.34
Strength, wife repair	0.14	2,41	2.92	2.47	2.93

[a] $p < .10$, * $p < .05$, ** $p < .01$, *** $p < .001$
$(W+)$ Wife Positive, $(W-)$ Wife Negative
$(H+)$ Husband Positive, $(H-)$ Husband Negative

their husbands' perception (before damping was triggered) than did the wives in stable marriages. There was also a marginal difference between the three groups in the negative half slope ($F(2, 43) = 2.74$, $p = .076$), but in this case there was no linear trend, and in fact it was the wives in the unhappy stable group who had more influence than the wives in the other two groups on their husbands' perception when they were feeling negative. The only significant difference between the three groups that arose from this model was in the husband's positive perception score that triggered wife damping, but again there was no linear trend. It was the unhappy stable group that stood out from the other two, with the wives in that group having to feel much more positive before their husbands started damping down the influence on their own perception.

In table 15.15, we see the results from Model 6, which paired wife perception with husband physiology. For this model, significant differences were found between the three groups that concerned the nature of physiological arousal in the husbands. The husbands in the divorced group started the conversation in a much greater (initial) state of physiological arousal than did the happy or unhappy stable husbands, and their physiological inertia was near zero as compared to a positive value in the two stable groups (for the divorced husbands, the contribution of their current physiological state to their state at the next time point was almost nil, and thus any change was driven almost entirely by the wife's influence). There was a significant linear trend across the three groups for both of these parameters ($F(1, 44) = 7.70$, $p = .008$ for linear trend in husband inertia; $F(1, 44) = 4.60$, $p = .038$ for linear trend in husband initial state). However, a comparison of the means showed that the divorced group was more different than the two stable groups, with the happy and unhappy stable husbands being relatively more similar to each other.

Table 15.16 shows the results from Model 7, which paired wife physiology with husband behavior. This model yielded little in the way of significant results, in sharp contrast with Model 3, which used the same two core triad measures, but with the spouses reversed. Model 3 showed significant differences between the three groups in which husbands in the divorced group were more physiologically aroused than the stable husbands, and the wives in the divorced group seemed to be driving their husbands' physiology more. We did not see the same sorts of patterns emerge from Model 7, where husband and wife are reversed. The only significant finding was for husband's behavioral initial state, which also showed a significant linear trend ($F(1, 46) = 7.07$, $p = .011$): quite negative in the divorced group, slightly negative (near neutral) in the unhappy stable group, and positive in the happy stable group.

Table 15.17 shows the results from Model 8, which paired wife physi-

Table **15.15:** Three Criterion Groups and Parameters
of Core Triad Model 6: Wife's Perception and Husband's
Physiology.

Variable	F-ratio	df	Happy, Stable	Unhappy, Stable	Div.
			\multicolumn{3}{Means}		
Number of Influenced Steady States					
where $(W+)$ and $(H-)$	0.07	2,44	0.76	0.67	0.64
where $(W-)$ and $(H-)$	0.09	2,44	0.82	1.00	0.93
where $(W+)$ and $(H+)$	1.50	2,44	0.59	0.13	0.29
where $(W-)$ and $(H+)$	0.03	2,44	0.24	0.27	0.29
Wife					
Inertia	0.75	2,44	0.88	0.80	0.89
Initial state	1.16	2,44	0.01	−0.43	0.11
Uninfluencedsteady state	0.60	2,44	1.05	5.88	−6.73
Influence on husband					
Positive half slope	1.13	2,43	0.44	0.66	1.47
Negative half slope	1.78	2,42	0.47	0.29	0.71
Trigger, husb damping	0.62	2,43	6.24	4.22	5.46
Strength, husb damping	0.32	2,43	−3.67	−3.34	−4.75
Trigger, husb repair	0.58	2,42	−5.26	−5.43	−7.21
Strength, husb repair	3.07[a]	2,42	3.28	1.98	4.79
Husband					
Inertia	4.75*	2,44	0.28	0.26	0.01
Initial state	3.69*	2,44	−1.05	−0.46	−4.86
Uninfluencedsteady state	2.28	2,44	−1.50	−1.22	−4.46
Influence on wife					
Positive half slope	0.70	2,44	0.49	0.48	0.32
Negative half slope	0.33	2,44	0.49	0.38	0.35
Trigger, wife damping	0.71	2,44	4.75	5.16	3.54
Strength, wife damping	1.07	2,44	−3.70	−4.01	−2.00
Trigger, wife repair	1.25	2,44	−6.32	−3.06	−5.51
Strength, wife repair	1.13	2,44	4.74	2.02	2.37

[a] $p < .10$, * $p < .05$, ** $p < .01$, *** $p < .001$
$(W+)$ Wife Positive, $(W-)$ Wife Negative
$(H+)$ Husband Positive, $(H-)$ Husband Negative

Table 15.16: Three Criterion Groups and Parameters of Core Triad Model 7: Wife's Physiology and Husband's Behavior.

				Means	
			Happy,	Unhappy,	
Variable	F-ratio	df	Stable	Stable	Div.
Number of Influenced Steady States					
where $(W+)$ and $(H-)$	0.82	2,46	0.24	0.01	0.31
where $(W-)$ and $(H-)$	2.19	2,46	0.41	0.83	1.08
where $(W+)$ and $(H+)$	0.95	2,46	0.35	0.11	0.15
where $(W-)$ and $(H+)$	1.38	2,46	0.65	0.67	0.23
Wife					
Inertia	0.20	2,46	0.40	0.38	0.35
Initial state	0.62	2,46	-3.91	-2.54	-2.83
Uninfluencedsteady state	0.50	2,46	-6.10	-5.30	-3.79
Influence on husband					
Positive half slope	0.02	2,46	0.78	0.80	0.83
Negative half slope	0.60	2,46	0.27	0.85	0.50
Trigger, husb damping	1.45	2,46	3.76	2.50	2.58
Strength, husb damping	2.52^a	2,46	-5.56	-3.35	-3.79
Trigger, husb repair	0.05	2,46	-7.12	-6.78	-6.35
Strength, husb repair	0.79	2,46	2.87	7.66	3.77
Husband					
Inertia	0.33	2,46	0.34	0.25	0.23
Initial state	3.78*	2,46	0.53	-0.05	-1.47
Uninfluencedsteady state	2.29	2,46	0.43	-1.14	-2.32
Influence on wife					
Positive half slope	1.56	2,46	0.66	0.55	0.39
Negative half slope	0.37	2,44	1.02	1.20	0.81
Trigger, wife damping	1.05	2,46	6.75	5.99	4.83
Strength, wife damping	1.74	2,46	-6.39	-6.93	-3.60
Trigger, wife repair	0.67	2,42	-3.84	-3.24	-4.34
Strength, wife repair	0.71	2,42	6.42	3.30	5.21

^{a} $p < .10$, * $p < .05$, ** $p < .01$, *** $p < .001$
$(W+)$ Wife Positive, $(W-)$ Wife Negative
$(H+)$ Husband Positive, $(H-)$ Husband Negative

Table 15.17: Three Criterion Groups and Parameters of Core Triad Model 8: Wife's Physiology and Husband's Perception.

			Means		
			Happy,	Unhappy,	
Variable	F-ratio	df	Stable	Stable	Div.
Number of Influenced Steady States					
where $(W+)$ and $(H-)$	0.26	2,41	0.38	0.31	0.18
where $(W-)$ and $(H-)$	0.53	2,41	0.69	1.06	1.18
where $(W+)$ and $(H+)$	1.68	2,41	0.75	0.31	0.18
where $(W-)$ and $(H+)$	0.27	2,41	1.00	0.75	0.91
Wife					
Inertia	2.29	2,41	0.49	0.22	0.34
Initial state	0.92	2,41	-2.80	-5.66	-1.89
Uninfluencedsteady state	1.89	2,41	-4.18	-6.65	0.02
Influence on husband					
Positive half slope	1.49	2,41	0.53	0.71	0.32
Negative half slope	0.78	2,41	0.24	0.39	0.32
Trigger, husb damping	0.13	2,41	3.49	3.06	3.44
Strength, husb damping	0.44	2,41	-3.33	-3.09	-2.60
Trigger, husb repair	0.51	2,41	-9.26	-9.58	-6.46
Strength, husb repair	1.03	2,41	2.29	3.70	2.68
Husband					
Inertia	2.26	2,41	0.87	0.86	0.68
Initial state	0.23	2,41	0.35	0.06	0.30
Uninfluencedsteady state	0.68	2,41	-121.61	-16.16	-1.49
Influence on wife					
Positive half slope	0.10	2,41	0.78	0.95	0.86
Negative half slope	0.77	2,39	1.02	0.66	0.69
Trigger, wife damping	3.66*	2,40	5.50	6.19	2.29
Strength, wife damping	1.21	2,40	-5.40	-4.38	-3.52
Trigger, wife repair	1.49	2,39	-3.17	-5.40	-4.92
Strength, wife repair	0.61	2,39	5.08	5.63	3.46

[a] $p < .10$, * $p < .05$, ** $p < .01$, *** $p < .001$
$(W+)$ Wife Positive, $(W-)$ Wife Negative
$(H+)$ Husband Positive, $(H-)$ Husband Negative

ology with husband perception. This model also yielded little in the way of significant results. The only significant finding was that the divorced wives began damping at a lower level, with the happy and unhappy stable wives having about the same positive score threshold for damping. That is, as their husband's perception became increasingly positive, the wives who eventually divorced began to moderate the positive influence on their own physiology sooner (i.e., at a lower level of husband perception) than did the wives in the other two groups.

Table 15.18 shows the results from Model 9, the third "pure" model, which explored the relationship between both partners' physiology (heart rate). This model yielded only two marginally significant results in terms of distinguishing the three groups. The husbands who eventually divorced had a more negative initial physiological state ($F(2, 43) = 3.05$, $p = .058$) than the husbands in the other two groups. They also had a more negative physiological uninfluenced steady state ($F(2, 43) = 2.89$, $p = .067$) than the husbands in the other two groups. For this parameter there was also a significant linear trend across the three groups ($F(1, 43) = 5.18$, $p = .028$), with the happy stable group slightly negative, the divorced group the most negative, and the unhappy stable group somewhere in between.

Summary of Results for the Three Criterion Groups

The results were strikingly similar to the divorce prediction results. Many of the same parameters that significantly predicted whether a couple would divorce or not were also able to discriminate predictively between the three groups. Model 1, our original model pairing both partners' behavior, had the most results and the most significant results; that is, it was the "best" at distinguishing the three groups.

As in the previous analysis, we found many more significant results from the models that involved at least one person's behavior (the exception again being Model 7, husband behavior and wife physiology). Models 1, 2, and 3, taken together, indicated differences between happy stable, unhappy stable, and divorced couples when the wife's behavior affected any of the three of the core triad measures in the husband (behavior, perception, and physiology). However, the reverse was not quite true. Model 1, of course, did indicate that husband behavior affected wife behavior. There was also some indication of a link between husband behavior and wife perception in Model 4, based on the linear trend in the number of steady states where both spouses were positive in their respective domain, with the happy stable couples having the highest number of positive steady states. However, the results for Model 7 did not suggest much of a linkage between husband behavior and wife physiology.

Table 15.18: Three Criterion Groups and Parameters of
Core Triad Model 9: Both Partners' Physiology.

Variable	F-ratio	df	Happy, Stable	Unhappy, Stable	Div.
				Means	
Number of Influenced Steady States					
where $(W+)$ and $(H-)$	0.59	2,43	0.44	0.13	0.36
where $(W-)$ and $(H-)$	1.36	2,43	0.94	0.53	1.07
where $(W+)$ and $(H+)$	1.47	2,43	0.56	0.13	0.00
where $(W-)$ and $(H+)$	0.99	2,43	0.69	0.33	0.29
Wife					
Inertia	0.21	2,43	0.43	0.37	0.48
Initial state	1.09	2,43	−2.61	−3.00	0.48
Uninfluencedsteady state	0.68	2,43	−3.70	−5.56	−8.10
Influence on husband					
Positive half slope	1.40	2,42	0.49	0.88	0.88
Negative half slope	0.32	2,43	0.32	0.39	0.38
Trigger, husb damping	0.44	2,42	3.20	2.99	2.26
Strength, husb damping	0.75	2,42	−3.12	−5.33	−4.13
Trigger, husb repair	0.35	2,43	−10.47	−8.57	−7.89
Strength, husb repair	0.63	2,43	5.04	3.38	3.29
Husband					
Inertia	2.19	2,43	0.37	0.12	0.11
Initial state	3.05[a]	2,43	−0.76	−0.61	−2.25
Uninfluencedsteady state	2.89[a]	2,43	−0.54	−1.01	−2.78
Influence on wife					
Positive half slope	0.60	2,42	0.83	1.02	1.53
Negative half slope	0.61	2,43	0.88	0.89	0.67
Trigger, wife damping	0.12	2,42	2.95	2.84	3.20
Strength, wife damping	0.58	2,42	−5.24	−5.48	−7.82
Trigger, wife repair	0.05	2,43	−5.92	−5.19	−5.99
Strength, wife repair	0.82	2,43	11.78	6.23	5.18

[a] $p < .10$, * $p < .05$, ** $p < .01$, *** $p < .001$
$(W+)$ Wife Positive, $(W-)$ Wife Negative
$(H+)$ Husband Positive, $(H-)$ Husband Negative

The fact that Model 7 is again the exception is quite interesting. It may mean that one factor that predicts marital outcome is whether the wife drives the husband's physiology, but not the reverse. This finding is consistent with predictions and with earlier findings in Gottman and Levenson (1988) and in Gottman, Coan, Carrère, and Swanson (1998).

Models 7, 8, and 9, taken together, showed few significant results and therefore the lack of a strong tie between wife's physiology and any of the three core triad measures in the husband (behavior, perception, or his own physiology), at least in terms of distinguishing between the three criterion groups. That is, the husband was not influencing the wife's heart rate no matter how we measured his influence in any of the three domains. Conversely, and probably not surprisingly, her physiology did not have an influence on his behavior, perception, or physiology.

15.6 Chapter Summary

In this chapter, we created an extension of the marriage model to show how the same principles could be applied to modeling other types of data than those emerging from behavioral coding. Such an extension allows the researcher to use the modeling approach to uncover new relationships. In this example, we explored what processes govern the interplay of objective behavior, physiology, and self-perception of feelings. The chapter also served as an example of how a researcher might need to work creatively with his or her data to reduce it to a scale that is amenable to the modeling framework.

The analyses were consistent with Gottman's (1994) theory that in marriages there is a core triad of balance and that newlywed marriages in which negative behavior drives the couples toward both negative perceptions and greater physiological arousal (of husbands only) will end up either in divorce or as stable but unhappy.

16

The Marriage Experiments

The mathematical model of marriage was the basis of a research grant application that proposed a novel idea: a series of studies in which the goal was not to change the entire marriage, but only to obtain proximal change in the marriage, which meant that our goal was to improve only the second of two conversations a couple would have in our laboratory. Between the two conversations, there would be an intervention. We called these proximal change studies the *marriage experiments.*

Previously, there had been approximately twenty-five controlled studies of clinical intervention in marriages. In these studies, it was very difficult to tell what was creating the effect when there was an effect. Actually, the picture about effectiveness is somewhat grim. Most of the effect is owing to the massive deterioration of couples in the no-treatment control groups, which means that, in fact, there is only a small experimental effect. Jacobson, Follette and Revenstorf (1984) estimated that only 35% of the couples in their behavioral marital intervention studies, which are among the most effective studies, had marriages that improved from the distressed range in marital satisfaction scores to just the "okay" range (not happy, but just at the national average). Furthermore, there is a huge relapse effect, such that one year after treatment approximately 30% to 50% of the couples who had made gains returned to their previous levels of marital satisfaction.

Of all the studies conducted, only two had conditions that produced lasting results after one year. These were one condition of a study by Jacobson with only nine couples (Jacobson *et al.*, 1985), and one condition of a study by Snyder and Wills with approximately thirty couples (Snyder and Wills, 1989). What is very interesting is that Snyder and Jacobson engaged in a debate in print about precisely what the Snyder and Wills intervention actually was. Jacobson analyzed the treatment manual of Snyder and Wills and determined that it had thirty-one components, twenty-six of which he considered identical to his own intervention. Snyder disagreed. However, Snyder's own coding of the tape recordings of the therapy sessions revealed that the therapist in the critical condition was judged as following the manual only 49% of the time. Furthermore, the manual was very complex.

So here are two studies that have produced lasting effects, but no one can agree what exactly one of the studies actually did. The other study, the one by Jacobson, was equally complex for other reasons. The point is that the rare clinical trial that worked has not greatly advanced knowledge because these interventions were multicomponent and so complicated.

The purpose of our "marriage experiments" was to perform a simple intervention designed to change one aspect of how a couple communicated with each other, with the goal of improving the second of two conversations a couple would have in our laboratory. In three years of pilot testing, we discovered that we could limit many of these interventions to about one-half hour in length and still obtain quite dramatic changes in approximately 80% of all couples who were quite distressed. The other 20% simply refused to go along with our experiment, even to change their thinking, physiology, or behavior for fifteen minutes.

We were quite surprised to be able to facilitate such dramatic change in so short a time. We fully expected most couples to relapse after they left our lab. In fact, both conditions, the refusal to cooperate and the initial gains and relapse of a proportion of our couples, became laboratory paradigms for important phenomena in marital therapy: resistance to change and relapse.

We also found that most couples who changed even temporarily obtained a renewed sense of hope. They saw that change was possible. We also informed them that it was the maintenance of change that would be the major challenge confronting them once they left our lab. These experiments led to the designing of weekend workshops for couples, to the training of clinicians, and to the building of a marriage clinic in Seattle.

This chapter illustrates some of the interplay between the mathematical modeling work, on the one hand, and the clinical work and theory building that it produced on the other. We present some clinical case material that illustrates how we moved from the couple's conversation to the on-line SPAFF coding and from there to the mathematical modeling of their data and its interpretation. That is, the mathematical modeling was at the heart of moving into intervention and clinical work.

16.1   Evaluation of Couples Therapy

In this section, we briefly review the results of marital intervention studies. There have been very few controlled studies with random assignment to groups. The evidence from these studies is that marital therapies are able to create statistically significant short-term effects compared to no-treatment control groups. There have been a number of meta-analyses to date and even a summary review of these meta-analyses (Bray and Jouriles, 1995). Hahlweg and Markman's (1988) meta-analysis assessed the effect size of behavioral marital therapies as 0.95 (an improvement rate of 44% over no-treatment control groups). However, by adding unpublished dissertations, Shadish, Montgomery, Wilson, Bright, and Okwumabua (1993) obtained a smaller effect size of 0.74 for behavioral marital interventions (an improvement rate of 35%) and an even smaller effect size of 0.51 (an improvement rate of 23%) for non-behavioral marital therapies.

However, these treatment effects may not actually be as powerful as they seem. It is clear that nondirective, nonspecific, and nonorganized treatment with a passive therapist causes people to drop out of marital treatment at high rates. But almost all organized interventions, in the short run, tend to exceed a no-treatment control. Although the effect sizes in these meta-analyses appear to be encouraging, the *effects of intervention may be primarily owing to the deterioration of marriages in the no-treatment control groups.* Gottman's friend, the late Neil Jacobson, was the first and only investigator to challenge the meta-analyses papers. Jacobson and Addis (1993) wrote, "The success that investigators have had establishing these effects for their preferred treatments is not as impressive as first thought. The improvement rate in the absence of treatment is so low that even small changes in an experimental treatment are likely to be statistically significant" (p. 85). Jacobson reanalyzed data from four of his own behavioral marital studies and concluded that although 55% of the couples improved after treatment, only 35% were in the nondistressed range at the end of therapy. Furthermore, he noted a pervasive problem that existed for almost all marital therapies that had been systematically evaluated using a long-term follow up: a ubiquitous *relapse effect.* Although it is estimated that about 50% to 75% of couples make initial gains, a sizable percentage of these couples relapse in two years (Jacobson and Addis, 1993).

Despite this pervasive relapse problem, we may ask, "What are the active ingredients of the effects?" First, it is important to point out that Jacobson (1978) has shown that the effects in behavioral marital therapy (problem-solving skills and either contingency or good-faith contracting) are *not owing to nonspecific factors,* such as the therapeutic alliance, therapist-client rapport, and so on. But if the effects are not owing to nonspecific factors, what then are the active ingredients of those effects? This is not easy to determine from the literature because of a paradoxical result that exists in this literature: for most studies, the addition of components to the marital therapy appears to contribute nothing to the effects of intervention. The strange conclusion is that every component appears to be as effective as the whole. Why might this be the case? For one thing, enormous similarity exists across so-called schools of marital therapy. The active core ingredient in almost all schools of marital intervention is Active Listening during conflict resolution. In Active Listening, the listener is supposed to listen nondefensively, not argue for his or her point of view, paraphrase the speaker, consider what was said, and then genuinely and empathetically validate the speaker's feelings. A number of writers have suggested that there is little empirical basis for this intervention and that it may be very difficult to do it when the listener is being criticized by the speaker (Johnson and Greenberg, 1985).

The intellectual roots of this intervention are Roger's client-centered psychotherapy, as translated into the marital arena by B. Guerney (Guerney, 1977; Guerney and Guerney, 1985; Harrell and Guerney, 1976). Yet the translation of Rogerian principles to the marital arena is less than perfect. In Rogerian therapy, the client is usually complaining about a third party, and the therapist empathizes. When the client complains about the therapist, this is called *resistance.* Yet in the marital arena each spouse is usually complaining precisely about the partner, whose task of listening empathetically and nondefensively may require some emotional gymnastics. Gottman, Coan, Carrère, and Swanson (1998) found no evidence that, among newlyweds, sequences of marital interaction indexing Active Listening predicted positive outcomes over a six-year period. Furthermore, according to the only study to evaluate this approach using observational data (Schindler, Hahlweg, and Revenstorf, 1983), Guerney's method only decreased negativity; it did not increase positivity, and there were substantial decreases in initial gains upon follow-up.

In the behavioral marital intervention literature, there is one exception to the pattern that every component is as effective as the whole. This exception is a follow-up of a study by Jacobson (1984) and his students on the combination of *behavior exchange* and *communication skill training.* Jacobson, Schmaling, and Holtzworth-Munroe (1987) reported the two year follow-up results of behavioral marital therapy. There were three treatment groups: behavior exchange (BE), communication problem-solving (CPT), and the complete treatment (CO). After two years, the percentages of couples who separated or divorced were 55% in the BE treatment, 36% in the CPT treatment, but only 9% in the complete treatment. Despite the small number of couples with this outcome, the CO couples were reported as significantly less likely to have separated or divorced than either BE or CPT couples ($p < 0.05$). Hence, one intervention stands out from the rest in terms of its long-term outcomes.

A careful reading of how these components were *actually* applied in Jacobson's manuals suggests to us that the contracting component of the intervention was aimed at increasing everyday positive affect exchanges in the marriage, and the communication skill training component was aimed at increasing the couple's ability to reduce negative affect during conflict. In the Shadish *et al.* (1993, 1995) meta-analysis, the separate immediate effect sizes of these two interventions were 0.85 for CPT and 0.88 for BE, but it is the combination that produces more lasting change. To summarize, the Jacobson treatment combination represents the only behavioral study that has demonstrated lasting effects beyond two years of follow-up.

Our hypothesis, then, is that *lasting effects in behavioral marital therapy are most likely when interventions accomplish at least three things: (1) they increase everyday positive affect during nonconflict contexts, (2) they reduce negative affect during conflict resolution, and (3) they increase positive affect during conflict.*

Not all marital interventions accomplish these three therapeutic goals. Baucom and Lester (1986) reported that as a result of treatment the only change in marital interaction was the reduction of negativity, not the increase of positivity. Furthermore, in the only study that used observational data to evaluate Guerney's Active Listening approach, Schindler, Hahlweg, and Revenstorf (1983) reported that this method only decreased negativity during conflict. It did not increase positivity, and there were substantial decreases in initial gains upon follow-up. Interestingly, Snyder and Wills's (1989) insight-oriented treatment, but not their behavioral treatment, showed significant gains in positiveness during conflict. Similarly, using a combined behavioral approach to communication training and problem-solving training on observational measures, Hahlweg, Revenstorf, and Schindler (1984) found both increases in positivity and decreases in negativity during conflict, but they included no long-term follow-up. The Jacobson study (1984) did not include observational data.

Our hypothesis about what is necessary to create lasting change in marriages relates to a recent finding in our divorce prediction studies. Recently, in a 14-year prospective longitudinal study, Gottman and Levenson (2000) found two high-risk points for divorce in the life course of the marriage. The first occurred early, in the first 7 years of marriage (average of 5.2 years), and the second occurred later in the life course (average of 16.4 years). We found that a different model, one emphasizing negative interaction at Time-1 during conflict, predicted early divorce, whereas a model involving the absence of positive affect at Time-1 predicted later divorce. Negative affect at Time-1—in particular criticism, defensiveness, contempt, and stonewalling, a pattern Gottman (1994a) called the "Four Horsemen of the Apocalypse"— predicted earlier divorce, but the lack of positive affect at Time-1 predicted later divorce. Clearly these results suggest the hypothesis that both the failure of marriages and their therapy must, in some way, involve both processes. None of these studies assessed positive affect in nonconflict contexts. We think that there is sufficient data to warrant suggesting the hypothesis that a three-pronged intervention is necessary for producing lasting changes in marriages.

The two critical time points for intervention (first seven years and sixteen to twenty years after the wedding) are also consistent with other literature. For example, Cherlin (1981) noted that the first seven years of marriage contain half the divorces, and Jacobson and Addis (1993) wrote, "Because there is a predictable decline in couple satisfaction that occurs after the birth of children, this seems to be an ideal time to intervene" (p. 90). It is also well-known that the low point in marital satisfaction in the life course of the marriage occurs around the time when the first child becomes a teenager.

The marital intervention literature includes one other study that has produced lasting effects, and that is Snyder, Wills, and Grady-Fletcher's (1991) "insight-oriented" intervention. Snyder et al. compared a behavioral intervention to an insight-oriented object-relations intervention and found that although there were no differences between treatments either upon termination or in a six month follow-up, after four years the divorce rate was 38% in the behavioral condition but only 3% in the insight-oriented condition. However, the exact nature of the Snyder et al. intervention led to a debate between Jacobson and Snyder et al. Jacobson (1991) maintained that a careful examination of the insight-oriented manual of Snyder et al. revealed that it was nearly identical to Jacobson's combined condition, and the Snyder et al. so-called behavioral intervention was similar to behavioral marital therapy as it had been practiced around 1980. Jacobson (1991) claimed that the Snyder and Wills and the Jacobson interventions were equivalent in twenty-six out of thirty-one separate elements. Snyder and Wills's (1989) own coding of their therapy sessions showed that the behavioral treatment was consistent and specific to the behavioral treatment 82% of the time, but the equivalent percentage for the insight condition was only 49% so that the insight-oriented intervention may have been eclectic. The debate may continue for some time. In the Snyder-Jacobson debate about what the Snyder and Wills intervention actually was, we can see dramatically the importance of the distinction we made previously between clinical interventions and experiments. In the Snyder and Wills clinical intervention, the planned changes were so complex that even after a remarkably successful study, little was learned about what actually produced the observed changes. We have proposed that the essential feature important in both the Snyder and Wills and the Jacobson *et al.* interventions is that they offered a two-pronged approach of increasing positive affect in everyday interaction and of decreasing negative affect during conflict resolution, with appropriate insights.

The current knowledge about the lasting effects of interventions is based on small sample sizes. For example, the Jacobson *et al.* intervention had nine couples per group, and the Snyder and Wills intervention had twenty-nine couples in the behavioral treatment and thirty in the insight-oriented treatment.

16.2   Gottman's New Theory and Marital Intervention

Figure 16.1 is an illustrative summary of Gottman's new theory. This theory is consistent with the hypothesis that three aspects of the marriage need to change in order to create lasting change. The first aspect is the overall level of positivity in the marriage, and the other two aspects involve the way the couple regulates conflict (i.e., by increasing positivity and by decreasing negativity). The theory is described in greater detail in two books, *The Seven Principles for Making Marriage Work* by Gottman and Silver (1999), and *The Marriage Clinic* by Gottman (1999). We provide only a very brief outline here.

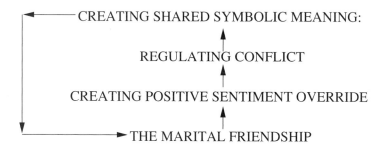

Figure 16.1: The Gottman theory of marriage—the "Sound Marital House."

Friendship is the Foundation: Three Components of Creating Positive Affect in Nonconflict Contexts

Rather than use contingency contracting to build positive affect, as Jacobson did quite effectively, the idea is that building a couple's friendship is probably the treatment of choice. Unfortunately, it is difficult to create positive affect or to re-create it in a distressed marriage that has lost it. The admonition to be positive or the setting up of behavioral exchanges is doomed. Vincent *et al.* (1979), after a neutral no-instruction condition, asked couples either to fake good or to fake bad. Although verbal behavior differentiated couples faking from the neutral condition, the positive or negative nonverbal behaviors of couples did not change. To change this dimension of positive affect, the therapy has to rebuild the friendship in the marriage. The technology involves creating positive affect and friendship in nonconflict contexts. This technology involves three steps, which we now briefly describe.

Love Maps, or Knowing One's Partner The first part of friendship is knowing one's partner, and this means being able to make a "Love Map." To introduce this concept in our workshops, we ask couples to play a game in which they cannot win points unless they know things about one another. In our research program, Love Maps are assessed from our Oral History Interview using the Oral History Coding System and are indexed by the amount of "cognitive room" each person has about the marriage, its history, and his or her spouse's psychological world.

The Fondness & Admiration System Gottman suggested this system as the antidote for contempt. In our research program, this system is also assessed from our Oral History Interview using the Oral History Coding System.

The Emotional Bank Account The third part of the marital friendship level of the Sound Marital House is the concept of "turning toward" versus "turning away" in everyday moments, or what might be called the "emotional bank account" that exists in every marriage. This aspect of a marriage is assessed in our research by coding "turning toward" versus "turning away" in our apartment laboratory, where the couple is spending time together in an unstructured manner. It involves reprogramming the way the couple moves through time together and makes connections during fairly mundane and mindless moments (Langer, 1992).

Creating Positive Sentiment Override

This level of the Sound Marital House theory is Weiss's (1980) idea of positive sentiment override. Positive and negative sentiment override

is assessed by combining the "outsider" behavioral observation data
stream with the "insider" rating dial data we obtain with our video
recall procedures. Negative sentiment override occurs when the spouse
views the partner's positive or neutral affect as negative. Positive sentiment override occurs when the spouse views the partner's negative
affect as positive. Negative sentiment override is like having "a chip on
one's shoulder"—that is, hypovigilance to being slighted and hurt. The
first level of the intervention builds the second level, which the theory
states is a consequence of the marital friendship going well. In a very
creative study, Notarius *et al.* (1989) provide evidence for negative sentiment override discriminating happily from unhappily married couples.
We have evidence for positive sentiment override in wives' perception
of their husbands' anger. Hawkins, Carrère, and Gottman (2002) found
that wives in happier marriages (as assessed by our Oral History Interview) viewed their husbands' anger as *neutral,* which was unlike unhappy
wives, who viewed their husbands' anger as negative. This result was
qualitative as well as quantitative.

Regulating Conflict

We have found that it is the regulation of most conflicts and not their
resolution that is predictive of longitudinal outcomes in marriages. In
our longitudinal research (Gottman and Levenson, 1999a, 1999b), we
found that there was enormous stability in marital interaction and that
couples studied four years apart had not resolved prior issues 69% of
the time. These issues were later called *perpetual* issues, and we suggest
that they stem from basic personality differences between spouses. The
other 31% of the time problems were apparently solvable: they appeared
at Time-1 but were resolved by Time-2. What mattered at Time-2
appeared to be not resolution of perpetual issues, but *the affect around
which the issues were not resolved.* These positive affect processes are
also operative in our long-term marriage study with couples in their
forties and sixties (Cherlin, 1981; Levenson, Carstensen, and Gottman,
1993, 1994), implying that it is the presence of positive affect within
the resolution of conflict, even perpetual conflicts, that matters. We
used the term *dialogue* to refer to the discussion of perpetual issues with
this positive affect present. When this positive affect was missing, we
saw either the Four Horsemen or emotional disengagement, a pattern
we called *gridlocked* marital conflict on perpetual issues.

How can one move a couple from gridlock to dialogue? Clinically it
entails exploring the *symbolic meaning* of each person's position in the
conflict, using our *dreams-within-conflict* intervention. First, we help
the couple identify the core perpetual gridlocked issues in the marriage.

Then we explore the symbolic meaning of each person's position on an issue by making the marriage feel safer; we call this *revealing the dreams within the conflict*. Physiological soothing is hypothesized as the major ingredient for making the marriage feel safer. Then we attempt to lead the couple toward "honoring" each person's dreams in this conflict. This latter process we think may change the influence functions of the couple, usually getting the husband to accept more influence from his wife.

- Type 1: For marital problems that are resolvable, we detail *the four parts of effective problem solving*. We have discovered, through detailed observational coding and sequential analysis in our newlywed study, that these components of effective conflict resolution (when the problem has a solution) are softened startup, accepting influence, repair and de-escalation, and compromise (Gottman, 1999). Use of positive affect in the service of de-escalation is a part of this process, too. Unfortunately, positive affect during conflict resolution is generally not programmable by intervention. Behavior exchange in the Jacobson intervention is one way of attempting to induce positive affect by changing the everyday interactions of the couple. Changing the nature of the couple's friendship is a conceptualization of this process. We have found, clinically, that positive affect during conflict resolution just happens by itself when positive sentiment override (Weiss, 1980) is in place. Our analyses have shown that the positive affect is in the service of de-escalation and physiological soothing.

- Type 2: Many conflicts occur because of basic personality and other differences (interests, preferences) between husband and wife that are perpetual in character. For perpetual marital problems (generally not resolvable), which in fact constitute most of the conflicts in marriages, it is necessary that the couple establishes what we call a dialogue with the perpetual problem to avoid marital gridlock.

- Physiological soothing (of both self and partner) is fundamental to both types of problems. The couple, and not the therapist, needs to be able to do this soothing to minimize relapse after treatment. In assessment, we look for two patterns: the presence of negativity (e.g., the Four Horsemen), but also the *absence of positive affect, even during conflict resolution*. Thus, many marriages that are at the stage of emotional detachment (farther down the distance and isolation cascade) will be identified in our assessment as problematic marriages.

Creating Shared Symbolic Meaning

Gottman has discovered clinically that it is the construction of shared
meanings that unlocks gridlocked marital conflict. This construction involves honoring and meshing each spouse's individual life dreams, narratives, myths, and metaphors. It is this meshing of the symbolic meanings
attached to aspects of marriage (goals, rituals, roles, symbols) and family that helps a couple to avoid marital gridlock. We have found that the
basis of a continued positive affective emotional connection involves the
perception of the marriage's effectiveness at making personal life dreams
and aspirations come true. Even if the two people come from the same
racial, ethnic, and geographic background, the two families they grew up
in will be very different, so their union will always involve the creation of
a new world of meaning. Here lie the narratives about what life means.

There are two salient interviews in assessing a couple. The first is
the Meta-emotion Interview. In this interview, we determine the history of each person's and the couple's feelings and philosophy about the
basic emotions: sadness, anger, fear, love, pride, embarrassment, guilt,
and shame. Levenson and Marchitelli (1995) discovered that emotion
metaphors during marital conflict were related to physiological arousal.
The second interview is the Meanings Interview. This is an interview
about rituals, roles, goals, and symbolic meanings. The levels of the
Sound Marital House are interconnected because the narratives, dreams,
metaphors, and myths about marriage actually cycle back to the foun-
dation, which is knowing one another (figure 16.1). We have discovered
that lack of affect and emotional disengagement in marriages result when
the marriage has not dealt adequately with the first *(and third)* levels
of the Sound Marital House, both of which make it possible for positive
affect to act in the service of de-escalation and physiological soothing so
that the marital conflict can proceed in a functional manner.

What Are the Potential Contributions of This Theory?

How does this theory alter current thinking about marital therapy?
First, it suggests that marital therapy should not be based only on how
couples resolve conflict. Instead, it presents a theory about intimacy in
marriage and its basis. It suggests that the effective resolution of conflict
itself is based on the first level of the Sound Marital House, which has
its roots in everyday marital interaction and thought, and has its effects
via positive sentiment override. Second, it suggests that when conflicts
have a solution, the conflict resolution skills that most therapies are tar-
geting (such as Active Listening) are the wrong skills, and it proposes
four alternative skills. Third, it suggests that most marital conflict is

about perpetual problems that never get resolved and that what matters most is the affect around which each problem doesn't get resolved. Either the couple establishes a dialogue with the perpetual problem and communicates acceptance to one another, or the conflict becomes gridlocked. When it becomes gridlocked, two patterns emerge, depending on the stage of the gridlock. One pattern involves the Four Horsemen, and it predicts early divorce (in the first seven years of marriage). The other pattern is emotional disengagement and affectlessness, and it predicts later divorce (around sixteen years into the marriage). Fourth, the theory proposes that the resolution of this gridlocked conflict is the same as its etiology; it involves the clash in people's life dreams and the clash in the symbolic meaning of people's stands on these issues. This part of the marriage—the metaphors, symbols, narratives, and dreams—is the engine that fuels both intimacy and estrangement. This aspect of people's lives is about *culture.* We do not deal with culture only when we think of how these processes vary with ethnic and racial groupings; rather, the theory says that we are always dealing with the culture that a couple creates when they create a marriage. This culture is their own unique blend of meanings, symbol systems, metaphors, narratives, philosophies, goals, roles, and rituals.

16.3   The Three Goals of an Empirically Based Marital Intervention and Rationale for the Marriage Experiments

Using the marital theory presented as figure 16.1, we can postulate what the goals might be of a minimal marital therapy program. As we do this, we discuss specific experimental interventions that may accomplish these goals. That is, to accomplish the speculation about the ingredients of a minimal marital intervention, we review literature in terms of which predictors may exist as parameters one wishes to change *that are derived from marital interaction.* Using the procedures of our laboratory (including video recall and rating dial procedures), these predictors can involve behavior, physiology, and self-report variables. The parameters selected will constitute *goals for changing marital interaction* in the series of proximal studies proposed, and they will eventually reappear as the parameters of our mathematical model.

The eight proximal experiments described in this chapter are guided by the theory described in figure 16.1. They are not an arbitrary set of experiments. Each experiment taps a different area related to divorce prediction. We discuss these eight experiments and the three goals in terms of the parameters of our mathematical model.

The First Goal: Reduce Emotional Inertia (Negative Affect Reciprocity)

The *inertia* parameter in the mathematical model represents each person's tendency to remain in a particular emotional state for some time. In the empirical literature, negative affect reciprocity, or the probability that one person's negative affect will be reciprocated by the partner and that the couple will remain in a negative affect state for some time, has emerged as *the* most consistent discriminator across laboratories (and cross-nationally) between happily and unhappily married couples. There is evidence that couples who are high in negative affect reciprocity are also high in positive affect reciprocity (e.g., Gottman, 1993), so that a concept such as "emotional inertia" instead of just "negative affect inertia" may be sensible. But why should the variable of negative affect reciprocity turn out to be the best and most consistent discriminator of happy from unhappy marriages? Gottman (1994a) speculated that negative affect reciprocity is theoretically very important because negativity becomes what has technically been named an *absorbing state* in the sequential analysis literature. An absorbing state is defined as one that is difficult to exit once it is entered. The cascade toward divorce involves being unhappily married for some time. The literature suggests that negative affect reciprocity is the most consistent correlate of marital satisfaction; we suggest that this finding argues for a "repair" intervention experiment. The existence of an absorbing state of negativity can have profound implications. One of these implications is that unhappiness in marriage results from the failure of repair processes. We next suggest three experiments whose goal is to reduce emotional inertia, and then we provide the rationale for these experiments.

Experiment 1: Improve the Success of Repair Attempts If one examines these repair attempts microanalytically, one finds that repair processes include feeling probes that explore feelings, information exchange, social comparison, humor, distraction, gossip, areas of common ground, and appeals to basic philosophy and expectations in the marriage. The repair attempts fail in unhappy marriages. Instead, what predominates in dissatisfied couples' use of these social processes is the negative affect. Why is negative affect reciprocity so destructive? What goes hand in glove is a constriction of other social processes with the greater reciprocity of negative affect in dissatisfied couples than in satisfied couples. Sequential analyses of the stream of behavior reveal that if one spouse expresses negative affect, the other spouse is more likely to respond with negative affect in a dissatisfied marriage than in a satisfied one. However, the constriction of available social processes is the fascinating structural dynamic that leads to the absorbing state. What happens if the repair attempt has two parts, one positive and one negative (which they often do)? For example, the message "Stop interrupting me!" is a metacommunicative attempt to repair the interaction, but it may have been said with some irritation (it usually is). In a happy marriage, there is a greater probability that the listener will focus on the repair component of the message, ignoring the negative affect, and respond by saying, "Sorry, what were you saying?" or even agree, but with some irritation, saying, "Go ahead and finish!" But the repair attempt eventually works and cuts the string of reciprocated negative affect. On the other hand, in an unhappy marriage, there is a greater probability that the listener will respond primarily to the irritation in the repair attempt, ignoring the repair attempt itself, and say something such as, "I wouldn't have to interrupt if I could get a word in edgewise," which may be responded to with, "Oh, now I talk too much, is that it?" which is responded to with, "You could say that you're a bit like your mother," and so on in a long chain of reciprocated negativity. In this case, the attempted repair mechanism does not work at all; it does not break the chain of negativity. Negativity being an absorbing state means that many social processes that are potential repair mechanisms have less of a chance of working because what people attend to and respond to is the negativity. The flip side of this coin is that many couples have a repertoire of repair tactics that can improve their marriages, but they do not have access to these repair mechanisms because negative affect has become an absorbing state. The obvious clinical prescription is to formalize the natural process of repair, which may drive a wedge into the sequential bond of negativity and thereby free up the repair mechanisms that the couple already has in the repertoire.

Other aspects of emotional inertia are defensiveness, the diffuse physiological arousal of distressed couples, and the concomitant "flooding" (see Gottman, 1994a, p.75) that goes along with diffuse physiological arousal. First, we consider defensiveness, one of the Four Horsemen of the Apocalypse.

Experiment 2: Reduce Defensiveness Defensiveness tends to fuel the cycle of reciprocated negative affect. We have found from video recall interviews that people behave defensively when they believe they are responding to an attack. It is clear that some ways of stating complaints are more likely to lead sequentially to a defensive response. These ways include adding blame to complaint (criticism) and expressing contempt. This "harsh start-up" is in part the residual effect of problems with the friendship in the marriage (Gottman and Levenson, 1999c). In many therapies, reducing defensiveness is addressed by attempting to alter the two-way communication—for example, by having each partner state complaints specifically, using nonblaming "XYZ statements," or "I statements" instead of "You statements," and so on, and by attempting to get the listener to respond to complaints less defensively, to "soften" anger with "more vulnerable affects," and so on. The key to ending defensiveness is taking responsibility for even a part of the problem. It is the denial of responsibility in the defensive response that fuels the conflict. In this experiment, we do two things. First we provide specific training in accepting influence, using three audio training tapes for men and three for women that present hypothetical problem situations with feedback on accepting influence and editing out negative affect in the presentation of an issue. Second, we teach couples how to process an argument in what Dan Wile (1988) calls a "recovery conversation" so that they will come to understand the specific things that created defensiveness and to find ways of avoiding these triggers and of accepting responsibility for a part of the problem after admitting their own defensiveness.

Experiment 3: Increasing Physiological Soothing We think that diffuse physiological arousal is part of why people reciprocate negative affect in long chains. This idea of physiological soothing in many cases could be considered the "nonspecifics" of most treatments because *the therapist* usually performs this task of soothing the couple with a variety of techniques, such as reframing or reinterpreting a comment, encouraging an empathic response, or soothing the receiver of a message that is perceived as an attack. We suggest that it may be far more effective in terms of minimizing relapse if *the couple* is taught the skills of soothing and if the couple, rather than the therapist, is required to do this job. It is clear that when the couple leaves the therapist's office and goes home, the therapist is no longer available to do the calming down. The couple's inability to self-soothe may be the primary active ingredient in causing relapse after treatment. Hence, we would suggest that a necessary ingredient of minimizing defensiveness is *soothing diffuse physiological arousal*. This component of marital intervention is also related to stress management.

The Second Goal: Make the Uninfluenced Steady States More Positive

To review, the uninfluenced steady state represents a parameter in our mathematical model that describes the initial marital affect before there has been much chance of social influence in a marital interaction and also those segments of marital interaction during which the partner can be presumed to be having zero influence (e.g., long periods of neutral affect). The uninfluenced steady state can be thought of as proportional to the resting affective state in the marriage to which each individual returns when uninfluenced by his or her spouse. It ought to be related to characteristic cognitions and affects the individuals have about the marriage when they are not together and when they just begin to interact. In almost any context in which distressed married couples have been observed, and in any type of interaction or conversation that has been sampled, the conclusion is always that distressed couples are either more negative or less positive affectively than nondistressed couples (Gottman, 1993; Margolin and Wampold, 1981; Wills, Weiss, and Patterson, 1974). This fact appears to be true no matter how brief the interaction, no matter what the couple is talking about, and even if the interaction does not involve the task of influencing one another (e.g., discussing events of the day, using the Rubin "fun deck," etc.).

Thus, variables such as positive minus negative affect appear to be remarkably stable across situations (Gottman, 1980). Therefore, we suggest that for each couple there exists a set point of positivity minus negativity of both husbands and wives, even when uninfluenced by the partner, which is more negative in distressed than it is in nondistressed couples. By *set point* we mean that like a person's weight, *this value will be regulated by the marital system*. The set point need not be functional, and, in fact, a ratio of 0.8 to 1 positive to negative interaction was characteristic of couples on the cascade toward divorce, whereas a ratio of 5 to 1 was characteristic of all three types of stable marriages. Despite its functional or dysfunctional nature, the marital system will defend this set point and resist changing so long as the conditions still exist that maintain it. Gottman, Swanson, and Murray (1999) found that these conditions are a combination of the couple's past interaction history and each person's enduring qualities. How accurate is divorce prediction using only a positive-minus-negative index? As we noted, Gottman and Levenson (1992) used one variable, the slope of a cumulated curve that plotted positive minus negative behaviors using our RCISS coding system, and the slope of these curves predicted marital stability or dissolution with 75% accuracy. If we add to this prediction by proposing that not all negative behaviors are equally corrosive (and use four behaviors that form a cascade: criticism, contempt, defensiveness, and stonewalling,) these variables improve the prediction to 85%. We now present the rationale for two experiments designed to change this parameter of the mathematical model.

Experiment 4: Softened Start-up We discovered that the way a conflict discussion starts determines much of what happens for the entire discussion. We can predict what will happen to a marriage in the future from the first three minutes of the interaction (Carrère and Gottman, 1999). Only 4% of all fifteen-minute interactions were significantly reversed once they started negatively. Although in our research primarily women played the predictive role of softened or hard start-up, we also found that men often play this role (particularly in volatile marriages). In our brief intervention, we employ an individual training program for teaching the principles of softened start-up to both spouses.

Experiment 5: Eliminating Contempt—Engaging the Affection and Admiration System This intervention emphasizes changing cognitions and attributions. The way people think about the relationship and their partner is predictive of stability or divorce (Gottman and Levenson, 1992; Booth and White, 1980). Holtzworth-Munroe and Jacobson (1985) used indirect probes to investigate when couples might "naturally" search for causes of events and what they conclude when they do search for causes. Holtzworth-Munroe and Jacobson found evidence for the hypothesis that distressed couples engage in more attributional activity than nondistressed couples and that attributional thoughts primarily surround negative impact events. Nondistressed couples engage in "relationship-enhancing" attributions, whereas distressed couples engage in "distress-maintaining" attributions. Distress-maintaining attributions maximize the impact of negativity and minimize the impact of positivity of the partner's behavior.

Moreover, Holtzworth-Munroe and Jacobson found that there is an important gender difference in attributional activity. Distressed husbands generate more attributions than nondistressed, but the two groups of wives do not differ. They suggested that although males normally may not engage in much attributional activity, they outstrip women once relationship conflict develops. Relationship-enhancing attributions are responses to positive partner behavior in both groups of couples. Relationship-enhancing attributions minimize the impact of negative behaviors and maximize the impact of positive behaviors of the partner.

In the proposed experiment, we would attempt to engage the cognitive system that involves relationship-enhancing cognitions. Admiration, which is the antidote for contempt, is a likely candidate for these relationship-enhancing cognitions. We currently employ a procedure in which couples are required to think about positive characteristics of their partner and share examples of events in which they displayed these positive traits. The hypothesis is that this experience can change the positivity with which couples start the second interaction. Similarly, we can use negative trait adjectives to engage distress-maintaining cognitions and thereby reduce the level of positivity with which couples begin the second interaction. Recall that the purpose of this latter intervention is to be able to show causally that we can push or pull this variable and affect the parameter of interest in the mathematical model—namely, to make the uninfluenced set points more positive or less positive.

The Third Goal: The Influenced Steady State Is More Positive Than the Uninfluenced

The *influenced* set point is the average value for those times for which a spouse has changed his or her behavior following a partner's behavior. The question here is, "What is the overall direction of this influence?" Does the partner's influence move the spouse in a more negative or a more positive direction? We can approach this issue by asking, "What gets couples into the cascade of the Four Horsemen?" in which complaining and criticizing leads to contempt, which leads to defensiveness, which leads to listener withdrawal from interaction (stonewalling). We suggest that it is actually quite easy to enter this sequence; in fact, we suggest that in everyday marital interaction it requires energy to avoid this sequence. Criticism is not very different from complaint; it simply is more global, with added blaming.

Experiment 6: Making an Emotional Connection—Responding to Anger We suggest that the most natural antecedent for criticism is *unrequited anger*. In our recent sequential analyses of older happy couples (who had been married an average of forty years) the only sequence that came out significant was the husband's positive response to the wife's anger (Coan, Gottman, Babcock and Jacobson, 1997). Hence, we suggest that a negative influenced set point is generally owing to the husband's failure to respond to his wife's anger, which leads to an escalation of the negativity, indicating that it is important to make an emotional connection at a lower level of negative affect intensity. The connection need not be an empathetic response or validation. We have found that actual validation of this sort is rare in response to anger. Hence, this experiment would use role playing and instruction to alter the conditional response of both partners to their spouse's anger (we include both spouses for tactical reasons even though the data support only the importance of the husband's responding positively to the wife's anger).

Experiment 7: Making an Emotional Connection—Responding to Positivity and to Bids for Connection Influence also occurs on the positive affect side of interaction. To explore what processes may be responsible for moving from a positive affect to one that is less positive we can ask the question, "What gets couples into the distance and isolation cascade that has loneliness as its endpoint?" We suggest that, once again, it is actually quite easy to enter this cascade and to become lonely in a marriage if people ignore what interests and excites their partner. In our apartment laboratory, we noticed that couples make what we now call "bids" for emotional connection. These bids can be as simple as bids for attention (e.g., "Isn't that a pretty boat?"), or they can be requests for emotional support (e.g., "I am worried about my sister"). Unhappily married couples make far fewer bids than happily married couples, and the probability of a partner turning away from a bid for connection is much higher among the unhappily married. In all marriages, the probability of rebidding once a partner turns away is nearly zero. Instead, the spurned partner seems to sink into a kind of loneliness. We have noticed in our events-of-the-day reunion conversations (couples meet in the lab at the end of the day after having been apart for eight hours) that loneliness appears in many cases to be the result of *interest or excitement*. This point can be illustrated very simply. One person comes into the bathroom in the morning and says to her spouse, "I just had a disturbing dream." The partner who responds with "What did you dream?" is making an emotional connection at a low level of positivity. It is remarkable that we see this kind of interchange often in our laboratory events-of-the-day discussion, in which one person in a distressed marriage will mention something exciting or interesting that happened that day, but there will be little or no response from the partner, which is deflating and leads the first person to withdraw emotionally or to become sad; the process is then usually repeated in identical form, with the partners switching roles. Hence, we suggest that a set point that moves negatively may also be owing to the partner's failure to respond to the spouse's interest or excitement, which suggests that it is important to make an emotional connection at a lower level of positive affect intensity. It need not be an empathetic response or validation. It can be genuine interest. The intervention is simply to make these moments mindful instead of mindless moments (in which people are on automatic pilot and not noticing their partners' bids for connection). The couple discusses areas on a checklist after each person picks three areas of their lives together in which he or she wants more emotional connection.

Experiment 8: Dreams-within-Conflict Intervention This intervention involves breaking up the logjam of two uncompromising, opposed positions by first uncovering what we call the "life dreams" that underlie each person's entrenchment in that uncompromising position. We suggest that in each of the two positions there are symbolic meanings: metaphors, stories, hopes, and dreams; these meanings are central to each person's sense of self. For example, a discussion about money is really about issues such as power, freedom, competence, security, and so on. Each of the positions involves images and associations that are latent and that first need to be uncovered and expressed in a safe marital climate. Even if the couple is not in a state of crisis, they may be in a state of intense pain because they are deadlocked on some central issues in their marriage. They have usually undergone a process involving entrenchment, vilification, and control struggles or emotional disengagement or both. After the dreams are uncovered and understood, the couple is led toward honoring each other's dreams. This second step of the intervention usually involves a change in influence patterns. That is, the intervention is designed to change the shape of the influence functions of the model.

Because of the large average delay of six years between the time a couple first detects that there is something seriously wrong with their marriage and the time they get any kind of help (Buongiorno, 1992), many marriages have compounded problems when they finally see a therapist. The usual problem of a couple experiencing gridlock on a problem is that, during a period of years, they undergo a process beginning with *dreams in opposition,* moving on to *entrenchment of positions, fears of accepting influence, vilification,* and finally *emotional disengagement.* Eventually, one of two states will be observed, the "hot" state in which all Four Horsemen of the Apocalypse are there, with possible imbalances in domineering behavior or belligerence, or the state of what could be called *affective death.* In this latter state, the couple seems very tired, energyless and emotionally uninvolved. There is very little humor and a pervasive, low-intensity sadness.

The *dreams-within-conflict* intervention involves exploring with each person, in the conjoint context, the symbolic meaning of that person's position and of that person's fears of accepting influence on an issue. Behind the position and the resistance to accepting influence, there are usually a set of metaphors, narratives, and mythological stories that go way back into the person's past and perhaps into the person's primary family.

16.4 The Dreams-Within-Conflict Intervention: An In-Depth Look

Here is the story of one of our interventions, the dreams-within-conflict intervention. In our longitudinal research, we discovered an interesting fact when over a four-year period we studied couples talking about their major area of continuing disagreement. First of all, approximately 69% of the time they seemed to be talking about the same problem in the same way. Most of the problems couples talked about as the major issues in their marriages were what we came to call *perpetual problems—* problems that kept recurring in the marriage. What turned out to be critical (in terms of the stability and happiness of the marriage) was not that couples resolved these problems, because they didn't resolve them. What was important was that they learned to live with them and not to hurt each other every time they discussed the issue. Couples whose marriages were on a healthy trajectory established what we called a *dialogue* with these perpetual problems. What was important was the affect (emotions) with which they didn't resolve their perpetual problems.

Couples who kept hurting each other every time they discussed their perpetual problems were what we started calling *gridlocked* on the problem. They were characterized at first by a great deal of criticism, defensiveness, and contempt, but after some time with a gridlocked problem these couples underwent a transformation. They began trying to expect less from one another, trying to "enclave" these problems so they didn't spill over to the rest of the marriage, and they started withdrawing emotionally from one another, establishing parallel lives that met less and less of the time (they would eat together less often, work more, and so on). Eventually they became lonely. Often they were not even aware of this transformation, thinking that they were not entitled to complain, that their own expectations for the marriage were unreasonable and that they should settle for less and become more realistic. Actually they were on the way out the door. They had entered what we call the *distance and isolation cascade* (Gottman, 1994a).

These findings suggest that people and therapists need to change their expectations about solving the fundamental problems in the relationship. In our marital workshops, we encourage couples to think of most of their relationship problems as inevitable, much the way people learn to deal with chronic physical ailments with increasing age. The chronic back pain, the trick knee or tennis elbow, or the irritable bowel do not go away, but people learn to have a dialogue with these problems.

People keep trying to make things a little better all the time, but they learn to live with these problems and manage their world so as to minimize them. So it is in marital relationships. This approach is very much like something Dan Wile (1988) wrote in *After the Honeymoon*: "choosing a partner is choosing a set of problems" (p. 12). He said that problems will be a part of any relationship and that a particular person will have some set of problems no matter whom that person married. Paul married Alice, who gets loud at parties, and Paul, who is shy, hates that. But if Paul had married Susan, he and Susan would have gotten into a fight before they even got to the party because Paul is always late, and Susan hates to be kept waiting. She would feel taken for granted, about which she is very sensitive. Paul would see her complaining about this problem as her attempt to dominate him, about which he is very sensitive. If Paul had married Gail, they wouldn't even have gone to the party because they would still be upset about an argument they had the day before about Paul's not helping with the housework. Gail claims that when Paul does not help her, she feels abandoned, about which she is sensitive, and to Paul, Gail's complaining is an attempt at domination, about which he is sensitive. The same is true about Alice. If she had married Steve, she would have the opposite problem because Steve gets drunk at parties, and she would get so angry at his drinking that they would get into a fight about it. If she had married Lou, she and Lou would have enjoyed the party, but then when they got home, the trouble would begin when Lou wanted sex because he always wants sex when he wants to feel closer, but sex is something Alice wants only when she already feels close. Wile (1988) wrote,

> "there is value, when choosing a long-term partner, in re-
> alizing that you will inevitably be choosing a particular set
> of unsolvable problems that you'll be grappling with for the
> next ten, twenty, or fifty years." (p. 13)

The goal of that part of our intervention that deals with problem solving is not to try to get couples to resolve their problems, but to turn the gridlocked perpetual problems into perpetual problems with which the couple has a dialogue. Only less than a third of their problems will have real solutions, and we teach the elements of effective problem solving based on what we have learned about effective problem solving on those issues that have a solution.

This idea is not so far-fetched. After all, does any one of us have a relationship—with siblings or friends—that is perfect? It is unlikely that we do. In fact, after having a friend over for an evening, we are unlikely to say, "I was expecting far more intimacy and community tonight. This friendship is over!" Instead we have learned to accept our friends as they are, grateful for what they do offer us, and accepting of their limitations. The only perfect relationship would probably result from our cloning ourselves as a member of the opposite sex, and we probably wouldn't even be attracted to that person!

There is a Woody Allen film in which he is searching for the perfect woman. He finds the perfect woman's body, but her brain is very limited; then he finds the perfect woman's brain, but the body is unattractive to him, so he gets a famous neurosurgeon to perform a delicate operation in which the brains are switched. He now has one woman with the perfect body and the perfect brain, and a second woman with an imperfect body and an imperfect brain. Then he proceeds to fall in love with the second woman!

But what is the nature of marital gridlock, and how can a couple be moved from gridlock to dialogue? The answer is in the dreams-within-conflict intervention. What we discovered about gridlocked marital conflict is that it is invariably conflict about the symbolic meaning of the issue and not about the issue itself. People, for example, cannot help but be gridlocked in talking about a financial issue if instead of really discussing money they are actually discussing power or freedom or competence or a man's role or security or any one of the thousands of things that money can stand for in a person's psyche.

We found that behind each person's position on a gridlocked conflict there was a hidden life dream. These dreams had great difficulty emerging in the unsafe climate of people vilifying one another and eventually becoming emotionally distant from one another. The goal of our intervention became to liberate the dreams and then to get people to set up the conditions under which they could honor one another's dreams. We illustrate this process with one dramatic case, the case of Dave and Angie.

16.5   Angie and Dave: Overview

The State of the Marriage

Dave scored in the average range in marital satisfaction and scored a zero on the Weiss-Cerreto divorce-proneness scale (the cutoff for predicting divorce is a score of 4), indicating that he seemed to be reasonably happily married. In contrast, Angie scored as unhappily married (85 on the Locke-Wallace marital satisfaction scale) and very high on the divorce-proneness scale (she scored 8), suggesting that not only was she unhappily married, but she had persistent thoughts about separation and divorce, and was quite likely to leave the marriage, because persistent thoughts about divorce are predictive of divorce. As we were to later discover, she had not shared any of these thoughts with Dave.

Oral History Interview

In the Oral History Interview, we ask couples about their perceptions of the marriage and its history. Our scoring of this interview has been consistently predictive of divorce or marital stability (Buehlman, Gottman, and Katz, 1992).

Challenges to the Marriage That Emerged from the Oral History Interview Based on our scoring of this interview and on our previous data, this couple was very low in *we-ness*, which is the amount of references to themselves as a team (using *us* or *we* often). The amount of disappointment the wife expressed toward the marriage was elevated, but for the the husband it was not. Both husband and wife scored high on the *chaos* scale, which means that they saw their lives as including many negative and stressful things beyond their control, things to which they would then have to adapt. For example, the husband's friend Johnny lived with them but turned out to be a very bad apple. Johnny later tried to sexually molest one of Angie's friends, who ran away from Johnny but later returned to confront him and force him to tell Dave and Angie what he had tried to do. At that point, Dave threw Johnny out of the house and called the naval base to report Johnny, but Angie was already very disappointed in Dave. She had been afraid of Johnny and had locked her bedroom door whenever she was alone with him in the house. She had kept telling Dave to ask him to leave, but Dave hadn't until the incident with Angie's friend. Johnny had apparently been stealing Angie's clothing; she had told Dave all of this, but he had done nothing, and Angie felt that he was not much of a protector.

They both scored high on *volatility,* which means that their arguments became very emotional. The emotion came from Angie, with Dave being the calm, rational, and unemotional one. She said that she was the only one who talked about feelings, whereas Dave kept his feelings to himself. This was an issue for her. She expressed feeling lonely because of this imbalance and as if she were the weird one. She thought that Dave stayed hidden.

One issue that emerged from the Oral History Interview was that Angie viewed herself as a "free spirit" before she married. She said that she would easily leave relationships whenever they became difficult for her. Later (after the first discussion) she would say that she had escaped from an impoverished environment, and she now had worked herself into a prestigious job that paid very well. She felt quite trapped by Dave's financial planning and dominated by his planning and controlling the finances. She was earning most of the money, yet he controlled how she could spend this money.

Strengths Determined by the Oral History Interview Both Angie and Dave were high in fondness and admiration for one another, and high on the amount of "cognitive room" for the relationship. They used a nice brand of teasing humor to defuse conflict. For example, they often stuck their tongues out at each other and laughed.

First Conversation

The major issue Angie and Dave discussed was money. They had differences on how it should be spent. Although Dave seemed financially conservative, he was actually in favor of spending on large-ticket items. They had a house, two new cars, and a boat, and he now wanted to buy a trailer home (a "fifth wheel") and to sell their current home and move into this trailer. This was his desire even though they had very little equity (about $7,000) in their home.

He began the conversation saying, "Want to discuss the future?" but she answered that she needed to discuss the past. She began talking about how let down she felt when his friend Johnny was living in their house but defaulting on his payment of the rent. She thought it was Dave's responsibility to collect money from Johnny, but that Dave had defaulted on this responsibility, and she said that she was still very angry with Dave.

The husband was quite defensive about this issue. At that point, Angie mentioned a friend of hers who had owed her money before she and Dave had married. Dave jumped on this opportunity to free himself of blame for not collecting money from Johnny. He said it was the same thing. Then he said that he did want Johnny to pay his bill.

She then took responsibility for spending too much. He agreed. He criticized her for expenditures on getting a professional resume done. She defended herself by saying that she needed to get a professional resume done. She then apparently felt that she had come on too strong and became self-deprecating, saying that she knew that she spent too much money. She said that she needed to quit carrying the checkbook.

They got together and trashed their "junk" TV viewing as getting in the way of their communication. He then said that he was worried that she was going to resent his spending time studying for his college classes when he got out of the navy. Actually, she also wanted to go to college and was clearly a very intelligent person who could complete college if she wanted to. She had some resentment that his education would come before hers, although she did subscribe to the view that the man needs to be head of the household. She was clearly torn about her role as a wife.

They discussed where he should study at home so that it would be least disruptive to her. Because she worked nights, she would get lonely not seeing him very much during the day, so his studying when they actually had time to be together would be a problem for her, she admitted.

He discussed wanting to sell the house, but she said that she did not want to sell it. Then it emerged that he wanted to buy a trailer for them to live in. She said that the "house was violated after Johnny left." This charge was not very well explained, but it was very clear that, despite her feeling that the house had been defiled, she did not want to live in a trailer. She said she did not see the house selling. He asked, "Where do you want to go if it does sell?" She evaded the issue and changed the topic to what they would do when he got out of the navy. They planned going to live in Oregon, which would mean a job transfer for her. She had a very demanding and high-powered job controlling traffic for the city's Metro system, similar to being an air traffic controller.

He discussed living in Portland. He wanted to keep the boat they owned. They went back to talking about the house. "I know you hate this," he said, "but we can go for a fifth wheel (trailer)." Her fear was that once they got into that lifestyle, they would never get out. He tried to reassure her, but he was unsuccessful. Then he said that they had no choice because of their two dogs and a cat (they couldn't move onto the base because of the animals). She very quickly added, "Get rid of the animals." He said, "No, they're our babies," and smiled. She did not smile back. She clearly would rather get rid of the dogs than move to a trailer. Both these issues were worth exploring.

This first conversation was generally very constrained and unemotional, but also quite tense. There was a sense that she was holding back from saying what she really thought and was therefore emotionally distant from him. She seemed to start to confront him but then quickly backed away from the issue. He was defensive and domineering and not very emotionally responsive when she confronted him. For example, she did say that she had lost respect for Dave around the "Johnny issue" and that she then stopped talking to him. Then she said something like, "I do understand this, and it really is over; we won't let our friends take advantage of us," so she acted as if the issue were over, when in her own mind it clearly wasn't resolved. When he returned to talking about the "fifth wheel," she was very opposed to this plan, but he kept trying to convince her. Although she tried gently to tell him no, he took her gentleness as weakness.

She said that he said that he didn't like to bring work concerns home, so she felt like an idiot for talking about her concerns. No, he said, he needed to become more emotional.

Gottman's Summary Questions

Clearly some powerful issues were dividing this couple. Gottman listed some issues to discuss with them:

- Angie seemed to be trapped by her ideas about what being a "good wife" means. It contrasted with the image of her unmarried self as a "free spirit" who was actually a very proud and strong woman. Gottman wondered if she thought that as a wife she should be subordinate, but then when she tried to do so, she wound up resenting her husband's domineering style. This conflict and its meaning in her mind were worth exploring.

- His lack of sharing his feelings and thoughts with her was a source of great emotional distance. What was this lack about? What was its history in his life and in their relationship?

- There was a need to understand more about the "Johnny issue" and what it meant to her that Dave failed her as a protector.

- There was a need to know more about the trailer issue, their plans of having babies while he was working and going to college but she was not doing either. These plans seemed antithetical to her personality as she had discussed her life.

These issues were all areas of "symbolic" meaning to explore in the dreams-within-conflict interview. Dave and Angie were then to talk to one another about these areas.

16.6 Angie and Dave: The Dreams-within-Conflict Intervention

Gottman told Angie and Dave that there were many conflicts in marriages that become "gridlocked," that are full of symbolic meaning, but that are never resolved until the symbolic meaning of each person's position becomes known. He reviewed the four issues that had been raised by the first conversation, but which they never acknowledged to one another. He told them about the questions he hadregarding what he couldn't understand in their conversations. They discussed these things briefly. They understood the idea. Gottman then told them that it would take courage to face these issues and to talk to one another about the meaning of each position, and he asked them if they thought they could do that. They said that they could and would.

What follows is a verbatim transcript of John Gottman's intervention with this couple. It illustrates the dreams-within-conflict intervention. Gottman is denoted as person (J) in the transcript; Dave and Angie are denoted as (D) and (A).

J: This Johnny episode was really a source of great pain.

D and **A**: (nodding) Yeah.

J: What was behind that "his defiling the place" part?

A: This is not being taped is it?

J: No, it's not being taped. (Gottman thought that the cameras were off, but that was not the case.)

D: Started out that he's an alcoholic and all this kind of stuff, and slowly he just quit paying the rent, and he and I are good friends, so I talked him into bringing himself into AA and try to take care of his alcoholism.

(knock on the door)

(Lab staff: "This *is* being taped.")

J: Oh, okay, this is being taped, so could you turn it off for a while? Thanks. (pause while recorder is turned off, then couple gives permission to tape again)

D: That caused a lot of problems, too, and that's some of what we have been talking about, too, and we have come to realize that our friends are just using us, and so we have withdrawn from friends, and we started communicating again, and we started trying to open all the avenues.

J: Well, one of the real strengths I see in your relationship, aside from the humor, is the fact that you (Dave) are really nondefensive. In the discussion, I saw before when you Angie were telling him how you felt, you didn't defend yourself, you just listened and acknowledged, and I think that's a real strength, particularly in a guy.

D: Yeah, that's something she's not used to.

A: Meow.

D: Because for a long time she would tell me she wouldn't tell me something because she thought I'd get mad. Well, I see myself that I can't get mad, but I also see myself that I will lose my temper once in a while, then I think she thinks . . .

A: Your dog side.

D: Yeah, when I'm a dog and barking all the time, but I mean I can understand why she felt some fear for me and why she didn't want to tell me stuff, but it's a different relationship between me and her, and I try to be more receptive.

J: But she may not be sure when loyalties are mixed what side you come down on.

D: That's something we hadn't actually defined, who we were loyal to.

J: That's probably still a question mark.

D: Yeah.

A: Not any more actually. I have to give my friend a lot of credit because when it happened, my friend she left the house; she didn't wake us up. I have to give her a lot of credit. She came back into our home and confronted him.

D: In the morning.

A: That next morning and made him tell us himself what had happened. Because if she hadn't, if Dave hadn't heard it ... I'm sorry, honey, but I think if you hadn't heard it from his own mouth, I don't think you would have believed her.

D: I don't think either one of us would have.

A: I don't think I would have not believed her, but I would have felt that there was more to the story. That she had done something to encourage this, but after he told us in his own words,

D: It had nothing to do with her; it was him.

A: And his next thing was "I'm leaving tomorrow," and I'm like "No you're leaving now. You're leaving now, you're out of the house. That's it." I was kind of waiting for Dave, I almost thought Dave was going to say, "Let him stay one more night," but

J: He backed you up.

A: Yeah, and at that point I left the house because I was really, really angry. I told Dave I would not come back to the house until he was gone, I was just not coming back to the house.

J: I see. How did you react to that?

D: I could understand where she was coming from, so I called the Command, and I called one of his friends, and I told him better come and pick him up, and I told him this is it, and we have not talked since that day; we have talked in court about each other but not to each other.

J: So that was an important moment for you. And for you too it was an important moment.

A: Yeah.

D: That was the end of the relationship, and before I even tried to call back, I had changed the locks in the house. I drew a close to that friendship once I realized him for what he was, once I realized that, then I could start working back on our relationship, trying to, but there was a lot of hurt, so it took us a while to get through it.

A: It wasn't a falling out for us, it wasn't.

D: Yeah, we are better people for it.

J: There's an issue that I see between you about this, and that's that I see you really approaching, for a short time approaching an issue that you're really worried about, with a lot of confidence and strength and then backing down.

A: Hmmm.

J: Really the finances is the big example of that, and how you really feel about it. All your feelings about all of these plans. Buying the RV, selling the house, not selling the house. And you approach them, and it seems like something goes on inside your mind, I don't really know what it is, that makes you say, well, back down from this, it's going to be all right, have more confidence. But I also hear in your words statements of doubt about whether you think this marriage is going to work, and then you convince yourself that it's okay. So I wonder if you're really scared about really approaching things and really talking to Dave about how you really feel.

A: Yeah, I feel that we've made some poor decisions together. Some things that we have done I haven't been vocal enough.

J: Yeah.

A: I felt I let Dave make some decisions that weren't right. And I still have some trepidation about those decisions, and sometimes I feel like I'm a little bit wiser than Dave on some things than he gives me credit for, and I'm afraid to say, "You may think I am materialistic or I'm money oriented, but I really feel that I know what I am talking about." But I don't want to upset him, and I don't want to undermine him because in a relationship, at least the way I was raised, the man is the head of the household. And it's my job as his wife to counsel him and to assist him, but it's not my job to lay down the law because the decisions have to be made jointly, but I have felt because I have not said "No, this isn't what I want,"

J: Right.

A: That I have ended up other than where I wanted.

J: So there's a tendency I see in you in which you kind of go inside yourself and kind of get distant and withdraw.

A: Yeah.

J: Which is pretty harmful to the relationship, isn't it?

A: Very.

J: Yeah.

A: But I feel like he'll get angry if I tell him, "No, that's just a stupid idea."

J: Maybe you want to check that out with him. See if that's true. Is that the way you really do feel?

D: I try to be open to what she says, and I try to process it. We were talking about renting the house instead of selling it; it's something to look into, but I have reservations about that.

J: But you know, I think on your part, Dave, what's difficult for Angie about you is that you stay so hidden and so rational. Then she is always the one with the feelings up front, and so you're being rational in this situation and being a good listener, sounds like it's a great thing to do, but she doesn't get to see you respond under fire, doesn't get to see you emerge. Is that an issue for you?

A: He's very, you're very one level. Even when you're mad, you're one level.

J: How does that affect you?

A: It feels fake. To me it feels fake. You're always trying to be so right about everything, and I really, really believe the RV thing is a bad idea. Because I really think we are going backwards, we are not going forwards.

J: Can I help here? Because I really think a lot of times conflicts are just conflicts, you know, they're about should we buy that box of tissues or not, a bigger box or a smaller box. But sometimes, and the hardest conflicts in a marriage, decisions have a symbolic, they have a meaning to them. It's not just the RV, but it symbolizes a whole thing for you in your mind. What moving into an RV means.

A: Mmm hmm.

J: And I think it's pretty loaded for you, isn't it?

A: Mmm hmmm.

J: And so in a way it's hard to make progress unless you talk about what it means. Not just about the decision, whether it's a good idea, a bad idea, how much money it should cost or not cost, where it should be and how long it should be and where it should be. But what does it symbolically mean to you, in terms of your life and what you've been through. And where you are now in your life especially, in terms of your earning power and the prestige of your job. So I think part of what would be helpful in the next conversation is for you to share that. And not back away because you really want to hear it.

A: See, I get the feeling that he doesn't want to hear it.

D: I do. But I also wanted you to listen because you haven't listened to what I wanted in it.

A: I listened to what you wanted in it, by paying off the bills and reducing the debt and being able to provide.

D: But I still ...

J: Let me try to be helpful on your end, too, Dave. The financial plan that you have and the way that you're thinking about your future together as a family, as a couple, your future as an individual is really trying to be successful and really have your life moving somewhere. That has a lot of symbolic meaning to you also. It's not just bucks. It's about who you are inside. And part of your challenge is to really be able to share that with her, what this all means, and how you see yourself as a person, as a husband, as a potential father. So part of your challenge is not to be hidden. And being very rational about it and talking about bottom line and ledgers and stuff like that, what's the wisest choice, is a way of staying hidden. What's the symbolic value for you? When I see symbolic value, I mean, you know when we come into a marriage we all have a set of stories and myths, and you know there's photo albums and stories that go with our families and beliefs that we have that come from our religious beliefs and our closeness to our families. And all those are connected to who you are now and where you want to go. And where you want to go, Angie. And there's also this part of you, Angie, that you're not letting out, this part of you that's a free spirit, independent and strong.

A: I feel like he doesn't want that.

J: Is that true?

D: Sometimes I want it, sometimes I don't.

J: See I think you can make tremendous progress by revealing all those sides of yourselves to each other when you talk about these financial issues. In other words, I think there's untapped strength in your friendship for one another. It involves you really revealing who you are. How do you reveal who you are? You have to talk about not whether to buy that box of Kleenex or a bigger box, but who you are as people. What some of these thoughts mean to you. Part of it is also having mixed feelings and being uncertain, part of it is really saying, "I don't really know what's right here. And this is what I'm scared about, this is what I'm worried about." And part of what we're seeing as you're talking to each other, in addition to the friendship, is a sadness; there's a sadness, and the sadness is coming from holding back. Because you're both holding back parts of who you are. Because you, Dave, need to be really strong and rational because you can't have two people falling apart and being real emotional. I don't think it's true. I think you're really an emotional person, and you can show these things to her. And it will build strength rather than detract. Because the way you're doing now you are holding back what these things mean to you; you're holding back parts of yourself, and it's hurting your friendship, I think.

D and **A**: (Nodding and smiling at one another)

J: Do you understand what I'm saying?

D and **A**: Umm hmm.

J: Okay, do you think you can try talking to each other with this in mind? The first thing you got to do is get rid of talking about what the right decision is to make. About the dogs, about the RV, about the boat, about all this stuff. Instead talk about how you feel about all this, and how you feel about the journey you're on together. All the feelings you have, the hopes and aspirations, the dreams, and the parts of yourself that you're hiding. And, in a way, that's a bad thing for you to do, Angie, because it winds up making you feel lonely. Am I right?

A: (nods)

J: Okay, we're going to get started now.

16.7 Angie and Dave: Second Conversation

Overview

Angie and Dave talked for thirty minutes instead of the usual fifteen, because so much emerged in this second conversation. She now explained that she did have this idea of an "ideal wife role," which meant that she would not be a strong force, but would "give him good counsel," as if he were a chief and would consider her counsel. But he let her down in the incident with Johnny. He didn't take her wise counsel; he ignored it. In fact, she later said that slow response was a big disappointment to her because even her niece was in the same room that Johnny had entered once during the night, so her own home was not safe, and the lack of safety was owing to Dave's lack of strength.

The issue of her concerns being minimized and her being ignored by him was not just limited to the Johnny incident. It was a general issue for her. She then confronted him about feeling put down and not respected by him and controlled by him, discussing the issue of his making sure she got rid of her old car, "the Mustang," and telling him what that car meant to her. She told him that she loved that car, that it represented her power and freedom, her ability to have worked herself out of having been "dirt poor" to a good $40,000 a year job. She said that she should never have let him take that car from her and that she resented him deeply for having done this. Dave then said that it was clearly a mistake on his part and that he did it because he was afraid of losing her. In the beginning of their marriage, he said, she kept saying that she would usually not stick with relationships once they became difficult, so he thought she would dump him if she had the Mustang.

She then confronted him about the trailer. She said she didn't want to go back to poverty, and that's what living in a trailer would mean to her. She did not want to go to the bathroom with a flashlight. Then she added that she didn't want "twelve babies on her hip either." She was referring to their plans of his going to college and having the career while she gave up her job and had babies. This plan was clearly not in her vision of her future, and she let him know so for the first time. She said she thought he didn't want her to be strong or have smart opinions and that he wanted to keep her down. He listened calmly to all of this and denied that he felt these ways.

She then told him that she couldn't trust him because he was so "clinical" and unemotional. After that he told her that he didn't want to lose her and that he wanted her help in becoming more emotional. He talked about why he thought he was so unemotional. It had to do, he said, with his violent and abusive father, and he feared that if he became emotionally expressive, he too would become violent and abusive with her.

She talked about wanting to help him, but Gottman had a sense that Dave's self-disclosure might be too little, too late.

Nonetheless, after this second conversation, Angie and Dave reaffirmed their love for each other, and she said that divorce was "just not an option" in this marriage. They had made an appointment to see a counselor (a clergyman) in a few days, and they were hopeful.

This second conversation was clearly much more affective. She cried, got angry, laughed, and Dave disclosed his fears of losing her.

Transcript of the Second Conversation

D: Okay.

A: I don't mean to hold stuff back from you. Self-preservation I guess. I lived in the projects. Don't want to go back to that. I was dirt poor. I don't want to go back to that. I don't want to have to go to the bathroom with shoes and a flashlight.

D: (laughs)

A: Did that. Now I don't want to be tied to your hip with twelve babies either. That Mustang, admitting you wanted that out because you wanted my independence. I didn't feel that we made the right decision by getting rid of the Mustang and getting the Pathfinder, and getting these two cars. Yeah, I am comfortable with my car now. But now I am hesitating to make those decisions to trade the house in for an RV; it's just ...

D: Another can of worms?

A: Yeah, I think it's like it's not just the RV stuff, but it's kind of our security right now. We'll have a roof over our heads. We have really different philosophies about money. My feeling is I'll just always make more. Like the other night you were talking about you'd be screwed if I left because you'd lose everything, and to me I thought you were more concerned about those things, the car, the house, the boat; I felt like you were more concerned about those things than I was. Okay, so what if I got bad credit, big deal. You know. I can still get things with bad credit, I can accumulate more. Things come and go. And every time we talk about money, it's like I'm going to lose that, I'm going to lose this; that's always your first priority, not that you're going to lose me. I just feel that I'm an added commodity.

D: You're my priority. And sometimes I talk about I'm going to lose other things; it's my way of saying or of dealing with my biggest hurt, which would be losing you. Sometimes it's easier for me to say that I would lose other things than to say that I would lose you.

A: I'd rather hear that than you're not going to have your boat type of thing. I know I joke around type of thing, and I say, "Oh, I make the payments," and I know that hurts your feelings and makes you feel bad. I just don't feel acknowledged for the contributions that I make. And I know you're always worrying about bills. And you're always worrying about bills, and I feel like I can never earn enough money to please you.

D: It's not what you earn. It's just that I want so bad to be able to take you on vacations. Treat you the way you've wanted to be treated, and you know . . .

A: Well, I don't.

D: Right now I can't do that, and right now my biggest heartache is I can't take you away; I can't take you on vacations because it will just add more bills to it.

A: I'm not even talking about that though.

D: I'm thinking about that because that's all you expressed for a long time is you wanted to go on vacation, you wanted to . . .

A: I was joking. I want to go somewhere warm. I get tired of the rain. (puts clipboard up to her face)

D: There's more to it, and I can see that in you. You want so bad to go on vacations and stuff; you want to go on the real honeymoon.

A: That's because I'm stressed out at work.

D: Yeah, well, you keep showing these things; it's just that I can't supply a lot of this stuff. (sighs) That's where I start worrying about what can I do, if I am able to do this or this, kind of the way you worry about how can you buy me something I want; well, that's what I'm trying to do, but I talk about trying to pay off bills and being stingy with money, and I end up having an adverse reaction rather than the reaction I need or want.

A: (pause) What should we do? (contemptuous facial expression)

D: We got to keep the communication lines open, we got to try to figure out how we can work on it. Some bills we got we can't pay off.

A: The bills aren't the issue. (contempt)

D: Usually it's how I can try to please you and how you . . .

A: No, I can please myself. I get happiness from my job, I get happiness from work, I get happiness from you, but I feel stifled; I feel like my creativity is stifled sometimes. Like when I talk to strangers, I always feel like you're looking down on me. Sometimes I feel like you're trying to mold me into something you want me to be that I can't be. People who have known me for years don't think I'm the person that I was. Or who I am. Like Evessa and Sandy, they're like, Sandy has known me since second grade. And she's asked me, "Are you happy? Because you're not the same person. You're much quieter, you're not so happy go lucky." It's like (contempt) I always feel like you're disapproving of me. I just want to be accepted for who I am.

D: Can you tell me when that happens so I can ...

A: Like when you told me not to bite my nails. It's like, okay, I know it's bad for me, but I'm thirty years old, I don't need to be scolded; if I want to bite my nails, damn it, I will bite my nails. I'm thirty years old. If I wanted to be married to my dad, I'd go live with my dad. You know sometimes I think you try and parent me, like if I swear. Oh, don't swear, don't swear. Yeah, sometimes I swear, but I'm just expressing emotion. I don't think I swear in excess that much. Sometimes I just feel like you're trying to control me at all times. And I get secretive, and I go do things, and I spend money and I don't tell you. (contempt) I guess I'm not used to having to answer to anybody. I am really concerned about some of the decisions I have allowed you to make because you always convince me that you know better. And I resent the fact that you think you know better than I do. I get angry because I think I am a fairly intelligent individual.

D: That's why I keep trying to solicit your inputs.

A: Yeah, I know, but you don't ask me. It's like you're so clinical. I feel that you have no respect for me. I feel like you talk down to me. (pause, D raises his hands slightly). Like the other day when we were talking, you're just real clinical. I guess I was looking for some kind of emotion, and I can't get that.

D: It's something we need to work on. I need to work on. But I don't try to talk down to you, and when I ask you for what you want, what you need, sometimes I just get the answer "whatever I want." And that's not the answer I'm looking for; I'm looking for inputs. I want you to be strong. I want you to tell me what you want, what you need.

A: I don't get that feeling that you want me to be strong.

D: But I do. That's why when you tell me something, I try very much to listen to it. Sometimes I do it, sometimes I don't. I can't say that I listen all the time, but I try to. I try very much to change and try to do the stuff that you expressed. Sometimes it takes time, sometimes I need an answer now. Whatever I want. I need some. I like to play devil's advocate a lot.

A: You like to analyze everything.

D: I like to play the wrong side. I need you to be the other half, when I say should we trade in this car or should we keep it. You may see that I want to trade it in, but I also need the other input of "No, I want to keep the car." And then ...

A: Dave, you were gonna get rid of that car no matter what. There's no two ways about it. You knew how I felt. You were gonna get me out of the Mustang no matter what. We went round and round with that car from the moment you got back from sea. And after we got married. I can see you're getting angry. You were going to get me out of that car. And I gave in. 'Cause I was doing what I thought a wife was supposed to do. I thought I was supposed to give in. And you took the car because you knew it was my freedom, because you didn't think I was going to stay. And you put me in a family car.

D: And now I look back on it and I think I was stupid.

A: We were stupid, because I didn't stand up for what I wanted.

D: And I was stupid because I was trying to do something to help myself out, to try to keep us in a relationship, because you keep on talking how you can just dump a relationship and go on without even blinking an eye and how you always saved yourself an out. I was trying to find those out;, it was a challenge for me. I was trying to knock them out. I was trying very hard to try and keep you because you are the one I want to spend the rest of my life with.

A: You would have kept me regardless.

D: Sometimes I'm not so sure. Sometimes, back at the car ...

A: The car is just a toy.

D: It's just a symbol. It's a symbol of your freedom; it was a symbol of what you were and of how you could keep away from me.

A: That's how you perceived it.

D: That's also how you expressed it to me.

A: (crying) That car was the first new car I had ever bought in the world. That car was probably the most important thing to me because I had been dirt poor. That was how I measured my success in getting myself out of the projects in going from four and a half dollars an hour to twenty-one dollars an hour. That was very important to me. And I took that as a personal attack, and I took that as your way of controlling me.

D: But I didn't mean it as a personal attack. I wanted someone who would be there and say that they were going to stay there forever, and I was not seeing it in you, and just start pulling us apart, and it doesn't need to be there. It's like we are constantly testing each other, but we don't need to. We know we love each other, why should we test each other. Neither one of us expressing our feelings for it. For being something I was raised with, something I taught myself, something that's been happening to me my whole life. And for you it's something that's new, but you're doing it because of me, and it's something I need to work on to change, but it's something you need to work on to keep. Yes, I do analyze everything. That's why they put me in the navy on nuclear power. That's the type of person I am. I have to analyze everything.

A: But how? I know it's your makeup, but you don't have to analyze everything.

D: That's what I need to work on changing, that's what I need you to help me with. I need you to help me with a lot of things. I couldn't do a lot of things. And as long as you're talking to me, telling me what I do wrong, or what things I need to improve on, I'm continually learning, I'm continually changing.

A: It doesn't show when you talk to me in this tone of voice. It's like you're so clinical. It's like you remove yourself from your body and talk. (contempt) Do you know what I mean?

D: I just haven't gotten to the point where I lose control of my emotions with you yet. I started to the other night, but like I told you, I didn't like it when I lost them. I don't like to lose control of my emotions. I don't like that.

A: I try to be more like you by controlling my emotions and not talking. But then you get mad at me.

D: I need to change. I need to start showing emotions. I know that. But I also don't know how to try to try to change it. I don't know what to say without thinking about stuff. I don't know how to react without thinking about it. It's kind of like I am a robot. I don't have a lot of natural stuff.

A: You have a good silly side.

D: But that's also learned too. I didn't grow up with it. I got that from people I hung out with. I am trying to learn all this stuff. I am starting out new because I have shut myself down so much. That's where I need you. I need your support. I need to learn to let go of my feelings. But I don't want to totally let go so much I don't know what's going on anymore.

A: How could you not know what's going on anymore?

D: The mouth runneth over and the hands taketh. It's when I get mad my mouth starts running.

A: Everybody's does, honey.

D: I know, but it's ... I lose control of what I am saying and what I am doing.

A: Are you talking about rugger?

D: And work. I mean I don't like not having control of myself. So that's why I try to clamp down on everything and control everything. And now I have to release the control on some of the feelings and stuff, and it's ... I was raised where my dad never got emotional. The only time he got emotional was when he was mad, and then he got aggressive not by some means, but aggressive by the means that I was raised. And I didn't like that. I don't like that in my father, and I don't like that in me. I was also very much raised where a man doesn't cry and a man doesn't show that much. I made the choice of no emotions, that's how I didn't get hurt; I would protect my heart that way. But I know that's not the way to be. And I want to change. And I want you to stay by me.

A: I told you divorce is not an option. It's a nice fantasy, but it's not what I want.

D: That's what I need to hear more often. I am always afraid if I do show my emotion, what's to say that you're not going to like my emotion.

A: Because I am an emotional person and I can understand emotions.

Debriefing

We recommended that Angie and Dave view the marriage as in a state of crisis and that they get couple's therapy. They had already made an appointment. A two-week follow-up visit was conducted by the TV station staff that was filming this couple in our laboratory. Angie and Dave told them that the intervention had created profound changes in their marriage, that they were now much closer and that they were continuing to talk about these issues. We followed this couple for the next three years. They continued talking with one another (without therapy) and reported resolving many of their issues. They have now had their first child, and their marital satisfaction is now also much higher.

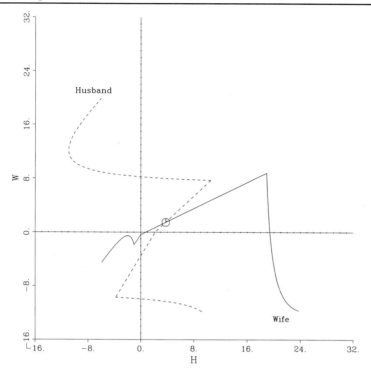

Figure 16.2: Dave and Angie before intervention. Discussion 1: Husband and wife null clines. The wife and husband scores are plotted on the vertical and horizontal axes respectively. The husband's null cline is shown as a dashed line, and the wife's null cline is shown as a solid line. The husband's score is shown on the x-axis and the wife's score is shown on the y-axis.

16.8   Angie and Dave: Math Model

In our SPAFF coding of Angie and Dave's first marital conversation (pre-intervention), we found that most of the affect was neutral (71.1% for husband, 63.4% for wife), with small percentages of domineeringness on the husband's part and defensiveness on the wife's part. This pattern was not very informative, but it was consistent with the previous qualitative observations.

The mathematical model was more informative. In their first conver-

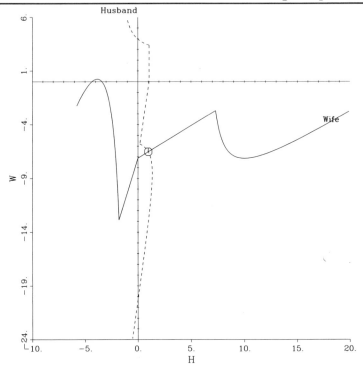

Figure 16.3: Dave and Angie after intervention. Discussion 2: Husband and wife null clines. The wife and husband scores are plotted on the vertical and horizontal axes respectively. The husband's null cline is shown as a dashed line, and the wife's null cline is shown as a solid line. The husband's score is shown on the x-axis and the wife's score is shown on the y-axis.

sation, the wife's emotional inertia was 0.31, not very high, but the husband's emotional inertia was 0.49, which is quite high and a level more characteristic of couples headed for divorce in the Cook *et al.* (1995) paper. The wife's uninfluenced steady state was −0.36, and the husband's was 2.17. This discrepancy was entirely consistent with their questionnaire scores, in which the husband reported being happily married and never thinking about divorce, whereas the wife reported being quite unhappy and often thinking about divorce. Their influenced steady states were 1.46 for the wife and 3.76 for the husband, which was a good sign.

Even though the wife's uninfluenced steady state was negative, her husband influenced her toward a far more positive point in phase space (see figure 16.2).

Their second conversation was dramatically different than the first. The husband showed a significant decrease in domineering behavior, and the wife showed a huge increase in sadness. Sadness moved from 5.7% in the first interaction to 44.1% of all her behavior in the second interaction. What about the math model? The wife's uninfluenced steady state in the second conversation was much more negative at -7.12, whereas the husband's stayed a positive 1.07, which exaggerated the differences observed in the first conversation. But now the influenced steady states were -6.52 for the wife and 0.98 for the husband. The new and more negative steady state reflected the fact that the intervention opened up a lot of suppressed negative affect. Hence, the couple looked *worse* in the second than in the first interaction (see figure 16.3).

16.9   Alan and Eve

To better understand the effects of the dreams-within-conflict intervention, we repeated the intervention with another couple who had a configuration similar to Dave and Angie's. This was also a young couple, but the differences were that the wife (Eve) was in her seventh month of pregnancy, and the husband (Alan) was the one who was unhappily married, whereas the wife was happy.

The intervention had the same effects qualitatively as it did with Dave and Angie. The first conversation had very little emotion in it, whereas in the second conversation the wife was very sad (she moved from 6.7% sadness in the first conversation to 40.2% sadness in the second conversation). The math model in the first conversation showed the following. The wife's inertia was 0.42, the husband's was 0.43, both high. The uninfluenced steady states were -0.58 and 0.51 for wife and husband respectively, and the influenced steady states were -0.48 and 0.37 for the wife and husband respectively (see figure 16.4). In the second conversation, the inertia parameter underwent little change; it was 0.42 for the wife and 0.43 for the husband. The uninfluenced steady states were -2.62 for the wife and 0.64 for the husband. The influenced steady states were -2.17 for the wife and 0.96 for the husband (see figure 16.5). Once again, this intervention unlocked a great deal of suppressed negative affect, so that the interaction looked *worse* than the emotionally disengaged preintervention conversation.

The dreams-within-conflict intervention may actually be only one necessary part of the required marital intervention. It does unlock sup-

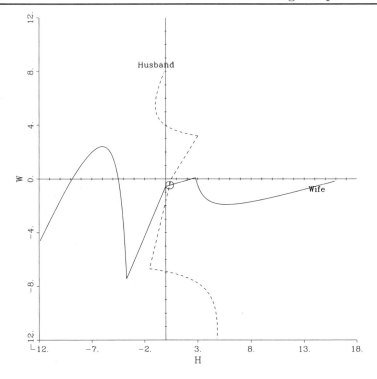

Figure 16.4: Alan and Eve before intervention. Discussion 1: Husband and wife null clines. The wife and husband scores are plotted on the vertical and horizontal axes respectively. The husband's null cline is shown as a dashed line, and the wife's null cline is shown as a solid line. The husband's score is shown on the x-axis and the wife's score is shown on the y-axis.

pressed or covert emotion, much of it having to do with sadness. However, it may not be enough to only unlock the dreams and uncover the sadness that has resulted from the emotional disengagement that follows gridlocked conflict. Ultimately we need an intervention that decreases emotional inertia, increases the positivity of the uninfluenced steady state, and increases the positivity of the influenced steady state. A combination of interventions may be necessary to produce these desired effects.

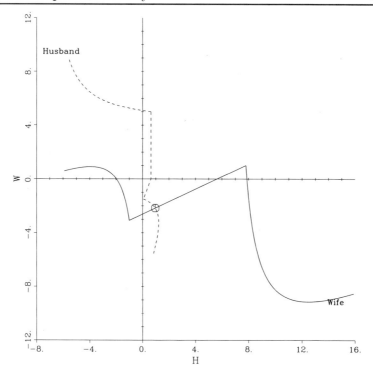

Figure 16.5: Alan and Eve after intervention. Discussion 2: Husband and wife null clines. The wife and husband scores are plotted on the vertical and horizontal axes respectively. The husband's null cline is shown as a dashed line, and the wife's null cline is shown as a solid line. The husband's score is shown on the x-axis and the wife's score is shown on the y-axis.

16.10   Chapter Summary

This chapter was written to demonstrate the dramatic interplay that has resulted from our mathematical modeling and from our goal of attempting to change clinical practices with specific marriage experiments designed to obtain proximal changes in the marriage. We are simultaneously studying the process of relapse following these brief interventions so that we can learn how to minimize such relapse. This chapter was designed to illustrate the integration of research and clinical practice that is our long-term objective.

The main point of the marriage experiments is precisely to reveal the advantages and limitations of the brief component interventions. In this manner, an empirically based intervention, or a library of components, will be produced, that may be tailored for the individual marital case. As noted, we would like to conduct eight studies, with each intervention having a control group in which couples do nothing for a half-hour between the two fifteen-minute conversations but read magazines. In the next five years, we will know the results of these specific experiments, but the main point we wish to make here is that the results of the mathematical modeling are driving the experimentation and the evaluation of the interventions' effects on interactive processes. The modeling thus has a quite central and directive role, and it creatively facilitates discovery.

17

How to Prepare Data for Modeling

It is our hope that the ideas presented in this book will inspire other researchers to try these methods with their own data. To encourage this kind of exploratory learning, we make our computer program available through a Web site. Because this site is still an evolving product at time of writing, the reader should always check there first for the most current instructions. However, we can discuss in a general way the concepts needed to convert a coding scale to data that is suitable for use with the model. That is the purpose of this chapter.

17.1 Obtaining the Model Program

The original program was developed by graduate students in the applied mathematics department at the University of Washington who were working with Dr. James Murray and Dr. John Gottman. This earliest incarnation of the model was written using MATLAB, a technical computing software package used for solving mathematical and engineering problems. It was run in a UNIX environment. One of its limitations was that it was unable to do batch processing of multiple datasets.

We converted the program when we began the process of exploring new forms of the influence function and moved away from the original RCISS data to using weighted data derived from the SPAFF. The model program was converted to FORTRAN and run in a DOS environment on an IBM-PC-type computer. At time of writing, that is the language and operating-system environment used for running the model. Future enhancements may include making the program more Windows compatible and possibly rewriting it in a different programming language that would facilitate porting it to different operating environments. As well, we may add new features and incorporate new theory into the model as our own ideas change and grow.

The program and documentation files will be maintained on the Web site of the Gottman Institute Web site at *http://www.gottman.com.* This site will contain a link to the current location of the model program and its documentation. Basic information regarding the operating system and computer requirements for using the program will be found on the Web site. For those who wish to proceed, instructions for downloading the program and documentation files will also be found there.

17.2   Basic Concepts in Data Preparation

The basic idea is that you must move from data gathered in the laboratory, which may or may not have a natural positive to negative range, to a variable that does have this property and is comparable across individuals. Most often this move means converting or translating data from a nominal scale to an ordinal scale. Because the model estimates the influence on the spouse of positive to negative values of whatever variable is being used, it is necessary to cast the data in those terms. It is also necessary for this variable to have a "neutral" value or range that makes sense in terms of what the variable is measuring and that occurs in the data often enough to allow for estimation of the uninfluenced steady state.

We have found that a minimum of 15% of the data must be coded or computed as being "neutral" in order to estimate the uninfluenced steady states. Ideally your data will satisfy this requirement for all subjects that were coded or measured in the laboratory. However, care must be taken not to expand the definition of "neutral" artificially to include data that are not truly representative of neutral (i.e., noninfluencing) behavior for the sake of obtaining enough data points in the neutral range. In other words, this may be a point at which you make a decision regarding the actual suitability of the data for use in this type of model.

Another basic idea is that the data must have been taken over time using some type of regular sampling. This is a model of what happens between two people over time; therefore, it must have time-based data. Summary coding of an interaction will not work. We suggest a minimum of seventy-five time points in order to obtain reasonable model parameter estimates. The time points themselves should represent an "interactive unit" that makes sense from a psychological standpoint.

Hopefully, you will be able to obtain a broad range of scores for each partner from your data. Such a range yields more data for the estimate of influence on the partner at each score. In other words, the estimated influence function will derive from a richer dataset when many different scores are found in the data and will better reflect the nuances of interaction between those two people. If the actual data are subsampled within the time unit or "interactive unit", they can be summed to obtain a total score for the time unit. This method has the potential to introduce a greater range of variability into the scores, which makes the parameter estimates more robust. An example of what we mean here will be given in section 17.3.

17.3   Example: Deriving Model Data from SPAFF

The extension of the marriage model to a sample of newlywed couples is described in chapter 12. The SPAFF system (Gottman *et al.*, 1996) was used to code the specific affects expressed during the couples' conflict interactions. It draws on facial expression (based on Ekman and Friesen's Facial Action Coding System; Ekman and Friesen, 1978), vocal tone, and speech content to characterize the emotions displayed. Coders categorized the affects displayed using five positive codes (interest, validation, affection, humor, joy), ten negative affect codes (disgust, contempt, belligerence, domineering, anger, fear/tension, defensiveness, whining, sadness, stonewalling), and a neutral affect code.

A weighting scheme for the SPAFF was devised. This scheme was the way we translated a nominal scale (the SPAFF) to an ordinal scale (the SPAFF code weights). We decided that we were able to distinguish degrees of negativity and positivity using a four-point scale – i.e., the negative SPAFF codes could be assigned a weight from -1 to -4, and the positive SPAFF codes could be assigned a weight from $+1$ to $+4$. The neutral code was considered to be slightly positive and was assigned a weight of $+0.1$.

Because previous research with the RCISS revealed the power of the negative codes in predicting divorce, the initial weighting scheme for the SPAFF codes weighted more heavily the subset of negative codes that were the best predictors of divorce in previous research. These negative codes were: contempt, defensiveness, criticism, and belligerence. The positive affects were not heavily weighted in this scheme, all being equally weighted at $+2$. For the newlywed data, we subsequently discovered that the SPAFF's positive affects were able to discriminate predictively the three criterion groups (see Gottman *et al.*, 1998). As a result of this finding, we reconsidered our weighting of the SPAFF codes and gave a higher positive weight of +4 to affection, validation, humor, and joy. The results of the marriage model using these two different weighting schemes are given in chapter 12.

SPAFF was coded in real time on observational coding stations that utilize a wheel with "click stops" for each code. The code at each "click stop" is sent as a digital value to the A/D converter board in a computer. The computer program that acquires the data takes samples from the A/D board multiple times per second and then determines the dominant code during each second. To convert these data for use in the math model, the nominal code for each second received the assigned weight, and then these weights were summed over 6-second time blocks or interactive units. We chose 6 seconds because it has become a fairly universally used time block for averaging social interaction data in human interaction across many laboratories and many contexts. The 900 seconds of the 15-minute conversation gave us 150 data points, or interactive units for husband and for wife. The potential range of data for any one second was -4 to $+4$, so for an interactive unit where the data are summed over 6 seconds, the potential range was -24 to $+24$, and we could expect more variability in the data by summing in this way.

Because we were summing over 6 seconds to obtain an interactive unit that would give us more variability in the data and also provide a time basis that had psychological meaning for the model, we needed to be sure we still had sufficient "neutral" data to estimate the uninfluenced parameters of the model. Recall that the SPAFF coding includes a neutral code that was assigned the weight 0.1. Therefore, interactive units or time points that had a summed score of 0.6 or less were considered to be "neutral" for the model. In our data, the neutral code occurred frequently and for long blocks of time (whenever another specific affect could not be definitely assigned), and as it turned out, we still had adequate neutral data even after summing to the level of interactive unit. The distribution of weighted summed data can be assessed using a standard statistics package to obtain frequency distributions for all data files.

The SPAFF coding system has evolved since the newlywed data was coded. The current version of the SPAFF contains twenty codes. The translation of these codes from nominal to ordinal data is as follows: disgust (-3), contempt (-4), belligerence (-2), low domineering (-1), high domineering (-1), criticism (-2), anger (-1), tension (0), tension/humor $(+2)$, defensiveness (-2), whining (-1), sadness (-1), stonewalling (-2), neutral (0.1), interest $(+2)$, low validation $(+4)$, high validation $(+4)$, affection $(+4)$, humor $(+4)$, and surprise/joy $(+4)$. For any couple that comes into our Family Research Laboratory, the SPAFF coding is weighted and summed as described above. The resulting file is an ASCII or text file with three columns of data: the interactive unit or time point number, followed by the data (weighted and summed SPAFF) for each partner at that time point.

Bibliography

[1] J.F. Alexander. Defensive and supportive communications in family systems. *Journal of Marriage and the Family*, 35:613–617, 1973.

[2] J.M. Andriote. *Victory Deferred: How AIDS Changed Gay Life in America*. University of Chicago Press, Chicago, Ill., 1999.

[3] V.I. Arnold. *Catastrophe Theory*. Springer–Verlag, Berlin, 1986.

[4] R. Bakeman and J. Gottman. *Observing Interaction: An introduction to sequential analysis*. Cambridge University Press, New York, 1986.

[5] R. Bakeman and V. Quera. *Analyzing interaction: Sequential analysis with SDIS and GSEQ*. Cambridge University Press, New York, 1995.

[6] G.L. Baker and J.P. Gollub. *Chaotic Dynamics: An Introduction*. Cambridge University Press, New York, second edition, 1995.

[7] L. Bank, T. Dishion, M. Skinner, and G.R. Patterson. Method variance in structural equation modeling: Living with "glop". In G.R. Patterson, editor, *Depression and Aggression in Family Interaction*, pages 247–280. Lawrence Erlbaum Associates, Hillsdale, NJ, 1990.

[8] G. Bateson. Critical evaluations. *International Journal of Psychiatry*, 2:415–417, 1966.

[9] G. Bateson, D.D. Jackson, J. Haley, and J. Weakland. Toward a theory of schizophrenia. *Behavioral Science*, 1:251–264, 1956.

[10] D.H. Baucom and G.W. Lester. The usefulness of cognitive restructuring as an adjunct to behavioral marital therapy. *Behavior Therapy*, 17:385–403, 1986.

[11] A.P Bell and M.S. Weinberg. *Homosexualities: A Study of Diversity Among Men and Women*. Simon and Schuster, New York, 1978.

[12] G.B. Bell and R.L. French. Consistency of individual leadership position in small groups of varying membership. *Journal of Abnormal and Social Psychology*, 45:764–767, 1950.

[13] R.Q. Bell. A reinterpretation of the direction of effects in studies of socialization. *Psychological Review*, 75:81–95, 1968.

[14] J. Belsky and J. Kelly. *The Transition to Parenthood*. Bantam, Doubleday and Dell, New York, 1994.

[15] P.M. Bentler and M.D. Newcomb. Longitudinal study of marital success and failure. *Journal of Consulting and Clinical Psychology*, 46:1053–1070, 1978.

[16] R.A. Berley and N.S. Jacobson. Causal attributions in intimate relationships: Toward a model of cognitive behavioral marital therapy. In P. Kendall, editor, *Advances in Cognitive-Behavioral Research and Therapy*, volume 3. Academic, New York, 1984.

[17] R.M. Beron, P.G. Amazoen, and P.J. Beek. Love and global dynamics of social relations. In R.R. Vallacher and A. Nowak, editors, *Dynamical Systems in Social Psychology*, pages 111–138. Academic, New York, 1994.

[18] Murstein B.I., M. Cerreto, and M.G. MacDonald. A theory and investigation of the effects of exchange- orientation on marriage and friendship. *Journal of Marriage and the Family*, 39:543–548, 1977.

[19] G. Birchler, R. Weiss, and J. Vincent. Multimethod analysis of social reinforcement exchange between maritally distressed and nondistressed spouse and stranger dyads. *Journal of Personality and Social Psychology*, 31:349–360, 1975.

[20] B. Bloom, S. Asher, and S. White. Marital disruption as a stressor: A review and analysis. *Psychological Bulletin*, 85:867–894, 1978.

[21] P. Blumstein and P. Schwartz. *American Couples: Money, Work, Sex*. William Morrow and Co., New York, 1983.

[22] A. Booth. Special issue on ethnicity and race. *Journal of Marriage and the Family*, 50(3), 1988.

[23] A. Booth. Special issue on ethnicity and race. *Journal of Marriage and the Family*, 51(4), 1989.

[24] A. Booth and L. White. Thinking about divorce. *Journal of Marriage and the Family*, 42:605–616, 1980.

[25] J.H. Bray and E.N. Jouriles. Treatment of marital conflict and prevention of divorce. *Journal of Marital and Family Therapy*, 21(4):461–473, 1995.

[26] P.C. Brown and T.W. Smith. Social influence, marriage, and the heart: Cardiovascular consequences of interpersonal control in husbands and wives. *Health Psychology*, 11:88–96, 1992.

[27] C.M. Buchanan, E.E. Maccoby, and S.M. Dornbusch. Caught between parents: Adolescents' experience in divorced homes. *Child Development*, 62:1008–1029, 1991.

[28] K. Buehlman, J.M. Gottman, and L. Katz. How a couple views their past predicts their future: Predicting divorce from an oral history interview. *Journal of Family Psychology*, 5:295–318, 1992.

[29] J. Buongiorno. Wait time until professional treatment in marital therapy. Unpublished master's thesis, Catholic University, 1992.

[30] E.W. Burgess, H.J. Locke, and M.M. Thomas. *The Family from Institution to Companionship*. American Books, New York, 1971.

[31] B. Burman and G. Margolin. Analysis of the association between marital relationships and health problems: An interactional perspective. *Psychological Bulletin*, 112:39–63, 1992.

[32] D.T. Campbell and D.W. Fiske. Convergent and discriminant validation by the multi-trait- multi-method matrix. *Psychological Bulletin*, 56:81–105, 1959.

[33] S. Carrère, K. Buehlman, J.M. Gottman, J. Coan, and L. Ruckstuhl. Predicting marital stability and divorce in newlywed couples. *Journal of Family Psychology*, 14(1):42–58, 2000.

[34] S. Carrère and J.M. Gottman. Predicting divorce among newlyweds from the first three minutes of a marital conflict discussion. *Family Process*, 38(3):293–301, 1999.

[35] D.P.L. Castrigiano and S.A. Hayes. *Catastrophe Theory*. Addison–Wesley, Reading, Mass., 1993.

[36] A. Cherlin. *Marriage, Divorce, Remarriage*. Harvard University Press, Cambridge, Mass., 1981.

[37] A. Christensen. Dysfunctional interaction patterns in couples. In P. Noller and M.A. Fitzpatrick, editors, *Perspectives on Marital Interaction*, pages 31–52. Multilingual Matters, Avon, England, 1988.

[38] A. Christensen and C.L. Heavey. Gender and social structure in the demand/withdraw pattern of marital conflict. *Journal of Personality and Social Psychology*, 59:73–82, 1990.

[39] J. Coan, J.M. Gottman, J. Babcock, and N.S. Jacobson. Battering and the male rejection of influence from women. *Aggressive Behavior*, 23:375–388, 1997.

[40] J. Cook, R. Tyson, J. White, R. Rushe, J.M. Gottman, and J.D. Murray. The mathematics of marital conflict: Qualitative dynamic mathematical modeling of marital interaction. *Journal of Family Psychology*, 9:110–130, 1995.

[41] P.A. Cowan and C.P. Cowan. Couple's relationships, parenting styles and the child's development at three, 1987. Paper presented at the Society for Research in Child Development, Baltimore, April.

[42] P.A. Cowan and C.P. Cowan. Becoming a family: Research and intervention. In I. Sigel and A. Brody, editors, *Family Research*. Lawrence Erlbaum Associates, Hillsdale, NJ, 1990.

[43] R.W. Cromwell and D.H. Olson. *Power in Families*. John Wiley and Sons, New York, 1975.

[44] E.M. Cummings and P. Davies. *Children and Marital Conflict: The Impact of Family Dispute Resolution*. Guilford, New York, 1994.

[45] P. Davies. *The Mind of God*. Simon and Schuster, New York, 1992.

[46] S.D. Duncan Jr. and D.W. Fiske. *Face-to-face Interaction: Research, Methods and Theory*. Lawrence Erlbaum Associates, Hillsdale, NJ, 1977.

[47] M.A. Easterbrooks. Early family development: Longitudinal impact of marital quality, 1987. Paper presented at the Society for Research in Child Development, Baltimore, April.

[48] M.A. Easterbrooks and R.A. Emde. Marital and parent-child relationships: The role of affect in the family system. In R.A. Hinde and J. Stephenson-Hinde, editors, *Relationships within Families: Mutual Influence*. Clarenden, Oxford, England, 1988.

[49] J.R. Eiser. Toward a dynamic conception of attitude consistency and change. In R.R. Vallacher and A. Nowak, editors, *Dynamical Systems in Social Psychology*, pages 198–218. Academic, New York, 1994.

[50] P. Ekman and W.V. Friesen. *Facial Action Coding System*. Consulting Psychologist, Palo Alto, Calif., 1978.

[51] R.E. Emery. Interparental conflict and the children of discord and divorce. *Psychological Bulletin*, 92:310–330, 1982.

[52] R.E. Emery. *Marriage, Divorce, and Children's Adjustment*. Sage, Newbury Park, Calif., 1988.

[53] R.E. Emery and K.D. O'Leary. Children's perceptions of marital discord and behavior problems of boys and girls. *Journal of Abnormal Child Psychology*, 10:11–24, 1982.

[54] C. J. Fankish. Warning! your marriage may be hazardous to your health: Spouse-pair visit factors and cardiovascular reactivity. *Dissertation Abstracts International*, 52:5532, 1992.

[55] F.D. Fincham and T.N. Bradbury. Assessing attributions in marriage: The relationship attributions measure. *Journal of Personality and Social Psychology*, 62:457–468, 1992.

[56] F.D. Fincham, T.N. Bradbury, and C.K. Scott. Cognition in marriage. In F.D. Fincham and T.D. Bradbury, editors, *The Psychology of Marriage*, pages 118–149. Guilford, New York, 1990.

[57] F.D. Fincham and T.N. Scott. The assessment of marital quality: A reevaluation. *Journal of Marriage and the Family*, 49:797–809, 1987.

[58] G.H. Fisher. Preparation of ambiguous stimulus materials. *Perception and Psychophysics*, 2:421–422, 1967.

[59] M. A. Fitzpatrick. *Between Husbands and Wives: Communication in Marriage*. Sage, Beverly Hills, Calif., 1988.

[60] E. Fivaz-Depeursinge. Documenting a time-bound, circular view of hierarchies: A microanalysis of parent-infant dyadic interaction. *Family Process*, 30:101–120, 1991.

[61] E. Fivaz-Depeursinge and A. Corboz-Warnery. *The Primary Triangle*. Basic, New York, 1995.

[62] R. Forehand, G. Brody, N. Long, J. Slotkin, and R. Fauber. Divorce/divorce potential and interparental conflict: The relationship to early adolescent social and cognitive functioning. *Journal of Adolescent Research*, 1:389–397, 1986.

[63] B.J. Fowers and D.H. Olson. Predicting marital success with prepare: A predicitve validity study. *Journal of Marital and Family Therapy*, 12:403–413, 1986.

[64] H.S. Friedman, J.S. Tucker, J.E. Schwartz, and K.C. Tomilson. Psychosocial and behavioral predictors of longevity: The aging and death of the "termites". *American Psychologist*, 50:69–78, 1995.

[65] R. Gilmore. *Catastrophe Theory for Scientists and Engineers*. Dover, New York, 1981.

[66] J. Gleick. *Chaos: Making a New Science*. Viking, New York, 1987.

[67] J. Gottman, J. Coan, S. Carrère, and C. Swanson. Predicting marital happiness and stability from newlywed interactions. *Journal of Marriage and the Family*, 60:5–22, 1998.

[68] J. Gottman, L. Katz, and C. Hooven. *Meta-Emotion*. Lawrence Erlbaum Associates, Hillsdale, NJ, 1996.

[69] J. Gottman, K. McCoy, J. Coan, and H. Collier. The specific affect coding system (SPAFF). In J.M. Gottman, editor, *What Predicts Divorce? The Measures*. Lawrence Erlbaum Associates, Hillsdale, NJ, 1996.

[70] J. Gottman and N. Silver. *The Seven Principles for Making Marriage Work*. Crown, New York, 1999.

[71] J. Gottman, C. Swanson, and J. Murray. The mathematics of marital conflict: Dynamic mathematical nonlinear modeling of newlywed marital interaction. *Journal of Family Psychology*, 13:3–19, 1999.

[72] J.M. Gottman. *Marital Interaction: Empirical Investigations*. Academic, New York, 1979.

[73] J.M. Gottman. The consistency of nonverbal affect and affect reciprocity in marital interaction. *Journal of Consulting and Clinical Psychology*, 48:711–717, 1980.

[74] J.M. Gottman. How marriages change. In G.R. Patterson, editor, *Depression and Aggression in Family Interaction*. Lawrence Erlbaum Associates, Hillsdale, NJ, 1990.

[75] J.M. Gottman. How marriages change. In G.R. Patterson, editor, *Depression and Aggression in Family Interaction*, pages 110–135. Lawrence Erlbaum Associates, Hillsdale, NJ, 1990.

[76] J.M. Gottman. A theory of marital dissolution and stability. *Journal of Family Psychology*, 7:57–75, 1993.

[77] J.M. Gottman. *What Predicts Divorce? The Relationship between Marital Processes and Marital Outcomes*. Lawrence Erlbaum Associates, Hillsdale, NJ, 1994a.

[78] J.M. Gottman. *Why Marriages Succeed or Fail*. Simon Schuster, New York, 1994b.

[79] J.M. Gottman, editor. *What Predicts Divorce? The Measures*. Lawrence Erlbaum Associates, Hillsdale, NJ, 1996.

[80] J.M. Gottman. *The Marriage Clinic*. W.W. Norton, New York, 1999.

[81] J.M. Gottman and R.W. Levenson. The social psychophysiology of marriage. In P. Noller and M.A. Fitzpatrick, editors, *Perspectives on Marital Interaction*, pages 182–200. Multilingual Matters, Clevedon, England, 1988.

[82] J.M. Gottman and R.W. Levenson. Marital processes predictive of later dissolution: Behavior, physiology, and health. *Journal of Personality and Social Psychology*, 63:221–233, 1992.

[83] J.M. Gottman and R.W. Levenson. What predicts change in marital interaction over time? A study of alternative models. *Family Process*, 38:143–158, 1999a.

[84] J.M. Gottman and R.W. Levenson. How stable is marital interaction over time? *Family Process*, 38:159–165, 1999b.

[85] J.M. Gottman and R.W. Levenson. Dysfunctional marital conflict: Women are being unfairly blamed. *Journal of Divorce and Remarriage*, 31:1–17, 1999c.

[86] J.M. Gottman and R.W. Levenson. The timing of divorce: Predicting when a couple will divorce over a 14-year period. *Journal of Marriage and the Family*, 62:737–745, 2000.

[87] J.M. Gottman, H. Markman, and C. Notarius. The topography of marital conflict: A study of verbal and nonverbal behavior. *Journal of Marriage and the Family*, 39:461–477, 1977.

[88] J.M. Gottman and C.I. Notarius. Decade review: Observing marital interaction. *Journal of Marriage and the Family*, 62:927–947, 2000.

[89] J.M. Gottman and A.K. Roy. *Sequential Analysis: A Guide for Behavioral Researchers*. Cambridge University Press, New York, 1990.

[90] J. P. Gray. The influence of female power in marriage on sexual behavior and attitudes: A holocultural study. *Archives of Sexual Behavior*, 13:223–231, 1984.

[91] B. Gray-Little and N. Burks. Power and satisfaction in marriage: A review and critique. *Psychological Bulletin*, 93:513–538, 1983.

[92] N.E. Gronlund. *Sociometry in the Classroom*. Harper and Brothers, New York, 1959.

[93] B.G. Guerney. *Relationship Enhancement*. Jossey Bass, San Francisco, 1977.

[94] B.G. Guerney and L. Guerney. Marital and family problem prevention and enrichment programs. In L. L'Abate, editor, *Handbook of Family Psychology and Therapy*, volume 2, pages 1179–1217. Dorsey, Homewood, Ill., 1985.

[95] L. Guttman. A basis for scaling qualitative data. *American Sociological Review*, 9:139–150, 1944.

[96] K. Hahlweg and H.J. Markman. Effectiveness of behavioral marital therapy: Empirical status of behavioral techniques in preventing and alleviating marital distress. *Journal of Consulting and Clinical Psychology*, 56(3):440–447, 1988.

[97] K. Hahlweg, D. Revenstorf, and L. Schindler. Effects of behavioral marital therapy on couples' communication and problem-solving skills. *Journal of Consulting and Clinical Psychology*, 52(4):553–566, 1984.

[98] K. Hahlweg, L. Schindler, D. Revenstorf, and J.C. Brengelmann. The Münich marital therapy study. In K. Hahlweg and N.S. Jacobson, editors, *Marital Interaction: Analysis and Modification*, pages 3–26. Guilford, New York, 1984.

[99] J. Harrell and B.G. Guerney. Training married couples in conflict resolution skills. In D.H. Olson, editor, *Treating Relationships*, pages 151–180. Graphic, Lake Mills, Iowa, 1976.

[100] J. Harry. Gay male and lesbian relationships. In E.D. Macklin and R.H. Rubin, editors, *Contemporary Families and Alternative Lifestyles*. Sage, Beverly Hills, Calif., 1983.

[101] M.W. Hawkins, S. Carrère, and J.M. Gottman. Marital sentiment override: Does it influence couples' perceptions? *Journal of Marriage and Family*, 64(1):193–201, 2002.

[102] C.L. Heavey, A. Christensen, and N.M. Malomuth. The longitudinal impact of demand and withdrawal during marital conflict. *Journal of Consulting and Clinical Psychology*, 63:797–801, 1995.

[103] F. Heider. *The Psychology of Interpersonal Relations*. Wiley, New York, 1958.

[104] H. Hendrix. *Getting the Love You Want*. Holt, New York, 1988.

[105] E.M. Hetherington and W.G. Clingempeel. Coping with marital transitions: A family systems perspective. *Monographs for the Society for Research in Child Development*, 1992.

[106] R.E. Heymar, J.M. Eddy, R.L. Weiss, and D. Vivian. Factor analysis of the marital interaction coding system "MICS". *Journal of Family Psychology*, 9:209–215, 1995.

[107] T.H. Holmes and R.H. Rahe. The social readjustment rating scale. *Journal of Psychosomatic Research*, 11:213–218, 1967.

[108] A. Holtzworth-Munroe and N.S. Jacobson. Causal attributions of married couples: When do they search for causes? what do they conclude when they do? *Journal of Personality and Social Psychology*, 48:1398–1412, 1985.

[109] D.D. Jackson. The question of family homeostasis. *Psychiatric Quarterly*, 31:79–90, 1957.

[110] T.C. Jacob. Family interaction and psychopathology: Historical overview. In T. Jacob, editor, *Family Interaction and Psychopathology*, pages 3–24. Plenum, New York, 1987.

[111] N.S. Jacobson. Specific and nonspecific factors in the effectiveness of a behavioral approach to the treatment of marital discord. *Journal of Consulting and Clinical Psychology*, 46(3):442–452, 1978.

[112] N.S. Jacobson. A component analysis of behavioral marital therapy: The relative effectiveness of behavior exchange and communication/problem-solving training. *Journal of Consulting and Clinical Psychology*, 52(2):295–305, 1984.

[113] N.S. Jacobson. The maintenance of treatment gains following social-learning-based marital therapy. *Behavior Therapy*, 20:325–336, 1989.

[114] N.S. Jacobson. Behavioral versus insight-oriented marital therapy: Labels can be misleading. *Journal of Consulting and Clinical Psychology*, 59(1):142–145, 1991.

[115] N.S. Jacobson and M.E. Addis. Research on couple therapy: What do we know? Where are we going? *Journal of Consulting and Clinical Psychology*, 61(1):85–93, 1993.

[116] N.S. Jacobson and A. Christensen. *Integrated Cognitive Behavioral Marital Therapy*. Guilford, New York, 1998.

[117] N.S. Jacobson, V.M. Follette, W.C. Follette, A. Holtzworth-Munroe, J.L. Katt, and K.B. Schmaling. A component analysis of behavioral marital therapy: 1-year follow-up. *Behavior Research and Therapy*, 23:549–555, 1985.

[118] N.S. Jacobson and G. Margolin. *Marital Therapy*. Mazel, New York, 1979.

[119] N.S. Jacobson, K. Schmaling, and A. Holtzworth-Munroe. Component analysis of behavioral marital therapy: 2-year followup and prediction of relapse. *Journal of Marital and Family Therapy*, 13:187–195, 1987.

[120] S.M. Johnson and L.S. Greenberg. Differential effects of experiential and problem-solving interventions in resolving marital conflict. *Journal of Consulting and Clinical Psychology*, 53(2):175–184, 1985.

[121] H.B. Kaplan, N.R. Burch, and S.W. Bloom. Physiological co-variation in small peer groups. In P.H. Liederman and D. Shapiro, editors, *Psychological Approaches to Social Behavior*, pages 21–43. Stanford University Press, Stanford, Calif., 1964.

[122] L.E. Kelly and J.J. Conley. Personality and compatibility: A prospective analysis of marital stability and marital satisfaction. *Journal of Personality and Social Psychology*, 52:27–40, 1987.

[123] J.M. Kolb and M.A. Strauss. Marital power and marital happiness in relation to problem-solving. *Journal of Marriage and the Family*, 36:756–766, 1974.

[124] L. Krokoff. Anatomy of negative affect in working class marriages. *Dissertation Abstracts International*, 45, 7A(84-22 109), 1987. University Microfilms.

[125] L.A. Kurdek. Relationship outcomes and their predictors: Longitudinal evidence from heterosexual married, gay cohabiting, and lesbian cohabiting couples. *Journal of Marriage and the Family*, 60:553–568, 1988.

[126] L.A. Kurdek. Predicting marital dissolution: A 5-year prospective longitudinal study of newlywed couples. *Journal of Personality and Social Psychology*, 64:221–242, 1993.

[127] B. Lantané and A. Nowak. Attitudes as catastrophes: From dimensions to categories with increasing involvement. In R. R. Vallacher and A. Nowak, editors, *Dynamical Systems in Social Psychology*, pages 219–250. Academic, New York, 1994.

[128] W.J. Lederer and D.D. Jackson. *The Mirages of Marriage*. Norton, New York, 1968.

[129] R.W. Levenson, L.L. Carstensen, and J.M. Gottman. Long-term marriage: Age, gender, and satisfaction. *Psychology and Aging*, 8:301–313, 1993.

[130] R.W. Levenson, L.L. Carstensen, and J.M. Gottman. The influence of age and gender on affect, physiology and their interrelations: A study of long-term marriages. *Journal of Personality and Social Psychology*, 67:56–68, 1994.

[131] R.W. Levenson and J.M. Gottman. Marital interaction: Physiological linkage and affective exchange. *Journal of Personality and Social Psychology*, 45:587– 597, 1983.

[132] R.W. Levenson and J.M. Gottman. Physiological and affective predictors of change in relationship satisfaction. *Journal of Personality and Social Psychology*, 49(1):85–94, 1985.

[133] R.W. Levenson and L. Marchitelli. Emotion metaphors during marital conflict discussions and physiological responses. Unpublished paper presented at the Society for Psychophysiological Research, 1995.

[134] G. Levinger. Toward the analysis of close relationships. *Journal of Experimental Social Psychology*, 16:510–544, 1980.

[135] M. Lewis and L.A. Rosenblum. *The Effect of the Infant on its Caregivers*. Wiley, New York, 1974.

[136] H. J. Locke and K. M. Wallace. Short marital adjustment and prediction tests: Their reliability and validity. *Marriage and Family Living*, 21:251–255, 1959.

[137] K. Lorenz. *On Aggression*. Harcourt, Brace, and World, New York, 1966.

[138] D. Ludwig, D. Jones, and C. Holling. Qualitative analsis of insect outbreak systems: The spruce budworm and forest. *Journal of Animal Ecology*, 47:315–332, 1978.

[139] E. Maccoby. *The Two Sexes*. Harvard University Press, Cambridge, Mass., 1998.

[140] W.B. Malarkey, J.K. Kiecolt-Glaser, D. Pearl, and R. Glaser. Hostile behavior during marital conflict alters pituitary and adrenal hormones. *Psychosomatic Medicine*, 56:41–51, 1994.

[141] G. Margolin and B.E. Wampold. Sequential analysis of conflict and accord in distressed and nondistressed marital partners. *Journal of Consulting and Clinical Psychology*, 49:554–567, 1981.

[142] T.C. Martin and L. Bumpass. Recent trends in marital disruption. *Demography*, 26:37–51, 1989.

[143] W.W. Meissner. The conceptualization of marriage and family dynamics from a psychoanalytic perspective. In T.J. Paolino and B.S. McCrady, editors, *Marriage and Marital Therapy*, pages 25–88. Brunner Mazel, New York, 1978.

[144] A.A. Milne. *The World of Christopher Robin*. E.P. Dutton and Co., New York, 1958.

[145] W. Mischel. *Personality and Assessment*. Wiley, New York, 1968.

[146] E.G. Mishler and N.E. Waxler. Family interaction processes in schizophrenia: A review of current theories. *International Journal of Psychiatry*, 2:375–415, 1966.

[147] W.J. Morgan. *The OSS and I*. Reinhold, New York, 1957.

[148] J.D. Murray. *Mathematical Biology*. Springer–Verlag, Berlin, 1989.

[149] D. Newtson. The perception and coupling of behavior waves. In R. R. Vallacher and A. Nowak, editors, *Dynamical Systems in Social Psychology*, pages 139–168. Academic, New York, 1994.

[150] C.I. Notarius, P.R. Benson, D. Sloane, N.A. Vanzetti, and L.M. Hornyak. Exploring the interface between perception and behavior: An analysis of marital interaction in distressed and nondistressed couples. *Behavioral Assessment*, 11:39–64, 1989.

[151] A. Nowak and R.R. Vallacher. *Dynamical Social Psychology*. Guilford, New York, 1998.

[152] F.I. Nye. *Role Structure and an Analysis of the Family*. Sage, Beverly Hills, Calif., 1976.

[153] F.I. Nye. Fifty years of family research, 1937-1987. *Journal of Marriage and the Family*, 50:305–316, 1988.

[154] G.M. Odell. Qualitative theory of systems of ordinary differential equations, including phase plane analysis and the use of the hopf bifurcation theorem. In L.A. Segel, editor, *Mathematical Models in Molecular and Cellular Biology*. Cambridge University Press, Cambridge, England, 1980.

[155] D.H. Olson and C. Rabunsky. Validity of four measures of family power. *Journal of Marriage and the Family*, 34:224–234, 1972.

[156] D.H. Olson and R.G. Ryder. Inventory of marital conflicts (imc): An experimental interaction procedure. *Journal of Marriage and the Family*, 32:443–448, 1970.

[157] G.R. Patterson. *Coercive Family Process*. Castalia, Eugene, Oregon, 1982.

[158] I. Peterson. *Newton's Clock: Chaos in the Solar System*. W.H. Freeman and Co., New York, 1993.

[159] H. Poincaré. *New methods of celestial mechanics*. American Institute of Physics, New York, 1993.

[160] T. Poston and I.N. Stewart. *Catastrophe Theory and Its Applications*. Pitman, London, 1978.

[161] A. Rapoport. *Fights, Games and Debates*. University of Michigan Press, Ann Arbor, 1960.

[162] H.L. Raush, W.A. Barry, R.K. Hertel, and M.A. Swain. *Communication, Conflict, and Marriage*. Jossey-Bass, San Francisco, Calif., 1974.

[163] J.B. Reid. Reliability assessment of observational data: A possible methodological problem. *Child Development*, 41:1143–1150, 1970.

[164] D. Revenstorf, B. Vogel, C. Wegener, K. Hahlweg, and L. Schindler. Escalation phenomena in interaction sequences: An empirical comparison of distressed and non-distressed couples. *Behavioral Analysis and Modification*, 2:97–116, 1980.

[165] L.E. Rogers and R.V. Farace. Relational communication analysis: New measurement procedures. *Human Communications Research*, 1:222–239, 1975.

[166] P.C. Rosenblatt. *Metaphors of Family Systems Theory: Toward New Constructions*. Guilford, New York, 1994.

[167] L. Rowell. *Human Circulation: Regulation during Physical Stress*. Oxford University Press, New York, 1986.

[168] R. Rushe. Tactics of power and influence in violent marriages. Ph.D. thesis, University of Washington, Seattle, 1996.

[169] M. Rutter. Protective factors in children's response to stress and disadvantage. In M.W. Kent and J.E. Rolf, editors, *Primary Prevention of Psychopathology, Vol. 3: Social Competence in Children*. University Press of New England, Hanover, NH, 1979.

[170] P.T. Saunders. *An Introduction to Catastrophe Theory*. Cambridge University Press, Cambridge, England, 1990.

[171] C. Schaap. *Communication and Adjustment in Marriage*. Swets–Zeitlinger, Netherlands, 1982.

[172] D.E. Scharff and S.S. Scharff. *Object Relations Couple Therapy*. Jason Aronson, Northvale, NJ, 1991.

[173] L. Schindler, K. Hahlweg, and D. Revenstorf. Short- and long-term effectiveness of two communication training modalities with distressed couples. *American Journal of Family Therapy*, 11(3):54–64, 1983.

[174] P. Schwartz. *Peer Marriage*. The Free Press, New York, 1994.

[175] M.E.P. Seligman. The effectiveness of psychotherapy: The *Consumer Reports* study. *American Psychologist*, 50:965–974, 1995.

[176] W.R. Shadish, L.M. Montgomery, P. Wilson, M.R. Wilson, I. Bright, and T. Okwumabua. Effects of family and marital psychotherapies: A meta-analysis. *Journal of Consulting and Clinical Psychology*, 61(6):992–1002, 1993.

[177] W.R. Shadish and K. Ragsdale. The efficacy and effectiveness of marital and family therapy: A perspective from meta-analysis. *Journal of Marital and Family Therapy*, 21(4):345–360, 1995.

[178] C. Shannon and W. Weaver. *The Mathematical Theory of Communication*. University of Illinois Press, Urbana, Ill., 1949.

[179] D.K. Snyder and R.M. Wills. Behavioral versus insight-oriented marital therapy: Effects on individual and interspousal functioning. *Journal of Consulting and Clinical Psychology*, 57(1):39–46, 1989.

[180] D.K. Snyder, R.M. Wills, and A. Grady-Fletcher. Long-term effectiveness of behavioral versus insight-oriented marital therapy: A 4-year followup study. *Journal of Consulting and Clinical Psychology*, 59(1):138–141, 1991a.

[181] D.K. Snyder, R.M. Wills, and A. Grady-Fletcher. Risks and challenges of long-term psychotherapy outcome research: Reply to jacobson. *Journal of Consulting and Clinical Psychology*, 59(1):146–149, 1991b.

[182] J. Sprey. Family power structure: A critical comment. *Journal of Marriage and the Family*, 34:235–238, 1972.

[183] I.N. Stewart. Catastrophe theory. *Mathematics Chronicle*, 5:140–165, 1977.

[184] M.A. Straus and I. Tallman. Simfam: A technique for observational measurement and experimental study of families. In J. Aldous, T. Concon, R. Hill, M. Straus, and I. Tallman, editors, *Family Problem Solving*. Dryden, Hinsdale, Calif., 1971.

[185] S.H. Strogatz. *Nonlinear Dynamics and Chaos: With Applications in Physics, Biology, Chemistry, and Engineering*. Addison–Wesley, Reading, Mass., 1994.

[186] L.M. Terman, P. Buttenweiser, L.W. Ferguson, W.B. Johnson, and D.P. Wilson. *Psychological Factors in Marital Happiness*. McGraw–Hill, New York, 1938.

[187] Seattle WA The Mathworks, Inc. Matlab 5.3.

[188] J.W. Thibaut and H.H. Kelley. *The Social Psychology of Groups*. Wiley, New York, 1959.

[189] R. Thom. *Stabilité Structurelle et morphogénése*. W.A. Benjamin, Reading, Mass., 1972.

[190] R. Thom and Translation D.H. Fowles. *Structural Stability and Morphogenesis*. W.A. Benjamin, Reading, Mass., 1975.

[191] S. Ting-Toomey. An analysis of verbal communications patterns in high and low marital adjustment groups. *Human Communications Research*, 9:306–319, 1982.

[192] J.L Turk and N.W. Bell. Measuring power in families. *Journal of Marriage and the Family*, 34:215–222, 1972.

[193] R.R. Vallacher and A. Nowak. *Dynamical Systems in Social Psychology*. Academic, New York, 1994.

[194] N.A. Vanzetti, C.I. Notarius, and D. NeeSmith. Specific and generalized expectancies in marital interaction. *Journal of Family Psychology*, 6:171–183, 1992.

[195] J.P. Vincent, L.C. Friedman, J. Nugent, and L. Messerly. Demand characteristics in observations of marital interaction. *Journal of Consulting and Clinical Psychology*, 47:557–566, 1979.

[196] L. von Bertalanffy. *General System Theory*. Braziller, New York, 1968.

[197] K. von Frisch. *The Dancing Bees: An Account of the Life and Senses of the Honey Bee*. Harcourt, Brace and World, New York, 1953.

[198] J. VonNeumann and O. Morgenstern. *Theory of Games and Economic Behavior*. University of Princeton Press, Princeton, NJ, 1947.

[199] P. Watzlawick, J.H. Beavin, and D.D. Jackson. *Pragmatics of Human Communication: A Study of Interactional Patterns, Pathologies and Paradoxes*. W.W. Norton, New York, 1967.

[200] M.S. Weinberg and C.J. Williams. *Male Homosexuals: Their Problems and Adaptations*. Oxford University Press, New York, 1974.

[201] R.L. Weiss, H. Hops, and G.R. Patterson. A framework for conceptualizing marital conflict, a technique for altering it, and some data for evaluating it. In L.A. Hamerlynck, L.C. Handy, and E.J. Mash, editors, *Behavior Change*. Research, Champaign, Calif., 1973.

[202] N. Wiener. *Cybernetics*. Wiley, New York, 1948.

[203] J.S. Wiggins. *Personality and Prediction*. Addison–Wesley, Reading, Mass., 1973.

[204] D.B. Wile. *After the Honeymoon: How Conflict Can Improve Your Relationship*. Wiley, New York, 1988.

[205] R.F. Winch. *Mate Selection: A Study of Complimentary Needs*. Harper and Row, New York, 1958.

[206] E.C. Zeeman. *Catastrophe Theory*. Addison–Wesley, New York, 1976.

[207] E.C. Zeeman. *Catastrophe Theory: Selected Papers 1972–1977*. Addison–Wesley, Reading, Mass., 1987.

Appendix A: Model Analysis

Recall the model is defined by equation (13.3). Along the nullclines: $W_{t+1} = W_t = W$ and $H_{t+1} = H_t = H$. Substitution of these expressions into the model equations (13.3) reveals

$$W = \quad I_{HW}(H) + R_W(H) + D_W(H) + r_1 W + a$$
$$H = \quad I_{WH}(W) + R_H(W) + D_H(W) + r_2 H + b \qquad \text{(A.1)}$$

Solving these gives the nullcines defined by equation (13.4).

Linear Stability Analysis. To determine the stability of the steady states (W^*, H^*) defined by the intersection of the nullclines, we linearize about the steady state and study the dynamics of the linear system. Write $W_t = W^* + w_t$ and $H_t = H^* + h_t$, then where w_t and h_t are small perturbations to the steady state. By definition, the steady state satisfies both of the nullcline equations yielding:

$$W^* = I_{HW}(H^*) + R_W(H^*) + D_W(H^*) + r_1 W^* + a,$$
$$H^* = I_{WH}(W^*) + R_H(W^*) + D_H(W^*) + r_2 H^* + b. \qquad \text{(A.2)}$$

Substitution of the linearization variables (B.11) into the model equations (B.1) with repair defined by (B.3) gives

$$W^* + w_{t+1} = I_{HW}(H^* + h_t) + r_1(W^* + w_t) + a$$
$$+ R_W(H^* + h_t) + D_W(H^* + h_t)$$
$$\approx I_{HW}(H^*) + \alpha_1 h_t + r_1 W^* + r_1 w_t + a$$
$$+ R_W(H^*) + D_W(H^*) + \beta_1 h_t$$

using Taylor series expansions of the right hand side and retaining only linear terms. Similarly,

$$
\begin{aligned}
H^* \mid h_{t+1} &= I_{WH}(W^* + w_t) + r_2(II^* + h_t) + b \\
&\quad + R_H(W^* + w_t) + D_H(W^* + w_t) \\
&\approx I_{WH}(W^*) + \alpha_2 w_t + r_2 H^* + r_2 h_t + b \\
&\quad + R_H(W^*) + D_H(W^*) + \beta_2 w_t
\end{aligned}
$$

where α_i for $i = 1, 2$ represent the slope of the respective influence functions:

$$
\alpha_1 = \left. \frac{dI_{HW}}{dH_t} \right|_{H^*} \qquad \alpha_2 = \left. \frac{dI_{WH}}{dW_t} \right|_{W^*}, \tag{A.3}
$$

and β_i for $i = 1, 2$ represent the slope of either the repair or damage functions depending on which is active at the steady state location:

$$
\beta_1 = \begin{cases} \left. \frac{dR_W}{dH_t} \right|_{H^*} & \text{if } H^* < K_{rh} \\ 0 & \text{if } K_{rh} < H^* < K_{dh} \\ \left. \frac{dD_W}{dH_t} \right|_{H^*} & \text{if } H^* > K_{dh} \end{cases} \tag{A.4}
$$

$$
\beta_2 = \begin{cases} \left. \frac{dR_H}{dH_t} \right|_{W^*} & \text{if } W^* < K_{rw} \\ 0 & \text{if } K_{rw} < W^* < K_{dw} \\ \left. \frac{dD_H}{dW_t} \right|_{W^*} & \text{if } W^* < K_{dw} \end{cases} \tag{A.5}
$$

Since we assume the influence functions are non-decreasing functions, we have $\alpha_i \geq 0$ for $i = 1, 2$. If the husband's steady state location is in a repairing region ($H^* < K_{rh}$), then

$$
\beta_1 = C_{rh} \, \frac{\frac{|H^* - K_{rh}|}{H^* - K_{rh}} - 1}{(1 - (H^* - K_{rh}))^2} < 0,
$$

and if the husband's steady state location is in a damping region ($H^* > K_{dh}$), then

$$
\beta_1 = -C_{dh} \, \frac{\frac{|H^* - K_{dh}|}{H^* - K_{dh}} + 1}{(1 + (H^* - K_{dh}))^2} < 0, \tag{A.7}
$$

and in all other cases $\beta_1 = 0$. If the wife's steady state location is in a repairing region ($W^* < K_{rw}$), then

$$
\beta_2 = C_{rw} \, \frac{\frac{|W^* - K_{rw}|}{W^* - K_{rw}} - 1}{(1 - (W^* - K_{rw}))^2} < 0, \tag{A.8}
$$

and if the wife's steady state location is in a damping region ($W^* > K_{dw}$), then

$$\beta_2 = -C_{dw} \frac{\frac{|W^* - K_{dw}|}{W^* - K_{dw}} + 1}{(1 + (W^* - K_{dw}))^2} < 0, \tag{A.9}$$

and in all other cases $\beta_2 = 0$.

We then have the following linearized equations for the perturbations w_{t+1} and h_{t+1}:

$$w_{t+1} = \alpha_1 h_t + r_1 w_t + \beta_1 h_t,$$
$$h_{t+1} = \alpha_2 w_t + r_2 h_t + \beta_2 w_t. \tag{A.10}$$

For $W^* \neq K_{rw}$ or K_{dw} and $H^* \neq K_{rh}$ or K_{dh}, the linearized system (B.21) can be written in matrix format as

$$\begin{pmatrix} w_{t+1} \\ h_{t+1} \end{pmatrix} = \begin{pmatrix} r_1 & \alpha_1 + \beta_1 \\ \alpha_2 + \beta_2 & r_2 \end{pmatrix} \begin{pmatrix} w_t \\ h_t \end{pmatrix}. \tag{A.11}$$

We seek solutions of the form $w_t \propto \lambda^t$ and $h_t \propto \lambda^t$. This requires that λ solve

$$\det \begin{pmatrix} r_1 - \lambda & \alpha_1 + \beta_1 \\ \alpha_2 + \beta_2 & r_2 - \lambda \end{pmatrix} = 0 \tag{A.12}$$

giving

$$\lambda^2 - \lambda(r_1 + r_2) + r_1 r_2 - (\alpha_1 + \beta_1)(\alpha_2 + \beta_2) = 0. \tag{A.13}$$

Solving for λ we find

$$\lambda_1, \lambda_2 = \frac{r_1 + r_2 \pm \sqrt{(r_1 - r_2)^2 + 4(\alpha_1 + \beta_1)(\alpha_2 + \beta_2)}}{2}. \tag{A.14}$$

The solutions for the perturbations w_t and h_t are given by

$$\begin{pmatrix} w_t \\ h_t \end{pmatrix} = \mathbf{A}\lambda_1^t + \mathbf{B}\lambda_2^t \tag{A.15}$$

where $\mathbf{A}$ and $\mathbf{B}$ are constant coefficient matrices. If $|\lambda_i| < 1$ then the perturbations w_t and h_t decay in time and the associated steady state (W^*, H^*) is stable; otherwise, the steady state is unstable.

For this case, stability of the steady state (W^*, H^*) requires

$$2 > 1 + r_1 r_2 - (\alpha_1 + \beta_1)(\alpha_2 + \beta_2) > |r_1 + r_2|. \tag{A.16}$$

Equivalently,

$$r_1 r_2 - 1 < (\alpha_1 + \beta_1)(\alpha_2 + \beta_2) < \min((r_1 - 1)(r_2 - 1), (r_1 + 1)(r_2 + 1)) \tag{A.17}$$

where $\alpha_i \geq 0$ for $i = 1, 2$.

Appendix B: More Complex Repair and Damping

The marital interaction equations are

$$W_{t+1} = I_{HW}(H_t) + r_1 W_t + a + R_W,$$
$$H_{t+1} = I_{WH}(W_t) + r_2 H_t + b + R_H. \tag{B.1}$$

where R_W, R_H represent repair and D_W, D_H represent damping. In the previous appendix, we demonstrate that both repair and damping are not active at a single steady state. For this reason, we choose to simplify the analysis in this appendix by simply considering only the contributions as a result of repair. Results are analogous when damping contributions are included.

Now, in the this chapter we have considered the case of a fairly simple repair model mechanism. In this appendix, we take the opportunity to consider cases of repair (and damping) that have a more complex model mechanism. Here we assume that the repair terms R_W and R_W will be active (nonzero) if two types of negativity conditions are satisfied as opposed to the single negativity condition required for the repair mechanism discussed in Chapter 9. The two negativity conditions we will consider are:

- Own or spouse's score is sufficiently negative

- Slope of own or spouse's cumulative score over the last two time steps is sufficiently negative

Clearly, there are various repair terms that can satisfy these conditions. We will explore several of these options in the following sections of this appendix.

Summary of Results

The introduction of repair into the marital interaction system affects the location of steady states and stability. Since the shape of the nullclines are adjusted by repair, the location of nullcline intersections (steady states) are also altered. Additionally, as a couple approaches a negative steady state, repair can be triggered sending the couple away from the negative steady state. This process introduces instability to certain negative steady states.

Consider a (sufficiently negative) stable steady state of the marital interaction model without repair (W^*, H^*). Under certain circumstances, with the addition of repair, this steady states may be moved more positively to $(W^{**}, H^{**}) \geq (W^*, H^*)$. In addition to the positive motion of the steady state. The new state (W^{**}, H^{**}) may be unstable if it is sufficiently close to the thresholds of repair. If the steady state is located far below the threshold at which repair is turned on, the stability is unaffected. The bulk effect of repair is to increase the positivity of certain negative steady state and destabilize.

When repair is too strong and influence functions are shallow, instability of the steady state can result. Alternatively, too little repair can account for instability when influence functions are steep. That is, both increasing the slope of the influence function or increasing the effectiveness of repair are destabilizing. So unless one is highly influenced by one's partner, repair is destabilizing. In some cases, for stability, repair must be very disparate between the spouse's. That is, one partner must have highly effective repair while the other does not.

In the next four sections, we describe the details of the model behavior with various repair criteria. The results described above are generically applicable to most of the repair term forms we discuss below.

B.1: Repair Determined by Own Slope and Own Score

Consider the couple is speaking and the wife observes that the conversation has become sufficiently negative. In particular, her score is below the threshold K_{rw} and the slope of her cumulative score is below the threshold S_{rw}:

$$W_t < K_{rw} \quad \text{and} \quad \frac{W_t + W_{t-1}}{2} < S_{rw}. \tag{B.2}$$

As a response to this negativity, a repair attempt by the wife is expected. Similarly, if the husbands score and cumulative score slope are sufficiently negative, a repair attempt by the husband is expected. In this case the repair terms in equation (B.1) are written:

$$R_W = C_{rw} \, \theta \left(S_{rw} - \frac{W_t + W_{t-1}}{2} \right) \frac{|W_t - K_{rw}| - (W_t - K_{rw})}{1 - (W_t - K_{rw})},$$

$$R_H = C_{rh} \, \theta \left(S_{rh} - \frac{H_t + H_{t-1}}{2} \right) \frac{|H_t - K_{rh}| - (H_t - K_{rh})}{1 - (H_t - K_{rh})} \qquad \text{(B.3)}$$

where $\theta(x) = \begin{cases} 1 & \text{if } x > 0 \\ 0 & \text{if } x < 0 \end{cases}$ is the Heaviside function.

Nullclines

Along the W-nullcline, the wife's score W_t does not change: $W_{t+1} = W_t = W_{t-1} = W$. Substitute this into the W_{t+1} equation defined by (B.1) and (B.3) to obtain

$$W = I_{HW}(H_t) + r_1 W + a +$$

$$C_{rw} \, \theta \left(S_{rw} - \frac{W + W}{2} \right) \frac{|W - K_{rw}| - (W - K_{rw})}{1 - (W - K_{rw})}$$

$$\implies (1 - r_1)W - I_{HW}(H_t) - a =$$

$$C_{rw} \, \theta(S_{rw} - W) \frac{|W - K_{rw}| - (W - K_{rw})}{1 - (W - K_{rw})}$$

$$\implies U(W; H_t) = V(W).$$

For each value of H_t, the intersection of the curves $U(W; H_t)$ and $V(W)$ is a point on the W-nullcline. Notice the ";" notation to denote the treatment of H_t as a parameter (not a variable). We wish to determine the portion of parameter space where repair affects the nullcline shape. That is, what parameter relation needs to be satisfied in order for the nullcline to not simply be a shift and stretch of the influence function I_{HW} determined by the system without repair.

$U(W; H_t)$ is a line with positive slope $1 - r_1$. The location of the y-intercept of the $U(W; H_t)$ line varies with $I_{HW}(H_t)$. For W less than $q_{rw} = \min(K_{rw}, S_{rw})$, $V(W)$ is nonzero. The qualitative form of $V(W)$ changes for different choices of the parameters K_{rw} and S_{rw}. figure B.1 exhibits the two cases for $V(W)$. If $K_{rw} \leq S_{rw}$ then $q_{rw} = K_{rw}$ and the function $V(W)$ is continuous; therefore, $U(W; H_t) = V(W)$ has one solution for each choice of H_t. If $K_{rw} > S_{rw}$, the function $V(W)$ is discontinuous and $U(W; H_t) = V(W)$ has at most one solution for each choice of H_t.

For each H_t, if $U(q_{rw}; H_t) < 0$ then the W-nullcline satisfies $U(W; H_t) =$

Case 1: $K_{rw} \leq S_{rw}$

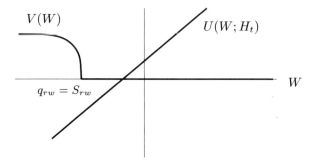

Case 2: $K_{rw} > S_{rw}$

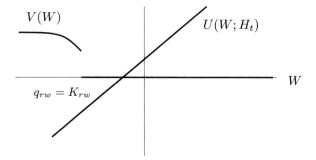

Figure B.1: Intersection of $U(W; H_t)$ and $V(W)$ for a given H_t value is a point on the W-nullcline.

0. Solving for W, we find

$$W = \frac{I_{HW}(H_t) + a}{1 - r_1}. \tag{B.4}$$

This is the case for which repair does not affect the nullcline. If $U(q_{rw}; H_t) \geq V(q_{rw})$ then repair affects the location of the nullcline and $V(W)$ is nonzero. In particular, the line $U(W, H_t)$ intersects the nonzero portion of $V(W)$. The W-nullcline satisfies

$$U(W; H_t) = V(W) \implies \tag{B.5}$$

$$(1 - r_1)W - I_{HW}(H_t) - a = C_{rw}\frac{|W - K_{rw}| - (W - K_{rw})}{1 - (W - K_{rw})}.$$

The intersection of the line $U(W)$ and the curve $V(W)$ occurs at some

$W < q_{rw} \leq K_{rw}$, so the above expression can be simplified to

$$(1 - r_1)W - I_{HW}(H_t) - a = C_{rw}\frac{-2(W - K_{rw})}{1 - (W - K_{rw})}. \quad (B.6)$$

Solving for W we find

$$W = \frac{P - M}{2(1 - r_1)} \quad (B.7)$$

where

$$P = (1 - r_1)(1 + K_{rw}) + a + I_{HW}(H_t) + 2C_{rw} \quad (B.8)$$

$$M = \sqrt{P^2 - 4(1 - r_1)((1 + K_{rw})(a + I_{HW}(H_t)) + 2C_{rw}K_{rw})}. \quad (B.9)$$

Notice that the location of the nullcline is adjusted positively. That is, the repair adjusted nullcline is greater than the nullcline defined by the model without repair. For each H_t,

W-nullcline with repair $\geq$ W-nullcline without repair

$$\frac{P - M}{2(1 - r_1)} \geq \frac{I_{HW}(H_t) + a}{1 - r_1}. \quad (B.10)$$

Now if $0 < U(q_{rw}; H_t) \leq V(q_{rw})$ then $U(W; H_t)$ does not intersect $V(W)$ and the W-nullcline value is undefined for the chosen H_t. Below we combine the above results and describe an algorithm for defining the nullclines of the system (B.1) with repair terms defined by (B.3).

W-nullcline Algorithm:

- Define $q_{rw} = min(K_{rw}, S_{rw})$

- For all values of H_t

    - If $U(q_{rw}; H_t) \geq V(q_{rw})$ then
      $W = \frac{P - M}{2(1 - r_1)}$.

    - Else if $U(q_{rw}; H_t) < 0$ then
      $W = \frac{I_{HW}(H_t) + a}{1 - r_1}$.

    - Else
      W is undefined.

    - End if

- End for

A similar algorithm can be defined for the H-nullcline.

Once the algorithms are used to plot the nullclines in the phase-plane (W-H plane), we can determine the steady states of the system. The intersection points of the two nullclines are the steady states. Without repair the W-nullcline is given by $W = \frac{I_{HW}(H_t)+a}{1-r_1}$. Clearly, the introduction of repair adjusts the location of the nullclines and, therefore, adjusts the location of some of the steady states. In particular, since both the husband and wife nullclines are positively adjusted by repair, we expect the steady states to be more positive than those without repair.

Besides adjusting the location of certain steady states, the repair terms in the model may have the ability to alter the stability of the steady states. To gain a better understand of the stability of the steady states we use the mathematical tool of linear stability analysis.

Linear Stability Analysis

To linearize the system about the steady state (W^*, H^*), we introduce the variables:

$$W_{t+1} = W^* + w_{t+1},$$
$$H_{t+1} = H^* + h_{t+1} \tag{B.11}$$

where w_{t+1} and h_{t+1} are small perturbations to the steady state. By definition of the steady state

$$W^* = I_{HW}(H^*) + r_1 W^* + a + R_W(W^*, W^*),$$
$$H^* = I_{WH}(W^*) + r_2 H^* + b + R_H(H^*, H^*). \tag{B.12}$$

Substitution of the linearization variables (B.11) into the model equations (B.1) with repair defined by (B.3) gives

$$\begin{aligned}
W^* + w_{t+1} &= I_{HW}(H^* + h_t) + r_1(W^* + w_t) + a \\
&\quad + R_W(W^* + w_t, W^* + w_{t-1}) \\
&\approx I_{HW}(H^*) + \alpha_1 h_t + r_1 W^* + r_1 w_t + a \\
&\quad + R_W(W^*, W^*) + \beta_1 w_t + \gamma_1 w_{t-1}.
\end{aligned}$$

using Taylor series expansions of the right hand side and retaining only linear terms. Similarly,

$$\begin{aligned}
H^* + h_{t+1} &= I_{WH}(W^* + w_t) + r_2(H^* + h_t) + b \\
&\quad + R_H(H^* + h_t, H^* + h_{t-1}) \\
&\approx I_{WH}(W^*) + \alpha_2 w_t + r_2 H^* + r_2 h_t + b \\
&\quad + R_H(H^*, H^*) + \beta_2 h_t + \gamma_2 h_{t-1}
\end{aligned}$$

where

$$\alpha_1 = \left.\frac{dI_{HW}}{dH_t}\right|_{H^*} \qquad \alpha_2 = \left.\frac{dI_{WH}}{dW_t}\right|_{W^*}, \qquad (B.13)$$

$$\beta_1 = \left.\frac{\partial R_W}{\partial W_t}\right|_{(W^*,W^*)} \qquad \beta_2 = \left.\frac{\partial R_H}{\partial H_t}\right|_{(H^*,H^*)}, \qquad (B.14)$$

$$\gamma_1 = \left.\frac{\partial R_W}{\partial W_{t-1}}\right|_{(W^*,W^*)} \qquad \gamma_2 = \left.\frac{\partial R_H}{\partial H_{t-1}}\right|_{(H^*,H^*)} \qquad (B.15)$$

By differentiation we have

$$\beta_1 = C_{rw}\ \theta(S_{rw} - W^*)\frac{1}{(1 - (W^* - K_{rw}))^2}\left(\frac{|W^* - K_{rw}|}{W^* - K_{rw}} - 1\right)$$

$$(B.16)$$

$$= \begin{cases} < 0 & \text{if } W^* < \min(S_{rw}, K_{rw}) = q_{rw} \\ DNE & \text{if } W^* = K_{rw} \\ 0 & \text{Otherwise} \end{cases} \qquad (B.17)$$

and

$$\beta_2 - C_{rh}\ \theta(S_{rh} - H^*)\frac{1}{(1 - (H^* - K_{rh}))^2}\left(\frac{|H^* - K_{rh}|}{H^* - K_{rh}} - 1\right) \quad (B.18)$$

$$= \begin{cases} < 0 & \text{if } H^* < \min(S_{rh}, K_{rh}) = q_{rh} \\ DNE & \text{if } H^* = K_{rh} \\ 0 & \text{Otherwise} \end{cases} \qquad (B.19)$$

Additionally,

$$\gamma_1 = \begin{cases} 0 & \text{if } W^* \neq S_{rw} \\ \infty & \text{if } W^* = S_{rw} \end{cases} \quad \text{and} \quad \gamma_2 = \begin{cases} 0 & \text{if } H^* \neq S_{rh} \\ \infty & \text{if } H^* = S_{rh} \end{cases} \qquad (B.20)$$

We then have the linearized equations for the perturbations w_{t+1} and h_{t+1}:

$$w_{t+1} = \alpha_1 h_t + r_1 w_t + \beta_1 w_t + \gamma_1 w_{t-1},$$
$$h_{t+1} = \alpha_2 w_t + r_2 h_t + \beta_2 h_t + \gamma_2 h_{t-1}. \qquad (B.21)$$

This is a linear difference system with delay terms (w_{t-1}, h_{t-1}).

For $W^* \neq S_{rw}$ and $H^* \neq S_{rh}$, $\gamma_1 = \gamma_2 = 0$ and the linearized system (B.21) can be written in matrix format as

$$\begin{pmatrix} w_{t+1} \\ h_{t+1} \end{pmatrix} = \begin{pmatrix} r_1 + \beta_1 & \alpha_1 \\ \alpha_2 & r_2 + \beta_2 \end{pmatrix}\begin{pmatrix} w_t \\ h_t \end{pmatrix}. \qquad (B.22)$$

Notice the delay terms have been eliminated, revealing a much simpler system to solve. We seek solutions of the form $w_t \propto \lambda^t$ and $h_t \propto \lambda^t$. This requires that λ solve

$$\det \begin{pmatrix} r_1 + \beta_1 - \lambda & \alpha_1 \\ \alpha_2 & r_2 + \beta_2 - \lambda \end{pmatrix} = 0 \tag{B.23}$$

giving

$$\lambda^2 - \lambda(r_1 + \beta_1 + r_2 + \beta_2) + (r_1 + \beta_1)(r_2 + \beta_2) - \alpha_1\alpha_2 = 0. \tag{B.24}$$

Solving for λ we find that $\lambda_1, \lambda_2 =$

$$\frac{r_1 + \beta_1 + r_2 + \beta_2}{2} \pm$$

$$\frac{\sqrt{(r_1 + \beta_1 + r_2 + \beta_2)^2 - 4[(r_1 + \beta_1)(r_2 + \beta_2) - \alpha_1\alpha_2]}}{2} \tag{B.25}$$

The solutions for the perturbations w_t and h_t are given by

$$\begin{pmatrix} w_t \\ h_t \end{pmatrix} = \mathbf{A}\lambda_1^t + \mathbf{B}\lambda_2^t \tag{B.26}$$

where $\mathbf{A}$ and $\mathbf{B}$ are constant coefficient matrices. If $|\lambda_i| < 1$ then the perturbations w_t and h_t decay in time and the associated steady state (W^*, H^*) is stable; otherwise, the steady state is unstable.

If we consider a general influence function form not necessarily with the o-jive form we obtain a more complete understanding of the behavior of the system. For stability we need $|\lambda_i| < 1$ for $i = 1, 2$. After some algebra, we find that stability requires

$$2 > 1 + (r_1 + \beta_1)(r_2 + \beta_2) - \alpha_1\alpha_2 > |r_1 + \beta_1 + r_2 + \beta_2|. \tag{B.27}$$

From Figure B.2 we see that those steady states $(W^*, H^*) \ll (q_{rw}, q_{rh})$ have $\beta_i \to 0$ and are therefore generally unaffected by the introduction of repair. Only those steady states near the thresholds $q_{rw} = \min(K_{rw}, S_{rw})$ and $q_{rh} = \min(K_{rh}, S_{rh})$ have $|\beta_i|$ large enough to strongly affect the stability requirements (B.27).

Without repair ($\beta_i = 0$), the stability condition (B.27) simplifies to

$$r_1 r_2 - 1 < \alpha_1\alpha_2 < \min((r_1 - 1)(r_2 - 1), (r_1 + 1)(r_2 + 1)) \tag{B.28}$$

From this we see that influence functions must have low or negative slope when the inertia is high ($|r_i|$ close to 1) for the steady state to be stable.

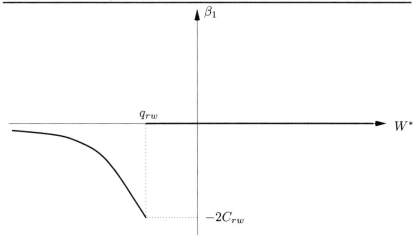

Figure B.2: Own Slope, Own Score. Plot of β_1 versus W. We plot only β_1 and can generalize to β_2. From this plot we see that only those steady states near the trigger q_{rw} strongly affect the stability conditions with repair.

Alternatively, steepening of the influence functions is destabilizing to the steady state.

When repair is present $\beta_i \neq 0$, we can rewrite the stability conditions (B.27) as

$$\gamma_1\gamma_2 - 1 < \alpha_1\alpha_2 < \min((\gamma_1 - 1)(\gamma_2 - 1), (\gamma_1 + 1)(\gamma_2 + 1)) \quad (B.29)$$

where $\gamma_i = r_i + \beta_i$ for $i = 1, 2$. Since $\beta_i < 0$, steady states that would be considered unstable without repair can be stabilized by repair.

Increasing Slope of Influence Function

The shaded regions of Figure B.3 show the portion of the C_{rw}-C_{rh} parameter space where solutions are stable. As the influence functions steepen (i.e. α_i increase), the region of stability for a steady state (W^*, H^*) in the neighborhood of and less than (q_{rw}, q_{rh}) decreases in size. Thus, higher rates of influence associated with larger α_i values, decreases the probability of a stable steady state. In other words, couples that are highly responsive to small changes in score (α_i large) have less of a chance for long term stability.

Interestingly this result also implies that for those couples with higher influence function slopes (α_i large), repair must be small or negligible

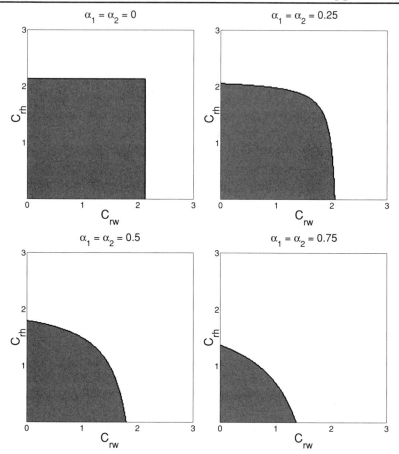

Figure B.3: Own Slope, Own Score. Evolution of stability region as slopes of the influence functions (α_i) increase. For this figure, the steady state (W^*, H^*) is chosen close to the switch (q_{rw}, q_{rh}) where we expect the maximum effect from the repair terms. Parameter values: $r_1 = r_2 = .25, S_{rw} = S_{rh} = -.25, K_{rw} = K_{rh} = -1.0, W^* = H^* = -1.1$.

for the steady state to be stable. Now since repair is only active for sufficiently negative steady states, it is important to notice that effective repair can induce an unstable negative steady state, leading the way for a possible postive stable steady state.

Note that in the stability conditions given by equation (B.27), α_1

and α_2 always appear in the form of the product $\alpha_1\alpha_2$. Therefore, increasing the slope of one of the influence functions has the same effect as increasing the slope of a combination of the two influence functions. For this reason, having one partner that can

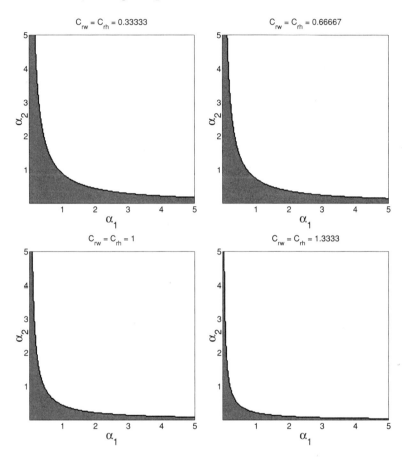

Figure B.4: Own Slope, Own Score. Evolution of stability region as the effectiveness of repair (C_{rw}, C_{dw}) increases (i.e. β_i decreases since $\beta_1 \propto -C_{rw}$ and $\beta_2 \propto -C_{dw}$. For this figure, the steady state is chosen close to the switch (q_{rw}, q_{rh}) where we expect the maximum effect from the repair terms. Parameter values: $r_1 = r_2 = .25, S_{rw} = S_{rh} = -.25, K_{rw} = K_{rh} = -1.0, W^* = H^* = -1.1$.

Increasing Effectiveness of Repair

Figure B.4 shows that increasing the effectiveness of repair decreases the size of the stability region. For fixed α_i (slope of the influence functions), increasing the effectiveness of repair can affect the stability of the steady state (W^*, H^*). For larger effectiveness of repair coefficients, the slopes of the influence functions for both the husband and the wife must decrease in magnitude. Note that there are stable steady states where, say, the wife's influence function slope is very large while the husband's is very small. However, once both partner's influence function slopes increase, stability is not possible.

B.2: Repair Determined by Spouse's Slope and Own Score

Consider it is the wife's turn to speak and she observes that the conversation has become sufficiently negative. In particular, her score is sufficiently negative and the slope of her spouse's cumulative score is sufficiently negative. In this case the repair terms are written:

$$
R_W = C_{rw} \; \theta \left(S_{rh} - \frac{H_t + H_{t-1}}{2} \right) \frac{|W_t - K_{rw}| - (W_t - K_{rw})}{1 - (W_t - K_{rw})},
$$

$$
R_H = C_{rh} \; \theta \left(S_{rw} - \frac{W_t + W_{t-1}}{2} \right) \frac{|H_t - K_{rh}| - (H_t - K_{rh})}{1 - (H_t - K_{rh})}. \tag{B.30}
$$

Nullclines

Along the wife's nullcline, $W_{t+1} = W_t = W$ and

$$
W = I_{HW}(H_t) + r_1 W + a +
$$
$$
C_{rw} \; \theta \left(S_{rh} - \frac{H_t + H_{t-1}}{2} \right) \frac{|W - K_{rw}| - (W - K_{rw})}{1 - (W - K_{rw})}. \tag{B.31}
$$

The wife's nullcline is in fact a surface in the H_t-H_{t-1} plane. Similarly, the H-nullcline is a surface in the W_{t+1}-W_t plane. In order to visualize the precise dynamics of the system we would have to plot the nullclines together in a 4-dimensional space (H_t-H_{t-1}-W_{t+1}-W_t space). But our ultimate goal is to determine the location and stability of the steady states of the system. So we take a slightly different approach to this problem.

A steady state of the system (B.1) with repair (B.30) satisfies ($W_{t+1} = W_t = W$ and $H_{t+1} = H_t = H$):

$$W = I_{HW}(H) + r_1 W + a + C_{rw}\, \theta\,(S_{rh} - H)\, \frac{|W - K_{rw}| - (W - K_{rw})}{1 - (W - K_{rw})},$$

$$H = I_{WH}(W) + r_2 H + b + C_{rh}\, \theta\,(S_{rw} - W)\, \frac{|H - K_{rh}| - (H - K_{rh})}{1 - (H - K_{rh})}.$$

$$(B.32)$$

These curves can be plotted in the W-H plane. Their intersection points are the steady states (W^*, H^*). Although these curves are not the actual nullclines for the system (B.1) and (B.30), they are projections of the nullcline equations defined in a four-dimensional space to curves defined in a two-dimensional space. From this point on we will refer to the set of curves (B.32) as the nullcurves (instead of nullclines). The first equation in (B.32) is the W-nullcurve and the second equation in (B.32) is the H-nullcurve.

To determine the steady states of the system, we must plot the null-curves (B.32) in the W-H plane. For brevity, we will only consider the W-nullcurve. For each H a point on the W-nullcurve satisfies

$$(1 - r_1)W - I_{HW}(H) - a = C_{rw}\, \theta\,(S_{rh} - H)\, \frac{|W - K_{rw}| - (W - K_{rw})}{1 - (W - K_{rw})}$$

$$(B.33)$$

$$U(W; H) = V(W; H) \tag{B.34}$$

Notice that there is always one solution to $U(W; H) = V(W; H)$.

If $H > S_{rh}$ then $V(W; H) = 0$ and W satisfies $U(W; H) = 0$:

$$W = \frac{I_{HW}(H) + a}{1 - r_1}. \tag{B.35}$$

For $H < S_{rh}$ then $V(W; H)$ may be nonzero. To solve for W in this case we refer to the graph of the function U and V. (See Figure B.5.)

If $H < S_{rh}$ and $U(K_{rw}; H) > 0$ then the line $U(W)$ intersects with the nonzero portion of $V(W)$ and W satisfies

$$(1 - r_1)W - I_{HW}(H) - a = C_{rw}\, \frac{|W - K_{rw}| - (W - K_{rw})}{1 - (W - K_{rw})}. \tag{B.36}$$

Graphically, it is clear that the intersection occurs for $W < K_{rw}$, so W now satisfies

$$(1 - r_1)W - I_{HW}(H) - a = C_{rw}\, \frac{-2(W - K_{rw})}{1 - (W - K_{rw})} \tag{B.37}$$

Case 1: $H < S_{rh}$

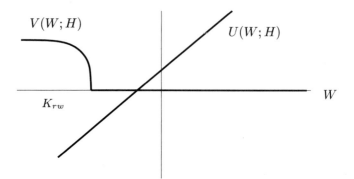

Case 2: $H > S_{rh}$

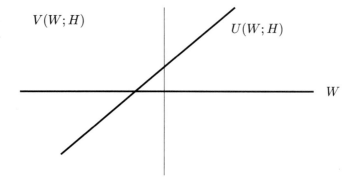

Figure B.5: Spouse's Slope, Own Score. Intersection of $U(W)$ and $V(W)$ for a given H value is a point on the W-nullcline.

which has solution

$$W = \frac{P - M}{2(1 - r_1)}$$ (B.38)

where

$$P = (1 - r_1)(1 + K_{rw}) + a + I_{HW}(H) + 2C_{rw},$$ (B.39)

$$M = \sqrt{P^2 - 4(1 - r_1)((1 + K_{rw})(a + I_{HW}(H)) + 2C_{rw}K_{rw})}.$$ (B.40)

Otherwise, the W-nullcurve is defined by equation (B.35).

We incorporate the above results to describe an algorithm for defining the nullcurves and therefore determining the steady states.

W-nullcurve Algorithm:

- For all values of H

    - If $H < S_{rh}$ and $U(K_{rw}) > 0$ then
        W is defined by equation (B.38)
    - Else
        $$W = \frac{a + I_{HW}(H)}{1 - r_1}$$
    - End if

- End for

A similar algorithm can be derived for the H-nullcurve.

Linear Stability Analysis

To linearize the system about the steady state (W^*, H^*), we introduce the variables:

$$W_{t+1} = W^* + w_{t+1},$$
$$H_{t+1} = H^* + h_{t+1} \tag{B.41}$$

where w_{t+1} and h_{t+1} are small. By definition of the steady state

$$W^* = I_{HW}(H^*) + r_1 W^* + a + R_W(H^*, H^*, W^*),$$
$$H^* = I_{WH}(W^*) + r_2 H^* + b + R_H(W^*, W^*, H^*). \tag{B.42}$$

Substitution of the linearization variables (B.41) into the model equations (B.1) gives

$$
\begin{aligned}
W^* + w_{t+1} &= I_{HW}(H^* + h_t) + r_1(W^* + w_t) + a \\
&\quad + R_W(H^* + h_t, H^* + h_{t-1}, W^* + w_t) \\
&\approx I_{HW}(H^*) + \alpha_1 h_t + r_1 W^* + r_1 w_t + a \\
&\quad + R_W(H^*, H^*, W^*) + \beta_1 h_t + \gamma_1 h_{t-1} + \epsilon_1 w_t.
\end{aligned}
$$

using Taylor series expansions of the right hand side and retaining only linear terms. Similarly,

$$
\begin{aligned}
H^* + h_{t+1} &= I_{WH}(W^* + w_{t+1}) + r_2(H^* + h_t) + b \\
&\quad + R_H(W^* + w_t, W^* + w_{t-1}, H^* + h_t) \\
&\approx I_{WH}(W^*) + \alpha_2 w_t + r_2 H^* + r_2 h_t + b \\
&\quad + R_H(W^*, W^*, H^*) + \beta_2 w_t + \gamma_2 w_{t-1} + \epsilon_2 h_t
\end{aligned}
$$

where α_i represent the slope of the influence functions:

$$\alpha_1 = \left.\frac{dI_{HW}}{dII_t}\right|_{H^*} \qquad\qquad \alpha_2 = \left.\frac{dI_{WH}}{dW_t}\right|_{W^*} \qquad (B.43)$$

and $\beta_i, \gamma_i, \epsilon_i$ represent the partial derivatives of the repair or damage terms:

$$\beta_1 = \left.\frac{\partial R_W}{\partial H_t}\right|_{(H^*,H^*,W^*)} \qquad \beta_2 = \left.\frac{\partial R_H}{\partial W_t}\right|_{(W^*,W^*,H^*)} \qquad (B.44)$$

$$\gamma_1 = \left.\frac{\partial R_W}{\partial H_{t-1}}\right|_{(H^*,H^*,W^*)} \qquad \gamma_2 = \left.\frac{\partial R_H}{\partial W_{t-1}}\right|_{(W^*,W^*,H^*)} \qquad (B.45)$$

$$\epsilon_1 = \left.\frac{\partial R_W}{\partial W_t}\right|_{(H^*,H^*,W^*)} \qquad \epsilon_2 = \left.\frac{\partial R_H}{\partial H_t}\right|_{(W^*,W^*,H^*)} \qquad (B.46)$$

We then have the linearized equations for the perturbations w_{t+1} and h_{t+1}:

$$w_{t+1} = \alpha_1 h_t + r_1 w_t + \beta_1 h_t + \gamma_1 h_{t-1} + \epsilon_1 w_t,$$
$$h_{t+1} = \alpha_2 w_t + r_2 h_t + \beta_2 w_t + \gamma_2 w_{t-1} + \epsilon_2 h_t. \qquad (B.47)$$

This is a linear difference system with delay terms (w_{t-1}, h_{t-1}). Before we attempt to solve this system, we need to obtain better knowledge of the coefficients $\alpha_i, \beta_i, \gamma_i, \epsilon_i$ for $i = 1, 2$.

$$\epsilon_1 = \gamma_1 = \begin{cases} 0 & \text{if } H^* \neq S_{rh} \\ \infty & \text{if } H^* = S_{rh} \end{cases} \qquad (B.48)$$

and

$$\epsilon_2 = \gamma_2 = \begin{cases} 0 & \text{if } W^* \neq S_{rw} \\ \infty & \text{if } W^* = S_{rw} \end{cases}. \qquad (B.49)$$

The singularities at $W^* = S_{rw}$ and $H^* = S_{rh}$ are due to the heaviside functions in the repair terms.

By differentiation we have

$$\beta_1 = C_{rw}\, \theta(S_{rh} - H^*)\frac{1}{(1 - (W^* - K_{rw}))^2}\left(\frac{|W^* - K_{rw}|}{W^* - K_{rw}} - 1\right) \quad (B.50)$$

$$= \begin{cases} < 0 & \text{if } W^* < K_{rw} \text{ and } H^* < S_{rh} \\ DNE & \text{if } W^* = K_{rw} \\ 0 & \text{Otherwise} \end{cases} \qquad (B.51)$$

and

$$\beta_2 = C_{rh}\, \theta(S_{rw} - W^*)\frac{1}{(1 - (H^* - K_{rh}))^2}\left(\frac{|H^* - K_{rh}|}{H^* - K_{rh}} - 1\right) \quad (B.52)$$

$$= \begin{cases} < 0 & \text{if } H^* < K_{rh} \text{ and } W^* < S_{rw} \\ DNE & \text{if } H^* = K_{rh} \\ 0 & \text{Otherwise} \end{cases} \quad (B.53)$$

where DNE means "does not exist". The DNE's are due to the kink in R_W and R_H at $W^* = K_{rw}$ and $H^* = K_{rh}$, respectively. Notice that only sufficiently negative steady states have nonzero β_1 and β_2. In addition, as $W^* \to -\infty$, $\beta_1 \to 0$ and as $H^* \to -\infty$, $\beta_2 \to 0$.

For $W^* \neq S_{rw}$ and $H^* \neq S_{rh}$, $\gamma_i = \beta_i = 0$ and the linearized system (B.47) can be written in matrix format as

$$\begin{pmatrix} w_{t+1} \\ h_{t+1} \end{pmatrix} = \begin{pmatrix} r_1 + \beta_1 & \alpha_1 \\ \alpha_2 & r_2 + \beta_2 \end{pmatrix}\begin{pmatrix} w_t \\ h_t \end{pmatrix}. \quad (B.54)$$

Notice the delay terms have been eliminated, revealing a much simpler system to solve. We seek solutions of the form $w_t \propto \lambda^t$ and $h_t \propto \lambda^t$. This requires that λ solve

$$\det\begin{pmatrix} r_1 + \beta_1 - \lambda & \alpha_1 \\ \alpha_2 & r_2 + \beta_2 - \lambda \end{pmatrix} = 0 \quad (B.55)$$

giving

$$\lambda^2 + (r_1 + \beta_1 + r_2 + \beta_2)\lambda + (r_1 + \beta_1)(r_2 + \beta_2) - \alpha_1\alpha_2 = 0 \quad (B.56)$$

Solving for λ gives $\lambda_1, \lambda_2 =$

$$\frac{r_1 + \beta_1 + r_2 + \beta_2}{2} \pm$$

$$\frac{\sqrt{(r_1 + \beta_1 + r_2 + \beta_2)^2 - 4[(r_1 + \beta_1)(r_2 + \beta_2) - \alpha_1\alpha_2]}}{2}. \quad (B.57)$$

This solution yields the same stability conditions as those given in the previous section for repair or damage defined by one's own slope and own score.

B.3: Repair Determined by Own Slope and Spouse's Score

Consider it is the wife's turn to speak and she observes that the conversation has become sufficiently negative. In particular, her spouse's score is sufficiently negative and the slope of her cumulative score is sufficiently negative. In this case the repair terms are written:

$$R_W = C_{rw}\,\theta\left(S_{rw} - \frac{W_t + W_{t-1}}{2}\right)\frac{|H_t - K_{rh}| - (H_t - K_{rh})}{1 - (H_t - K_{rh})},$$

$$R_H = C_{rh}\,\theta\left(S_{rh} - \frac{H_t + H_{t-1}}{2}\right)\frac{|W_t - K_{rw}| - (W_t - K_{rw})}{1 - (W_t - K_{rw})}. \quad (B.58)$$

Nullclines

Along the wife's nullcline, $W_{t+1} = W_t = W$ and

$$W = I_{HW}(H_t) + r_1 W + a + C_{rw}\,\theta\,(S_{rw} - W)\frac{|H_t - K_{rh}| - (H_t - K_{rh})}{1 - (H_t - K_{rh})}$$

$$\implies (1 - r_1)W - I_{HW}(H_t) - a =$$

$$C_{rw}\,\theta\,(S_{rw} - W)\frac{|H_t - K_{rh}| - (H_t - K_{rh})}{1 - (H_t - K_{rh})}$$

$$\implies U(W; H_t) = V(W; H_t)$$

Notice there is either 0 or 1 solutions to $U(W; H_t) = V(W; H_t)$ for each H_t.

If $H_t > K_{rh}$ then $V(W; H_t) = 0$ and W satisfies $U(W; H_t) = 0$:

$$W = \frac{I_{HW}(H_t) + a}{1 - r_1}. \quad (B.59)$$

For $H_t < K_{rh}$ then $V(W; H_t)$ may be nonzero. To solve for W in this case we refer to the graph of the function U and V. (See Figure B.6.) If $H_t < K_{rh}$ and $U(S_{rw}; H_t) > \frac{|H_t - K_{rh}| - (H_t - K_{rh})}{1 - (H_t - K_{rh})}$ then the line $U(W; H_t)$ intersects with the nonzero portion of $V(W; H_t)$ and W satisfies

$$(1 - r_1)W - I_{HW}(H_t) - a = C_{rw}\frac{|H_t - K_{rh}| - (H_t - K_{rh})}{1 - (H_t - K_{rh})} \quad (B.60)$$

$$\implies (1 - r_1)W - I_{HW}(H_t) - a = C_{rw}\frac{-2(H_t - K_{rh})}{1 - (H_t - K_{rh})} \quad (B.61)$$

which has solution

$$W = \frac{a + I_{HW}(H_t) - C_{rw}\frac{2(H_t - K_{rh})}{1 - (H_t - K_{rh})}}{1 - r_1} > \frac{I_{HW}(H_t) + a}{1 - r_1}. \quad (B.62)$$

If $H_t < K_{rh}$ and $U(S_{rw}; H_t) < 0$ then the line $U(W; H_t)$ intersects $V(W; H_t) = 0$ and the W-nullcline is defined by equation (B.59). For other choices of H_t, the W-nullcline is undefined since the line $U(W; H_t)$ passes through the vertical portion of $V(W; H_t)$.

Case 1: $H_t < K_{rh}$

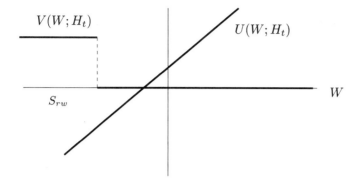

Case 2: $H_t > K_{rh}$

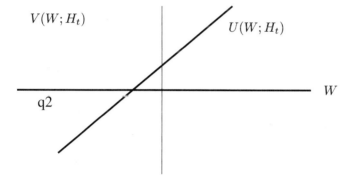

Figure B.6: Own Slope, Spouse's Score. Intersection of $U(W; H_t)$ and $V(W; H_t)$ for a given H_t value is a point on the W-nullcline.

W-nullcline Algorithm:

- For H_t from $hmin$ to $hmax$

    - If $H_t > K_{rh}$ then
      $$W = \frac{a + I_{HW}(H_t)}{1 - r_1}.$$
    - End if
    - If $H_t < K_{rh}$ then
        * If $U(S_{rw}; H_t) < 0$ then
          $$W = \frac{a + I_{HW}(H_t)}{1 - r_1}.$$

* Else if $U(S_{rw}; H_t) > C_{rw} \frac{|H_t - K_{rh}| - (H_t - K_{rh})}{1 - (H_t - K_{rh})}$ then

$$W = \frac{1}{1 - r_1}\left(a + I_{HW}(H_t) - C_{rw}\frac{2(H_t - K_{rh})}{1 - (H_t - K_{rh})}\right).$$

    * Else

        W is undefined.

    * End if

   – End if

- End for

A similar algorithm can be defined for the H-nullcline.

Linear Stability Analysis

To linearize the system about the steady state (W^*, H^*), we introduce the variables:

$$W_{t+1} = W^* + w_{t+1},$$
$$H_{t+1} = H^* + h_{t+1} \tag{B.63}$$

where w_{t+1} and h_{t+1} are small. By definition of the steady state

$$W^* = I_{HW}(H^*) + r_1 W^* + a + R_W(W^*, W^*, H^*),$$
$$H^* = I_{WH}(W^*) + r_2 H^* + b + R_H(H^*, H^*, W^*). \tag{B.64}$$

Substitution of the linearization variables (B.63) into the model equations (B.1) gives

$$\begin{aligned}
W^* + w_{t+1} &= I_{HW}(H^* + h_t) + r_1(W^* + w_t) + a \\
&\quad + R_W(W^* + h_t, W^* + h_{t-1}, H^* + w_t) \\
&\approx I_{HW}(H^*) + \alpha_1 h_t + r_1 W^* + r_1 w_t + a \\
&\quad + R_W(W^*, W^*, H^*) + \beta_1 w_t + \gamma_1 w_{t-1} + \epsilon_1 h_t.
\end{aligned}$$

using Taylor series expansions of the right hand side and retaining only linear terms. Similarly,

$$\begin{aligned}
H^* + h_{t+1} &= I_{WH}(W^* + w_{t+1}) + r_2(H^* + h_t) + b \\
&\quad + R_H(H^* + h_t, H^* + h_{t-1}, W^* + w_t) \\
&\approx I_{WH}(W^*) + \alpha_2 w_t + r_2 H^* + r_2 h_t + b \\
&\quad + R_H(H^*, H^*, W^*) + \beta_2 h_t + \gamma_2 h_{t-1} + \epsilon_2 w_t
\end{aligned}$$

where α_i are the slopes of the influence functions:

$$\alpha_1 = \left.\frac{dI_{HW}}{dH_t}\right|_{H^*} \qquad\qquad \alpha_2 = \left.\frac{dI_{WH}}{dW_{t+1}}\right|_{W^*} \tag{B.65}$$

and $\beta_i, \gamma_i, \epsilon_i$ are the partial derivatives of the repair or damage terms:

$$\epsilon_1 = \left.\frac{\partial R_W}{\partial W_t}\right|_{(W^*,W^*,H^*)} \qquad \epsilon_2 = \left.\frac{\partial R_H}{\partial H_t}\right|_{(H^*,H^*,W^*)} \qquad \text{(B.66)}$$

$$\gamma_1 = \left.\frac{\partial R_W}{\partial W_{t-1}}\right|_{(W^*,W^*,H^*)} \qquad \gamma_2 = \left.\frac{\partial R_H}{\partial H_{t-1}}\right|_{(H^*,H^*,W^*)} \qquad \text{(B.67)}$$

$$\beta_1 = \left.\frac{\partial R_W}{\partial H_t}\right|_{(W^*,W^*,H^*)} \qquad \beta_2 = \left.\frac{\partial R_H}{\partial W_t}\right|_{(H^*,H^*,W^*)} \qquad \text{(B.68)}$$

We then have the linearized equations for the perturbations w_{t+1} and h_{t+1}:

$$w_{t+1} = \alpha_1 h_t + r_1 w_t + \epsilon_1 w_t + \gamma_1 w_{t-1} + \beta_1 h_t,$$
$$h_{t+1} = \alpha_2 w_t + r_2 h_t + \epsilon_2 h_t + \gamma_2 h_{t-1} + \beta_2 w_t. \qquad \text{(B.69)}$$

This is a linear difference system with delay terms (w_{t-1}, h_{t-1}). Before we attempt to solve this system, we need to obtain better knowledge of the coefficients $\alpha_i, \beta_i, \gamma_i, \epsilon_i$ for $i = 1, 2$.

Differentiation defines

$$\epsilon_1 = \gamma_1 = \begin{cases} 0 & \text{if } W^* \neq S_{rw} \\ \infty & \text{if } W^* = S_{rw} \end{cases} \qquad \text{(B.70)}$$

and

$$\epsilon_2 = \gamma_2 = \begin{cases} 0 & \text{if } H^* \neq S_{rh} \\ \infty & \text{if } H^* = S_{rh} \end{cases}. \qquad \text{(B.71)}$$

The singularities at $W^* = S_{rw}$ and $H^* = S_{rh}$ are due to the heaviside functions in the repair terms.

By differentiation we have

$$\beta_1 = C_{rw}\, \theta(S_{rw} - W^*) \frac{1}{(1 - (H^* - K_{rh}))^2} \left(\frac{|H^* - K_{rh}|}{H^* - K_{rh}} - 1\right) \qquad \text{(B.72)}$$

$$= \begin{cases} < 0 & \text{if } H^* < K_{rh} \text{ and } W^* < S_{rw} \\ DNE & \text{if } H^* = K_{rh} \\ 0 & \text{otherwise} \end{cases}$$

and

$$\beta_2 = C_{rh}\, \theta(S_{rh} - H^*) \frac{1}{(1 - (W^* - K_{rw}))^2} \left(\frac{|W^* - K_{rw}|}{W^* - K_{rw}} - 1\right) \qquad \text{(B.73)}$$

$$= \begin{cases} < 0 & \text{if } W^* < K_{rw} \text{ and } H^* < S_{rh} \\ DNE & \text{if } W^* = K_{rw} \\ 0 & \text{otherwise} \end{cases}$$

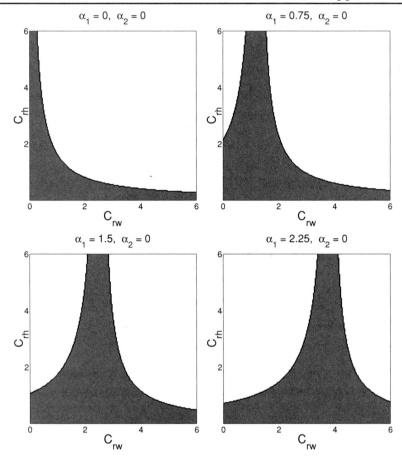

Figure B.7: Own Slope, Spouse's Score. Evolution of stability region as slope of wife's influence function (α_1) changes for $(s_i > k_i)$ where $i = w, k$. For this figure, the steady state is chosen close to the switch (q_{rw}, q_{rh}) where we expect the maximum effect from the repair terms. Parameter values: $r_1 = r_2 = .25, S_{rw} = S_{rh} = -.25, K_{rw} = K_{rh} = -1.0, W^* = H^* = -1.1$.

where DNE means "does not exist". The DNE's are due to the kinks in R_W and R_H at $H^* = K_{rh}$ and $W^* = K_{rw}$, respectively. Notice that only sufficiently negative steady states have nonzero β_1 and β_2. In addition, as $W^* \to -\infty$, $\beta_1 \to 0$ and as $H^* \to -\infty$, $\beta_2 \to 0$.

For $W^* \neq S_{rw}$ and $H^* \neq S_{rh}$, $\gamma_i = \epsilon_i = 0$ and the linearized system

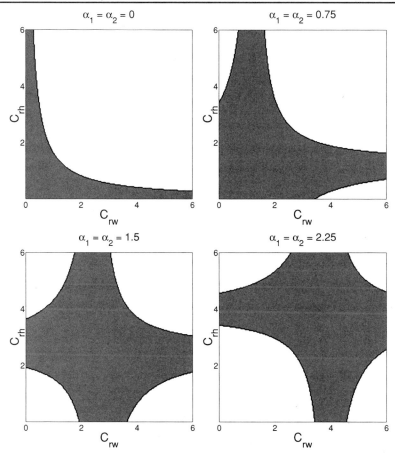

Figure B.8: Own Slope, Spouse's Score. Evolution of stability region as slope of both influence functions (α_1 and α_2) are increased. Parameter values: $r_1 = r_2 = .25, S_{rw} = S_{rh} = -.25, K_{rw} = K_{rh} = -1.0, W^* = H^* = -1.1$.

(B.69) can be written in matrix format as

$$\begin{pmatrix} w_{t+1} \\ h_{t+1} \end{pmatrix} = \begin{pmatrix} r_1 & \alpha_1 + \beta_1 \\ \alpha_2 + \beta_2 & r_2 \end{pmatrix} \begin{pmatrix} w_t \\ h_t \end{pmatrix}. \qquad \text{(B.74)}$$

Notice the delay terms have been eliminated, revealing a much simpler system to solve. We seek solutions of the form $w_t \propto \lambda^t$ and $h_t \propto \lambda^t$.

This requires that λ solve

$$\det \begin{pmatrix} r_1 - \lambda & \alpha_1 + \beta_1 \\ \alpha_2 + \beta_2 & r_2 - \lambda \end{pmatrix} = 0 \tag{B.75}$$

giving

$$\lambda_1, \lambda_2 = \frac{r_1 + r_2 \pm \sqrt{(r_1 - r_2)^2 + 4(\alpha_1 + \beta_1)(\alpha_2 + \beta_2)}}{2}. \tag{B.76}$$

The solutions for the perturbations w_t and h_t are given by

$$\begin{pmatrix} w_t \\ h_t \end{pmatrix} = \mathbf{A}\lambda_1^t + \mathbf{B}\lambda_2^t \tag{B.77}$$

where $\mathbf{A}$ and $\mathbf{B}$ are constant coefficient matrices. If $|\lambda_i| < 1$ then the perturbations w_t and h_t decay in time and the associated steady state (W^*, H^*) is stable; otherwise, the steady state is unstable.

We consider a general influence function form such that at any given steady state α_i (the slope of each influence function) is a parameter. In this way we can determine the behavior of the marital system under an arbitrary influence function form. For stability we need $|\lambda_i| < 1$ for $i = 1, 2$ which implies

$$2 > 1 + r_1 r_2 - (\alpha_1 + \beta_1)(\alpha_2 + \beta_2) > |r_1 + r_2|. \tag{B.78}$$

Since $\alpha_i \geq 0$, then without repair ($\beta_i = 0$), the stability condition (B.78) simplifies to

$$\max(0, r_1 r_2 - 1) < \alpha_1 \alpha_2 < \min((r_1 - 1)(r_2 - 1), (r_1 + 1)(r_2 + 1)) \tag{B.79}$$

The influence function must have low or negative slope for the steady state to be stable when inertia is high ($r_i \approx 1$). That is, steepening of the influence function destabilizes the steady state.

When repair is active ($\beta_i \neq 0$), the stability condition (B.78) is written

$$r_1 r_2 - 1 < (\alpha_1 + \beta_1)(\alpha_2 + \beta_2) < \min((r_1 - 1)(r_2 - 1), (r_1 + 1)(r_2 + 1)) \tag{B.80}$$

Since $\beta_1 \propto C_{rw}$ and $\beta_2 \propto C_{rh}$, the stability condition (B.78) can be violated by increasing the effectiveness of repair C_{rw} and/or C_{rh}.

Figure B.9 shows the regions of the $\alpha_1 - \alpha_2$ plane where the steady state is stable as one of the effectiveness of repair coefficients C_{rw} is increased.

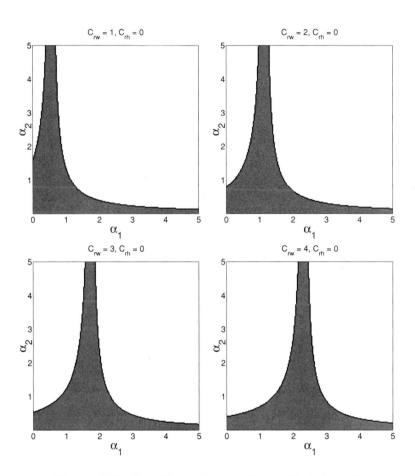

Figure B.9: Own Slope, Spouse's Score. Evolution of stability region of the $\alpha_1 - \alpha_2$ plane for increasing values of the wife's effectiveness of repair coefficients C_{rw}. Parameter values: $r_1 = r_2 = .25, S_{rw} = S_{rh} = -.25, K_{rw} = K_{rh} = -1.0, W^* = H^* = -1.1$.

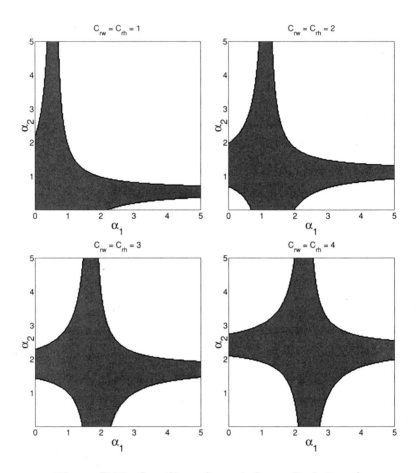

Figure B.10: Own Slope, Spouse's Score. Evolution of stability region of the $\alpha_1 - \alpha_2$ plane for increasing values of the effectiveness of repair coefficients C_{rw}, C_{rh}. Parameter values: $r_1 = r_2 = .25, S_{rw} = S_{rh} = -.25, K_{rw} = K_{rh} = -1.0, W^* = H^* = -1.1$.

Increasing Slope of Influence Function

Figure B.7 demonstrates the regions in the C_{rw}-C_{rh} parameter space where steady state solutions to (B.1) with (B.58) are stable. As the wife's influence function steepens (i.e. α_1 increases), the region of stability for a steady state (W^*, H^*) near (and below) (q_{rw}, q_{rh}) move right and eventually falls from the the domain of reasonable repair effectiveness coefficients C_{rw} and C_{rh}.

Increasing slope of the wife's influence function requires the wife to increase her effectiveness of repair for stability. That is, if the wife is strongly influenced by the husband, then, to retain stability, the wife must counter this with an augmented repair term. The husband's repair term is free to vary.

Figure B.8 indicates that if both influence function are steepened, the stability domain moves in the positive C_{rw} and C_{rh} directions. Therefore, for stability with increasing influence, effectiveness of repair by both partners must be increased for stability.

Increasing Effectiveness of Repair

Figure B.10 indicates that increasing the effectiveness of repair requires the slope of the wife's influence function to increase for stability. Also, for a fixed α_1 (slope of the wife's influence function), increasing the effectiveness of repair can affect the stability to the steady state (W^*, H^*). Additionally, as the wife's effectiveness of repair increases, the stability region moves rightward thereby requiring the wife's influence function slope to increase for stability. From this we expect that if both partners increase the effectiveness of repair, both influence functions must steepen for stability.

B.4: Repair Determined by Spouse's Slope and Spouse's Score

Consider it is the wife's turn to speak (W_{t+1} is about to be determined). She observes that the conversation has become sufficiently negative. In particular, her spouse's score is below the threshold K_{rh} and the slope of her spouse's cumulative score is below the threshold S_{rh}:

$$\frac{H_t + H_{t-1}}{2} < S_{rh}. \tag{B.81}$$

As a response to this negativity, a repair attempt by the wife is expected. Similarly, if the wife's score and cumulative score slope are sufficiently negative, a repair attempt by the husband is expected. In this case the repair terms are written:

$$R_W = C_{rw} \ \theta \left(S_{rh} - \frac{H_t + H_{t-1}}{2} \right) \frac{|II_t - K_{rh}| - (H_t - K_{rh})}{1 - (H_t - K_{rh})},$$

$$R_H = C_{rh} \ \theta \left(S_{rw} - \frac{W_t + W_{t-1}}{2} \right) \frac{|W_t - K_{rw}| - (W_t - K_{rw})}{1 - (W_t - K_{rw})}. \quad \text{(B.82)}$$

Nullclines

Along the W-nullcline, the wife's score W_t does not change: $W_{t+1} = W_t = W_{t-1} = W$. Substitute this into the W_{t+1} equation defined by (B.1) and (B.82) to obtain

$$W = I_{HW}(H_t) + r_1 W + a$$
$$+ C_{rw} \ \theta \left(S_{rh} - \frac{H_t + H_{t-1}}{2} \right) \frac{|H_t - K_{rh}| - (H_t - K_{rh})}{1 - (H_t - K_{rh})}.$$

The wife's nullcline is in fact a surface in the H_t-H_{t-1} plane. Similarly, the H-nullcline is a surface in the W_t-W_{t-1} plane. In order to visualize the precise dynamics of the system we would have to plot the nullclines together in a 4-dimensional space (H_t-H_{t-1}-W_t-W_{t-1} space). But our ultimate goal is to determine the location and stability of the steady states of the system. So we take a slightly different approach to this problem. A steady state of the system (B.1) with repair (B.82) satisfies $W_{t+1} = W_t = W$ and $H_{t+1} = H_t = H$:

$$W = I_{HW}(H) + r_1 W + a + C_{rw} \ \theta \left(S_{rh} - H \right) \frac{|H - K_{rh}| - (H - K_{rh})}{1 - (H - K_{rh})},$$

$$H = I_{WH}(W) + r_2 H + b + C_{rh} \ \theta \left(S_{rw} - W \right) \frac{|W - K_{rw}| - (W - K_{rw})}{1 - (W - K_{rw})}.$$
$$\text{(B.83)}$$

These curves can be plotted in the W-H plane. Their intersection points are the steady states (W^*, H^*). Although these curves are not the actual nullclines for the system (B.1), they are projections of the nullcline equations defined in a four-dimensional space to curves defined in a two-dimensional space. From this point on we will refer to the set of curves (B.83) as the nullcurves (instead of nullclines). The first equation in (B.83) is the W-nullcurve and the second equation in (B.83) is the H-nullcurve.

For each H, the W nullcurve satisfies

$$W = \frac{1}{1 - r_1} \Big(I_{HW}(H) + a + $$

$$C_{rw} \, \theta \, (S_{rh} - H) \frac{|H - K_{rh}| - (H - K_{rh})}{1 - (H - K_{rh})} \Big). \qquad (B.84)$$

If $H < q_{rh} = \min(S_{rh}, K_{rh})$, then repair is active and the W nullcurve without repair is increased in the W-H plane. For each W, the H nullcurve satisfies

$$H = \frac{1}{1 - r_2} \Big(I_{WH}(W) + b + $$

$$C_{rh} \, \theta \, (S_{rw} - W) \frac{|W - K_{rw}| - (W - K_{rw})}{1 - (W - K_{rw})} \Big). \qquad (B.85)$$

If $W < q_{rw} = \min(S_{rw}, K_{rw})$, then repair is active and the H nullcurve without repair is increased in the H-W plane. The effect of the repair term is to increase sufficiently negative steady states. That is, the repair adjusted nullcurve is greater than the nullcline defined by the model without repair. For each H,

W-nullcurve with repair $\geq$ W-nullcurve without repair

Below we combine the above results and describe an algorithm for defining the nullcurves of the system (B.1) with repair terms defined by (B.82).

W-nullcurve Algorithm:

- Define $q_{rw} = min(K_{rw}, S_{rw})$

- For H from $hmin$ to $hmax$

  - If $H < q_{rh}$ then
    W is defined by (B.84)
  - Else
    $$W = \frac{a + I_{HW}(H)}{1 - r_1}$$

- End for

A similar algorithm can be defined for the H-nullcurve. Once we use the algorithms to plot the nullclines in the phase-plane (W-H plane), we can determine the steady states of the system. The intersection points of the two nullclines are the steady states.

Besides adjusting the location of certain steady states, the repair terms in the model may have the ability to alter the stability of the steady states. To gain a better understand of the stability of the steady states we use the mathematical tool of linear stability analysis.

Linear Stability Analysis

To linearize the system about the steady state (W^*, H^*), we introduce the variables:

$$W_{t+1} = W^* + w_{t+1},$$
$$H_{t+1} = H^* + h_{t+1} \tag{B.86}$$

where w_{t+1} and h_{t+1} are small. By definition of the steady state

$$W^* = I_{HW}(H^*) + r_1 W^* + a + R_W(H^*, H^*),$$
$$H^* = I_{WH}(W^*) + r_2 H^* + b + R_H(W^*, W^*). \tag{B.87}$$

Substitution of the linearization variables (B.11) into the model equations (B.1) with repair defined by (B.3) gives

$$\begin{aligned}
W^* + w_{t+1} &= I_{HW}(H^* + h_t) + r_1(W^* + w_t) + a \\
&\quad + R_W(H^* + h_t, H^* + h_{t-1}) \\
&\approx I_{HW}(H^*) + \alpha_1 h_t + r_1 W^* + r_1 w_t + a \\
&\quad + R_W(H^*, H^*) + \beta_1 h_t + \gamma_1 h_{t-1}.
\end{aligned}$$

using Taylor series expansions of the right hand side and retaining only linear terms. Similarly,

$$\begin{aligned}
H^* + h_{t+1} &= I_{WH}(W^* + w_t) + r_2(H^* + h_t) + b \\
&\quad + R_H(W^* + w_t, W^* + w_{t-1}) \\
&\approx I_{WH}(W^*) + \alpha_2 w_t + r_2 H^* + r_2 h_t + b \\
&\quad + R_H(W^*, W^*) + \beta_2 w_t + \gamma_2 w_{t-1}
\end{aligned}$$

where

$$\alpha_1 = \left.\frac{dI_{HW}}{dH_t}\right|_{H^*} \qquad \alpha_2 = \left.\frac{dI_{WH}}{dW_t}\right|_{W^*}, \tag{B.88}$$

$$\beta_1 = \left.\frac{\partial R_W}{\partial H_t}\right|_{(H^*, H^*)} \qquad \beta_2 = \left.\frac{\partial R_H}{\partial W_t}\right|_{(W^*, W^*)}, \tag{B.89}$$

$$\gamma_1 = \left.\frac{\partial R_W}{\partial H_{t-1}}\right|_{(H^*, H^*)} \qquad \gamma_2 = \left.\frac{\partial R_H}{\partial W_{t-1}}\right|_{(W^*, W^*)} \tag{B.90}$$

We then have the linearized equations for the perturbations w_{t+1} and h_{t+1}:

$$w_{t+1} = \alpha_1 h_t + r_1 w_t + \beta_1 h_t + \gamma_1 h_{t-1},$$
$$h_{t+1} = \alpha_2 w_t + r_2 h_t + \beta_2 w_t + \gamma_2 w_{t-1}. \tag{B.91}$$

This is a linear difference system with delay terms (w_{t-1}, h_{t-1}).

By differentiation we have

$$\beta_1 = C_{rw}\ \theta(S_{rh} - H^*)\frac{1}{(1 - (H^* - K_{rh}))^2}\left(\frac{|H^* - K_{rh}|}{H^* - K_{rh}} - 1\right) \quad \text{(B.92)}$$

$$= \begin{cases} < 0 & H^* < \min(S_{rh}, K_{rh}) = q_{rh} \\ DNE & H^* = K_{rh} \\ 0 & \text{Otherwise} \end{cases}$$

and

$$\beta_2 = C_{rh}\ \theta(S_{rw} - W^*)\frac{1}{(1 - (W^* - K_{rw}))^2}\left(\frac{|W^* - K_{rw}|}{W^* - K_{rw}} - 1\right) \quad \text{(B.93)}$$

$$= \begin{cases} < 0 & W^* < \min(S_{rw}, K_{rw}) = q_{rw} \\ DNE & W^* = K_{rw} \\ 0 & \text{Otherwise} \end{cases}$$

Also,

$$\gamma_1 = \begin{cases} 0 & H^* \neq S_{rh} \\ \infty & H^* = S_{rh} \end{cases} \quad \text{and} \quad \gamma_2 = \begin{cases} 0 & W^* \neq S_{rw} \\ \infty & W^* = S_{rw} \end{cases}. \quad \text{(B.94)}$$

For $W^* \neq S_{rw}$ and $H^* \neq S_{rh}$, $\gamma_1 = \gamma_2 = 0$ and the linearized system (B.21) can be written in matrix format as

$$\begin{pmatrix} w_{t+1} \\ h_{t+1} \end{pmatrix} = \begin{pmatrix} r_1 & \alpha_1 + \beta_1 \\ \alpha_2 + \beta_2 & r_2 \end{pmatrix}\begin{pmatrix} w_t \\ h_t \end{pmatrix}. \quad \text{(B.95)}$$

Notice the delay terms have been eliminated, revealing a much simpler system to solve. We seek solutions of the form $w_t \propto \lambda^t$ and $h_t \propto \lambda^t$. This requires that λ solve

$$\det\begin{pmatrix} r_1 - \lambda & \alpha_1 + \beta_1 \\ \alpha_2 + \beta_2 & r_2 - \lambda \end{pmatrix} = 0 \quad \text{(B.96)}$$

giving

$$\lambda^2 - \lambda(r_1 + r_2) + r_1 r_2 - (\alpha_1 + \beta_1)(\alpha_2 + \beta_2)) = 0 \quad \text{(B.97)}$$

Solving for λ we find

$$\lambda_1, \lambda_2 = \frac{r_1 + r_2 \pm \sqrt{(r_1 - r_2)^2 + 4(\alpha_1 + \beta_1)(\alpha_2 + \beta_2)}}{2}. \quad \text{(B.98)}$$

This solution yields the same stability conditions as those given in the previous section for repair and damage defined by sufficient negativity in one's own slope and spouse's score.

Index